THE LOEB CLASSICAL LIBRARY

FOUNDED BY JAMES LOEB, LL.D.

EDITED BY [Latin authors], 414]

†T. E. PAGE, c.h., litt.d.

†E. CAPPS, ph.d., ll.d.   †W. H. D. ROUSE, litt.d.

L. A. POST, l.h.d.   E. H. WARMINGTON, m.a., f.r.hist.soc.

SAINT AUGUSTINE

THE CITY OF GOD AGAINST THE PAGANS

IV

BOOKS XII—XV

414

SAINT
AUGUSTINE

THE CITY OF GOD AGAINST THE PAGANS

IN SEVEN VOLUMES

IV

BOOKS XII—XV

WITH AN ENGLISH TRANSLATION BY

PHILIP LEVINE

PROFESSOR OF CLASSICS
UNIVERSITY OF CALIFORNIA, LOS ANGELES

CAMBRIDGE, MASSACHUSETTS
HARVARD UNIVERSITY PRESS
LONDON
WILLIAM HEINEMANN LTD
MCMLXVI

Printed in Great Britain

CONTENTS

v

PREFACE

THE present volume has been made to conform, so far as it was possible, to the pattern of the others in the series comprising St. Augustine's *City of God*.[1] The fourth edition of B. Dombart's Teubner text, prepared by A. Kalb (1928–1929) and reprinted with additional bibliography, some corrections and numerous new errors in *Corpus Christianorum*, series latina, vols. 47–48 (Turnholt, 1955), has provided the text upon which this translation has been essentially based. Yet the significant manuscript variants have in all cases been carefully considered, and the Latin text here presented does in fact depart occasionally from that of Dombart–Kalb. Very ancient, perhaps almost contemporary, evidence for the textual tradition of the four books in this volume is found in Verona, cod. XXVIII (26), designated as V in the apparatus. This uncial manuscript containing Books XI–XVI is assigned by Lowe to the first part of the fifth century (" post A.D. 420 ").[2]

[1] See G. E. McCracken's Introduction, vol. 1, p. lix, note 1, on the practice followed in translating St. Augustine's scriptural quotations in the *City of God*. Basic bibliography is found in his Bibliographical Note, *ibid*. pp. lxxxiii-lxxxix.

[2] Cf. E. A. Lowe, *Codices Latini Antiquiores* vol. 4, 491, where the manuscript is characterized as " conspicuous for the excellence of its calligraphy rather than of its text." See also A. Kalb, " Bemerkungen zum Text der ' Civitas Dei ' Augustins," *Philologus* 87 (1932), 477–480, where the codex is

PREFACE

St. Augustine's *City of God* is not an easy work to read and, for all its importance in the history of thought, still lacks a modern detailed commentary sufficient for its needs. The extensive notes of T. Waleys (Wallensis, † *ca.* 1350)–N. Trivet (Trevet or Treveth, † *ca.* 1335) (Strasbourg, 1468 ?), J. L. Vives (Basel, 1522) and L. Coqueau (Coquaeus) (Paris, 1613) are products of their own times and neither always relevant nor readily accessible nowadays. J. E. C. Welldon's commentary (London, 1924), helpful as it sometimes is, more often than not leaves the reader in the lurch. Hence for assistance and guidance in the interpretation of the Latin text of the *City of God*, a translator inevitably turns to the versions of his predecessors, for a translation properly done is in fact an essential, and perhaps the most creative, part of a commentary on the text. Thus the present translator too is indebted to his predecessors, especially English,[1] German,[2] and French,[3]

---

assigned to *saec.* VI; A. Wilmart, " La tradition des grands ouvrages de saint Augustin," in *Miscellanea Agostiniana*, vol. 2 (Rome, 1931), 290, note 349.

[1] Cf. the translations of J. Healey (London, 1610, and then variously revised and reprinted); M. Dods in the *Library of Nicene and Post-Nicene Fathers*, 2 vols. (Edinburgh, 1872, and then variously reprinted); D. B. Zema, G. G. Walsh, G. Monahan, and D. J. Honan in *The Fathers of the Church*, vols. 8, 14 and 24 (New York, 1950–1954).

[2] Cf. the recent German translation of W. Thimme in *Die Bibliothek der Alten Welt*, Reihe Antike und Christentum, 2 vols. (Zürich, 1955).

[3] Cf. the recent French translation of G. Combès, with introduction and notes by G. Bardy, in *Bibliothèque Augustinienne*, Oeuvres de Saint Augustin, 5ᵉ série, vols. 33–37 (Paris–Bruges, 1959–1960). The Notes Complémentaires to each book at the end of every volume are especially helpful and informative.

SAINT AUGUSTINE

THE CITY OF GOD AGAINST THE PAGANS

S. AURELII AUGUSTINI

DE CIVITATE DEI CONTRA PAGANOS

LIBER XII

I

De una bonorum angelorum malorumque natura.

ANTEQUAM de institutione hominis dicam, ubi
duarum civitatum, quantum ad rationalium mortalium genus adtinet, apparebit exortus, sicut superiore
libro apparuisse in angelis iam videtur, prius mihi
quaedam de ipsis angelis video esse dicenda, quibus
demonstretur, quantum a nobis potest, quam non
inconveniens neque incongrua dicatur esse hominibus
angelisque societas, ut non quattuor (duae scilicet
angelorum totidemque hominum), sed duae potius
civitates, hoc est societates, merito esse dicantur, una
in bonis, altera in malis non solum angelis, verum
etiam hominibus constitutae.

Angelorum bonorum et malorum inter se con-
trarios adpetitus non naturis principiisque diversis,
cum Deus omnium substantiarum bonus auctor et
conditor utrosque creaverit, sed voluntatibus et

---

[1] See above, 11.9, 33–34.

PREFACE

but he has tried to exercise his own independent judgement at every point and to resist (with some measure of success, it is hoped) the temptation to skirt a difficulty either by an opaque literalism or by an evasive paraphrase.

P. L.

SAINT AURELIUS AUGUSTINE

THE CITY OF GOD AGAINST THE PAGANS

BOOK XII

I

On the identical nature of good and bad angels.

THE subject of man's creation is now to be discussed. We shall observe here too the emergence of two cities comprising all rational mortals, just as we have already seen the same phenomenon among angels.[1] Before I proceed, however, I see that I must make some remarks about the angels too to demonstrate, as best I can, that there is no impropriety or incongruity in speaking of social union between men and angels, so that we are justified in speaking, not of four cities, namely, two of angels and as many of men, but rather of two cities or fellowships —one of the good and one of the bad, not merely good and bad angels, but good and bad men as well.

It is not permissible to doubt that the contrary pursuits of good and bad angels arose, not from differences in their original natures, since God, the good author and creator of all forms of being, created both classes, but from differences in their acts of will

3

cupiditatibus extitisse dubitare fas non est, dum alii
constanter in communi omnibus bono, quod ipse illis
Deus est, atque in eius aeternitate veritate caritate
persistunt, alii sua potestate potius delectati, velut
bonum suum sibi ipsi essent, a superiore communi
omnium beatifico bono ad propria defluxerunt et
habentes elationis fastum pro excelsissima aeternitate, vanitatis astutiam pro certissima veritate, studia
partium pro individua caritate superbi fallaces
invidi effecti sunt.

Beatitudinis igitur illorum causa est adhaerere
Deo; quocirca istorum miseriae causa ex contrario
est intellegenda, quod est non adhaerere Deo. Quam
ob rem si, cum quaeritur quare illi beati sint, recte
respondetur: Quia Deo adhaerent, et cum quaeritur
cur isti sint miseri, recte respondetur: Quia non
adhaerent Deo, non est creaturae rationalis vel intel-
lectualis bonum, quo beata sit, nisi Deus.

Ita quamvis non omnis beata possit esse creatura
(neque enim hoc munus adipiscuntur aut capiunt
ferae ligna saxa et si quid huius modi est), ea tamen
quae potest non ex se ipsa potest, quia ex nihilo
creata est, sed ex illo a quo creata est. Hoc enim
adepto beata, quo amisso misera est. Ille vero qui
non alio, sed se ipso bono beatus est, ideo miser non
potest esse, quia non se potest amittere.

and desires. For while the good angels steadfastly remain in the good that is shared by all—in their case this is God himself—and so enjoy his eternity, truth and love, the bad angels, exulting rather in their own power, as though they themselves were their own good, sank from the higher good that brings happiness and is shared by all to the level of merely private good. They preferred the pinnacle of pride to the summit of eternity, the cunning of folly to the absolute certainty of truth and zeal for a faction to oneness in love; and this made them in the end arrogant, deceitful and full of spite.

Thus it is their clinging to God that brings happiness to the good angels; and consequently the opposite, or failure to cling to God, must be regarded as causing the unhappiness of the bad angels. Therefore, if the right answer to the question why good angels are happy is that they cling to God, and if the right answer to the question why bad angels are unhappy is that they do not cling to God, then the only good that can make a rational or intellectual being happy is God.

To be sure, not every kind of being or thing can be happy, for this boon is beyond the reach or capacity of beasts, stocks, stones and the like. Yet the being that can be happy cannot draw happiness from himself, since he was created out of nothing, but from him by whom he was created. For the attainment of this good makes such a being happy, just as the loss of it makes him unhappy. But he whose happiness comes from his own good self rather than from an alien good cannot be unhappy because he cannot lose this self.

SAINT AUGUSTINE

Dicimus itaque inmutabile bonum non esse nisi unum verum beatum Deum; ea vero quae fecit bona quidem esse, quod ab illo, verum tamen mutabilia, quod non de illo, sed de nihilo facta sunt. Quamquam ergo summa non sint quibus est Deus maius bonum, magna sunt tamen ea mutabilia bona quae adhaerere possunt, ut beata sint, inmutabili bono, quod usque adeo bonum eorum est ut sine illo misera esse necesse sit.

Nec ideo cetera in hac creaturae universitate meliora sunt, quia misera esse non possunt; neque enim cetera membra corporis nostri ideo dicendum est oculis esse meliora quia caeca esse non possunt. Sicut autem melior est natura sentiens et cum dolet quam lapis qui dolere nullo modo potest, ita rationalis natura praestantior etiam misera quam illa quae rationis vel sensus est expers, et ideo in eam non cadit miseria. Quod cum ita sit, huic naturae quae in tanta excellentia creata est ut, licet sit ipsa mutabilis, inhaerendo tamen incommutabili bono, id est summo Deo, beatitudinem consequatur nec expleat indigentiam suam nisi utique beata sit eique explendae non sufficiat nisi Deus, profecto non illi adhaerere vitium est.

Omne autem vitium naturae nocet ac per hoc contra naturam est. Ab illa igitur quae adhaeret Deo non natura differt ista, sed vitio; quo tamen etiam vitio valde magna multumque laudabilis ostenditur

6

I say therefore that there is no unchangeable good but the one true and happy God, and that, while the things that he has made are indeed good because they were made by him, yet they are changeable because they were not made of anything that came from him but of nothing. Accordingly, although the goods that are surpassed by the greater good of God are not greatest, yet the changeable goods that can cling for their happiness to the unchangeable Good are great; and the latter is so very much their good that they are bound to be unhappy without it.

It does not follow that the other things in this universe of creation are better because they cannot be unhappy, for neither can we say that the other members of our body are better than the eyes because they cannot be blind. Rather, just as a sentient being is better, even when he feels pain, than a stone, which is wholly incapable of feeling pain, so a rational being is superior, even when unhappy, to that which is devoid of reason or sensation and consequently beyond the reach of unhappiness. Surely then it is a defect in this rational being not to cling to God, for he is created on so high a plane that, despite his own mutability, he may nevertheless achieve happiness by clinging to the intransmutable Good, that is, to the supreme God; he is unable to fill his own need except by being happy somehow, and God alone can fill this need.

Moreover, every defect violates nature and is consequently contrary to nature. The nature then that does not cling to God differs from that which does in respect not of its nature but of its defect. Yet this defect shows that the nature itself is very great and

7

ipsa natura. Cuius enim recte vituperatur vitium, procul dubio natura laudatur. Nam recta vitii vituperatio est, quod illo dehonestatur natura laudabilis.

Sicut ergo, cum vitium oculorum dicitur caecitas, id ostenditur, quod ad naturam oculorum pertinet visus, et cum vitium aurium dicitur surditas, ad earum naturam pertinere demonstratur auditus, ita, cum vitium creaturae angelicae dicitur, quo non adhaeret Deo, hinc apertissime declaratur, eius naturae ut Deo adhaereat convenire. Quam porro magna sit laus adhaerere Deo ut ei vivat, inde sapiat, illo gaudeat tantoque bono sine morte sine errore sine molestia perfruatur, quis digne cogitare possit aut eloqui? Quapropter etiam vitio malorum angelorum, quo non adhaerent Deo, quoniam omne vitium naturae nocet, satis manifestatur Deum tam bonam eorum creasse naturam cui noxium sit non esse cum Deo.

II

Nullam essentiam Deo esse contrariam, quia ab eo qui summe et semper est hoc in totum videtur diversum esse quod non est.

HAEC dicta sint ne quisquam, cum de angelis apostaticis loquimur, existimet eos aliam velut ex alio principio habere potuisse naturam, nec eorum naturae

---

[1] Cf. Psalms 145.3.

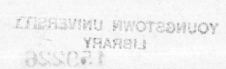

greatly to be praised.[1] For just denunciation of a
defect in some natural creature doubtless implies
praise of the creature itself, since a defect is justly
denounced precisely because a praiseworthy creature
is degraded by that defect.

Now, when we say that blindness is a defect of the
eyes, we indicate that sight belongs to the nature of
eyes, and when we say that deafness is a defect of
the ears, we prove that hearing belongs to their
nature. So, in like manner, when we say that it is a
defect in one created an angel not to cling to God,
this is very clearly a statement that it is essential
for such a nature to cling to God. Moreover, no one
can adequately imagine or express in words how
great a theme for praise there is in so clinging to God
as to live for him, derive wisdom from him, find gladness in him and enjoy this great good without death,
deviation or trouble. Therefore, even the defect
which prevents bad angels from clinging to God
serves to make it quite clear, since every defect
violates nature, that God created so good a nature in
them that separation from God is harmful to it.

II

*That no kind of being is contrary to God, because not-
being is clearly the direct opposite of him who
supremely and for ever is.*

LET these remarks suffice to warn anyone who
might suppose, when we speak of apostate angels,
that they might have received a different nature as
if from a different principle, and that God was not

auctorem Deum. Cuius erroris impietate tanto
quisque carebit expeditius et facilius quanto per-
spicacius intellegere potuerit quod per angelum
Deus dixit quando Moysen mittebat ad filios Israel:
Ego sum qui sum.

Cum enim Deus summa essentia sit, hoc est
summe sit, et ideo inmutabilis sit, rebus, quas ex
nihilo creavit, esse dedit, sed non summe esse sicut
est ipse; et aliis dedit esse amplius, aliis minus, atque
ita naturas essentiarum gradibus ordinavit (sicut
enim ab eo quod est sapere vocatur sapientia, sic ab
eo quod est esse vocatur essentia, novo quidem
nomine, quo usi veteres non sunt Latini sermonis
auctores, sed iam nostris temporibus usitato, ne
deesset etiam linguae nostrae quod Graeci appellant
οὐσίαν; hoc enim verbum e verbo expressum est ut
diceretur essentia); ac per hoc ei naturae quae summe
est, qua faciente sunt quaecumque sunt, contraria
natura non est, nisi quae non est. Ei quippe quod

---

[1] Exodus 3.14. The AV renders: "I am that I am," and
the RSV: "I am who I am," with alternative versions in a
footnote: "I am what I am," "I will be what I will be."
The translation given above best suits the context; cf. the
Septuagint: Ἐγώ εἰμι ὁ ὤν.
[2] The novelty of this coinage was long in wearing off.
Seneca the Younger (d. A.D. 65), *Epistulae* 58.6, and Sidonius
Apollinaris (d. *ca.* A.D. 480), *Carmen* 14, *Epistula Dedicatoria*
4, cite Cicero (d. 43 B.C.) as their authority for this word,
though it is nowhere found in his extant works. Quintilian
(d. *ca.* A.D. 100), *Institutio Oratoria* 2.14.2 and 3.6.23, attributes
its invention to a certain Plautus, but in 8.3.33, ascribes it to
a person whose name seems to be Sergius Flavus. The

the author of their being. Each man will the more speedily and easily avoid the sin of falling into this heresy, the deeper he is able to penetrate into the meaning of God's words delivered by the angel when he dispatched Moses to the children of Israel: " I am he that is." [1]

For, since God is the summit of being, that is to say, he *is* supremely and is therefore unchangeable, he granted being to the objects that he created out of nothing, but not the supreme kind of being such as belongs to him. He also granted a larger measure of being to some but less of it to others and so ordered natural entities according to a system of degrees of being. The word ' being ' (*essentia*) bears the same relation to the verb ' to be ' (*esse*) as the noun ' wisdom ' (*sapientia*) to the verb ' to be wise ' (*sapere*). The word *essentia* [2] is admittedly a new coinage not used by the earlier Latin writers, but it has become good usage in our era, else our language would still lack a word for what the Greeks call *ousia*; for the Latin *essentia* is obtained by a literal translation of the Greek term. And that is why there is no natural entity contrary to the nature that *is* supremely and to whose agency are due all things that are, unless it be an entity that has no being. The opposite of

Council of Nicaea (A.D. 325) notwithstanding, Greek theologians differentiated οὐσία from ὑπόστασις and defined the Trinity as μία οὐσία, τρεῖς ὑποστάσεις; Latin theologians, as Augustine points out in *De Trinitate* 5.9.10 and 7.4.7–8, equated the corresponding terms *essentia* and *substantia* and spoke of the Trinity as *una essentia* or *substantia, tres personae*. Cf. J. De Ghellinck, " L'entrée d'essentia, substantia et autres mots apparentés, dans le latin médiéval," *Archivum Latinitatis Medii Aevi* (Bulletin Du Cange) 16(1941), 77–112.

est non esse contrarium est. Et propterea Deo, id est summae essentiae et auctori omnium qualiumcumque essentiarum, essentia nulla contraria est.

III

De inimicis Dei non per naturam, sed per contrariam voluntatem, quae, cum ipsis nocet, bonae utique naturae nocet quia vitium, si non nocet, non est.

DICUNTUR autem in scripturis inimici Dei qui non natura, sed vitiis adversantur eius imperio, nihil ei valentes nocere, sed sibi. Inimici enim sunt resistendi voluntate, non potestate laedendi. Deus namque inmutabilis est et omni modo incorruptibilis. Idcirco vitium, quo resistunt Deo qui eius appellantur inimici, non est Deo, sed ipsis malum, neque hoc ob aliud nisi quia corrumpit in eis naturae bonum. Natura igitur contraria non est Deo, sed vitium, quia malum est, contrarium est bono.

Quis autem neget Deum summe bonum? Vitium ergo contrarium est Deo, tamquam malum bono. Porro autem bonum est et natura quam vitiat; unde et huic bono utique contrarium est; sed Deo tan-

being is surely not to be. And for that very reason
there is no form of being that is contrary to God, that
is, to him who has supreme being and is author of all
beings, whatever their kind.

III

*On the enemies of God who are such not by nature but
by contrariety of will, which, in so far as it hurts
them, violates a nature that is certainly good,
for a defect that does not violate nature
does not exist.*

In Scripture those who fight against the authority
of God not because of their original nature but because of their defects are called enemies of God,
though they cannot hurt him but only themselves.
They are his enemies because they have a will to
thwart him, not because they have power to hurt
him. God is in fact unchangeable and in no way
subject to deterioration. Consequently, the defect
that brings resistance to God on the part of those
who are called his enemies is a bad thing not for
God but for them, and it is bad for no other reason
save that it vitiates the good of their original nature.
Nothing in nature then is contrary to God; but a
defect, since it is a bad thing, is contrary to what is
good.

Moreover, who can deny that God is supremely
good? It follows then that a defect is contrary to
God as evil to good. Furthermore, the original
nature that it vitiates is also good. Hence a defect
must needs be contrary to this good as well. But

13

tummodo tamquam bono malum, naturae vero quam vitiat non tantum malum, sed etiam noxium. Nulla quippe mala Deo noxia, sed mutabilibus corruptibilibusque naturis, bonis tamen ipsorum quoque testimonio vitiorum. Si enim bonae non essent, eis vitia nocere non possent.

Nam quid eis nocendo faciunt nisi adimunt integritatem pulchritudinem salutem virtutem et quidquid boni naturae per vitium detrahi sive minui consuevit? Quod si omnino desit, nihil boni adimendo non nocet ac per hoc nec vitium est. Nam esse vitium et non nocere non potest. Unde colligitur, quamvis non possit vitium nocere incommutabili bono, non tamen posse nocere nisi bono quia non inest nisi ubi nocet. Hoc etiam isto modo dici potest, vitium esse nec in summo posse bono nec nisi in aliquo bono.

Sola ergo bona alicubi esse possunt, sola mala nusquam, quoniam naturae etiam illae quae ex malae voluntatis initio vitiatae sunt, in quantum vitiosae sunt, malae sunt, in quantum autem naturae sunt, bonae sunt. Et cum in poenis est natura vitiosa, excepto eo, quod natura est, etiam hoc ibi bonum est, quod inpunita non est. Hoc enim est iustum et omne iustum procul dubio bonum. Non

---

[1] Here and elsewhere, *e.g. De Natura Boni* 9, Augustine echoes Plato's doctrine of the intrinsic value of just punishment, as expounded by Socrates in the *Gorgias* (see especially 472e).

whereas it is contrary to God only as evil to good, in the case of the original nature that it vitiates, it is contrary not only as a bad thing but also as a hurtful thing. Evil things are in fact not hurtful to God but to natural beings that are changeable and perishable, but still good beings, as the defects themselves also testify. For if the beings were not originally good, no defects could be hurtful to them.

For what is effected when there is hurt? Is it not some deprivation of completeness, beauty, health, virtue or any good thing of which a being has been wont to suffer removal or diminution through a defect? But if the good thing were not there at all, then there could be no removal of it, hence no hurt, and in consequence there is no defect either. For there can be no defect where there is no hurt. Hence we deduce that, although a defect cannot do hurt to an unchangeable good, still it can do hurt only to a good thing, for a defect cannot be present where no hurt is done. Here is another way of putting it: there can be no defect either in the highest good or where some good does not exist.

Accordingly, good things can exist unalloyed in some cases, but unalloyed evils can in no case exist. For even those beings that have incurred a defect by the entrance of an evil will, though they are evil in so far as they are defective, yet are good in so far as they are natural beings. And when a defective being is undergoing punishment, there is in this circumstance, apart from its goodness as a natural being, further good in that it does not go unpunished.[1] For there is justice in this and any justice is doubtless good. No one suffers punishment because of natural

enim quisquam de vitiis naturalibus, sed de voluntariis
poenas luit.   Nam etiam quod vitium consuetudine
nimiove progressu roboratum velut naturaliter inole-
vit a voluntate sumpsit exordium.   De vitiis quippe
nunc loquimur eius naturae cui mens inest capax
intellegibilis lucis, qua discernitur iustum ab iniusto.

IV

De naturis inrationalium aut vita carentium, quae in
suo genere atque ordine ab universitatis decore
non discrepant.

CETERUM vitia pecorum et arborum aliarumque
rerum mutabilium atque mortalium vel intellectu vel
sensu vel vita omnino carentium, quibus eorum dis-
solubilis natura corrumpitur, damnabilia putare ridi-
culum est, cum istae creaturae eum modum nutu
Creatoris acceperint ut cedendo ac succedendo
peragant infimam pulchritudinem temporum in
genere suo istius mundi partibus congruentem.
Neque enim caelestibus fuerant terrena coaequanda,
aut ideo universitati deesse ista debuerunt, quoniam
sunt illa meliora.   Cum ergo in his locis ubi esse talia
competebat aliis alia deficientibus oriuntur et suc-

---

[1] Cf. the notion of succession in Lucretius 1.262–264;
551–564; 3.964–965.

defects; his defects spring from the will. For even
the defect that has, as it were, naturally become
ingrained through reinforcement by habit or excessive progress derived originally from an act of the
will. Here I refer in fact only to such defects as are
found in a created being with a mind that can possess
the light of reason by virtue of which right and
wrong are discriminated.

IV

*On the nature of things that are irrational or lifeless,
but yet in their own kind and order are not out of
tune with the harmony of the universe.*

On the other hand, in the case of cattle, trees and
the other changeable and perishable things that lack
understanding or sensation or life altogether, it is
absurd to think that the defects by which their
perishable nature is sullied are subject to adverse
judgement. It is absurd because these created
things by decree of their creator have been endowed
with a pattern whereby, coming and going one after
another, they produce a beauty of the lowest order,
namely, that of the seasons, such as harmonizes on its
own level with the parts of this world. For while it
would not have been right to put earthly things on an
equality with heavenly things, neither was there any
need to omit them from the universe just because
heavenly things are higher. Accordingly, when in
the region where this sort of thing might fittingly
have a place it happens that some things arise as
others pass away,[1] the less succumbs to the greater,

cumbunt minora maioribus atque in qualitates superantium superata vertuntur, rerum est ordo transeuntium. Cuius ordinis decus nos propterea non delectat, quoniam parti eius pro condicione nostrae mortalitatis intexti universum, cui particulae quae nos offendunt satis apte decenterque conveniunt, sentire non possumus. Unde nobis, in quibus eam contemplari minus idonei sumus, rectissime credenda praecipitur providentia Conditoris, ne tanti artificis opus in aliquo reprehendere vanitate humanae temeritatis audeamus.

Quamquam et vitia rerum terrenarum non voluntaria neque poenalia naturas ipsas, quarum nulla omnino est cuius non sit auctor et conditor Deus, si prudenter adtendamus, eadem ratione commendant, quia et in eis hoc nobis per vitium tolli displicet quod in natura placet; nisi quia hominibus etiam ipsae naturae plerumque displicent, cum eis fiunt noxiae, non eas considerantibus, sed utilitatem suam, sicut illa animalia, quorum abundantia Aegyptiorum superbia vapulavit. Sed isto modo possunt et solem vituperare, quoniam quidam peccantes vel debita non reddentes poni a iudicibus iubentur ad solem.

Non itaque ex commodo vel incommodo nostro, sed

---

[1] The allusion is to the creatures of the plagues mentioned in Exodus 8 and 10.

and the characteristics of the conqueror are assumed
by the conquered, here we have an order which is that
of transitory phenomena. But the harmony of this
order gives us no enjoyment because, being ourselves by virtue of our mortal condition but threads
in a part of the fabric, we are unable to perceive the
whole, into which the details that displease us fit as
neatly and prettily as need be. Hence, in cases
where we are not properly situated to behold the
prudence of the Founder, we are very rightly enjoined to accept it on faith; we must not with the
futile rashness of mere men make bold to find fault
with the work of so mighty an artist in any particular.

And yet, if we bring our best judgement to bear,
even the defects of earthly things, where no free will
or punishment is involved, speak in favour of them as
originally created, and by the same argument as
before; there is absolutely none of them but that
God is its originator and creator. Here is the argument: even in the case of these earthly things we
are displeased when a defect removes something that
pleases us in the natural object. Men, to be sure,
are in most cases critical even of natural objects
when they become a nuisance, for they do not view
them disinterestedly but consider their own convenience. Take for instance those animals that by
multiplying beyond measure smote the pride of the
Egyptians.[1] By this rule, however, they might even
inveigh against the sun, since there are certain male-
factors and delinquent debtors who are sentenced by
their judges to be exposed to the sun.

This shows that it is not nature as seen in the light
of our own convenience or inconvenience, but nature

per se ipsam considerata natura dat artifici suo
gloriam. Sic est et natura ignis aeterni sine ulla
dubitatione laudabilis, quamvis damnatis impiis
futura poenalis. Quid enim est igne flammante
vigente lucente pulchrius? quid calfaciente curante
coquente utilius, quamvis eo nihil sit urente moles-
tius? Idem igitur ipse aliter adpositus perniciosus,
qui convenienter adhibitus commodissimus invenitur.
Nam eius in universo mundo utilitates verbis explicare
quis sufficit?

Nec audiendi sunt qui laudant in igne lucem,
ardorem autem vituperant, videlicet non ex vi
naturae,[1] sed ex suo commodo vel incommodo.
Videre enim volunt, ardere nolunt. Sed parum adtendunt eam ipsam lucem, quae certe et illis placet,
oculis infirmis per inconvenientiam nocere, et in illo
ardore, qui eis displicet, nonnulla animalia per con-
venientiam salubriter vivere.

V

Quod in omnium naturarum specie [2] ac modo lauda-
bilis sit Creator.

NATURAE igitur omnes, quoniam sunt et ideo habent
modum suum, speciem suam et quandam secum

---

[1] vi naturae *some MSS.:* sui natura *other MSS. The 5th-*
century cod. Veronesis xxviii (26), designated as V, reads vi
naturae *but has above the first letter an* s *that was later deleted.*

[2] omnium naturarum specie *conjectured by Dombart from*
omnium natura et specie *found in V and two other MSS.:*
another MS. reads omni natura specie.

seen in her own light that gives glory to her maker. Thus the natural substance of eternal fire too is doubtless deserving of approval although it will be a means of punishment for condemned sinners. For what is more beautiful than a fire blazing stoutly and brightly? What more useful than a fire that gives us heat, promotes healing and cooks food, although nothing is more annoying than a fire when it burns us? The very same fire then, which, if properly applied, is found very serviceable, is, if otherwise employed, destructive. Who can set forth in words all the services of fire throughout the entire world?

We should not listen to those who, though they praise in fire its light, yet find fault with its burning heat, for they do so plainly in consideration not of its natural function but of their own convenience or inconvenience. They want to see, but they do not want to burn. They fail to observe, however, that this very light, which even they do not hesitate to approve, is injurious to weak eyes because it is not the proper thing for them, and that in that burning heat, which displeases them, some animals enjoy a healthful existence because it is the proper thing for them.[1]

V

*That for every design and rank of being the
Creator merits praise.*

ALL physical things then, since they exist and have therefore their own rank, design and, as it were,

---

[1] Augustine probably has in mind here some creature like the salamander; cf. below, 21.4: *salamandra in ignibus vivit.*

pacem suam, profecto bonae sunt; et cum ibi sunt, ubi esse per naturae ordinem debent, quantum acceperunt, suum esse custodiunt; et quae semper esse non acceperunt, pro usu motuque rerum, quibus Creatoris lege subduntur, in melius deteriusve mutantur, in eum divina providentia tendentes exitum quem ratio gubernandae universitatis includit, ita ut nec tanta corruptio quanta usque ad interitum naturas mutabiles mortalesque perducit sic faciat non esse quod erat, ut non inde fiat consequenter quod esse debebat.

Quae cum ita sint, Deus, qui summe est atque ob hoc ab illo facta est omnis essentia quae non summe est (quia neque illi aequalis esse deberet quae de nihilo facta esset, neque ullo modo esse posset si ab illo facta non esset), nec ullorum vitiorum offensione vituperandus et omnium naturarum consideratione laudandus est.

VI

Quae causa sit beatitudinis angelorum bonorum et quae causa sit miseriae angelorum malorum.

PROINDE causa beatitudinis angelorum bonorum ea verissima reperitur, quod ei adhaerent qui summe est. Cum vero causa miseriae malorum angelorum

---

[1] On the concept of peace implied here cf. below, 19.12–13 (vol. 6, 163–181).

internal law of peace,[1] are surely good. And when they are in the places where they should be according to the natural order, they keep their own being safe and in such measure as they have received it. Those things in nature that were not granted everlasting being suffer changes for better or for worse as they serve the course of events to which they are subject by the law of the Creator, thereby moving through divine providence toward the end marked out for them on the guiding chart of the universe. Thus not even such decay as brings destruction of changeable and mortal things can make what was cease to be in the sense that what was ordained to be is not in due sequence created out of it.

Therefore not only should God not be denounced for any defects that we encounter, but he should receive our praise for every part of creation that we contemplate. For he has supreme being and is for that reason the author of every entity that does not have supreme being; this is so because no being that has been made out of nothing can claim equality with him, nor could a thing have any being at all if it had not been made by him.

VI

Why good angels enjoy happiness and why bad angels suffer unhappiness.

Accordingly, the truest reason for the happiness of good angels is found in their clinging to him who has supreme being. And when we inquire into the reason for the unhappiness of bad angels, we are

quaeritur, ea merito occurrit, quod ab illo qui summe est aversi ad se ipsos conversi sunt qui non summe sunt; et hoc vitium quid aliud quam superbia nuncupetur? *Initium* quippe *omnis peccati superbia.*[1] Noluerunt ergo ad illum custodire fortitudinem suam, et qui magis essent, si ei qui summe est adhaererent, se illi praeferendo id quod minus est praetulerunt.

Hic primus defectus et prima inopia primumque vitium eius naturae quae ita creata est ut nec summe esset et tamen ad beatitudinem habendam eo qui summe est frui posset, a quo aversa non quidem nulla, sed tamen minus esset atque ob hoc misera fieret. Huius porro malae voluntatis causa efficiens si quaeratur, nihil invenitur. Quid est enim quod facit voluntatem malam cum ipsa faciat opus malum? Ac per hoc mala voluntas efficiens est operis mali, malae autem voluntatis efficiens nihil est. Quoniam si res aliqua est, aut habet aut non habet aliquam voluntatem; si habet, aut bonam profecto habet aut malam; si bonam, quis ita desipiat ut dicat quod bona voluntas faciat voluntatem malam? Erit enim, si ita est, bona voluntas causa peccati, quo absurdius putari nihil potest.

Si autem res ista quae putatur facere voluntatem malam ipsa quoque habet voluntatem malam, etiam eam quae fecerit res consequenter interrogo, atque ita, ut sit aliquis inquirendi modus, causam primae

---

[1] Ecclesiasticus 10.13(15). The thought is inverted in the Septuagint: ἀρχὴ ὑπερηφανίας ἁμαρτία, but the original reading of the codex Alexandrinus appears to have agreed with the version in Augustine and the Vulgate.

right in thinking that it is this: that, after turning
away from him who has supreme being, they turn
wholly to themselves who do not have supreme being.
What else can we call this defect save pride? For
" pride is the start of all sin." [1] They chose then not
to keep their strength for him,[2] and though they
would have more being if they clung to him who has
supreme being, by preferring themselves to him they
preferred that which has less being.

Here we have the first failing, the first weakness,
the first defect of that nature which was so created
that, though it did not have supreme being, yet it
could, in order to possess happiness, rejoice in him
who has supreme being. In turning from him it
would not, to be sure, lose all its being, yet it would
have less being and so would become unhappy.
Further, if we should seek for an efficient cause of this
evil will, we find none. For what makes the will bad
when it is the will itself that makes a deed bad?
And therefore an evil will is the efficient cause of an
evil deed, but nothing is the efficient cause of an evil
will. For if something is the cause, it either has or
has not a will; if it has, the will must be definitely
either good or bad; if good, no one surely would be
foolish enough to say that a good will makes a will
bad, since in that case a good will would be the cause
of sin, which is the most absurd notion possible.

On the other hand, if this thing which is supposed
to make a will bad also has a bad will, I ask next what
thing made it too, and finally, to put an end to this
questioning, I inquire after the cause of the first bad

[2] Cf. Psalms 59.9 (Vulgate), on which see below, 13.21 (p.
218, note 3).

25

malae voluntatis inquiro. Non est enim prima voluntas mala quam fecit voluntas mala; sed illa prima est
quam nulla fecit. Nam si praecessit a qua fieret, illa
prior est quae alteram fecit. Si respondetur quod
eam nulla res fecerit et ideo semper fuerit, quaero
utrum in aliqua natura fuerit. Si enim in nulla fuit,
omnino non fuit; si autem in aliqua, vitiabat eam et
corrumpebat eratque illi noxia ac per hoc bono
privabat.

Et ideo in mala natura voluntas mala esse non
poterat, sed in bona, mutabili tamen, cui vitium hoc
posset nocere. Si enim non nocuit, non utique vitium
fuit, ac per hoc nec mala voluntas fuisse dicenda est.
Porro si nocuit, bonum auferendo vel minuendo
utique nocuit. Non igitur esse potuit sempiterna
voluntas mala in ea re in qua bonum naturale praeces-
serat quod mala voluntas nocendo posset adimere.

Si ergo non erat sempiterna, quis eam fecerit
quaero. Restat ut dicatur quod ea res fecerit malam
voluntatem in qua nulla voluntas fuit. Haec utrum
superior sit requiro, an inferior, an aequalis. Sed
superior utique melior; quo modo ergo nullius ac non
potius bonae voluntatis? Hoc idem profecto et aequalis. Duo quippe quamdiu sunt pariter voluntatis
bonae, non facit alter in altero voluntatem malam.

will. For the bad will that was made by a bad will is not the first bad will; the first is the one that was not made by any will. If there came before it a will to make it what it is, the one that made the other is prior. If I am given the answer that nothing made it and that it therefore always was, I ask whether it existed in some creature. If it did not exist in any creature, it did not exist at all; but if it did exist in some creature, it vitiated that creature and made it deteriorate. It did it hurt and thereby deprived it of good.

And for this reason an evil will could not have existed in an evil creature but was bound to reside in one that was good yet changeable—a creature such as to suffer hurt by this defect. For if no hurt was done, there was no defect whatever, and hence we must say that there was no evil will either. Further, if it did hurt, it did that hurt surely by the subtraction or diminution of a good. Accordingly, an evil will could not have existed from all eternity in a thing in which there was originally some natural good that the evil will could diminish by doing hurt to the thing.

If then the evil will did not exist from all eternity, I want to know who made it. The remaining possibility is to say that this evil will was made by something in which no will existed. My next question is whether this thing is superior or inferior or of equal rank. But if it is superior, then it is certainly better, and in that case how has it no will and not rather a good will? The same argument holds again if it is equal. For as long as two beings are possessed of a will equally good, one does not create an evil will in

Relinquitur ut inferior rés, cui nulla voluntas est, fecerit angelicae naturae, quae prima peccavit, voluntatem malam.

Sed etiam res ipsa quaecumque est inferior usque ad infimam terram, quoniam natura et essentia est, procul dubio bona est, habens modum et speciem suam in genere atque ordine suo. Quo modo ergo res bona efficiens est voluntatis malae? Quo modo, inquam, bonum est causa mali? Cum enim se voluntas relicto superiore ad inferiora convertit, efficitur mala, non quia malum est quo se convertit, sed quia perversa est ipsa conversio. Idcirco non res inferior voluntatem malam fecit, sed rem inferiorem prave atque inordinate, ipsa quia [1] facta est, adpetivit.

Si enim aliqui duo aequaliter affecti animo et corpore videant unius corporis pulchritudinem, qua visa unus eorum ad inlicite fruendum moveatur, alter in voluntate pudica stabilis perseveret, quid putamus esse causae ut in illo fiat, in illo non fiat voluntas mala? Quae illam res fecit in quo facta est? Neque enim pulchritudo illa corporis; nam eam non fecit in ambobus quando quidem amborum non dispariliter occurrit aspectibus. An caro intuentis in causa est? cur non et illius? An vero animus? cur non utriusque? Ambos enim et animo et corpore aequaliter affectos fuisse praediximus. An dicendum est alterum eorum occulta maligni spiritus sug-

---

[1] quia *most MSS.:* a qua *or* a que *other MSS.*

the other. Hence by reduction it was an inferior thing with no will that created the evil will of the angelic nature that was the first to sin.

But even this very thing, whatever it is, though it be lower even to the lowest deep of earth, is a creature and entity and therefore most indubitably good, possessing its own rank and design after its own kind and order. How then can a good thing be the efficient cause of an evil will? How, pray, can good be the cause of evil? For when a will leaves something higher and turns to what is lower, it becomes evil, not because that to which it turns is evil, but because this act of turning is itself a wrong turn. Therefore the lower thing did not make the will evil, but the will, because it was itself brought to be, basely and perversely craved a lower thing.

Let us suppose that two persons in the same mental and physical state see the beauty of a single body, and that the sight of it drives one of them to seek illicit enjoyment while the other maintains steadfastly the chastity of his will. Now what do we think is the reason that the will to do evil is produced in one but not in the other? What created such a will in the man in whom it was created? It cannot be the aforesaid beauty of the body, for that did not create a bad will in both when in fact it struck the sight of both with no concomitant variation. If we suppose that the flesh of the beholder is the cause, then why not also that of the other? If we suppose that it is the mind of one, then why not of both? Remember, our premise was that both had the same mental and physical state. Are we then to say that one of them was tempted by the secret prompting of

29

gestione temptatum, quasi non eidem suggestioni et qualicumque suasioni propria voluntate consenserit?

Hanc igitur consensionem, hanc malam quam male suadenti adhibuit voluntatem quae in eo res fecerit quaerimus. Nam ut hoc quoque inpedimentum ab ista quaestione tollatur, si eadem temptatione ambo temptentur et unus ei cedat atque consentiat, alter idem qui fuerat perseveret, quid aliud apparet nisi unum noluisse, alterum voluisse a castitate deficere? Unde nisi propria voluntate, ubi eadem fuerat in utroque corporis et animi affectio? Amborum oculis pariter visa est eadem pulchritudo, ambobus pariter institit occulta temptatio; propriam igitur in uno eorum voluntatem malam res quae fecerit scire volentibus, si bene intueantur, nihil occurrit.

Si enim dixerimus quod ipse eam fecerit, quid erat ipse ante voluntatem malam nisi natura bona cuius auctor Deus, qui est inmutabile bonum? Qui ergo dicit eum qui consensit temptanti atque suadenti, cui non consensit alius, ad inlicite utendum pulchro corpore, quod videndum ambobus pariter adfuit, cum ante illam visionem ac temptationem similes ambo animo et corpore fuerint, ipsum sibi fecisse voluntatem malam, qui[1] utique bonus ante voluntatem

---

[1] quia *a few MSS.*

a malicious spirit, as if he had not of his own free will fallen in with that prompting or any other influence whatsoever?

The object then of our inquiry is to determine what created in the one person this concurrence, this evil will that was provided by him to abet the evil counsellor. Now, to eliminate this obstacle too from our inquiry, let us suppose that both persons experience the same temptation and that one yields to it and consents while the other steadfastly remains the same as he had been. In that case it is quite apparent that, whereas one refused, the other chose to be wanting in chastity. And in a circumstance where the state of body and mind had been the same in each of the two, this situation can only result from the individual will. The same beauty was seen by the eyes of both alike, a secret temptation assailed both alike. Accordingly, even if they study the matter ever so carefully, those who are curious to know what thing created the individual will of one of them evil are at a loss for an idea.

For if we should say that the person himself created it, then what was he before the evil will if not a good natural being whose creator was God, who is an unchangeable good? Let us again suppose that the two men had the same view of a beautiful body and that one yielded, whereas the other did not, to the tempter who urged him to make unlawful use of it, although they both were alike in mind and body before the sight and temptation. Now if anyone says that the one who yielded was himself responsible for making his will evil, although he was certainly good before the evil will, let him put the

31

SAINT AUGUSTINE

malam fuerit, quaerat cur eam fecerit, utrum quia
natura est, an quia ex nihilo facta est, et inveniet
voluntatem malam non ex eo esse incipere quod
natura est, sed ex eo quod de nihilo facta natura [1] est.
Nam si natura causa est voluntatis malae, quid aliud
cogimur dicere nisi a bono fieri malum et bonum esse
causam mali, si quidem a natura bona fit voluntas
mala? Quod unde fieri potest, ut natura bona,
quamvis mutabilis, antequam habeat voluntatem
malam, faciat aliquid mali, hoc est ipsam voluntatem
malam?

VII

*Causam efficientem malae voluntatis non esse
quaerendam.*

Nemo igitur quaerat efficientem causam malae
voluntatis; non enim est efficiens sed deficiens quia
nec illa effectio sed defectio. Deficere namque ab
eo quod summe est ad id quod minus est, hoc est
incipere habere voluntatem malam. Causas porro
defectionum istarum, cum efficientes non sint, ut dixi,
sed deficientes, velle invenire tale est ac si quisquam
velit videre tenebras vel audire silentium, quod
tamen utrumque nobis notum est, neque illud nisi
per oculos neque hoc nisi per aures, non sane in

---

[1] natura *bracketed by Welldon.*

32

question why he did this, whether it is because he is a natural creature or because he was made out of nothing. It will then be discovered that the evil will derives not from the fact that he is a natural creature, but from the fact that he is a natural being created out of nothing. For if a natural being is the cause of an evil will, are we not forced to conclude that evil is created by good and that good is the cause of evil, since on this hypothesis a will is made evil by a natural being that is good? But how is this possible? How can a natural being that is good though changeable, before he comes to have an evil will, create something that is evil, I mean, the evil will itself?

VII

That an efficient cause of an evil will should not be sought.

No one then should look for an efficient cause of an evil will, for the cause is not one of efficiency but of deficiency even as the evil will itself is not an effect but a defect. For to defect from that which has supreme being to that which has less is to make a start in having an evil will. Further, since the causes of such defections are not efficient but deficient causes, to wish to trace them is as if someone were to set his heart on seeing darkness or hearing silence. To be sure, each of these two things is known to us, and one only through our eyes, the other only through our ears, yet clearly we know them not by their definite shape, but by the absence of shape or

33

specie, sed in speciei privatione. Nemo ergo ex me scire quaerat quod me nescire scio, nisi forte ut nescire discat quod sciri non posse sciendum est.

Ea quippe quae non in specie, sed in eius privatione sciuntur, si dici aut intellegi potest, quodam modo nesciendo sciuntur ut sciendo nesciantur. Cum enim acies etiam oculi corporalis currit per species corporales, nusquam tenebras videt nisi ubi coeperit non videre. Ita etiam non ad aliquem alium sensum, sed ad solas aures pertinet sentire silentium, quod tamen nullo modo nisi non audiendo sentitur. Sic species intellegibiles mens quidem nostra intellegendo conspicit; sed ubi deficiunt, nesciendo condiscit. *Delicta* enim *quis intellegit?*

VIII

De amore perverso, quo voluntas ab incommutabili
bono ad mutabile bonum deficit.

Hoc scio, naturam Dei numquam, nusquam, nulla ex parte posse deficere, et ea posse deficere quae ex nihilo facta sunt. Quae tamen quanto magis sunt et bona faciunt (tunc enim aliquid faciunt), causas habent efficientes; in quantum autem deficiunt et ex hoc mala faciunt (quid enim tunc faciunt nisi vana?),

---

[1] Psalms 19.12.

form. Hence let no one seek from me to know what I know that I do not know, except it be in order to learn how not to know what we should know cannot be known.

The fact is that in the case of those things which are known not by definite form, but by the absence of it, our knowledge is in a way, if the notion can be put or understood thus, a matter of unknowing, so that our unknowing is a matter of knowing. For when the keen glance even of the physical eye darts among concrete forms, it sees darkness only where it begins not to see. So too the perception of silence concerns only the ears and no other sense. Yet the only way to perceive silence is by not hearing. So too our mind glimpses objects of thought by thinking them, but where they are deficient in something, the mind is instructed through unknowing. For " who can discern lapses?" [1]

VIII

On misdirected love, which causes the will to fall away from an unchangeable to a changeable good.

THIS I do know, that the nature of God cannot be deficient at any time, at any place, or to any degree, and that those things which were created out of nothing can be deficient. Yet the more they have being and the more they produce good results, the more they have efficient causes, for it is then that they accomplish something. On the other hand, they have deficient causes in so far as they are deficient and because of this produce bad results, for

SAINT AUGUSTINE

causas habent deficientes. Itemque scio, in quo fit
mala voluntas, id in eo fieri quod, si nollet, non fieret,
et ideo non necessarios, sed voluntarios defectus
iusta poena consequitur. Deficitur enim non ad mala,
sed male, id est non ad malas naturas, sed ideo male,
quia contra ordinem naturarum ab eo quod summe
est ad id quod minus est.

Neque enim auri vitium est avaritia, sed hominis
perverse amantis aurum iustitia derelicta, quae incomparabiliter auro debuit anteponi; nec luxuria
vitium est pulchrorum suaviumque corporum, sed
animae perverse amantis corporeas voluptates neg-
lecta temperantia, qua rebus spiritaliter pulchriori-
bus et incorruptibiliter suavioribus coaptamur; nec
iactantia vitium est laudis humanae, sed animea
perverse amantis laudari ab hominibus spreto testimonio conscientiae; nec superbia vitium est dantis
potestatem vel ipsius etiam potestatis, sed animae
perverse amantis potestatem suam potentioris iustiore
contempta. Ac per hoc qui perverse amat cuiuslibet
naturae bonum, etiamsi adipiscatur, ipse fit in bono
malus et miser meliore privatus.

what do they accomplish then but futility? I likewise know that, where the will goes bad, there a
result is produced which, if there were no will to it,
would not happen. And that is why, since the
lapses are not inevitable but wilful, the punishment
that follows is righteous. The lapse is not to what is
bad, but to lapse is bad. In other words, the natural
objects to which there is a lapse are not bad, but to
lapse is bad because the will lapses against the natural
order from what has supreme being to what has less
being.

Thus avarice is not a defect of gold but a defect of
the man who misguidedly loves gold and so deserts
righteousness, which should have been immeasurably
preferred to gold. Nor is dissipation a defect of
beautiful and delightful bodies but a defect of the
soul that misguidedly loves bodily pleasures, dis-
regarding the virtue of moderation, by which we are
brought into harmony with things of greater spiritual
beauty and more unfading delight. Nor is boastful-
ness a defect in glory among men but a defect in the
soul that misguidedly loves glorification by men while
it rejects the witness borne by conscience. Nor,
finally, is pride a defect of Him who gives power or
even of power itself but a defect of the soul that misguidedly loves its own power while it despises the
more righteous power of a higher Power. Hence
whoever loves misguidedly the good of any natural
being, even if he should obtain it, becomes evil himself through this good as well as wretched by the loss
of a higher good.

IX

An sancti angeli, quem habent creatorem naturae,
eundem habeant bonae voluntatis auctorem per
Spiritum sanctum in eis caritate diffusa.[1]

CUM ergo malae voluntatis efficiens naturalis vel, si
dici potest, essentialis nulla sit causa (ab ipsa quippe
incipit spirituum mutabilium malum, quo minuitur
atque depravatur naturae bonum, nec talem voluntatem facit nisi defectio, qua deseritur Deus, cuius
defectionis etiam causa utique deficit), si dixerimus
nullam esse efficientem causam etiam voluntatis
bonae, cavendum est ne voluntas bona bonorum
angelorum non facta, sed Deo coaeterna esse credatur.

Cum ergo ipsi facti sint, quo modo illa non esse
facta dicetur? Porro quia facta est, utrum cum ipsis
facta est, an sine illa fuerunt prius? Sed si cum
ipsis, non dubium quod ab illo facta sit a quo et ipsi;
simulque ut facti sunt, ei a quo facti sunt amore cum
quo facti sunt adhaeserunt; eoque sunt isti ab
illorum societate discreti, quod illi in eadem bona
voluntate manserunt, isti ab ea deficiendo mutati
sunt, mala scilicet voluntate hoc ipso quod a bona

[1] *After* diffusa *some MSS. add* semper fuisse existimant
from the heading of the next chapter.

IX

*Whether the creator of the substance of the holy
angels is also the author of their good will
by the diffusion of love in them through
the Holy Spirit.*

THERE is then no natural or, if the term is permissible, substantial efficient cause of an evil will.
For it is with the evil will itself that the evil starts in
changeable spirits, the evil by which the good of
their own nature is diminished and defiled. Such a
will is created only by the lapse of forsaking God, and
the cause of this lapse or lack is also lacking.
On the other hand, if we should say that there is no
efficient cause of a good will either, we must guard
against the belief that the good will of good angels
was not created but is coeternal with God.

Now, since the angels themselves were created,
how can one say that their good will was not created?
Further, since it was created, there arises the question whether it was created with the angels themselves or whether they existed first without it. But
if it was created with the angels, then there is no
doubt that it was created by him who also created
them. As soon as they were created, they clung to
their creator with the love with which they were
created. And the reason why the evil angels were
separated from the company of the good angels is
that, while the latter remained steadfast in the same
good will, the former underwent a change when they
lapsed from it, their will obviously being evil precisely
because they lapsed from a will that was good; nor

defecerunt; a qua non defecissent, si utique noluissent.

Si autem boni angeli fuerunt prius sine bona voluntate eamque in se ipsi Deo non operante fecerunt, ergo meliores a se ipsis quam ab illo facti sunt. Absit. Quid enim erant sine bona voluntate nisi mali? Aut si propterea non mali, quia nec mala voluntas eis inerat (neque enim ab ea quam nondum coeperant habere defecerant), certe nondum tales, nondum tam boni quam esse cum bona voluntate coeperunt. At si non potuerunt se ipsos facere meliores quam eos ille fecerat quo nemo melius quicquam facit, profecto et bonam voluntatem, qua meliores essent, nisi operante adiutorio Creatoris habere non possent.

Et cum id egit eorum voluntas bona, ut non ad se ipsos, qui minus erant, sed ad illum qui summe est converterentur eique adhaerentes magis essent eiusque participatione sapienter beateque viverent, quid aliud ostenditur nisi voluntatem quamlibet bonam inopem fuisse in solo desiderio remansuram, nisi ille qui bonam naturam ex nihilo sui capacem fecerat ex se ipso faceret inplendo meliorem, prius faciens excitando avidiorem?

Nam et hoc discutiendum est, si boni angeli ipsi in se fecerunt bonam voluntatem, utrum aliqua eam an

would they have lapsed from this good will if they had been truly unwilling to do so.

On the other hand, if good angels existed first without a good will and if they created it in themselves without the help of God, then they were made better by themselves than by him. Heaven forbid! For without a good will they could only have been evil. Or if they were not evil for the reason that an evil was not in them either, since they had not lapsed from the good will which they had not yet come to possess, at any rate they were not yet of such sort, that is, not yet as good as they were as soon as they had a good will. But if they were incapable of making themselves better than they were created by him whose work is improved upon by none, then surely the good will also, which was an improvement in them, could not have been in their possession without the co-operative help of their creator.

Granted that the good will of these angels had for its effect this, that they turned not to themselves who had less being but to him who has supreme being and that by clinging to him they had more being and by communion with him lived a wise and happy life, what else does this mean but that the will, however good, would have remained destitute with only its desire, except that he who created out of nothing a good being, fitted to receive him, went on making it better by filling it with himself, having already awakened in it a greater yearning for him?

Moreover, we have another point that demands discussion. Supposing that the good angels were alone responsible for creating the good will in themselves, was it with or without a will that they did this?

nulla voluntate fecerunt. Si nulla, utique nec
fecerunt. Si aliqua, utrum mala an bona? Si mala,
quo modo esse potuit mala voluntas bonae voluntatis
cffcctrix? Si bona, iam ergo habebant. Et istam
quis fecerat nisi ille qui eos cum bona voluntate, id
est cum amore casto quo illi adhaererent, creavit
simul eis et condens naturam et largiens gratiam?
Unde sine bona voluntate, hoc est Dei amore, numquam sanctos angelos fuisse credendum est.

Isti autem qui, cum boni creati essent, tamen mali
sunt (mala propria voluntate, quam bona natura non
fecit nisi cum a bono sponte defecit, ut mali causa
non sit bonum, sed defectus a bono) aut minorem
acceperunt divini amoris gratiam quam illi qui in
eadem perstiterunt aut, si utrique boni aequaliter
creati sunt, istis mala voluntate cadentibus illi amplius adiuti ad eam beatitudinis plenitudinem unde
se numquam casuros certissimi fierent pervenerunt;
sicut iam etiam in libro quem sequitur iste tracta-
vimus.

Confitendum est igitur cum debita laude Creatoris
non ad solos sanctos homines pertinere, verum etiam
de sanctis angelis posse dici quod caritas Dei diffusa
sit in eis per Spiritum sanctum, qui datus est eis;
nec tantum hominum, sed primitus praecipueque
angelorum bonum esse quod scriptum est: *Mihi autem*

---

[1] See above, 11.13
[2] Cf. Romans 5.5.

If they had no will, then they certainly created
nothing. If they had a will, was it a good or a bad
will? If bad, how could a bad will have been productive of a good will? If good, then they already had
it. And who else had made this will save him who,
creating their substance and at the same time granting them grace, made them with a good will, that is,
with a pure love which enabled them to cling to him?
Hence we must believe that the holy angels were
never without a good will, that is, without the love of
God.

But let us consider now the angels who, in spite of
being created good, are evil. They are evil through
their own evil will, which their good nature did not
create except for that spontaneous lapse from the
good. Hence the cause of evil is not a good thing;
it is lapsing from a good thing. In the case of
these angels either they received less of the grace of divine
love than did those angels who persevered in this
grace, or, if both were created equally good, it must
have happened that, while the evil angels fell through
their evil will, the others with more help achieved
such fulness of bliss as brought them the utmost certainty that they would never fall from it. But this
subject has already been treated by me in the preceding book.[1]

We must then acknowledge with praise due to the
Creator that it is not merely of holy men that it is
said that the love of God has been poured forth in
them through the Holy Spirit bestowed upon them.[2]
This may refer also to holy angels. Nor is it only
men but rather, first and foremost, angels to whom
pertains the good of which it is written: " But it is

43

adhaerere Deo bonum est. Hoc bonum quibus commune est, habent et cum illo cui adhaerent et inter se sanctam societatem et sunt una civitas Dei eademque vivum sacrificium eius vivumque templum eius.

Cuius pars, quae coniungenda inmortalibus angelis ex mortalibus hominibus congregatur et nunc mutabiliter [1] peregrinatur in terris vel in eis qui mortem [2] obierunt secretis animarum receptaculis sedibusque requiescit, eodem Deo creante quem ad modum exorta sit, sicut de angelis dictum est, iam video esse dicendum. Ex uno quippe homine, quem primum Deus condidit, humanum genus sumpsit exordium secundum sanctae scripturae fidem, quae mirabilem auctoritatem non inmerito habet in orbe terrarum atque in omnibus gentibus, quas sibi esse credituras inter cetera vera quae dixit vera divinitate praedixit.

X

De opinione eorum, qui humanum genus sicut ipsum mundum semper fuisse existimant. [3]

OMITTAMUS igitur coniecturas hominum nescientium quid loquantur de natura vel institutione generis

[1] mortaliter *many MSS.*
[2] mortem *V and the first hand of another MS.:* morte *most MSS.*
[3] *Chapter heading omitted in some MSS.*

---

[1] Psalms 73.28.
[2] Cf. above, 10.16.
[3] Cf. Ephesians 2.19–22.

good for me to cling to God."¹   Those who hold this
good in common enjoy a holy fellowship both with
him to whom they cling and with one another, and
they constitute one city of God, which is also his living
sacrifice ² and his living temple.³

Thus this city has one division which is gathered
from among mortal men and is destined to be united
with the immortal angels.   In our day it endures the
vicissitudes of a pilgrimage on earth or else, as far
as those who have met death are concerned, is at
rest in the secret repositories and abiding places of
souls.⁴   I see that I must now explain, just as I did
with reference to the angels, how this division also
came into being through creation by the same God.
The fact is that the human race took its rise from one
man whom God created first, as we are assured in
holy Scripture, which has, and rightly so, marvellous
authority throughout the world and among all
nations.⁵   That the nations would put faith in it is a
true prediction divinely made by Scripture among its
other true utterances.⁶

X

*On the opinion of those who think that the human
race, like the world itself, always existed.*

LET us then pass over the guesses of men who
know not what they are saying about the birth or

---

⁴ On the intermediate state of souls awaiting resurrection,
see below, 13.8 (p. 159); also Augustine's *Enchiridion* 29.109.
⁵ Cf. Mark 14.9.
⁶ See below, 12.11 (p. 51).

humani. Alii namque, sicut de ipso mundo crediderunt, semper fuisse homines opinantur. Unde ait
et Apuleius, cum hoc animantium genus describeret:
" Singillatim mortales, cuncti tamen universo genere
perpetui." Et cum illis dictum fuerit, si semper fuit
humanum genus, quonam modo verum eorum
loquatur historia narrans qui fuerint quarumque
rerum inventores, qui primi liberalium disciplinarum
aliarumque artium institutores, vel a quibus primum
illa vel illa regio parsque terrarum, illa atque illa
insula incoli coeperit, respondent diluviis et con-
flagrationibus per certa intervalla temporum non
quidem omnia, sed plurima terrarum ita vastari ut
redigantur homines ad exiguam paucitatem, ex
quorum progenie rursus multitudo pristina reparetur;
ac sic identidem reperiri et institui quasi prima, cum
restituantur potius, quae fuerant illis nimiis vasta-
tionibus interrupta et extincta; ceterum hominem
nisi ex homine existere omnino non posse. Dicunt
autem quod putant, non quod sciunt.

---

[1] Cf. above, 11.4.
[2] Apuleius, *De Deo Socratis* 4.
[3] Cf. Critias' account of Solon's conversation with an
Egyptian priest in Plato's *Timaeus* 22c–23c. On the Stoic

creation of the human race. For there are some who hold the view that men have always existed, just as they have already come to this conclusion about the universe itself.[1] Hence, when Apuleius in particular is describing this race of animate beings, his words are: " Individually, they are mortal, yet collectively, as a comprehensive species, they are everlasting." [2] And when we ask these people, on the assumption that the human race has always existed, what truth there can be in their historical accounts relating who the inventors were and what things they invented, who the first founders of liberal studies and of other arts were, or who first settled this or that region and section of the earth, and this or that island, they reply [3] that floods and conflagrations, occurring at fixed chronological intervals, lay waste most, but not all, of the earth's surface so that mankind is reduced to very scanty remnants, and that from the offspring of these the original numbers are again renewed. Thus things that were cut short or destroyed by those immense disasters are again and again introduced as novel discoveries and practices, though really only a reintroduction takes place. Man, however, can spring only from pre-existing man. But in saying this they express what they think, not what they know.

doctrine of periodic destruction of the world, see Pease's notes on Cicero's *De Natura Deorum* 2.118, and the references there given.

SAINT AUGUSTINE

XI

*De falsitate eius historiae quae multa milia annorum
praeteritis temporibus ascribit.*[1]

FALLUNT eos etiam quaedam mendacissimae lit-
terae, quas perhibent in historia temporum multa
annorum milia continere, cum ex litteris sacris ab
institutione hominis nondum completa annorum sex
milia computemus. Unde, ne multa disputem quem
ad modum illarum litterarum in quibus longe plura
annorum milia referuntur vanitas refellatur et nulla
in illis rei huius idonea reperiatur auctoritas, illa
epistula Alexandri Magni ad Olympiadem matrem
suam quam scripsit narrationem cuiusdam Aegyptii
sacerdotis insinuans, quam protulit ex litteris quae
sacrae apud illos haberentur, continet etiam regna
quae Graeca quoque novit historia.

In quibus regnum Assyriorum in eadem epistula
Alexandri quinque milia excedit annorum; in Graeca
vero historia mille ferme et trecentos habet ab ipsius
Beli principatu, quem regem et ille Aegyptius in
eiusdem regni ponit exordio; Persarum autem et

---

[1] *In earlier editions this inscription was placed at the head of
chapter 10, with which chapter 11 was combined.*

---

[1] On this letter see above, 8.5 and 27.
[2] Cf. above, 4.6 (vol. 2, 23–25), where Augustine, following
the chronology in Jerome's translation of Eusebius' *Chronica*,
gives 1,240 years as the duration of the Assyrian empire,
beginning with the reign of Ninus, legendary son of Belus.

XI

*On the mistaken history which ascribes many
thousands of years to times past.*

THESE same people are deceived also by certain
false documents, which, so they assure us, cover in
their chronology many thousands of years, though
from sacred Scripture we calculate that 6,000 years
have not yet elapsed since the creation of man.
Hence, to avoid extended argument showing how the
vain character of those writings which record far
more thousands of years is refuted and how no
authority worthy of the subject is found in them, let
us take the famous letter that Alexander the Great
wrote to his mother Olympias.[1] In it he introduces
the account of events given by a certain Egyptian
priest, which the latter extracted from writings held
sacred among that people. There appear in its
narrative certain monarchies, among others, that are
also known to Greek history.

Among these monarchies, that of the Assyrians,
according to this letter of Alexander, lasted more
than 5,000 years, whereas, according to Greek
history, it endured only about 1,300 years [2] from the
reign of Belus himself whom the Egyptian priest too
makes first king of the same monarchy. Again, he
assigned more than 8,000 years to the duration of the

Below, 18.21, Augustine, including the reign of Belus, says
that the empire lasted about 1,305 years. Diodorus Siculus,
Bibliotheca Historica 2.21.8, and Pompeius Trogus, in Justin's
Epitoma 1.2.13, state its duration as 1,300 years; cf. also
Eusebius, *Chronica* 1.14.1. Velleius Paterculus, 1.16.1, sets
it at 1,070 years.

Macedonum imperium[1] usque ad ipsum Alexandrum, cui loquebatur, plus quam octo annorum milia ille constituit, cum apud Graecos Macedonum usque ad mortem Alexandri quadringenti octoginta quinque reperiantur, Persarum vero, donec ipsius Alexandri victoria finiretur, ducenti et triginta tres computentur.

Longe itaque hi numeri annorum illis Aegyptiis sunt minores, nec eis, etiamsi ter tantum computarentur, aequarent. Perhibentur enim Aegyptii quondam tam breves annos habuisse ut quaternis mensibus finirentur; unde annus plenior et verior, qualis nunc et nobis et illis est, tres eorum annos complectebatur antiquos. Sed ne sic quidem, ut dixi, Graeca Aegyptiae numero temporum concordat historia. Et ideo Graecae potius fides habenda est, quia veritatem non excedit annorum qui litteris nostris, quae vere sacrae sunt, continentur.

Porro si haec epistula Alexandri, quae maxime innotuit, multum abhorret in spatiis temporum a probabili fide rerum, quanto minus credendum est illis litteris quas plenas fabulosis velut antiquitatibus proferre voluerint contra auctoritatem notissimorum divinorumque librorum, quae totum orbem sibi crediturum esse praedixit, et cui totus orbis, sicut ab ea praedictum est, credidit; quae vera se narrasse

---

[1] imperium *MSS.:* imperio *conjectured by Dombart.*

---

[1] Cf. Velleius Paterculus, 1.6.5. Pompeius Trogus, in Justin's *Epitoma* 33.2.6, sets the duration at 924 years.

empire of the Persians and Macedonians down to the time of Alexander himself, whom he was addressing, though in the records of the Greeks we find that the Macedonian empire down to the death of Alexander covered 485 years,[1] while the Persian empire, till the victory of Alexander put an end to it, completed the sum of 233 years.[2]

Thus we see that the Greek accounts give much smaller figures than the Egyptian accounts, nor could we make the figures equal even if we multiplied by three. For it is reported that the Egyptians had in former times years so short that a year ended every four months, and hence the full and true year, such as both they and we now have in common, covered three of their former years.[3] But not even so, as I say, does Greek history agree with Egyptian in chronology. And we have a reason to give credit to Greek history in that it does not exceed the true tale of years that appears in our own truly sacred writings.

Further, if this widely known letter of Alexander disagrees so strikingly in its chronology with acceptable trustworthy history, how much less faith must we put in those other documents which, though they abound in fantastic tales supposedly of ancient times, our foes may have chosen to offer as a counterpoise to the authority of the familiar and divinely inspired books of Scripture, which predicted that the entire world would put faith in them, and in which, as it predicted, the entire world has put faith.[4] The truth

---

[2] Quintus Curtius, 4.14.20 and 6.4.9, and Jerome, *Commentarii in Danielem* 9, give 230 years for its duration.

[3] Cf. below, 15.12 (p. 473).

[4] Cf. above, 12.9 (p. 45).

praeterita ex his quae futura praenuntiavit, cum
tanta veritate inplentur, ostendit.

XII

De his qui hunc quidem mundum non sempiternum
putant, sed aut innumerabiles aut eundem unum
certa conclusione saeculorum semper nasci et
resolvi opinantur.

ALII vero, qui mundum istum non [1] existimant
sempiternum, sive non eum solum, sed innumerabiles
opinentur, sive solum quidem esse, sed certis saeculorum intervallis innumerabiliter oriri et occidere,
necesse est fateantur hominum genus prius sine
hominibus gignentibus extitisse. Neque enim ut
alluvionibus incendiisque terrarum, quas illi non putant toto prorsus orbe contingere, et ideo paucos
homines, ex quibus multitudo pristina reparetur,
semper remanere contendunt, ita et hi possunt putare
quod aliquid [2] hominum pereunte mundo relinquatur [3]
in mundo; sed sicut ipsum mundum ex materia sua
renasci existimant, ita in illo ex elementis eius genus

---

[1] non *omitted in some MSS.*
[2] aliqui *some MSS.*
[3] relinquantur *some MSS.*

---

[1] Cf. below, 18.41 (vol. 6, 23). The theory of innumerable
worlds was held by Anaximander, Democritus and the Epicureans; cf. Lucretius, 2.1023–1174, and Bailey's introductory
note *ad loc.*
[2] This was the doctrine of Heraclitus and the Stoics. Cf.

of its narrative of past events is manifest in it through such true fulfilment of the future events that it prophesied.

XII

*On those who think that this world is not everlasting
but believe either that there are countless worlds
or that one and the same world constantly
suffers birth and dissolution at the end
of a fixed cycle of ages.*

Now there are other schools that do not think that this world is everlasting. Either they believe that this is not the only world and that there are countless other worlds,[1] or they believe, to be sure, in a single world but hold that in fixed cycles it rises and perishes times without number.[2] But either way they are forced to agree that a human race first arose without human parents. For they are barred from the theory of floods and conflagrations,[3] which, according to those who hold it, do not affect the whole world absolutely; this permits them to urge that a few people are always left to replenish the original population. In this case, the theory that any human beings would be left in the world when the world perishes is impossible. But just as they think that the world itself is regenerated out of its own matter, so they think that the human race is regenerated in it out of its elements and that only then do the

Jerome, *Epistulae* 124.2.5, who accuses Origen of holding this view.

[3] Cf. above, 12.10 (p. 47).

SAINT AUGUSTINE

humanum ac deinde a parentibus progeniem pullulare
mortalium, sicut aliorum animalium.

XIII

*Quid respondendum sit his qui primam conditionem
hominis tardam esse causantur.*

Quod autem respondimus, cum de mundi origine
quaestio verteretur, eis qui nolunt credere non eum
semper fuisse, sed esse coepisse, sicut etiam Plato
apertissime confitetur, quamvis a nonnullis contra
quam loquitur sensisse credatur, hoc etiam de prima
hominis conditione responderim propter eos qui similiter moventur cur homo per innumerabilia atque
infinita retro tempora creatus non sit tamque sero sit
creatus ut minus quam sex milia sint annorum ex
quo esse coepisse in sacris litteris invenitur. Si enim
brevitas eos offendit temporis quod tam pauci eis
videntur anni ex quo institutus homo in nostris
auctoritatibus legitur, considerent nihil esse diutur-
num in quo est aliquid extremum, et omnia saeculorum spatia definita, si aeternitati interminae com-
parentur, non exigua existimanda esse, sed nulla.
Ac per hoc si non quinque vel sex, verum etiam
sexaginta milia sive sescenta, aut sexagiens aut
sescentiens aut sescentiens miliens dicerentur annorum, aut itidem per totidem totiens multiplicaretur haec summa ubi iam nullum numeri nomen

---

[1] See above, 11.4–5.
[2] Cf. Plato, *Timaeus* 28b.

54

generations of mortal men, like those of other animals, come teeming from parents.

XIII

*What answer is to be given to those who bring
up the late date of man's creation.*

WHEN the origin of the world was under consideration,[1] I gave an answer to those who refuse to believe, not that the world always existed, but that it had a beginning, even as Plato too very plainly acknowledges,[2] although some believe that he held a view opposed to what he states. This same answer I should also give in discussing the original creation of man for the benefit of those who are likewise disturbed by the question why man was not created during the countless and infinite ages past but was created so late that it is less than 6,000 years since he came into existence, according to sacred Scripture.[3] If they are bothered by the short lapse of time because they regard the years as so few since man, as we read in our authorities, was created, let them reflect that nothing that has some limit is really long and that all finite measures of ages, if compared with unbounded eternity, must be regarded not merely as minute but as naught. It follows too that, if there were said to be not 5,000 or 6,000 years since God created man but even 60,000 or 600,000, or 60 or 600 or 600,000 times that number, or if this sum were likewise squared again and again until we came to numbers

[3] See above, 12.11 (p. 49).

haberemus, ex quo Deus hominem fecit, similiter quaeri posset cur ante non fecerit.

Dei quippe ab hominis creatione cessatio retrorsus aeterna sine initio tanta est ut, si ei conferatur quamlibet magna et ineffabilis numerositas temporum, quae tamen fine conclusa certi spatii terminatur, nec saltem tanta videri debeat quanta si umoris brevissimam guttam universo mari, etiam quantum oceanus circumfluit, comparemus, quoniam istorum duorum unum quidem perexiguum est, alterum incomparabiliter magnum, sed utrumque finitum. Illud vero temporis spatium quod ab aliquo initio progreditur et aliquo termino cohercetur, magnitudine quantacumque tendatur, comparatum illi quod initium non habet nescio utrum pro minimo an potius pro nullo deputandum est.

Hinc enim si a fine vel brevissima singillatim momenta detrahantur, decrescente numero licet tam ingenti ut vocabulum non inveniat, retrorsum redeundo (tamquam si hominis dies ab illo in quo nunc vivit usque ad illum in quo natus est detrahas) quandoque ad initium illa detractio perducetur. Si autem detrahantur retrorsus in spatio quod a nullo coepit exordio non dico singillatim minuta momenta vel horarum aut dierum aut mensum [1] aut annorum etiam quantitates, sed tam magna spatia quanta illa summa conprehendit annorum quae iam dici a quibuslibet computatoribus non potest, quae tamen momentorum minutatim detractione consumitur, et

[1] mensium *some MSS.*

for which we no longer had a name, the same question could be asked, " Why did he not create man before that ? "

For the eternity that extends backward without any starting point, during which God refrained from the creation of man, is so great that, if there be compared with it any number of eons, however large and inexpressible it be, if it is still bounded by the limit of a definite measure, this number ought not to be regarded as even so big as the tiniest drop of water compared with the entire sea, even all that is enclosed by the flowing ocean. For of these two things one is, to be sure, extremely minute and one incomparably big, but both are finite. On the other hand, that measure of time, starting out from some beginning and limited by some end, no matter how greatly extended it may be, must, in comparison with that which has no beginning, be esteemed as infinitesimal or perhaps rather even as naught.

For if even the briefest moments should be taken away, one by one, from the end of that time span, the number, albeit so huge that it has no name, decreases and, as you work backward, this subtraction will eventually bring you to the beginning. It is like beginning with the present day of a man's life and subtracting from his days until you come down to that in which he was born. On the other hand, take the time span which is without beginning and, working back, subtract from it not merely tiny moments, one by one, or even large numbers of hours, days, months or years, but periods as great as are contained in that sum of years which, though no computer can designate it, yet is diminished by the subtraction of

57

detrahantur haec tanta spatia non semel atque iterum saepiusque, sed semper, quid fit, quid agitur, quando numquam ad initium, quod omnino nullum est, pervenitur?

Quapropter quod nos modo quaerimus post quinque milia et quod excurrit annorum, possent et posteri etiam post annorum sescentiens miliens eadem curiositate requirere, si in tantum haec mortalitas hominum exoriendo et occubando et inperita perseveraret infirmitas. Potuerunt et qui fuerunt ante nos ipsis recentibus hominis creati temporibus istam movere quaestionem. Ipse denique primus homo vel postridie vel eodem die postea quam factus est potuit inquirere cur non ante sit factus; et quandocumque antea factus esset, non vires tunc alias et alias nunc vel etiam postea ista de initio rerum temporalium controversia reperiret.

XIV

De revolutione saeculorum, quibus certo fine conclusis universa semper in eundem ordinem eandemque speciem reditura quidam philosophi crediderunt.

Hanc autem se philosophi mundi huius non aliter putaverunt posse vel debere dissolvere nisi ut circuitus temporum inducerent, quibus eadem semper

moments, one by one, and subtract these great periods not once or twice or time and again but evermore. If all this be done, what happens, what is accomplished, since you never reach a beginning, which does not at all exist?

Therefore the question which we now ask after 5,000-odd years could also be raised by posterity with the same curiosity after 600,000,000 years if our mortal condition with its ignorance and weakness were to endure so long through the rise and fall of generations. The same question might also have been raised by those who lived before us when the era of man's creation was still in its infancy. In fact, the first man himself, on the day after, or even on the very day, he was created, could have asked why he had not been created before. And no matter how much sooner he might have been created, this dispute over the beginning of temporal events would have had no less force then than now or for that matter at any later time.

XIV

On the periodic succession of ages, which are completed at a definite moment so that the universe, as certain philosophers believed, will always come back to the same pattern and the same appearance.

PHILOSOPHERS of this world have thought that they could not or should not resolve this dispute in any other way than by introducing periodic cycles, in which, according to their contention, there has been

fuisse renovata atque repetita in rerum natura atque
ita deinceps fore sine cessatione adseverarent volumina venientium et praetereuntium saeculorum, sive
in mundo permanente isti circuitus fierent, sive certis
intervallis oriens et occidens mundus eadem semper
quasi nova quae transacta et ventura sunt exhiberet.
A quo ludibrio prorsus inmortalem animam, etiam
cum sapientiam perceperit, liberare non possunt,
euntem sine cessatione ad falsam beatitudinem et ad
veram miseriam sine cessatione redeuntem.

Quo modo enim vera beatitudo est de cuius numquam aeternitate confiditur, dum anima venturam
miseriam aut inperitissime in veritate nescit aut
infelicissime in beatitudine pertimescit? At[1] si ad
miserias numquam ulterius reditura ex his ad beatitudinem pergit, fit ergo aliquid novi in tempore, quod
finem non habet temporis. Cur non ergo et mundus,
cur non et homo factus in mundo, ut illi nescio qui
falsi circuitus a falsis sapientibus fallacibusque com-
perti in doctrina sana tramite recti itineris evitentur?

Nam quidam et illud quod legitur in libro Salomonis, qui vocatur ecclesiastes: *Quid est quod fuit?
Ipsum quod erit. Et quid est quod factum est? Ipsum*

[1] aut *or* ac *some MSS.*

---

[1] Augustine may here be thinking, in part, of the concept
of the 'Great Year,' when all the planets in their orbits
return to their same relative positions at the same time;
cf. Plato, *Timaeus* 39d; Cicero, *De Natura Deorum* 2.51–52
and Pease's notes *ad loc.*

an everlasting renewal and repetition of the same
events in nature;[1] there will likewise be hereafter
an uninterrupted series of revolving ages that come
and go by. Either these cycles took place in a
permanent world or else the world, rising and setting
at fixed intervals, always displayed as though new the
same events as had happened in the past and were
to come again in the future. From this whirligig
they are quite unable to free their immortal soul even
though it has attained wisdom, for in its own uninterrupted circular course it moves back and forth
between false happiness and genuine unhappiness.

For how can that happiness which has no assurance
of eternity be genuine when the soul either is totally
uninstructed in the truth so that it knows nothing of
its future unhappiness or in its happiness has a most
unhappy apprehension of it? But if the soul passes
to happiness from unhappiness to which it is nevermore to return, then there takes place in time something new that is without an end in time. Why then
can this not be the case with the world too? Why
not also with man created in the world? In this way,
by following the straight path of sound doctrine, we
may avoid those circuitous routes, whatever they
are, the feigned discoveries of feigned and fallacious
philosophers.

Indeed, certain people[2] also allege, in support of
their theory of repeated returns and universal restoration, the passage that occurs in the book of Solomon,
called *Ecclesiastes*: " What is that which has been?
The very thing that shall be. And what is that

[2] Origen is included here; cf. his *De Principiis* 2.3.1;
3.5.3.

quod fiet; et non est omne recens sub sole. Qui[1] *loque-tur*[2] *et dicet:*[3] *Ecce hoc novum est, iam fuit saeculis*[4] *quae fuerunt ante nos,* propter hos circuitus in eadem redeuntes et in eadem cuncta revocantes dictum intellegi volunt; quod ille aut de his rebus dixit de quibus superius loquebatur, hoc est de generationibus aliis euntibus, aliis venientibus, de solis anfractibus, de torrentium lapsibus, aut certe de omnium rerum generibus quae oriuntur atque occidunt.

Fuerunt enim homines ante nos, sunt et nobiscum, erunt et post nos; ita quaeque animantia vel arbusta. Monstra quoque ipsa quae inusitata nascuntur, quamvis inter se diversa sint et quaedam eorum semel facta narrentur, tamen, secundum id quod generaliter miracula et monstra sunt, utique et fuerunt et erunt, nec recens et novum est ut monstrum sub sole nascatur. Quamvis haec verba quidam sic intellex-erint, tamquam in praedestinatione Dei iam facta fuisse omnia sapiens ille voluisset intellegi et ideo nihil recens esse sub sole.

Absit autem a recta fide ut his Salomonis verbis illos circuitus significatos esse credamus quibus illi putant sic eadem temporum temporaliumque rerum volumina repeti ut, verbi gratia, sicut isto saeculo Plato philosophus in urbe Atheniensi et in ea schola

---

[1] qui *most MSS. (cf. Septuagint:* ὅς): quis *other MSS.*

[2] loquetur *Dombart (Cf. Septuagint:* λαλήσει): loquitur *MSS.*

[3] dicet *a few MSS. (cf. Septuagint:* ἐρεῖ): dicit *most MSS.*

[4] in saeculis *some MSS.,* Vulg. *(cf. Septuagint:* ἐν τοῖς αἰῶσιν, *but* ἐν *omitted in cod. Alexandrinus).*

---

[1] Ecclesiastes 1.9–10.

which has been done? The very thing that shall be done; and there is nothing new under the sun. If anyone speaks and says, ' Lo, this is new,' it has already been in the ages that have gone before us." [1] But these observations were made by Solomon either concerning those matters about which he had just been speaking, that is, the generations that come and go, the spiral course of the sun, the swift descent of torrents, or, at any rate, concerning the things of every kind that have a rising and a setting.

For there were men before us, there are men with us now, there will also be men after us; and such is the case with all animals and plants. Even the very monstrosities which are abnormal creatures of birth, although they differ from one another and certain of them are said to have been created but once, yet, since they belong to the general category of wonders and monstrosities, certainly both have been before and will be hereafter, and it is not a new event of recent days for a monstrous birth to occur under the sun. And yet certain people have understood our famous sage to mean by these words that in the predestination of God all things had already been created and that, therefore, there is nothing new under the sun.

But heaven forbid that our true faith should allow us to believe that these words of Solomon denoted those cycles in which, as those others think, the same measures of time and the same events in time are repeated in circular fashion: on the basis of this cyclic theory, it is argued, for example, that, just as in a certain age the philosopher Plato taught his students in the city of Athens and in the school

quae Academia dicta est discipulos docuit, ita per
innumerabilia retro saecula multum quidem prolixis
intervallis, sed tamen certis, et idem Plato et eadem
civitas et eadem schola idemque discipuli repetiti et
per innumerabilia deinde saecula repetendi sint.
Absit, inquam, ut nos ista credamus. Semel enim
Christus mortuus est pro peccatis nostris; *surgens*
autem *a mortuis iam non moritur, et mors ei ultra non
dominabitur*; et nos post resurrectionem semper cum
Domino erimus, cui modo dicimus, quod sacer admonet psalmus: *Tu, Domine, servabis nos et custodies
nos a generatione hac et in aeternum.* Satis autem istis
existimo convenire quod sequitur: *In circuitu impii
ambulabunt*,[1] non quia per circulos, quos opinantur,
eorum vita est recursura, sed quia modo talis est
erroris eorum via, id est falsa doctrina.

XV

*De temporali conditione generis humani, quam Deus
nec novo consilio instituerit nec mutabili voluntate.*

QUID autem mirum est si in his circuitibus errantes
nec aditum nec exitum inveniunt? quia genus
humanum atque ista nostra mortalitas nec quo initio

---

[1] ambulant *many MSS., Vulg. (cf. Septuagint:* περιπατοῦσιν).

---

[1] Romans 6.9.
[2] 1 Thessalonians 4.17.
[3] Psalms 12.7.

called the Academy, so during countless past ages,
at very prolonged yet definite intervals, the same
Plato, the same city, and the same school with the
same students had existed again and again, and
during countless ages to come will exist again and
again. Heaven forbid, I repeat, that we should believe that. For Christ died once for our sins, but
" rising from the dead he dies no more, and death
shall no longer have dominion over him ";[1] and after
the resurrection " we shall always be with the Lord,"[2]
to whom we now say, as the holy psalm tells us:
" Thou, O Lord, wilt preserve us and guard us from
this generation forever." [3] Moreover, the verse that
follows is, I think, quite applicable to these philosophers: " The wicked shall walk around in circles," [4]
not because their life is going to run again and again
in cycles, as they suppose, but because the path of
their present deviation, that is, the way of their false
doctrine, is just like that.

XV

*On the creation of the human race in time, which God
effected without any novelty of purpose or change
of will.*

WHAT wonder is it, moreover, that those who go
astray in these roundabouts find neither entrance nor
exit? This is so because they know neither at what
point the human race started and with it that death-

---

[4] Psalms 12.8. Augustine departs from the usual interpretation of the text to suit his purpose; cf. the RSV: " On
every side the wicked prowl."

65

coepta sit sciunt, nec quo fine claudatur, quando quidem altitudinem Dei penetrare non possunt, qua,[1] cum ipse sit aeternus et sine initio, ab aliquo tamen initio exorsus est tempora et hominem, quem numquam antea fecerat, fecit in tempore, non tamen novo et repentino, sed inmutabili aeternoque consilio.

Quis hanc valeat altitudinem investigabilem vestigare et inscrutabilem perscrutari secundum quam Deus hominem temporalem, ante quem nemo umquam hominum fuit, non mutabili voluntate in tempore condidit et genus humanum ex uno multiplicavit? Quando quidem psalmus ipse cum praemisisset atque dixisset: *Tu, Domine, servabis nos et custodies nos a generatione hac et in aeternum,* ac deinde repercussisset eos in quorum stulta impiaque doctrina nulla liberationis et beatitudinis animae servatur aeternitas, continuo subiciens: *In circuitu impii ambulabunt,* tamquam ei diceretur: "Quid ergo tu credis, sentis, intellegis? Numquidnam existimandum est subito Deo placuisse hominem facere, quem numquam antea infinita retro aeternitate fecisset, cui nihil novi accidere potest, in quo mutabile aliquid non est?" continuo respondit ad ipsum Deum loquens: *Secundum altitudinem tuam multiplicasti filios hominum.* Sentiant, inquit, homines quod putant, et quod eis

---

[1] quam *or* quia *some MSS.*

---

[1] Psalms 12.7–8.
[2] Psalms 12.8. Augustine's interpretation of the scriptural

doom of ours nor at what point its story ends. For they cannot, of course, reach to the sublimity of God, whereby, though he himself is eternal and without beginning, he nevertheless did start at some first point when he created measures of time and man in time, whom he had never before created; yet he did so by a plan that was not new or suddenly conceived but unchangeable and eternal.

Who could trace and search out the untraceable and unsearchable sublimity wherewith God, without any change of will, created time-bound man, before whom no man ever existed, and produced the multiplicity of the human race from but one? Indeed, after the psalmist himself had laid down the premiss in the words: " Thou, O Lord, wilt preserve us and guard us from this generation forever," he thereupon rebutted those in whose foolish and impious doctrine no eternity of the soul's freedom and happiness is preserved, for he at once subjoined: " The wicked shall walk around in circles ";[1] then, as though he were asked: " What then is your belief, your opinion, your understanding? Are we to infer that God suddenly decided to create man, whom he had never created before during the endless past of eternity, that God for whom there is nothing accidental or new, in whom there is nothing subject to change? " the psalmist straightway replies, addressing God himself: " In keeping with thy sublimity thou didst multiply the sons of men."[2] Let men, he says, deliver what opinions they hold, and let them suppose

passage, whose text here agrees with that of the Vulgate, differs radically from the AV and RSV; in the latter we read: " as vileness is exalted among the sons of men."

placet opinentur et disputent: *Secundum altitudinem tuam*, quam nullus potest nosse hominum, *multiplicasti filios hominum.* Valde quippe altum est et semper fuisse et hominem, quem numquam fecerat, ex aliquo tempore primum facere voluisse, nec consilium voluntatemque mutasse.

XVI

An ut Deus semper etiam dominus fuisse intellegatur, credendum sit creaturam quoque numquam defuisse cui dominaretur, et quo modo dicatur semper creatum quod dici non potest coaeternum.

Ego quidem sicut Dominum Deum aliquando dominum non fuisse dicere non audeo, ita hominem numquam antea fuisse et ex quodam tempore primum hominem creatum esse dubitare non debeo. Sed cum cogito cuius rei dominus semper fuerit, si semper creatura non fuit, adfirmare aliquid pertimesco quia et me ipsum intueor et scriptum esse recolo: *Quis hominum potest scire consilium Dei, aut quis poterit cogitare quid velit Dominus? Cogitationes enim mortalium timidae et incertae adinventiones nostrae. Corruptibile enim corpus adgravat animam, et deprimit terrena inhabitatio sensum multa cogitantem.*

Ex his igitur quae in hac terrena inhabitatione

---

[1] Wisdom 9.13–15.

and argue as they choose: "In keeping with thy sublimity," which no man can discover, "thou didst multiply the sons of men." For it is indeed something very sublime always to have existed and to have willed to create at some point of time a first man, whom he had never created before, and this with no change of purpose or will.

XVI

Whether, in order to grasp the truth that God has also been Lord, we must believe that there was never lacking some creature too over whom he might be lord, and in what sense a thing may be said always to have been created that cannot be said to be coeternal.

In fact, just as I dare not say that the Lord God at some time was not lord, so I am bound not to doubt that man never existed previously and that the first man was created at a certain point of time. But when I would conceive what there was of which he always was lord if there was not always some creature in existence, I fear to make a positive assertion, for I both contemplate what I am and recall what Scripture says: "Who among men can know the counsel of God, or who shall be able to conceive what the will of the Lord is? For the thoughts of mortal men are timid, and our devices are uncertain. For the corruptible body is heavy upon the soul, and the earthly tabernacle encumbers the mind in its many thoughts." [1]

Accordingly, I shall give some of my many thoughts

69

multa cogito (ideo utique multa, quia unum quod ex
illis vel praeter illa, quod forte non cogito, verum est
invenire non possum), si dixero semper fuisse creaturam cuius dominus esset, qui semper est dominus
nec dominus umquam non fuit, sed nunc illam, nunc
aliam per alia atque alia temporum spatia, ne aliquam
Creatori coaeternam esse dicamus, quod fides ratioque
sana condemnat, cavendum est ne sit absurdum et a
luce veritatis alienum mortalem quidem per vices
temporum semper fuisse creaturam, decedentem
aliam, aliam succedentem, inmortalem vero non esse
coepisse nisi cum ad nostrum saeculum ventum est,
quando et angeli creati sunt, si eos recte lux illa
primum facta significat aut illud potius caelum de quo
dictum est: *In principio fecit Deus caelum et terram*,[1]
cum tamen non fuerint, antequam fierent, ne inmortales, si semper fuisse dicuntur, Deo coaeterni esse
credantur.

Si autem dixero non in tempore creatos angelos,
sed ante omnia tempora et ipsos fuisse, quorum Deus
dominus esset, qui numquam nisi dominus fuit,
quaeretur a me etiam, si ante omnia tempora facti
sunt, utrum semper potuerint esse qui facti sunt.
Hic respondendum forte videatur: Quo modo non

---

[1] Genesis 1.1.

in this earthly tabernacle. There must indeed be many because I cannot discover the one that is true, whether it be one among mine or one outside them that perhaps does not occur to me. Well, suppose I say that there always was in existence a creature for him who always is Lord and never has not been Lord to be lord over, but that there was a succession of different creatures during different periods of time, for we must not imply that any creature is coeternal with the Creator, a statement rejected by faith and sound reason alike. Then we must avoid the absurdity, which is contrary to true enlightenment, of inferring that, though some mortal creature always existed, one succeeding as another passed away, through one period after another, yet no immortal creature began its existence until our own age was reached when the angels were also created. I take it that we are right in supposing that they are symbolized by that light which was the first thing created or better still by that heaven of which it is said: " In the beginning God created heaven and earth." [1] For indeed they could not exist before they were created; otherwise, being immortal, they might, if we say that they have always existed, be believed to be coeternal with God.

On the other hand, if I say that the angels were not created in time but before all measures of time and that they existed for God, who was never other than Lord, to be lord over, I shall next be asked whether, if they were created before all measures of time, created beings could always have existed. The proper answer to this question might perhaps be as follows: Why can we not say that they always ex-

semper, cum id quod est omni tempore non inconvenienter semper esse dicatur? Usque adeo autem isti omni tempore fuerunt ut etiam ante omnia tempora facti sint, si tamen a caelo coepta sunt tempora, et illi iam erant ante caelum. At si tempus non a caelo, verum et ante caelum fuit, non quidem in horis et diebus et mensibus et annis (nam istae dimensiones temporalium spatiorum, quae usitate ac proprie dicuntur tempora, manifestum est quod a motu siderum coeperint; unde et Deus, cum haec institueret, dixit: *Et sint in signa et in tempora et in dies et in annos*), sed in aliquo mutabili motu, cuius aliud prius, aliud posterius praeterit, eo quod simul esse non possunt—si ergo ante caelum in angelicis motibus tale aliquid fuit et ideo tempus iam fuit atque angeli, ex quo facti sunt, temporaliter movebantur, etiam sic omni tempore fuerunt quando quidem cum illis facta sunt tempora. Quis autem dicat: Non semper fuit quod omni tempore fuit?

Sed si hoc respondero, dicetur mihi: Quo modo ergo non coaeterni Creatori si semper ille, semper illi fuerunt? Quo modo etiam creati dicendi sunt si semper fuisse intelleguntur? Ad hoc quid respondebitur? An dicendum est et semper eos fuisse, quoniam omni tempore fuerunt qui cum tempore facti sunt aut cum quibus facta sunt tempora, et tamen

---

[1] Genesis 1.14. On these measures of time cf. Augustine, *Confessions* 11.23.29–30.

[2] Cf. Augustine, *De Genesi ad Litteram* 8.20.39.

isted since that which exists at every time may properly be said to exist always? Indeed, so surely did they exist at every time that they were created as well before all measures of time, that is, if measures of time began with the heaven and they already existed before the heaven. But let us suppose that time did not begin with the heaven but existed even before the heaven. Now, by time I do not mean time calculated in hours, days, months and years, for these measures of periods of time, which are properly and commonly called ' units of time,' manifestly began with the motion of the heavenly bodies; hence, when God created them, he said: " And let them be for signs and for seasons and for days and for years." [1] But by time I mean that indicated in some changing motion, of which one part passes earlier, another later, because they cannot exist simultaneously. If then before the heaven existed there was something of this sort in the movements of the angels [2] and thus time already existed and the angels from the moment of creation were subject to movement in time, even so they existed at every time since periods of time came into being with them. Now who would say that what existed at every time did not always exist?

But if I give this answer, I shall be asked: " Why then are they not coeternal with the Creator if they as well as he have always existed? How can we say, moreover, that they were created if we understand that they have always existed? " What reply shall we give to this? Are we to say that they did indeed always exist, since they who were created simultaneously with time or with whom periods of time were simultaneously created existed at every time, but

creatos? Neque enim et ipsa tempora creata esse
negabimus, quamvis omni tempore tempus fuisse
nemo ambigat.

Nam si non omni tempore fuit tempus, erat ergo
tempus quando nullum erat tempus. Quis hoc stul-
tissimus dixerit? Possumus enim recte dicere: Erat
tempus quando non erat Roma; erat tempus quando
non erat Hierusalem; erat tempus quando non erat
Abraham; erat tempus quando non erat homo, et si
quid huius modi. Postremo si non cum initio temporis, sed post aliquod tempus factus est mundus,
possumus dicere: Erat tempus quando non erat
mundus. At vero: Erat tempus quando nullum erat
tempus, tam inconvenienter dicimus ac si quisquam
dicat: Erat homo quando nullus erat homo, aut:
Erat iste mundus quando iste non erat mundus. Si
enim de alio atque alio intellegatur, potest dici aliquo
modo, hoc est: Erat alius homo quando non erat iste
homo. Sic ergo: Erat aliud tempus quando non erat
hoc tempus, recte possumus dicere. At vero: Erat
tempus quando nullum erat tempus, quis vel insi-
pientissimus dixerit?

Sicut ergo dicimus creatum tempus, cum ideo semper fuisse dicatur, quia omni tempore tempus fuit,
ita non est consequens ut, si semper fuerunt angeli,
ideo non sint creati, ut propterea semper fuisse
dicantur, quia omni tempore fuerunt; et propterea
omni tempore fuerunt, quia nullo modo sine his ipsa

that they nevertheless were created? For indeed we shall not deny that periods of time were also created, although no one is in doubt that time existed at every time.

For if time did not exist at every time, then there was a time when there was no time. Who, no matter how foolish, would say this? We can, to be sure, properly say: "There was a time when Rome was not; there was a time when Jerusalem was not; there was a time when Abraham was not; there was a time when man was not"; and so on. Lastly, if the world was not created with the beginning of time but after some time, we can say: "There was a time when the world was not." But when we say that there was a time when there was no time, we speak as incongruously as if someone should say that there was a man when there was no man, or that this world was when this world was not. For if two different things are understood, we can find some way to say it: for instance, "There was another man when this man was not." Similarly then, we can rightly say: "There was another time when this time was not." But, really, would even the greatest fool say that there was a time when there was no time?

Accordingly, if we say, as in fact we do, that time was created, although it is said always to have existed because time has existed at every time, then it is not logical to conclude that, if angels have always existed, they were therefore not created. Hence we may say that they have always existed because they have existed at every time, and they have existed at every time because the very periods of time could in no way have existed without them.

75

tempora esse potuerunt. Ubi enim nulla creatura
est cuius mutabilibus motibus tempora peragantur,
tempora omnino esse non possunt. Ac per hoc etsi
semper fuerunt, creati sunt, nec si semper fuerunt,
ideo Creatori coaeterni sunt. Ille enim semper fuit
aeternitate inmutabili; isti autem facti sunt. Sed
ideo semper fuisse dicuntur, quia omni tempore fuerunt, sine quibus tempora nullo modo esse potuerunt.

Tempus autem quoniam mutabilitate transcurrit,
aeternitati inmutabili non potest esse coaeternum.
Ac per hoc etiamsi inmortalitas angelorum non
transit in tempore, nec praeterita est quasi iam non
sit, nec futura quasi nondum sit, tamen eorum motus,
quibus tempora peraguntur, ex futuro in praeteritum
transeunt, et ideo Creatori, in cuius motu dicendum
non est vel fuisse quod iam non sit vel futurum esse
quod nondum sit, coaeterni esse non possunt.

Quapropter si Deus semper dominus fuit, semper
habuit creaturam suo dominatui servientem, verum
tamen non de ipso genitam, sed ab ipso de nihilo
factam nec ei coaeternam; erat quippe ante illam,
quamvis nullo tempore sine illa, non eam spatio
transcurrente, sed manente perpetuitate praecedens.
Sed hoc si respondero eis qui requirunt quo modo
semper creator, semper dominus fuit si creatura
serviens non semper fuit, aut quo modo creata est et
non potius creatori coaeterna est si semper fuit, vereor

---

[1] On Augustine's distinction between eternity and time cf.
above, 11.6.

[2] On the precedence of God's eternity over time cf. Augustine, *Confessions* 11.13.16.

For where there is no creature to produce the passage of time by its changing motions, there can be no periods of time at all. Therefore, although angels have always existed, they were created, but it does not follow that, if they have always existed, they are for that reason coeternal with the Creator. For he has always existed in unchanging eternity, whereas they were created. But we say that they have always existed because they have existed at every time. Without them there could have been no periods of time at all.

Moreover, since the course of time involves changeableness, time cannot be coeternal with unchanging eternity.[1] And therefore, although the immortality of angels does not pass in time, being neither past as if it no longer were, nor future as if it were not yet, nevertheless their movements, by which periods of time are produced, do pass from future to past, and for that reason they cannot be coeternal with the Creator, in whose movement we cannot say either that there has been that which no longer is or that there will be that which is not yet.

Wherefore, if God has always been Lord, he has always had some creature subject to his lordship—a creature, however, not begotten of him but created by him out of nothing, and not coeternal with him; for he was before it existed, yet at no time was he without it, preceding it not by a transient interval but by an abiding continuity.[2] But if I give this answer to those who ask how he was always Creator and always Lord if there was not always some subject creature, or how it is a created being and not rather one coeternal with the Creator if it existed always,

ne facilius iudicer adfirmare quod nescio quam docere quod scio.

Redeo igitur ad id quod creator noster scire nos voluit. Illa vero quae vel sapientioribus in hac vita scire permisit vel omnino perfectis in alia vita scienda servavit ultra vires meas esse confiteor. Sed ideo putavi sine adfirmatione tractanda, ut qui haec legunt videant a quibus quaestionum periculis debeant temperare, nec ad omnia se idoneos arbitrentur potiusque intellegant quam sit apostolo obtemperandum praecipienti salubriter ubi ait: *Dico autem per gratiam Dei quae data est mihi omnibus qui sunt in vobis, non plus sapere quam oportet sapere, sed sapere ad temperantiam, unicuique sicut Deus partitus est mensuram fidei.* Si enim pro viribus suis alatur infans, fiet ut crescendo plus capiat; si autem vires suae capacitatis excedat, deficiet antequam crescat.

XVII

Quo modo intellegenda sit promissa homini a Deo vita aeterna ante tempora aeterna.

Quae saecula praeterierint antequam genus institueretur humanum, me fateor ignorare; non tamen dubito nihil omnino creaturae Creatori esse coaeter-

---

[1] Romans 12.3. Augustine understands *sapere* as meaning ' to be wise,' a sense required for his argument, but the verb in Greek is ὑπερφρονεῖν, ' to be over-proud '; the RSV renders here: "I bid every one among you not to think of himself more highly than he ought to think, but to think with sober judgment, *etc.*"

I fear that I may more readily be thought to assert what I do not know than to teach what I do know.

I return then to what our Creator chose that we should know. As for those matters which he either allowed wiser men to know in this life or reserved for the knowledge of those altogether perfect in the next life, I confess that they are beyond my powers to comprehend. But I thought that I should discuss them without making any positive assertions in order that my readers may see from what dangerous problems they should stay clear, and, instead of thinking that they are equipped to deal with all matters, may rather understand that they should follow the wholesome instruction of the Apostle when he says: " By the grace of God given to me I bid every one among you not to be wiser than he ought, but to be wise in moderation, each according to the measure of faith which God has assigned him." [1] For if an infant should be nourished in accordance with his strength, the result will be that he takes more nourishment as he grows; but if he should go beyond what his capacity can manage, he will dwindle before he grows.

XVII

How we are to understand God's promise of ever-lasting life to man before the everlasting periods of time.

I confess that I do not know what ages passed before the human race was created. I have no doubt, however, that no creature of any sort is coeternal with the Creator. The Apostle also speaks of ever-

num. Dicit etiam apostolus tempora aeterna, nec
ea futura, sed, quod magis est mirandum, praeterita.
Sic enim ait: *In spem vitae aeternae quam promisit non
mendax Deus ante tempora aeterna; manifestavit autem
temporibus suis verbum suum.*

Ecce dixit retro quod fuerint tempora aeterna,
quae tamen non fuerint Deo coaeterna si quidem ille
ante tempora aeterna non solum erat verum etiam
promisit vitam aeternam, quam manifestavit temporibus suis, id est congruis. Quid aliud quam Verbum suum? Hoc est enim vita aeterna. Quo modo
autem promisit, cum hominibus utique promiserit,
qui nondum erant ante tempora aeterna, nisi quia in
eius aeternitate atque in ipso Verbo eius eidem
coaeterno iam praedestinatione fixum erat quod suo
tempore futurum erat?

XVIII

*Quid de incommutabili consilio ac voluntate Dei fides
sana defendat contra ratiocinationes eorum, qui
opera Dei ex aeternitate repetita per eosdem
semper volunt saeculorum redire circuitus.*

ILLUD quoque non dubito, antequam homo primus
creatus esset, numquam quemquam fuisse hominem,
nec eundem ipsum nescio quibus circuitibus nescio
quotiens revolutum nec alium aliquem natura similem.

---

[1] Titus 1.2–3. For Augustine's *ante tempora aeterna*, to
which the Greek πρὸ χρόνων αἰωνίων corresponds, the Vulgate
reads *ante tempora saecularia*; the RSV renders: ' ages ago.'
[2] Cf. above, 12.14 (p. 59).

lasting periods of time, referring not to times to come but (and this is all the more remarkable) to times gone by. For his words are these: " In hope of eternal life which God, who does not lie, promised before the everlasting periods of time; and in his own right times he made his word manifest." [1]

Observe, he said that in the past there were everlasting periods of time, although these were still not coeternal with God since before the everlasting periods of time he not only existed but also promised eternal life, which he made manifest in his own, that is, in fitting times. What else was this than his Word? For this is eternal life. But how did he make his promise, since he made it surely to men, who were not yet in existence before the everlasting periods of time, unless it be that in his eternity and in his very Word that is coeternal with him there had already been determined by predestination the event which was to happen in its own time?

XVIII

What defence sound faith presents concerning the unchangeable purpose and will of God against the theories of those who hold that the works of God have been repeated from eternity and return always in the same cycles of ages.

I HAVE no doubt also of this, that, before the first man had been created, there was never any man in existence, whether it be the very same person brought back in cycles,[2] whatever they are and however many times, or anyone else by nature like him.

Neque ab hac fide me philosophorum argumenta
deterrent, quorum acutissimum illud putatur, quod
dicunt nulla infinita ulla scientia posse conprehendi;
ac per hoc Deus, inquiunt, rerum quas facit omnium
finitarum [1] omnes finitas apud se rationes habet.
Bonitas autem eius numquam vacua fuisse credenda
est, ne sit temporalis eius operatio cuius retro fuerit
aeterna cessatio, quasi paenituerit eum prioris sine
initio vacationis ac propterea sit operis adgressus
initium.

Et ideo necesse est, inquiunt, eadem semper repeti
eademque semper repetenda transcurrere, vel manente mundo mutabiliter, qui, licet numquam non
fuerit et sine initio temporis, tamen factus est, vel
eius quoque ortu et occasu semper illis circuitibus
repetito semperque repetendo, ne videlicet, si aliquando primum Dei opera coepta dicuntur, priorem
suam sine initio vacationem tamquam inertem ac
desidiosam et ideo sibi displicentem damnasse quodam
modo atque ob hoc mutasse credatur.

Si autem semper quidem temporalia, sed alia atque
alia perhibetur operatus ac sic aliquando etiam ad
hominem faciendum, quem numquam antea fecerat,

---

[1] infinitarum *some MSS.*

Nor am I deterred from this belief by the arguments of philosophers. Of these the most penetrating is reckoned to be the statement that no infinite things can be comprehended by any knowledge and that, consequently, the conceptions which God has in his mind of all the finite things that he makes are all finite. We must believe, however, so these philosophers continue, that his goodness was never inoperative, lest his activity should be taken to be bounded in time, while behind that there lay an eternity of idleness, as if he had repented of his earlier leisure that was without beginning and for that reason had taken it upon himself to begin working.

Therefore it must needs be, according to their argument, that the same events are always repeated and also always race past with repetition due to recur. Either the world continues to exist while it undergoes change, the world which, though it has always been in existence and had no beginning in time, nevertheless was created, or else its coming-to-be and passing away have also always been and are always to be included in these recurrent cycles. Otherwise, plainly, if it is said that the works of God first began at some point of time, he might be thought to have condemned in a sense as unsatisfactory his earlier inactivity that had no beginning, counting it sluggish and slothful, and to have changed it for that reason.

Suppose, on the other hand, the theory be maintained that God was indeed always engaged in creating things in time, but different things at different times, and thus one day arrived also at the making of man, whom he had never previously made.

pervenisse, non scientia, qua putant non posse quaecumque infinita conprehendi, sed quasi ad horam,
sicut veniebat in mentem, fortuita quadam incon-
stantia videatur fecisse quae fecit. Porro si illi
circuitus admittantur, inquiunt, quibus, vel manente
mundo vel ipso quoque revolubiles ortus suos et
occasus eisdem circuitibus inserente, eadem temporalia repetuntur, nec ignavum otium, praesertim
tam longae sine initio diuturnitatis, Deo tribuitur nec
inprovida temeritas operum suorum, quoniam si non
eadem repetantur, non possunt infinita diversitate
variata ulla eius scientia vel praescientia conprehendi.

Has argumentationes, quibus impii nostram sim-
plicem pietatem, ut cum illis in circuitu ambulemus,
de via recta conantur avertere, si ratio refutare non
posset, fides inridere deberet. Huc accedit quod in
adiutorio Domini Dei nostri hos volubiles circulos,
quos opinio confingit, ratio manifesta confringit.
Hinc enim maxime isti errant ut in circuitu falso
ambulare quam vero et recto itinere malint, quod
mentem divinam omnino inmutabilem, cuiuslibet in-
finitatis capacem et innumera omnia sine cogitationis
alternatione numerantem, de sua humana mutabili
angustaque metiuntur. Et fit illis quod ait apostolus:

---

[1] Cf. Psalms 12.8; see also above, p. 65, note 4.

But in this case it would seem that he did what he did, not by virtue of knowledge, which they think cannot comprehend such things as are infinite, but on the spur of the moment, as it were, just as it entered his mind, with a kind of haphazard instability. Further, they contend, if we should accept this theory of cycles, in accordance with which there is a repetition of the same things created in time, whether the world remains unchanged or whether it too merges its own revolving sequence of coming-to-be and passing away with the same cycles, then neither slothful ease, especially ease of so long a duration without beginning, nor blind rashness in his works is predicated of God. For if there were no recurrence of the same events, it is impossible that their infinitely varied diversity should be encompassed by any knowledge or foreknowledge of God.

These are the arguments by which the wicked endeavour to turn our simple piety from the straight path and make us walk in circles with them.[1] But if reason could not refute these arguments, our faith should laugh them to scorn. Besides, by the help of the Lord our God these revolving circles, which owe their construction to superficial thinking, find their destruction in clear reasoning. Now the particular reason for the deviation of these men, whence they prefer to walk around in an imaginary circle instead of taking the straight path of reality, is that they measure by the narrowness of their own changeable human mind the wholly unchangeable mind of God, which can grasp no matter what infinity and counts all uncountable things without any shifting of thought from one to another. And the words of the Apostle

85

SAINT AUGUSTINE

Comparantes enim *semet ipsos sibimet ipsis non intellegunt.*

Nam quia illis quidquid novi faciendum venit in mentem novo consilio faciunt (mutabiles quippe mentes gerunt), profecto, non Deum, quem cogitare non possunt, sed semet ipsos pro illo cogitantes, non illum, sed se ipsos, nec illi, sed sibi comparant. Nobis autem fas non est credere aliter affici Deum cum vacat, aliter cum operatur, quia nec affici dicendus est, tamquam in eius natura fiat aliquid quod ante non fuerit. Patitur quippe qui afficitur, et mutabile est omne quod aliquid patitur. Non itaque in eius vacatione cogitetur ignavia desidia inertia, sicut nec in eius opere labor conatus industria. Novit quiescens agere et agens quiescere. Potest ad opus novum non novum, sed sempiternum adhibere consilium; nec paenitendo quia prius cessaverat, coepit facere quod non fecerat.

Sed et si prius cessavit et posterius operatus est (quod nescio quem ad modum ab homine possit intellegi), hoc procul dubio quod dicitur prius et posterius in rebus prius non existentibus et posterius existentibus fuit. In illo autem non alteram praecedentem altera subsequens mutavit aut abstulit voluntatem, sed una eademque sempiterna et inmutabili voluntate res quas condidit et ut prius non essent

---

[1] 2 Corinthians 10.12. Augustine's text agrees with the Greek: συνκρίνοντες ἑαυτοὺς ἑαυτοῖς οὐ συνιᾶσιν. The Vulgate reads here: *comparantes nosmet ipsos nobis.*

are applicable to them; for " comparing themselves with one another, they are without understanding." [1]

In fact, whenever the thought of doing something occurs to them, they do it with a new resolution since they are equipped with changeable minds. Thus surely, since they do not imagine God, whom they cannot imagine, but themselves in his place, they are comparing, not him, but themselves, and, not with him, but with themselves. As for us, our religion does not permit us to believe that God is in a different state when he is active and when he works, because he cannot be even said to have states at all, as if something that did not exist before could come to be in his substance. For the one who is brought into a certain state suffers an effect, and everything that suffers an effect is changeable. We should not then imagine indolence, sloth or idleness in connexion with his activity any more than we should think of toil, effort or diligence in connexion with his work. God knows how to act while resting and to rest while acting. He can bring to a new work a plan that is not new but eternal; nor did he start doing what he had not been doing because he regretted his former inactivity.

But grant even that he previously did nothing and later did something, though I know not how this may be understood by a man. Now the terms 'previously' and 'later' doubtless refer to things that previously were not, and later were, in existence. In the case of God, however, there was no previous act of will that was changed or removed by a subsequent one. Rather with one and the same will, eternal and unchanging, he caused the things that he created both not to be

egit, quamdiu non fuerunt, et ut posterius essent,
quando esse coeperunt, hinc eis qui talia videre
possunt mirabiliter fortassis ostendens quam non eis
indiguerit, sed eas gratuita bonitate condiderit, cum
sine illis ex aeternitate initio carente in non minore
beatitate permansit.

XIX

Contra eos qui dicunt ea quae infinita sunt nec Dei
posse scientia conprehendi.

Illud autem aliud quod dicunt, nec Dei scientia
quae infinita sunt posse conprehendi, restat eis ut
dicere audeant (atque huic se voragini profundae in-
pietatis inmergant) quod non omnes numeros Deus
noverit. Eos quippe infinitos esse certissimum est,
quoniam in quocumque numero finem faciendum
putaveris, idem ipse, non dico uno addito augeri, sed
quamlibet sit magnus et quamlibet ingentem multitudinem continens, in ipsa ratione atque scientia
numerorum non solum duplicari verum etiam multiplicari potest. Ita vero suis quisque numerus proprietatibus terminatur ut nullus eorum par esse cuicumque alteri possit. Ergo et dispares inter se atque
diversi sunt; et singuli quique finiti sunt, et omnes
infiniti sunt. Itane numeros propter infinitatem

in existence previously, so long as they were not, and
to be in existence later, as soon as they began to be.
Thereby he perhaps demonstrated admirably to those
who can discern such matters how little he had need
of these things, but rather created them by gratuitous
benevolence, since he had continuously enjoyed no
less bliss without them from an eternity that had no
beginning.

XIX

*Against those who contend that the things which are
infinite cannot be comprehended even by God's
knowledge.*

Now let us turn to that other statement of those
philosophers. They say that not even the wisdom
of God can comprehend what is infinite. Well, the
only thing left is for them to say boldly (and so
plunge into this deep abyss of irreligion) that God
does not know all numbers. That numbers are
infinite is indeed beyond all doubt, for at no matter
what number one may think to make an end, this
very same number, to say nothing of increasing it by
adding one, can, regardless of its magnitude and the
huge quantity that it expresses, not only be doubled
but also multiplied in accordance with the basic
principle and theory of numbers. Moreover, each
number is so delimited by its own characteristics that
no one of them can be equal to any other. Accordingly, they are unlike one another and different;
individually they are all finite, and collectively they
are all infinite. Does this mean that God does not

nescit omnes Deus, et usque ad quandam summam numerorum scientia Dei pervenit, ceteros ignorat? Quis hoc etiam dementissimus dixerit?

Nec audebunt isti contemnere numeros et eos dicere ad Dei scientiam non pertinere, apud quos Plato Deum magna auctoritate commendat mundum numeris fabricantem.[1] Et apud nos Deo dictum legitur: *Omnia in mensura et numero et pondere disposuisti.*[2] De quo et propheta dicit: *Qui profert numerose saeculum*,[3] et Salvator in evangelio: *Capilli*, inquit, *vestri omnes numerati sunt.* Absit itaque ut dubitemus quod ei notus sit omnis numerus *cuius intellegentiae*, sicut in psalmo canitur, *non est numerus.* Infinitas itaque numeri, quamvis infinitorum numerorum nullus sit numerus, non est tamen inconprehensibilis ei cuius intellegentiae non est numerus. Quapropter si quidquid scientia conprehenditur scientis conprehensione finitur, profecto et omnis infinitas quodam ineffabili modo Deo finita est quia scientiae ipsius inconprehensibilis non est.

Quare si infinitas numerorum scientiae Dei, qua conprehenditur, esse non potest infinita, qui tandem nos sumus homunculi qui eius scientiae limites figere praesumamus, dicentes quod, nisi eisdem circuitibus temporum eadem temporalia repetantur, non potest

---

[1] Cf. Plato, *Timaeus* 31c–36d.

[2] Wisdom 11.20.

[3] Isaiah 40.26. Augustine's text reflects that of the Septuagint: ὁ ἐκφέρων κατὰ ἀριθμὸν τὸν κόσμον αὐτοῦ. The Vulgate reads: *qui educit in numero militiam eorum*; the RSV renders: " He who brings out their host by number."

know all numbers because of their infinity and that his knowledge extends to a certain sum total of numbers but is ignorant of the rest? Who, no matter how demented, would say that?

Nor will those philosophers be so bold as to scorn numbers and say that they do not fall within the realm of God's knowledge, for Plato, who is one of them, with his great authority represents God as fashioning the world on numerical principles.[1] And in our own Scripture we read the words addressed to God: "Thou hast ordered all things by measure and number and weight."[2] The prophet also says of God: "He who brings forth an age by number,"[3] and in the gospel the Saviour says: "Your hairs are all numbered."[4] Let us then not doubt that every number is known to him "of whose understanding," as the psalm goes, "there is no set number."[5] Accordingly, the infinity of number, although there is no set number of infinite numbers, nevertheless is not incomprehensible to him "of whose understanding there is no set number." Wherefore, if whatever is comprehended by knowledge is limited by the comprehension of him who knows, assuredly all infinity also is in some ineffable way finite to God because it is not incomprehensible for his knowledge.

Consequently, if the infinity of numbers cannot be without limit for the knowledge of God by which it is comprehended, who indeed are we petty men to presume to set limits to his knowledge by saying that, unless the same temporal things are repeated in the same periodic cycles, God cannot either foreknow

[4] Matthew 10.30.
[5] Psalms 147.5.

Deus cuncta quae facit [1] vel praescire ut faciat vel scire cum fecerit? Cuius sapientia simpliciter multiplex et uniformiter multiformis tam inconprehensibili conprehensione omnia inconprehensibilia conprehendit ut, quaecumque nova et dissimilia consequentia praecedentibus si semper facere vellet, inordinata et inprovisa habere non posset, nec ea provideret [2] ex proximo tempore, sed aeterna praescientia contineret.

XX

De saeculis saeculorum.

Quod utrum ita faciat et continuata sibi conexione copulentur quae appellantur saecula saeculorum, alia tamen atque alia ordinata dissimilitudine procurrentia, eis dumtaxat qui ex miseria liberantur in sua beata inmortalitate sine fine manentibus, an ita dicantur saecula saeculorum ut intellegantur saecula in sapientia Dei inconcussa stabilitate manentia istorum quae cum tempore transeunt tamquam efficientia saeculorum, definire non audeo. Fortassis enim possit dici saeculum quae sunt saecula, ut nihil aliud perhibeatur saeculum saeculi quam saecula saeculorum, sicut nihil aliud dicitur caelum caeli quam caeli caelorum. Nam caelum Deus vocavit firmamentum super quod sunt aquae, et tamen

[1] fecit *some MSS.*
[2] praevideret *a few MSS.*

---

[1] Cf. Psalms 115.16, where the Vulgate reads: *Caelum caeli,* cited by Augustine in his *Confessions* 12.2.2; 8.8; 11.12; 15.20; 21.30; 13.5.6; 8.9.

all that he does in order to do it or know it when he
has done it? For his wisdom, which is simple in its
multiplicity and uniform in its multiformity, compre-
hends all incomprehensible things with a comprehension so incomprehensible that, if he willed always
to make all subsequent events novel and unlike those
that preceded, he could not have them so without a
pattern or without foresight, nor would he foresee
them only at the last moment, but they would be
included in his eternal foreknowledge.

XX

On ages of ages.

I do not venture to pronounce whether this is how
God proceeds, and whether the so-called ages of
ages are joined in a continuous series, yet running
on, each after the other, in ordered dissimilarity,
while only those who gain freedom from their
wretched state remain without end in their blessed
immortality, or whether the ages of ages are so
designated in order that we may understand the
ages that abide in the wisdom of God with unshaken
steadfastness as being the efficient causes of those
ages that pass with time. Perhaps the term ' ages '
may mean no more than ' age ' so that ' ages of ages '
is just another expression for ' age of age,' just as
' heavens of heavens ' is for ' heaven of heaven.' [1]
For God called the firmament that lies beneath the
waters ' heaven,' [2] and yet the psalm says: " And

[2] Cf. Genesis 1.7–8.

psalmus: *Et aquae*, inquit, *quae super caelos* [1] *laudent nomen Domini.*

Quid ergo istorum duorum sit, an praeter haec duo aliquid aliud de saeculis saeculorum possit intellegi, profundissima quaestio est; neque hoc quod nunc agimus inpedit si indiscussa interim differatur, sive aliquid in ea definire valeamus sive nos faciat cautiores diligentior ipsa tractatio, ne in tanta obscuritate rerum adfirmare temere aliquid audeamus. Nunc enim contra opinionem disputamus qua illi circuitus asseruntur quibus semper eadem per intervalla temporum necesse esse repeti existimantur. Quaelibet autem illarum sententiarum de saeculis saeculorum vera sit, ad hos circuitus nihil pertinet, quoniam, sive saecula saeculorum sint non eadem repetita, sed alterum ex altero conexione [2] ordinatissima procurrentia, liberatorum beatitudine sine ullo recursu miseriarum certissima permanente, sive saecula saeculorum aeterna sint temporalium tamquam dominantia subditorum, circuitus illi eadem revolventes locum non habent, quos maxime refellit aeterna vita sanctorum.

[1] caelos sunt *many MSS.*, *Vulg.*
[2] conexione *most MSS.:* contextione *V, according to Kalb, Philologus 87 (1932), 478, and one other MS.*

let the waters that are above the heavens praise the name of the Lord." [1]

It is then a very profound question to decide which of these two is correct, or whether, besides these two meanings, the phrase 'ages of ages' may admit of some other interpretation. But it does not hinder our present discussion to postpone the problem meanwhile without examination, and this holds true whether we should prove capable of arriving at some conclusion of the matter or whether the very consideration of it with closer attention should render us more cautious for fear of making any rash assertion where the subject is so obscure. For our present concern is to refute that cyclic theory according to which the same things must always be repeated at periodic intervals. Yet no matter which of the interpretations mentioned of 'ages of ages' is correct, it has no bearing on these cycles. For whether the term 'ages of ages' means, not a repetition of the same ages, but a succession of different ages, running on one after the other, with perfectly ordered connexion, while the bliss of delivered souls remains most secure without any return of miseries, or whether the 'ages of ages' are eternal, standing in relation to those of time as master to subject, there is no place for those cyclic repetitions, which are utterly refuted by the eternal life of the saints. [2]

---

[1] Psalms 148.4.
[2] Matthew 25.46.

SAINT AUGUSTINE

XXI

De impietate eorum qui asserunt animas summae veraeque beatitudinis participes iterum atque iterum per circuitus temporum ad easdem miserias laboresque redituras.

Quorum enim aures piorum ferant post emensam tot tantisque calamitatibus vitam (si tamen vita ista dicenda est quae potius mors est ita gravis ut mors quae ab hac liberat mortis huius amore timeatur), post tam magna mala tamque multa et horrenda tandem aliquando per veram religionem atque sapientiam expiata atque finita ita pervenire ad conspectum Dei atque ita fieri beatum contemplatione incorporeae lucis per participationem inmutabilis inmortalitatis eius, cuius adipiscendae amore flagramus, ut eam quandoque necesse sit deseri et eos qui deserunt ab illa aeternitate veritate felicitate deiectos tartareae mortalitati, turpi stultitiae, miseriis exsecrabilibus implicari, ubi Deus amittatur, ubi odio veritas habeatur, ubi per inmundas nequitias bcatitudo quaeratur, et hoc itidem atque itidem sine ullo fine priorum et posteriorum certis intervallis et dimensionibus saeculorum factum et futurum; et hoc propterea, ut possint Deo circuitibus definitis euntibus semper atque redeuntibus per nostras falsas beatitudines et veras miserias alternatim quidem,

---

[1] Cf. below, 13.10 (pp. 163–167); Cicero, *De Re Publica* 6.14.14; *Tusculanae Disputationes* 1.31.75.

XXI

On the irreligion of those who maintain that souls
which partake of supreme and true happiness will
return again and again in periodic cycles to the
same miseries and toils.

For who of the truly religious could endure to hear
such words as these? After life has been lived amid
so many and so great unhappy circumstances—if
indeed life is the proper word for what is rather a
death so burdensome that the death which frees us
from it is feared because of our love for this living
death [1]—after the many great and frightful evils have
at long last been expiated and finished thanks to
true religion and wisdom, we are to arrive, so we are
told, at the vision of God and find bliss in the con-
templation of incorporeal light through participation
in his unchangeable immortality, which we yearn to
attain with a burning passion, only on the condition
that we must some time abandon it. And those
who abandon it are then doomed to be hurled from
that everlasting life, that truth, that happiness and
to be caught in the toils of hellish mortality, ugly
folly, abominable miseries, where God is taken from
them, hatred for truth prevails, and the pursuit of
bliss goes on amid unclean frivolities. Further, this
has happened and will happen again and again without end at fixed intervals and measures of ages past
and future. And those philosophers maintain all
this to enable God to know his own works through
the eternal revolution of defined cycles, wherein our
false bliss and true misery alternate with one another

97

sed revolutione incessabili sempiternas nota esse
opera sua, quoniam neque a faciendo quiescere
neque sciendo potest ea quae infinita sunt indagare?

Quis haec audiat? Quis credat? Quis ferat?
Quae si vera essent, non solum tacerentur prudentius,
verum etiam (ut quo modo valeo dicam quod volo)
doctius nescirentur. Nam si haec illic in memoria
non habebimus et ideo beati erimus, cur hic per
eorum scientiam gravatur amplius nostra miseria?
Si autem ibi ea necessario scituri sumus, hic saltem
nesciamus, ut hic felicior sit expectatio quam illic
adeptio summi boni, quando hic aeterna vita conse-
quenda expectatur, ibi autem beata, sed non aeterna,
quandoque amittenda cognoscitur.

Si autem dicunt neminem posse ad illam beatitudinem pervenire nisi hos circuitus, ubi beatitudo et
miseria vicissim alternant, in huius vitae eruditione
cognoverit, quo modo ergo fatentur, quanto plus
quisque amaverit Deum, tanto eum facilius ad
beatitudinem perventurum, qui ea docent quibus
amor ipse torpescat? Nam quis non remissius et
tepidius amet eum quem se cogitat necessario deser-
turum et contra eius veritatem sapientiamque sen-
surum, et hoc cum ad eius plenam pro sua capacitate
notitiam beatitudinis perfectione pervenerit, quando
nec hominem amicum possit quisque amare fideliter

but yet are everlasting because of the ceaseless rotation; for otherwise, according to them, God can neither rest from creating nor encompass by his knowledge an infinity of events.

Now who would lend ear to such views as these? Who would believe or tolerate them? Even if they were true, not only would it be more sensible to say nothing about the facts, but also, to speak my mind as best I can, it would be more intelligent to know nothing about them. For if we are not to remember them in the world beyond and are thus to enjoy happiness, why is the burden of our misery in this world increased by the knowledge of them? On the other hand, if we must perforce get to know them there, let us be ignorant of them here at least, that our expectation of the highest good may be happier in this life than its attainment in the life beyond, for here we expect a future of eternal life, whereas there it is found to be a happy life, but not eternal, a life that must at some time be lost.

Again, if they say that no one can arrive at that bliss unless he has learned in this life and come to know those cyclic alternations of happiness and misery, how then can they aver that the more each one loves God, the more readily he will arrive at bliss, and yet teach doctrines to make that very love grow cold? Who indeed would not be more careless and lukewarm in his love for someone when he imagines that he will perforce leave him and disagree with his truth and wisdom, and this when he has reached, in the perfection of bliss, the fullest knowledge of him of which he is capable? For no one can love loyally even a human friend when he knows

cui se futurum novit inimicum? Sed absit ut vera
sint quae nobis minantur veram miseriam numquam
finiendam, sed interpositionibus falsae beatitudinis
saepe ac sine fine rumpendam.

Quid enim illa beatitudine falsius atque fallacius
ubi nos futuros miseros aut in tanta veritatis luce
nesciamus aut in summa felicitatis arce timeamus?
Si enim venturam calamitatem ignoraturi sumus,
peritior est hic nostra miseria, ubi venturam beatitudinem novimus. Si autem nos illic clades inminens
non latebit, beatius tempora transigit anima misera,
quibus transactis ad beatitudinem sublevetur, quam
beata, quibus transactis in miseriam revolvatur.
Atque ita spes nostrae infelicitatis est felix et felicitatis infelix. Unde fit ut, quia hic mala praesentia
patimur, ibi metuimus inminentia, verius semper
miseri quam beati aliquando esse possimus.

Sed quoniam haec falsa sunt clamante pietate, con-
vincente veritate (illa enim nobis veraciter promittitur vera felicitas cuius erit semper retinenda et
nulla infelicitate rumpenda certa securitas), viam
rectam sequentes, quod nobis est Christus, eo duce ac
salvatore, a vano et inepto impiorum circuitu iter
fidei mentemque avertamus. Si enim de istis cir-

---

[1] Cf. Cicero, *De Amicitia* 16.59.   [2] Cf. John 14.6.
[3] See above, 12.14 (p. 61).

that in the future he will be an enemy.[1]   But heaven
forbid that there be any truth in the threats that
these philosophers make to us of a misery destined
never to be ended but often and endlessly to be
interrupted by intervals of false bliss.

Truly, nothing is more false or fallacious than that
kind of bliss which leaves us either in so great a light
of truth ignorant that we shall be wretched or on the
highest pinnacle of happiness fearful because we
shall be so.   For if in the world beyond we are to be
ignorant of future misfortune, then our present
misery on earth is better informed, since it allows us
to know of future bliss.   On the other hand, if in the
world beyond impending disaster is not to be concealed from us, the soul passes its periods of time
more happily in misery than it does in happiness;
for in the former case, when the periods are completed, the soul is to be raised to bliss, but in the
latter the soul is at the end to come full circle to
misery.   And thus the prospect that we have in our
unhappiness is happy and that which we have in our
happiness is unhappy.   Consequently, since we suffer
present evils here on earth and fear impending evils
there in heaven, it is truer to say that we may always
be in misery than that we may sometimes be in bliss.

But these views, as religion cries out and truth
proves, are false, for we are truthfully promised that
true happiness whose assured serenity will be ours
to possess forever unbroken by unhappiness.   Let
us then follow the straight way that we have in
Christ,[2] and with him as our leader and saviour let us
turn away our minds and the route of our faith from
the vain and bungling gyrations of the irreligious.[3]

cuitibus et sine cessatione alternantibus itionibus et
reditionibus animarum Porphyrius Platonicus suorum
opinionem sequi noluit, sive ipsius rei vanitate
permotus sive iam tempora Christiana reveritus, et,
quod in libro decimo commemoravi dicere maluit
animam propter cognoscenda mala traditam mundo,
ut ab eis liberata atque purgata, cum ad Patrem
redierit, nihil ulterius tale patiatur, quanto magis nos
istam inimicam Christianae fidei falsitatem detestari
ac devitare debemus!

His autem circuitibus evacuatis atque frustratis,
nulla necessitas nos compellit ideo putare non habere
initium temporis ex quo esse coeperit genus humanum, quia per nescio quos circuitus nihil sit in
rebus novi quod non et antea certis intervallis temporum fuerit et postea sit futurum. Si enim liberatur
anima non reditura ad miserias, sicut numquam antea
liberata est, fit in illa aliquid quod antea numquam
factum est, et hoc quidem valde magnum, id est
quae numquam desinat aeterna felicitas. Si autem
in natura inmortali fit tanta novitas nullo repetita,
nullo repetenda circuitu, cur in rebus mortalibus fieri
non posse contenditur? Si dicunt non fieri in anima
beatitudinis novitatem quoniam ad eam revertitur

---

[1] On Porphyry see above, vol. 2, 466, note 1.
[2] See above, 10.30.

Concerning these cycles and the ceaseless ebb and flow of souls going and returning the Platonist Porphyry [1] declined to follow the opinion of his school—I am not sure whether it was because he was agitated by the implicit nonsense of the very idea or because he already had some respect for the Christian era. As I mentioned in the tenth book,[2] he preferred to say that the soul was entrusted to the world to become acquainted with evils, in order that, after it had been delivered and purified from them and had returned to the Father, it might never again suffer such a thing. How much more ought we to abominate and avoid that false doctrine which is hostile to our Christian faith!

Moreover, once this theory of cycles has been disposed of and refuted, we are under no compulsion to think that the human race did not have a beginning in time, with which it first came into existence, because of any argument that cycles, whatever they are, ensure that nothing new happens in history that did not occur previously at certain periodic intervals and is not destined to occur hereafter. For if the soul is freed and, just as it was never before freed, so is destined never to return to miseries, there is created in it something never before created, and this something is indeed a very great thing, namely, an eternal felicity that is nevermore to cease. Now if there occurs in an immortal being so great an innovation that has not been and will not be repeated by any gyration, why do they argue that no such thing can occur in mortal entities? Suppose they say that the bliss that occurs in the soul is nothing new since it merely returns to that happy state in

in qua semper fuit, ipsa certe liberatio nova fit, cum
de miseria liberatur in qua numquam fuit, et ipsa
miseriae novitas in ea facta est quae numquam fuit.
Haec autem novitas si non in rerum quae divina
providentia gubernantur ordinem venit sed casu
potius evenit, ubi sunt illi determinati dimensique
circuitus, in quibus nulla nova fiunt sed repetuntur
eadem quae fuerunt?

Si autem et haec novitas ab ordinatione providentiae non excluditur, sive data sit anima sive lapsa
sit, possunt fieri nova quae neque antea facta sint nec
tamen a rerum ordine aliena sint.   Et si potuit anima
per inprudentiam facere sibi novam miseriam quae
non esset inprovisa divinae providentiae ut hanc
quoque in rerum ordine includeret et ab hac eam non
inprovide liberaret, qua tandem temeritate humanae
vanitatis audemus negare divinitatem facere posse
res, non sibi, sed mundo novas, quas neque antea
fecerit nec umquam habuerit inprovisas?

Si autem dicunt liberatas quidem animas ad
miseriam non reversuras, sed, cum hoc fit in rebus,
nihil novi fieri quoniam semper aliae atque aliae
liberatae sunt et liberantur et liberabuntur, hoc certe
concedunt, si ita est, novas animas fieri quibus sit et
nova miseria et nova liberatio.   Nam si antiquas eas
esse dicunt et retrorsum sempiternas, ex quibus

---

1 The Neoplatonists debated whether the soul was united
with a body by God's will or " lapsed " into it as retribution
for sin.

which it always was. Then, at any rate, the freeing
itself that occurs is new, when the soul is freed from
misery in which it never was before, and the misery
itself that never before existed in the soul is a new
thing produced in it. But if these innovations do
not enter into the order of things governed by divine
providence but happen rather by chance, then what
about those fixed and measured cycles, in which
nothing new is created but the same things that have
been are repeated?

If, however, these innovations too gain admittance
to the order of providence, whether the soul was
delivered to this experience or fell into it,[1] there can
be new events that neither occurred previously nor
yet are unrelated to the pattern of history. And if
the soul could through its own improvidence create
new misery for itself that was not unforeseen by
divine providence, which could thus include it too
in the order of things and set the soul free from it
not without foresight, what rash human vanity
prompts us that we dare deny that God can create
things which are new not to him but to the world,
things which were neither created previously nor
yet at any time unforeseen by him?

But if, granting that freed souls will not return to
misery, they say that, when this release occurs in the
world, nothing new occurs since there always have
been, now are and ever will be souls gaining freedom,
group after group, they at any rate yield the point,
if this is so, that there come into being new souls that
are to have both misery and freedom as novelties.
For if they maintain that the souls are not new but
have existed from past eternity, that is, souls where-

cotidie novi fiant homines, de quorum corporibus, si
sapienter vixerint, ita liberentur ut numquam ad
miserias revolvantur, consequenter dicturi sunt
infinitas. Quantuslibet namque finitus numerus
fuisset animarum, infinitis retro saeculis sufficere non
valeret ut ex illo semper homines fierent quorum
essent animae ab ista semper mortalitate liberandae,
numquam ad eam deinceps rediturae. Nec ullo
modo explicabunt quo modo in rebus quas, ut Deo
notae esse possint, finitas volunt infinitus sit numerus
animarum.

Quapropter, quoniam circuitus illi iam explosi sunt,
quibus ad easdem miserias necessario putabatur anima
reditura, quid restat convenientius pietati quam
credere non esse inpossibile Deo et ea quae numquam
fecerit nova facere et ineffabili praescientia voluntatem mutabilem non habere? Porro autem utrum
animarum liberatarum nec ulterius ad miserias redi-
turarum numerus possit semper augeri, ipsi viderint
qui de rerum infinitate cohibenda tam subtiliter
disputant. Nos vero ratiocinationem nostram ex
utroque latere terminamus. Si enim potest, quid
causae est ut negetur creari potuisse quod numquam
antea creatum esset, si liberatarum animarum
numerus, qui numquam antea fuit, non solum factus
est semel, sed fieri numquam desinet? Si autem
oportet ut certus sit liberatarum aliquis numerus

with each day there are created new men, from whose
bodies, if they have lived wisely, they will be freed
with no need to rotate back to miseries, they will, to
be consistent, have to say that the souls are infinite
in number. For no matter how large a finite number of souls there may have been, it could not be
enough for infinite past ages to ensure the perpetual
creation of men whose souls were always to be set
free from this mortality and never thereafter to
return to it. And they will be quite unable to explain how there can be an infinite number of souls in
a world where, according to them, events must be
finite for God to know them.

Wherefore, since we have now exploded that
theory of cycles, according to which the soul was
bound to return to the same miseries, nothing can
be more in harmony with our faith than to believe
that it is not impossible for God both to create new
things which he never before created and at the same
time, because of his ineffable foreknowledge, not to
have a will that changes. Further, the question
whether the number of souls that have been set free
and are no longer to return to miseries can always go
on increasing is recommended to the attention of
those who so subtly debate about putting a limit on
things infinite. We, for our part, conclude our
argument in the form of a dilemma. For if the
answer is yes, why should it be denied that what had
never before been created can have been created, if,
in the case of souls set free, a number which never
before existed not only was created once but will
never cease to be created? On the other hand, if
there must be some fixed number of souls set free

animarum quae ad miseriam numquam redeant,
neque iste numerus ulterius augeatur, etiam ipse sine
dubio, quicumque erit, ante utique numquam fuit,
qui profecto crescere et ad suae quantitatis terminum
pervenire sine aliquo non posset initio; quod initium
eo modo antea numquam fuit. Hoc ergo ut esset,
creatus est homo, ante quem nullus fuit.

XXII

De conditione unius primi hominis atque in eo generis
humani.

Hac igitur quaestione difficillima propter aeternitatem Dei nova creantis sine novitate aliqua voluntatis,
quantum potuimus, explicata, non est arduum videre
multo fuisse melius quod factum est, ut ex uno
homine quem primum condidit multiplicaret genus
humanum quam si id incohasset a pluribus. Nam
cum animantes alias solitarias et quodam modo
solivagas, id est, quae solitudinem magis adpetant,
sicuti sunt aquilae milvi, leones lupi et quaecumque
ita sunt, alias congreges instituerit, quae congre-
gatae atque in gregibus malint vivere, ut sunt co-
lumbi sturni, cervi dammulae et cetera huius modi,
utrumque tamen genus non ex singulis propagavit,
sed plura simul iussit existere.

that are never to return to misery, and if this number must not be further increased, then even this very number doubtless, whatever it will be, was certainly never in existence before, nor could it surely increase and reach the limit of its size without some beginning. But this beginning never before existed in that way. Accordingly, in order that there might be this beginning, a man, before whom none existed, was created.

XXII

On the creation of the one first man and of the human race in him.

WE have therefore explained, as best we could, the extremely difficult problem regarding the eternity of God and his creation of new things without any innovation in his will. Now that we have done this, it is not hard to see that what happened, namely, God's propagation of the human race from the single man whom he first created, was much better than if he had begun it with several. For in the case of other animals he created some to be solitary and, so to say, lone-ranging, that is, animals who are more attracted to separate living, like eagles, kites, lions, wolves and so on, while others he created to be gregarious, animals preferring to live together in groups, like doves, starlings, deer, little fallow-deer and so on. Yet when he created these animals, he did not propagate both kinds from single specimens but ordered more than one to take up existence at the same time.

SAINT AUGUSTINE

Hominem vero, cuius naturam quodam modo mediam inter angelos bestiasque condebat ut, si Creatori suo tamquam vero domino subditus praeceptum eius pia oboedientia custodiret, in consortium transiret angelicum, sine morte media beatam inmortalitatem absque ullo termino consecutus,[1] si autem Dominum Deum suum libera voluntate superbe atque inoboedienter usus offenderet, morti addictus bestialiter viveret, libidinis servus aeternoque post mortem supplicio destinatus, unum ac singulum creavit, non utique solum sine humana societate deserendum, sed ut eo modo vehementius ei commendaretur ipsius societatis unitas vinculumque concordiae, si non tantum inter se naturae similitudine verum etiam cognationis affectu homines necterentur; quando ne ipsam quidem feminam copulandam viro sicut ipsum creare illi placuit, sed ex ipso ut omnino [2] ex homine uno diffunderetur genus humanum.

[1] consecuturus *some MSS.*
[2] omne *a few MSS.*

In the case of man, however, he proceeded differently. For he created man's nature to be midway,
so to speak, between angels and beasts in such a way
that, if he should remain in subjection to his creator
as his true lord and with dutiful obedience keep his
commandment, he was to pass into the company of
the angels, obtaining with no intervening death [1]
a blissful immortality that has no limit; but if he
should make proud and disobedient use of his free
will and go counter to the Lord his God, he was to
live like a beast, at the mercy of death, enthralled by
lust and doomed to eternal punishment after death.
That God created man one and alone did not, however, mean that he was to be left in his solitary state
without human fellowship. The purpose was rather
to ensure that unity of fellowship itself and ties of
harmony might be more strongly impressed on him,
if men were bound to one another not only by their
similar nature but also by their feeling of kinship.[2]
For not even woman herself, who was to be joined to
man, did he choose to create as he did that very man,
but he created her out of that man in order that the
human race might derive entirely from one man.[3]

---

[1] Cf. below, 13.1 (p. 135); 13.3 (p. 141). Augustine opposed
the doctrine of the Pelagians, who held that death was a
necessary condition of man's mortal nature even if Adam had
not sinned; cf. his *De Haeresibus* 88.

[2] Cf. below, 14.1 (p. 259).

[3] Cf. Genesis 2.22.

SAINT AUGUSTINE

XXIII

Quod praescierit Deus hominem quem primum condidit peccaturum simulque praeviderit quantum piorum populum ex eius genere in angelicum consortium sua esset gratia translaturus.

Nec ignorabat Deus hominem peccaturum et morti iam obnoxium morituros propagaturum eoque progressuros peccandi inmanitate mortales ut tutius atque pacatius inter se rationalis voluntatis expertes bestiae sui generis viverent, quarum ex aquis et terris plurium [1] pullulavit exordium, quam homines quorum genus ex uno est ad commendandam concordiam propagatum. Neque enim umquam inter se leones aut inter se dracones qualia homines bella gesserunt. Sed praevidebat etiam gratia sua populum piorum in adoptionem vocandum remissisque peccatis iustificatum Spiritu sancto sanctis angelis in aeterna pace sociandum, novissima inimica morte destructa; cui populo esset huius rei consideratio profutura, quod ex uno homine Deus ad commendandum hominibus quam ei grata sit etiam in pluribus unitas genus instituisset humanum.

[1] plurimum *many MSS.*

---

[1] Cf. Horace, *Epodes* 7.11–12; Pliny the Elder, *Naturalis Historia* 7, Praefatio 5; Juvenal, 15.159–171; Seneca the Younger, *De Clementia* 1.26.3; *Epistulae Morales* 95.31.

XXIII

That God foreknew that the first man whom he created would sin, and at the same time foresaw how large a company of righteous men he would translate by his grace from the human race into the society of the angels.

GOD was not unaware that man would sin and that, being already doomed to death, he would propagate mortals destined to die. Further, these mortals, he knew, would go so far in the enormity of their sins that even beasts without a rational will, such as arose in teeming numbers from the waters and the lands, would live more securely and peaceably with their own kind than men, whose race was propagated from one individual for the purpose of inspiring harmony. For never did lions or dragons wage such wars with one another as men have waged.[1] But he foresaw also that by his grace a company of righteous men would be called to adoption and that, after they were forgiven their sins and made righteous by the Holy Spirit, they would be united with the holy angels in eternal peace, when the last enemy, death, was destroyed.[2] And this company, he knew, would profit by a consideration of the historical fact that God had created the human race out of one man to make it clear to men how pleasing to him is oneness even among many.[3]

[2] Cf. 1 Corinthians 15.26.
[3] Cf. Psalms 133.1.

SAINT AUGUSTINE

XXIV

De natura humanae animae creatae ad imaginem Dei.

Fecit ergo Deus hominem ad imaginem suam. Talem quippe illi animam creavit qua per rationem atque intellegentiam omnibus esset praestantior animalibus terrestribus et natatilibus et volatilibus, quae mentem huius modi non haberent. Et cum virum terreno formasset ex pulvere eique animam qualem dixi sive quam iam fecerat sufflando indidisset sive potius sufflando fecisset eumque flatum quem sufflando fecit (nam quid est aliud sufflare quam flatum facere ?), animam hominis esse voluisset, etiam coniugem illi in adiutorium generandi ex eius latere osse detracto fecit, ut Deus. Neque enim haec carnali consuetudine cogitanda sunt, ut videre solemus opifices ex materia quacumque terrena corporalibus membris quod artis industria potuerint fabricantes. Manus Dei potentia Dei est, qui etiam visibilia invisibiliter operatur. Sed haec fabulosa potius quam vera esse arbitrantur qui virtutem ac sapientiam Dei, qua novit et potest etiam sine seminibus ipsa certe facere semina, ex his usitatis et cotidianis metiuntur operibus. Ea vero quae primitus instituta sunt, quoniam

---

[1] Cf. Genesis 1.26–27.
[2] Cf. Genesis 2.7.
[3] As proposed by Augustine, *De Genesi ad Litteram* 7.24.35.
[4] Cf. Genesis 2.21–22.
[5] For Augustine's stand against an anthropomorphic view of God's creative acts, see his *De Genesi ad Litteram* 6.12.20.

XXIV

On the nature of the human soul created in the image of God.

God therefore fashioned man in his own image.[1] That is, he endowed him with a soul that enabled him through reason and intelligence to surpass all other animals that move on land or swim or fly, since they had no mind of this sort. Now God shaped man from the dust of the earth [2] and then endowed him with the soul that I mentioned. Either he had implanted in him by breathing a soul that he had already made,[3] or had rather created it by breathing and willed that this breath, made by breathing, should be the soul of man. (' To breathe ' means, of course, ' to make breath.') Next, out of a bone taken from the man's side he also made him a wife to help him in the work of procreation.[4] He accomplished all this as God. For we must not, in typical carnal fashion, imagine this work as wrought after the manner of artisans, whom we frequently see shaping with physical hands earthly material of every sort into such products as their professional skill enables them to make. The hand of God is the power of God, who produces even visible things in an invisible way.[5] But this is deemed myth rather than true history by those who use our commonplace, everyday works as standards to measure the might and wisdom of God, which give him the knowledge and power to make assuredly even without seeds the very seeds themselves. As for those things that were first created, they regard them sceptically since

non noverunt, infideliter cogitant, quasi non haec
ipsa quae noverunt de humanis conceptibus atque
partubus, si inexpertis narrarentur, incredibiliora
viderentur, quamvis et ea ipsa plerique magis
naturae corporalibus causis quam operibus divinae
mentis adsignent.

XXV

An ullius vel minimae creaturae possint dici angeli
creatores.

SED cum his nullum nobis est in his libris negotium
qui divinam mentem facere vel curare ista non
credunt. Illi autem qui Platoni suo credunt non ab
illo summo Deo qui fabricatus est mundum, sed ab
aliis minoribus, quos quidem ipse creaverit, permissu
sive iussu eius, animalia facta esse cuncta mortalia,
in quibus homo praecipuum diisque ipsis cognatum
teneret locum, si superstitione careant qua quaerunt
unde iuste videantur sacra et sacrificia facere quasi
conditoribus suis, facile carebunt etiam huius opinionis
errore. Neque enim fas est ullius naturae quamlibet
minimae mortalisque creatorem nisi Deum credere
ac dicere, et antequam possit intellegi. Angeli
autem, quos illi deos libentius appellant, etiamsi
adhibent vel iussi vel permissi operationem suam

---

[1] Such was the view of the Epicureans, who held that any
creative activity or concern over affairs would be incompatible
with the supreme happiness of the gods.

they do not know them, as though those very facts
that they do know about human conceptions and
births would not seem more unbelievable if they were
told to those unfamiliar with them. And yet these
very matters, too, many people attribute to natural
physical causes rather than to the working of the
divine mind.

XXV

*Whether the creation of any creature, even the smallest,
can be attributed to the angels.*

BUT in these books we are not concerned with those
who do not believe that the divine mind makes or
cares for these things,[1] There are, however, those
who, following their master Plato, believe that all
mortal animals, among whom man holds a position of
pre-eminence and kinship with the gods themselves,
were made not by the supreme God who fashioned
the world but, at his leave or behest, by other lesser
gods, who were, to be sure, created by him.[2] But if
only they could be rid of the superstition which
prompts them to seek to justify their performance of
rites and sacrifices to their supposed creators, they
will easily be rid also of the error of this belief. For
it is wrong to believe and say that the creation of
any nature, however small and mortal, was effected
by anyone save God, even before we can understand
why. As for the angels, whom those philosophers
prefer to call gods, even though they directly participate, whether by order or by leave, in the production

[2] Cf. Plato, *Timaeus* 41a–d; 69c.

rebus quae gignuntur in mundo, tam non [1] eos dicimus creatores animalium quam nec agricolas frugum
atque arborum.

XXVI

*Omnem naturam et omnem speciem universae
creaturae non nisi opere Dei fieri atque
formari.*

Cum enim alia sit species quae adhibetur extrinsecus cuicumque materiae corporali, sicut operantur
homines figuli et fabri atque id genus opifices, qui
etiam pingunt et effingunt formas similes corporibus
animalium, alia vero quae intrinsecus efficientes
causas habet de secreto et occulto naturae viventis
atque intellegentis arbitrio, quae non solum naturales
corporum species verum etiam ipsas animantium
animas, dum non fit, facit, supra dicta illa species
artificibus quibusque tribuatur, haec autem altera
non nisi uni artifici, creatori et conditori Deo, qui
mundum ipsum et angelos sine ullo mundo et sine
ullis angelis fecit.

Qua enim vi divina et, ut ita dicam, effectiva, quae
fieri nescit sed facere, accepit speciem, cum mundus
fieret, rutunditas caeli et rutunditas solis, eadem vi
divina et effectiva, quae fieri nescit, sed facere,
accepit speciem rutunditas oculi et rutunditas pomi

---

[1] tamen non *some MSS.*; tamen tam non *some early editors.*

of things in the world, we can no more call them creators of animals than we in fact call farmers creators of crops and trees.

XXVI

That every natural thing and every form of all creation is made and shaped by the work of God.

Now there are two kinds of forms. First, there is the form that is applied externally to each and every physical substance, as is done by potters, smiths and other artisans of this sort, who even paint and fashion shapes that resemble the bodies of animals. And second, there is also the form that has inherent efficient causes deriving from the secret and hidden discretion of a living and intelligent nature, which, without being made itself, makes not only natural physical forms but also the very souls of living beings. The first-mentioned kind of form we may attribute to the several craftsmen, but the latter only to one craftsman, creator and founder, God, who made the world itself and the angels when no world and no angels existed.

For there is a divine and, if I may say, productive force, that is capable only of making and not of being made, from which came the roundness of the sky and the roundness of the sun when the world was being made. It is the same divine and productive force, that is capable only of making and not of being made, from which came the roundness of the eye and the roundness of a fruit as well as the

et ceterae figurae naturales, quas videmus in rebus quibusque nascentibus non extrinsecus adhiberi, sed intima Creatoris potentia, qui dixit: *Caelum et terram ego impleo*, et cuius sapientia est quae *adtingit a fine usque ad finem fortiter et disponit omnia suaviter*.[1] Proinde facti primitus angeli cuius modi ministerium praebuerint Creatori cetera facienti nescio. Nec tribuere illis audeo quod forte non possunt, nec debeo derogare quod possunt. Creationem tamen conditionemque omnium naturarum, qua fit ut omnino naturae sint, eis quoque faventibus illi Deo tribuo cui se etiam ipsi debere quod sunt cum gratiarum actione noverunt.

Non solum igitur agricolas non dicimus fructuum quorumque creatores, cum legamus: *Neque qui plantat est aliquid neque qui rigat, sed qui incrementum dat Deus*, sed ne ipsam quidem terram, quamvis mater omnium fecunda videatur quae germinibus erumpentia promovet et fixa radicibus continet, cum itidem legamus: *Deus illi dat corpus quo modo voluerit et unicuique seminum proprium corpus*. Ita nec feminam sui puerperii creatricem appellare debemus sed potius illum qui cuidam famulo suo dixit: *Priusquam te formarem in utero, novi te.* Et quamvis anima sic vel sic affecta praegnantis valeat aliquibus velut induere qualitatibus fetum, sicut de virgis variatis fecit

---

[1] suaviter *most MSS., Vulg.:* sapienter *V. The Septuagint reads here:* χρηστῶς.

---

[1] Jeremiah 23.24.　　　[2] Wisdom 8.1.
[3] 1 Corinthians 3.7.　　[4] 1 Corinthians 15.38.
[5] Jeremiah 1.5.

forms of other natural objects that we see bestowed
on each several thing at birth not from without but
by the inmost power of the Creator, who said: " I
fill heaven and earth," [1] and whose wisdom it is that
" reaches from one end to another mightily and
sweetly orders all things." [2]   Accordingly, I do not
know what kind of service was rendered by the angels,
who were first to be made, when the Creator went
on to make other things.   I am not so bold as to
ascribe to them something that perchance they
cannot do, and I ought not to deny them anything
that they can do.   Nevertheless, I attribute, with
the approval of the angels as well, the creation and
formation of all natural things, whereby it comes that
things exist at all, to that God to whom even they
themselves gratefully recognize that they are indebted for their existence.

Not only then do we not call farmers the creators
of each kind of fruit, for we read: " Neither he who
plants nor he who waters is anything, but only God
who gives the growth," [3] but we do not give the name
creator even to the earth herself, although she shows
herself the fruitful mother of all the things that she
thrusts up when they burst with young shoots, while
she holds them fast by the roots; for we likewise
read: " God gives it a body as he has chosen and to
each of the seeds its own body." [4]   Similarly, it is
also wrong to call a woman creator of her own
progeny but rather him who said to one of his servants: " Before I formed you in the womb, I knew
you." [5]   And granted that the different states of a
pregnant woman's spiritual being can, as it were,
endow her unborn child with certain qualities, just

SAINT AUGUSTINE

Iacob ut pecora colore varia [1] gignerentur, naturam tamen illam quae gignitur tam ipsa non fecit quam nec ipsa se fecit.

Quaelibet igitur corporales vel seminales causae gignendis rebus adhibeantur, sive operationibus angelorum aut hominum aut quorumque animalium sive marium feminarumque mixtionibus, quaelibet etiam desideria motusve animae matris valeant aliquid liniamentorum aut colorum aspergere teneris mollibusque conceptibus, ipsas omnino naturas, quae sic vel sic in suo genere afficiantur, non facit nisi summus Deus, cuius occulta potentia cuncta penetrans incontaminabili praesentia facit esse quidquid aliquo modo est, in quantumcumque est, quia nisi faciente illo non tale vel tale esset,[2] sed prorsus esse non posset.

Quapropter si in illa specie quam forinsecus corporalibus opifices rebus inponunt urbem Romam et urbem Alexandriam non fabros et architectos sed reges, quorum voluntate consilio imperio fabricatae sunt, illam Romulum, illam Alexandrum habuisse dicimus conditores, quanto potius non nisi Deum debemus conditorem dicere naturarum, qui neque ex ea materia facit aliquid quam ipse non fecerit nec operarios habet nisi quos ipse creaverit. Et si potentiam suam, ut ita dicam, fabricatoriam rebus subtrahat, ita non erunt sicut ante quam fierent non

---

[1] vario colore *or* colore vario *some MSS.*
[2] esse *V and one other MS.*

---

[1] Cf. Genesis 30.37–39.
[2] Augustine develops this argument at considerable length in *De Trinitate* 3.8.13–9.16.

as Jacob with the variegated rods caused flocks of varied colours to be born,[1] yet she no more made the natural being that is born than she made herself.

Therefore, so far as creation is concerned, neither the material nor the seminal causes that are brought into play for the generation of things make any difference, whether there is action of angels or human beings or any kind of animal or mingling of male and female; nor does it matter whether any desires or emotions of the mother act to impart something in the way of features or colours to the tender and impressionable foetus. For the natural beings themselves, though they may be affected one way or another after their kind, are made by the supreme God alone. His hidden power, pervading all things with its undefilable presence, gives being to every thing that exists on every level, in so far as it has being; for, were it not for his action, a thing would not only not be like this or like that, but it could not be at all.[2]

So then, to return to that form which artisans impose from without on physical objects, we say that the cities of Rome and Alexandria had as their founders not the carpenters and the architects but the kings, Romulus and Alexander, respectively, by whose will, plan and power they were built. Now, if this be so, all the more ought we to call none but God alone creator of natural beings, for he makes nothing out of material that he himself has not made nor has he any workmen whom he himself has not created. And if he were to take away his constructive energy, so to speak, from objects, they will no more be than they were before they were created.

fuerunt. Sed ante dico aeternitate, non tempore.
Quis enim alius creator est temporum nisi qui fecit
ea quorum motibus currerent tempora?

XXVII

*De Platonicorum opinione qua putaverunt angelos
quidem a Deo conditos, sed ipsos esse humanorum
corporum conditores.*

Ita sane Plato minores et a summo Deo factos
deos effectores esse voluit animalium ceterorum, ut
inmortalem partem ab ipso sumerent, ipsi vero mortalem adtexerent. Proinde animarum nostrarum
eos creatores noluit esse, sed corporum. Unde
quoniam Porphyrius propter animae purgationem
dicit corpus omne fugiendum simulque cum suo
Platone aliisque Platonicis sentit eos qui inmoderate
atque inhoneste vixerint propter luendas poenas ad
corpora redire mortalia, Plato quidem etiam bestiarum, Porphyrius tantummodo ad hominum, sequitur eos, ut dicant deos istos quos a nobis volunt quasi
parentes et conditores nostros coli, nihil esse aliud
quam fabros compedum carcerumve nostrorum, nec
institutores sed inclusores adligatoresque nostros
ergastulis aerumnosis et gravissimis vinculis. Aut
ergo desinant Platonici poenas animarum ex istis

---

[1] Cf. above, 11.6; 12.16 (p. 71–77).

[2] See above, 12.25 (p. 117, note 2).

[3] In his *De Regressu Animae*, for which see J. Bidez, *Vie de
Porphyre* (Gand-Leipzig, 1913), appendices, p. 41 *. Cf.
above, 10.29; below, 22.12; 22.26–28.

[4] See above, 10.30; below, 13.19 (pp. 207–209).

But I mean ' before ' with reference to eternity, not to time. For who else is the creator of periods of time except him who created the objects whose movements mark the course of time ? [1]

XXVII

On the belief of the Platonists who, granting that the angels were created by God, held that the angels themselves were the creators of human bodies.

WHEN Plato held that lesser gods, who were created by the supreme God, were the makers of the other living beings, he doubtless meant that, while they received the immortal part from God himself, they themselves attached to it the mortal part.[2] His view therefore was that they were creators not of our souls but of our bodies. Now Porphyry says that we must avoid all touch of body for the purification of the soul,[3] and at the same time he shares with Plato and the other Platonists the belief that those whose lives were licentious and disgraceful return by way of atonement to mortal bodies—even of beasts according to Plato, but only of men according to Porphyry.[4] Hence it follows that, if these philosophers are to bestow the name of gods upon those whom they would have us cherish as though they were our parents and creators, these gods are nothing but the artificers of our fetters or prisons, and not our creators but our gaolers, shutting us up in grievous workhouses and binding us fast in most burdensome chains. Let the Platonists therefore either cease threatening us with the punishment of

corporibus comminari aut eos nobis deos colendos non praedicent quorum in nobis operationem ut, quantum possumus, fugiamus et evadamus hortantur, cum tamen sit utrumque falsissimum.

Nam neque ita luunt poenas animae cum ad istam vitam denuo revolvuntur, et omnium viventium sive in caelo sive in terra nullus est conditor nisi a quo facta sunt caelum et terra. Nam si nulla causa est vivendi in hoc corpore nisi propter pendenda supplicia, quo modo dicit idem Plato aliter mundum fieri non potuisse pulcherrimum atque optimum nisi omnium animalium, id est et inmortalium et mortalium, generibus impleretur? Si autem nostra institutio, qua vel mortales conditi sumus, divinum munus est, quo modo poena est ad ista corpora, id est ad divina beneficia, remeare? Et si Deus, quod adsidue Plato commemorat, sicut mundi universi, ita omnium animalium species aeterna intellegentia continebat, quo modo non ipse cuncta condebat? An aliquorum esse artifex nollet, quorum efficiendorum artem ineffabilis eius et ineffabiliter laudabilis mens haberet?

our souls through these bodies or cease preaching that it is our duty to worship as gods those from whose handiwork in our persons they exhort us to escape and detach ourselves as much as we can—though for that matter both doctrines are utterly mistaken.

The fact is that souls do not pay the penalty in this way by returning once again to this life, and there is no creator of any living thing, whether in heaven or in earth, but him by whom the heaven and earth were made. Indeed, if our only reason for living in this body is to suffer punishment, how can Plato also say that the world could not have been made supremely beautiful and good except by being filled with all kinds of animate beings, that is both immortal and mortal?[1] On the other hand, if our creation even as mortals is a divine gift, how can the return to these bodies, that is, to God's good works, be a punishment? And if God, as Plato repeatedly mentions,[2] held in his eternal intelligence the forms not only of the entire universe but also of all animate beings, how comes it that he did not create them all himself? Could it be that he was unwilling to be the craftsman of some things, though the requisite craft for producing them existed in his mind, which no tongue can describe or sufficiently praise?

[1] Cf. Plato, *Timaeus* 30d; 92c.
[2] Cf. Plato, *Timaeus* 30b–d; *Republic* 597b–c.

SAINT AUGUSTINE

XXVIII

In primo homine exortam fuisse omnem plenitudinem generis humani, in qua praeviderit Deus quae pars honoranda esset praemio, quae damnanda supplicio.

MERITO igitur vera religio quem mundi universi, eum animalium quoque universorum, hoc est et animarum et corporum, conditorem agnoscit et praedicat. In quibus terrenis praecipuus ab illo ad eius imaginem homo propter eam causam quam dixi, et si qua forte alia maior latet, factus est unus, sed non relictus est solus. Nihil enim est quam hoc genus tam discordiosum vitio, tam sociale natura. Neque commodius contra vitium discordiae, vel cavendum ne existeret vel sanandum cum extitisset, natura loqueretur humana quam recordationem illius parentis quem propterea Deus creare voluit unum de quo multitudo propagaretur, ut hac admonitione etiam in multis concors unitas servaretur. Quod vero femina illi ex eius latere facta est, etiam hic satis significatum est quam cara mariti et uxoris debeat esse coniunctio.

Haec opera Dei propterea sunt utique inusitata, quia prima. Qui autem ista non credunt nulla facta prodigia debent credere; neque enim et ipsa, si usitato naturae curriculo gignerentur, prodigia dicerentur. Quid autem sub tanta gubernatione divinae providentiae, quamvis eius causa lateat,

---

[1] Cf. Genesis 2.22–24; Matthew 19.5; Ephesians 5.28 and 31.

XXVIII

That in the first man appeared the entire plenitude of
the human race, wherein God foresaw what part was
to be honoured with reward and what part was to
be condemned to punishment.

TRUE religion then rightly recognizes and pro-
claims that the creator of the entire universe is also
creator of all living things, that is, of both souls and
bodies. And chief among those on earth, one man,
and one alone, was created by him in his image for
the reason that I gave and perhaps for some greater
reason not yet discovered, but he was not left solitary.
For there is nothing so discordant when it deteriorates
or so sociable in its true nature as the human race. Nor
could a better argument be offered by man's nature
for either the cure or the prevention of the defect of
discord than the recollection of our common parent
whom God chose to create as a single being for the
propagation of a multitude in order that we might
thus be reminded to preserve a single-minded unity
even when we are many. Moreover, the fact that
the woman was made for him out of his side is also
an effective symbol of the conjugal love that should
unite husband and wife.[1]

These works of God are in any case extraordinary
because they are his first. But those who do not believe in them ought not to believe in the reality of any
marvels, for these would not be called marvels either if
they occurred in the ordinary course of nature. But
what, under so mighty a governance of divine providence, occurs without a purpose, although the reason

129

frustra gignitur? Ait quidam psalmus sacer: *Venite et videte opera Domini, quae posuit prodigia super terram.* Cur ergo ex latere viri femina facta sit, et hoc primum quodam modo prodigium quid praefiguraverit, dicetur [1] alio loco, quantum me Deus adiuverit.

Nunc quoniam liber iste claudendus est, in hoc primo [2] homine qui primitus factus est nondum quidem secundum evidentiam, iam tamen secundum Dei praescientiam exortas fuisse existimemus in genere humano societates tamquam civitates duas. Ex illo enim futuri erant homines, alii malis angelis in supplicio, alii bonis in praemio sociandi, quamvis occulto Dei iudicio sed tamen iusto. Cum enim scriptum sit: *Universae viae Domini misericordia et veritas,* nec iniusta eius gratia nec crudelis potest esse iustitia.

[1] dicam, *placed after* adiuverit *in a few MSS.*
[2] primo *omitted in* V *and one other MS., bracketed by some editors.*

for it may not be apparent? One of the sacred psalms tells us: " Come and behold the works of the Lord, what marvels he has placed upon the earth." [1] Elsewhere,[2] I shall set forth, as best I can with God's aid, the reason why woman was made out of the side of man and what this first marvel, as we may call it, foreshadowed.

Now, since I must bring this book to an end, let us imagine that with this first man who was created in the beginning there had arisen, not as yet indeed in plain sight, but already in the foreknowledge of God, two societies or cities among the human race. For it was from him that mankind was destined to arise, of which one part was to be joined in fellowship with evil angels for punishment and the other with good angels for reward. Such was God's decree, which, though hidden, was yet righteous. For, since we read in Scripture: " All the paths of the Lord are mercy and truth," [3] we know that neither can his grace be unjust nor his justice cruel.

---

[1] Psalms 46.8. The translation here suits the context, but the RSV renders the last part differently: ". . . how he has wrought desolations in the earth."

[2] Cf. below, 22.17.

[3] Psalms 25.10.

BOOK XIII

LIBER XIII

I

De lapsu primorum hominum, per quem est contracta mortalitas.

EXPEDITIS de nostri saeculi exortu et de initio generis humani difficillimis quaestionibus, nunc iam de lapsu primi hominis, immo primorum hominum, et de origine ac propagine mortis humanae disputationem a nobis institutam rerum ordo deposcit. Non enim eo modo quo angelos condiderat Deus homines ut, etiam si peccassent, mori omnino non possent, sed ita ut perfunctos oboedientiae munere sine interventu mortis angelica inmortalitas[1] et beata aeternitas sequeretur, inoboedientes autem mors plecteret damnatione iustissima; quod etiam in libro superiore iam diximus.

II

De ea morte quae animae semper utcumque victurae accidere potest et ea cui corpus obnoxium est.

SED de ipso genere mortis video mihi paulo diligentius disserendum. Quamvis enim anima humana

---

[1] inmutabilitas *a few MSS.*

---

[1] See above, 12.22 (p. 111 and note 1).

BOOK XIII

I

On the fall of the first human beings and the mortality that it entailed.

Now that I have settled the very difficult problem respecting the rise of our present world and the beginning of the human race, I next take up in my discussion, as the logical order of my subject matter requires, the fall of the first human being, or rather human beings, and the origin and dissemination of human death. For God had not made human beings in the same way as angels, that is, incapable of dying under any circumstances, even though they should have sinned. Rather, in their case, fulfilment of their duty of obedience was to bring angelic death-lessness and an eternity of bliss with no intervening period of death, whereas disobedience would be very justly punished with death. This is a point that I have already made in the preceding book too.[1]

II

On the death that can befall the soul, which is destined to live on somehow, and the death to which the body is subject.

But I see that I should explain somewhat more carefully what is actually meant by death. To begin

135

veraciter inmortalis perhibeatur, habet tamen quandam etiam ipsa mortem suam. Nam ideo dicitur
inmortalis, quia modo quodam quantulocumque non
desinit vivere atque sentire; corpus autem ideo
mortale, quoniam deseri omni vita potest nec per se
ipsum aliquatenus vivit. Mors igitur animae fit cum
eam deserit Deus, sicut corporis cum id deserit
anima. Ergo utriusque rei, id est totius hominis,
mors est cum anima Deo deserta deserit corpus. Ita
enim nec ex Deo vivit ipsa nec corpus ex ipsa.

Huius modi autem totius hominis mortem illa
sequitur quam secundam mortem divinorum eloquiorum appellat auctoritas. Hanc Salvator signi-
ficavit ubi ait: *Eum timete qui habet potestatem et corpus
et animam perdere in gehenna.*[1] Quod cum ante non
fiat quam cum anima corpori sic fuerit copulata ut
nulla diremptione separentur, mirum videri potest
quo modo corpus ea morte dicatur occidi qua non
anima deseritur sed animatum sentiensque cruciatur.
Nam in illa ultima poena ac sempiterna, de qua suo
loco diligentius disserendum est, recte mors animae
dicitur quia non vivit ex Deo. Mors autem corporis

---

[1] in gehenna *some MSS.* (*cf. the corresponding Greek:* ἐν γεέννῃ): in gehennam *other MSS., Vulg.*

---

[1] Cf. Revelation 2.11; 20.6 and 14; 21.8, on which see J. C. Plumpe, "Mors secunda," in *Mélanges Joseph de Ghellinck* (Gembloux, 1951), vol. 1, 387–403, especially pp. 392–400 for Augustine.

with, although the human soul is correctly said to be immortal, yet it too is subject to its own sort of death. For when the soul is termed immortal, the meaning is that it does not cease to have life and feeling in some degree no matter how slight. On the other hand, when the body is termed mortal, the meaning is that it may be abandoned by life completely and has no life of its own at all. Consequently, it is the death of a soul when God abandons it, just as it is the death of a body when its soul abandons it. Hence the death of both combined, that is, of the whole human being, occurs when a soul abandoned by God abandons a body. For under these circumstances neither does the soul derive life from God nor the body life from the soul.

Moreover, death of the whole human being in this way leads to the second death,[1] a term sanctioned by the authority of God's word. It is to this death that our Saviour referred when he said: " Fear him who has power to destroy both body and soul in hell." [2] But since this does not happen until after the soul and body have been so closely welded that they are utterly inseparable, we may wonder how it can be said that the body is slain if in its death it is not abandoned by the soul but tormented while it is animated by a soul and possessed of feeling. In connexion with that final and everlasting punishment, a subject on which I must discourse more fully in its proper place,[3] we can, it is true, rightly speak of the death of the soul because it derives no life from God. But how can we speak here of any death of the

[2] Matthew 10.28.
[3] See below, 19.28 (vol. 6, 243-245).

quonam modo, cum vivat ex anima? Non enim aliter potest ipsa corporalia quae post resurrectionem futura sunt sentire tormenta. An quia vita qualiscumque aliquod bonum est, dolor autem malum, ideo nec vivere corpus dicendum est in quo anima non vivendi causa est, sed dolendi?

Vivit itaque anima ex Deo cum vivit bene; non enim potest bene vivere nisi Deo in se operante quod bonum est. Vivit autem corpus ex anima cum anima vivit in corpore, seu vivat ipsa seu non vivat ex Deo. Impiorum namque in corporibus vita non animarum sed corporum vita est; quam possunt eis animae etiam mortuae, hoc est Deo desertae,[1] quantulacumque propria vita, ex qua et inmortales sunt, non desistente, conferre. Verum in damnatione novissima quamvis homo sentire non desinat, tamen, quia sensus ipse nec voluptate suavis nec quiete salubris sed dolore poenalis est, non inmerito mors est potius appellata quam vita. Ideo autem secunda, quia post illam primam est, qua fit cohaerentium diremptio naturarum, sive Dei et animae sive animae et corporis. De prima igitur corporis morte dici potest quod bonis bona sit, malis mala. Secunda vero sine dubio sicut nullorum bonorum est, ita nulli bona.

---

[1] deserente *a few MSS.*

body since that does derive life from the soul?
Indeed, the body cannot otherwise experience those
physical pains that it is destined to feel after the
resurrection. The answer is perhaps this: since life
of any sort constitutes some good, and pain some
evil, we ought not to say that a body is alive if the
soul resides in it, not in order to make it live, but to
make it hurt.

The soul is therefore deriving life from God when
it lives a good life, for it can live a good life only if
God works in it for good. The body, however,
derives life from the soul when the soul lives in it,
whether or not the soul itself derives life from God.
For in the bodies of the irreligious life is not a life of
their souls but of their bodies; and souls, even when
dead, that is, when abandoned by God, can contrib
ute life to them since their own life, no matter how
slight, which is the source of their immortality, does
not come to a halt. But in the punishment of the
last judgement such existence may well be called
death rather than life, for, although the man does
not cease to have feelings, yet his feelings are neither
sweetened by pleasure nor made wholesome by calm;
rather, sensation is painful and thereby punitive.
Moreover, it is called the second death because it
comes after the first, which effects the separation of
two substances that are joined, whether it be God
and the soul or the soul and the body. Consequently,
we may say of the first death, that of the body, that
it is good for those who are good and evil for those
who are evil. But as for the second death, just as it
happens to no one who is good, so doubtless it is good
for no one.

SAINT AUGUSTINE

III

Utrum mors, quae per peccatum primorum hominum
in omnes homines pertransiit, etiam in sanctis
poena peccati sit.

NON autem dissimulanda nascitur quaestio utrum
re vera mors, qua separantur anima et corpus, bonis
sit bona; quia, si ita est, quo modo poterit obtineri
quod etiam ipsa sit poena peccati? Hanc enim
primi homines, nisi peccavissent, perpessi utique non
fuissent. Quo pacto igitur bona esse possit bonis
quae accidere non posset nisi malis? Sed rursus, si
non nisi malis posset accidere, non deberet bonis bona
esse, sed nulla. Cur enim esset ulla poena in quibus
non essent ulla punienda?

Quapropter fatendum est primos quidem homines
ita fuisse institutos ut, si non peccassent, nullum
mortis experirentur genus, sed eosdem primos peccatores ita fuisse morte multatos ut etiam quidquid
de [1] eorum stirpe esset exortum eadem poena
teneretur obnoxium. Non enim aliud ex eis quam
quod ipsi fuerant nasceretur. Pro magnitudine
quippe culpae illius naturam damnatio mutavit in
peius, ut quod poenaliter praecessit in peccantibus
hominibus primis etiam naturaliter sequeretur in
nascentibus ceteris.

[1] de, *found in a late MS., was apparently omitted in the
archetype by haplology.*

III

*Whether death, which by reason of the sin of the first
human beings has spread among all human beings,
is punishment for sin even in the case of saints.*

BUT this raises a question that cannot be ignored,
namely, whether, in actual fact, death, by which soul
and body are separated, is good for those who are
good; because, if this is the case, how shall we maintain that it is also the punishment of sin? For if the
first human beings had not sinned, they doubtless
would not have suffered this death. How then can
it be good for those who are good if it could not happen except to bad men? Conversely, if it could not
happen except to bad men, it ought not to be good
for the good but non-existent. For how could there
be any punishment for those in whom there was
nothing to be punished for?

Therefore we must admit that, although the first
human beings were indeed so created that they
would not have known any kind of death if they had
not sinned, yet these same persons, as the first
sinners, received punishment by death on such terms
that whatever should spring from their stock was also
to be held liable to the same penalty; for they were
to have no progeny other than that which resembled
them. Their punishment, in fact, was commensurate
with the enormity of their guilt and effected in their
original nature a change for the worse. As a result,
what came initially as punishment to the first human
beings who sinned also follows as a natural consequence in the rest who are born.

Neque enim ita homo ex homine sicut homo ex pulvere. Pulvis namque homini faciendo materies fuit, homo autem homini gignendo parens. Proinde quod est terra, non hoc est caro, quamvis ex terra facta sit caro; quod est autem parens homo, hoc est et proles homo. In primo igitur homine per feminam in progeniem transiturum universum genus humanum fuit quando illa coniugum copula divinam sententiam suae damnationis excepit, et quod homo factus est, non cum crearetur, sed cum peccaret et puniretur, hoc genuit, quantum quidem adtinet ad peccati et mortis originem.

Non enim ad infantilem hebetudinem et infirmitatem animi et corporis, quam videmus in parvulis, peccato vel poena ille redactus est; quae Deus voluit [1] esse tamquam primordia catulorum, quorum parentes in bestialem vitam mortemque deiecerat. Sicut enim scriptum est: *Homo in honore cum esset, non intellexit; comparatus est pecoribus non intellegentibus et similis factus est eis;* [2] nisi quod infantes infirmiores etiam cernimus in usu motuque membrorum et sensu adpetendi atque vitandi quam sunt aliorum tenerrimi fetus animalium, tamquam se tanto adtollat excellentius supra cetera animantia vis humana quanto magis impetum suum, velut sagitta cum arcus extenditur, retrorsum reducta distulerit.

[1] Deus voluit *most MSS.:* noluit *V.*
[2] illis *some MSS.*, *Vulg.*

---

[1] Psalms 49.12 and 20. Augustine's text, the Vulgate and the Septuagint are in substantive agreement here. The RSV, however, renders: '' Man cannot abide in his pomp, he is like the beasts that perish.''

Now the reason for this is that man's genesis from man is not like man's genesis from dust. For dust served as the material used for the manufacture of man, but man serves as parent for the procreation of man. Accordingly, whereas flesh is not the same thing as earth, though flesh was manufactured from earth, yet man the offspring is just the same thing as man the parent. Therefore the entire human race that was to pass through woman into offspring was contained in the first man when that conjugal couple received the divine sentence condemning them to punishment, and man reproduced what man became, not when he was being created, but when he was sinning and being punished, at least as far as the origin of sin and death is concerned.

For the first man was not reduced by sin or punishment to an infantile state of mental dullness and bodily weakness, such as we see in small children. God meant that these traits should represent the first stages, as it were, of the puppies or cubs whose parents he had cast down to a beast-like level of life and death. For as we read in Scripture, " Man, when he was in honour, did not understand; he was compared to beasts that lacked understanding and became like them." [1] And so it is, except that infants, as we see, are even weaker in the use and movement of their limbs and in their sense of desire and aversion than the most delicate new-born offspring of other animals. This suggests that a man's powers shoot up all the higher above those of other animals, according as they have been drawn back like an arrow when the bow is bent and have thus increased the tension of their thrust.

SAINT AUGUSTINE

Non ergo ad ista infantilia rudimenta praesump-
tione inlicita et damnatione iusta prolapsus vel inpulsus est primus homo. Sed hactenus in eo natura
humana vitiata atque mutata est ut repugnantem
pateretur in membris inoboedientiam concupiscendi
et obstringeretur necessitate moriendi atque ita id
quod vitio poenaque factus est, id est obnoxios
peccato mortique, generaret. A quo peccati vinculo
si per mediatoris Christi [1] gratiam solvuntur infantes,
hanc solam mortem perpeti possunt quae animam
seiungit a corpore; in secundam vero illam sine fine
poenalem liberati a peccati obligatione non transeunt.

IV

*Cur ab his qui per gratiam regenerationis absoluti
sunt a peccato non auferatur mors, id est
poena peccati.*

Si quem vero movet cur vel ipsam patiantur, si et
ipsa peccati poena est, quorum per gratiam reatus
aboletur, iam ista quaestio in alio nostro opere, quod
scripsimus de baptismo parvulorum, tractata ac
soluta est; ubi dictum est ad hoc relinqui animae
experimentum separationis a corpore, quamvis ablato
iam criminis nexu, quoniam, si regenerationis sacramentum continuo sequeretur inmortalitas corporis,

---

[1] Christi *omitted in some MSS.*

[1] The full title of the work seems to have been *De Peccatorum Meritis et Remissione et De Baptismo Parvulorum Ad
Marcellinum Libri Tres;* cf. Augustine, *Retractationes* 2.33
(59).

144

The first man then neither fell nor was plunged into this undeveloped state of infancy for all his unlawful presumption and just punishment. But his human nature was so corrupted and changed within him that he suffered in his members a rebellious disobedience of desire, was bound by the necessity of dying and thus reproduced what he himself had come to be through vice and punishment, that is, offspring liable to sin and death. If infants are released from this bond of sin through the grace of Christ the Mediator, they can suffer only the death that separates a soul from the body; but, once freed from the bondage of sin, they do not pass on to that second death of endless punishment.

IV

Why those who have been absolved of sin through the grace of regeneration are not rid of death, that is, the punishment of sin.

SOMEONE may be puzzled why people whose guilt is erased through grace suffer even the first death, if it too is the punishment of sin. I have already treated and resolved this problem in another work of mine entitled *On the Baptism of Children.*[1] There the point was made that, although the bond of guilt was already removed, the experience of the soul's separation from the body was allowed to remain for the reason that, if the sacrament of regeneration [2] were immediately followed by immortality of the body,

[2] That is, baptism; see the next paragraph and cf. Titus 3.5.

ipsa fides enervaretur, quae tunc est fides quando expectatur in spe quod in re nondum videtur.

Fidei autem robore atque certamine, in maioribus dumtaxat aetatibus, etiam mortis fuerat superandus timor, quod in sanctis martyribus maxime eminuit. Cuius profecto certaminis esset nulla victoria, nulla gloria (quia nec ipsum omnino posset esse certamen) si post lavacrum regenerationis iam sancti non possent mortem perpeti corporalem. Cum parvulis autem baptizandis quis non ad Christi gratiam propterea potius curreret, ne a corpore solveretur? Atque ita non invisibili praemio probaretur fides, sed iam nec fides esset, confestim sui operis quaerendo et sumendo mercedem.

Nunc vero maiore et mirabiliore gratia Salvatoris in usus iustitiae peccati poena conversa est. Tunc enim dictum est homini: Morieris, si peccaveris, nunc dicitur martyri: Morere, ne pecces. Tunc dictum est: Si mandatum transgressi fueritis, morte moriemini, nunc dicitur: Si mortem recusaveritis, mandatum transgrediemini.[1] Quod tunc timendum fuerat ut non peccaretur, nunc suscipiendum est ne peccetur.

Sic per ineffabilem Dei misericordiam et ipsa poena vitiorum transit in arma virtutis et fit iusti meritum etiam supplicium peccatoris. Tunc enim mors est

---

[1] transgrediemini *some MSS.*

---

[1] Cf. *De Peccatorum Meritis et Remissione* 3.31.50; 34.55.
[2] Cf. Genesis 2.17.

faith itself would be weakened. Faith is really faith
only when we await in hope what we do not yet see
in fact.[1]

Moreover, it was by the strength and struggle of
faith, at least in earlier times, that even the fear of
death had to be overcome, and this was most conspicuously exemplified in the fate of our holy martyrs.
There could surely be neither victory nor renown to
be won in this struggle if after the baptism of regeneration the saints could no longer suffer bodily death;
for, under these circumstances, there could not even
be a contest at all. Further, who would not rather
run with children yet to be baptized to the grace of
Christ just so as not to be parted from the body? And
in this way faith would not be put to the test by an
invisible prize—indeed, it would no longer even be
faith if it sought and took at once the reward for its
action.

As it is, however, through a greater and more
wonderful act of grace on the part of the Saviour our
punishment of sin has been converted to serve the
ends of righteousness. For whereas once man was
told: " You will die if you sin," the martyr is now
told: " Die that you may not sin." Whereas once
man was told: " If you break the commandment, you
shall surely die," [2] we are now told: " If you refuse to
die, you will be breaking the commandment." The
thing that was once duly feared to prevent sin is now
duly accepted to avoid sin.

Thus through the ineffable mercy of God the very
penalty for failings passes over into the arsenal of
virtue, and even the punishment of the sinner becomes the reward of the righteous man. For where-

adquisita peccando, nunc inpletur iustitia moriendo.
Verum hoc in sanctis martyribus, quibus alterutrum
a persecutore proponitur, ut aut deserant fidem aut
sufferant mortem. Iusti enim malunt credendo perpeti quod sunt primi iniqui non credendo perpessi.
Nisi enim peccassent illi, non morerentur; peccabunt
autem isti nisi moriantur. Mortui sunt ergo illi quia
peccaverunt; non peccant isti quia moriuntur.
Factum est per illorum culpam ut veniretur in poenam; fit per istorum poenam ne veniatur in culpam,
non quia mors bonum aliquod facta est, quae antea
malum fuit, sed tantam Deus fidei praestitit gratiam
ut mors, quam vitae constat esse contrariam, instru-
mentum fieret per quod transiretur ad vitam.

V

Quod sicut iniqui male utuntur lege, quae bona est,
ita iusti bene utantur morte, quae mala est.

Apostolus cum vellet ostendere quantum peccatum, gratia non subveniente, ad nocendum valeret,
etiam ipsam legem, qua prohibetur peccatum, non
dubitavit dicere virtutem esse peccati. *Aculeus,*
inquit, *mortis est peccatum, virtus autem peccati lex.*
Verissime omnino. Auget enim prohibitio desi-
derium operis inliciti quando iustitia non sic diligitur

---

[1] 1 Corinthians 15.56.

as once man gained death by sinning, he now satisfies the demands of righteousness by dying. This is true in the case of the holy martyrs who are confronted by their persecutor with the alternative of abandoning their faith or suffering death. For the righteous choose to suffer for their belief what the first wicked men suffered for their lack of it. If the latter had not sinned, they would not have died, but the righteous will sin if they do not die. Accordingly, whereas the first human beings died because they sinned, the righteous do not sin because they die. The guilt of the first human beings resulted in their incurrence of punishment, but the punishment of the righteous results in their avoidance of guilt. And this so happens, not because death, which was previously an evil thing, has become something good, but because God has bestowed so great a gift of grace on faith that death, which is held to be the opposite of life, became the means by which men pass to life.

V

That even as the wicked put law, which is good, to ill use, so the righteous put death, which is evil, to good use.

WHEN the Apostle wanted to indicate the extent to which sin could effect harm if grace did not lend aid, he did not hesitate to assert that even the very law which forbade sin was the power of sin. He said: "The sting of death is sin, and the power of sin is the law."[1] This is quite true, for prohibition increases longing for a forbidden action when righteousness is

ut peccandi cupiditas eius delectatione vincatur. Ut autem diligatur et delectet vera iustitia, non nisi divina subvenit gratia.

Sed ne propterea lex putaretur malum, quoniam virtus est dicta peccati, ideo ipse alio loco versans huius modi quaestionem: *Itaque*, inquit, *lex quidem sancta et mandatum sanctum et iustum et bonum. Quod ergo bonum est*, inquit, *mihi factum est mors? Absit. Sed peccatum, ut appareat peccatum, per bonum mihi operatum est mortem, ut fiat super* [1] *modum peccator aut peccatum per mandatum. Super* [1] *modum* dixit quia etiam praevaricatio additur cum, peccandi aucta libidine, etiam lex ipsa contemnitur.

Cur hoc commemorandum putavimus? Quia scilicet, sicut lex non est malum quando auget peccantium concupiscentiam, ita nec mors bonum est quando auget patientium gloriam, cum vel illa pro iniquitate deseritur et efficit praevaricatores vel ista pro veritate suscipitur et efficit martyres. Ac per hoc lex quidem bona est, quia prohibitio est peccati; mors autem mala, quia stipendium est peccati. Sed quem ad modum iniustitia male utitur non tantum malis verum etiam bonis, ita iustitia bene non tantum bonis sed etiam malis. Hinc fit ut et mali male lege utantur quamvis sit lex bonum et boni bene moriantur quamvis sit mors malum.

[1] supra *some MSS.*, *Vulg.*

---

[1] Romans 7.12–13.
[2] Cf. Romans 6.23.

not loved enough for delight in it to be victorious over desire to sin. And there is no help but the grace of God to ensure our love of true righteousness and our delight in it.

To prevent law, however, from being thought an evil because it was called the power of sin, the Apostle, considering a similar problem in another connexion, said: " And so the law is holy, and the commandment is holy and just and good. Did that which is good then bring death to me? By no means! It was sin, working death in me through that which is good, in order that sin might be shown to be sin and through the commandment sinner or sin might go beyond measure."[1] He said ' beyond measure ' because there is a further transgression when the lust to sin is increased and the very law is despised as well.

Why did I think this worth mentioning here? It was, in fact, because, just as the law is not an evil though it increases the evil desire of sinners, so neither is death a good though it increases the glory of sufferers, when either the law is abandoned for the sake of unrighteousness and so creates transgressors, or death is undergone for the sake of truth and so creates martyrs. And whereas the law is good because it is the prohibition of sin, death is evil because it is the wage of sin.[2] Even as unrighteousness, however, makes evil use not only of evil things but also of good things, so righteousness makes good use not only of good things but also of evil things. And so it happens that evil men make evil use of the law although the law is a good thing, and that good men die a good death although death is an evil thing.

VI

*De generali mortis malo, quo animae et corporis
societas separatur.*

QUAPROPTER, quod adtinet ad corporis mortem, id
est separationem animae a corpore, cum eam patiuntur qui morientes appellantur, nulli bona est. Habet
enim asperum sensum et contra naturam vis ipsa
qua utrumque divellitur quod fuerat in vivente coniunctum atque consertum, quamdiu moratur, donec
omnis adimatur sensus, qui ex ipso inerat animae
carnisque complexu. Quam totam molestiam nonnumquam unus ictus corporis vel animae raptus
intercipit nec eam sentiri, praeveniente celeritate,
permittit.

Quidquid tamen illud est in morientibus quod cum
gravi sensu adimit sensum, pie fideliterque tolerando
auget meritum patientiae, non aufert vocabulum
poenae. Ita cum ex hominis primi perpetuata propagine procul dubio sit mors poena nascentis, tamen,
si pro pietate iustitiaque pendatur, fit gloria renascen-
tis; et cum sit mors peccati retributio, aliquando
inpetrat ut nihil retribuatur peccato.

VI

*On the evil of death in general, whereby the union
of soul and body is sundered.*

WHEREFORE, so far as the death of the body or, in
other words, the separation of the soul from the body
is concerned, it is not good for anyone when those
who are said to be dying are undergoing it. For a
grating and unnatural feeling is produced by the
force itself that rends asunder the two things that
were joined and interwoven in the living person; and
this experience lasts until there is a complete loss of
sensation, which was present precisely because of the
union of soul and flesh. But all this anguish is sometimes cut short by a single blow to the body or by a
sudden seizure of the soul, the swiftness of which
prevents its being felt.

Yet, whatever it is in the dying that removes with
a feeling of distress the power of feeling, it adds to
the merit of patience when it is borne with religious
faith, but it does not expunge the term 'penalty.'
Thus, although death is doubtless the penalty incurred by a man at birth as a direct descendant of
the first man, yet, if it is paid on behalf of religion
and righteousness, it becomes the glory of a man at
rebirth; and although death is recompense of sin,
it sometimes succeeds in bringing it about that there
is no recompense for sin.

VII

De morte quam quidam non regenerati pro Christi confessione suscipiunt.

NAM quicumque, etiam non percepto regenerationis lavacro, pro Christi confessione moriuntur, tantum eis valet ad dimittenda peccata quantum si abluerentur sacro fonte baptismatis. Qui enim dixit: *Si quis non renatus fuerit ex aqua et spiritu,*[1] *non intrabit in regnum caelorum,* alia sententia istos fecit exceptos, ubi non minus generaliter ait: *Qui me confessus fuerit coram hominibus, confitebor* [*et ego*][2] *eum coram Patre meo qui in caelis est;* et alio loco: *Qui perdiderit animam suam propter me inveniet eam.*

Hinc est quod scriptum est: *Pretiosa in conspectu Domini mors sanctorum eius.* Quid enim pretiosius quam mors per quam fit ut et delicta omnia dimittantur et merita cumulatius augeantur? Neque enim tanti sunt meriti qui, cum mortem differre non possent, baptizati sunt deletisque omnibus peccatis, ex hac vita emigrarunt quanti sunt hi qui mortem, cum possent, ideo non distulerunt, quia maluerunt

---

[1] spiritu *some MSS.* (*cf. the corresponding Greek:* πνεύματος): spiritu sancto *other MSS., Vulg.*

[2] et ego *omitted in most MSS. and probably rightly bracketed by editors as an interpolation from the Vulgate.*

---

[1] John 3.5.	[2] Matthew 10.32.
[3] Matthew 16.25.	[4] Psalms 116.15.

VII

On the death which certain persons who are not
regenerated undergo for their acknowledgement
of Christ.

FOR all those who perish for their acknowledgement of Christ, even though they have not experienced the cleansing water of regeneration, are just as
effectively delivered from their sins as they would be
if they were washed by the holy font of baptism.
Christ, to be sure, stated: " Unless a man is born
again of water and the Spirit, he shall not enter the
kingdom of heaven." [1] But in another utterance he
made an exception of those persons of whom I am
speaking, when he said in equally general terms:
" Whoever acknowledges me before men, him will I
also acknowledge before my father who is in the
heavens." [2] And elsewhere he declares: " Whoever
loses his life for my sake shall find it." [3]

Hence we read in the Scriptures: " Precious in the
sight of the Lord is the death of his saints." [4] Indeed, nothing is more precious than the death which
makes it possible for all transgressions to be remitted,
and merits to be accumulated in greater store. For
those who were baptized when they could not postpone death and departed from this life with all sins
wiped out [5] are not as deserving as those who did not
postpone death when they might have done so, just
because they preferred to acknowledge Christ and

[5] Augustine several times mentions his own postponed
baptism; cf. his *Confessions* 1.11.17–18; 5.9.16; 6.13.23;
9.2.4; 6.14.

Christum confitendo finire vitam quam eum negando
ad eius baptismum pervenire. Quod utique si
fecissent, etiam hoc eis in illo lavacro dimitteretur,
quod timore mortis negaverant Christum, in quo
lavacro et illis facinus tam inmane dimissum est qui
occiderant Christum. Sed quando sine abundantia
gratiae Spiritus illius qui ubi vult spirat tantum
Christum amare possent ut eum in tanto vitae dis-
crimine sub tanta spe veniae negare non possent?

Mors igitur pretiosa sanctorum, quibus cum tanta
gratia est praemissa [1] et praerogata mors Christi ut
ad eum adquirendum suam non cunctarentur in-
pendere, in eos usus redactum esse monstravit quod
ad poenam peccati [2] antea fuerat constitutum ut inde
iustitiae fructus uberior nasceretur. Mors ergo non
ideo bonum videri debet, quia in tantam utilitatem
non vi sua, sed divina opitulatione conversa est ut
quae tunc metuenda proposita est ne peccatum com-
mitteretur, nunc suscipienda proponatur ut peccatum
non committatur commissumque deleatur magnaeque
victoriae debita iustitiae palma reddatur.

---

[1] praemissa *adopted by editors from an 11th-century MS.:*
promissa *most MSS.*
[2] peccantis *many MSS.*

terminate life rather than to deny him and survive to gain his baptism. Yet surely, if they had done so, they would have been forgiven even the sin of denying Christ through fear of death in that cleansing rite whereby even the slayers of Christ were forgiven their so monstrous crime. But how, apart from the abounding grace of that Spirit who ' blows where he wills,' [1] could they have loved Christ so much that they were unable to deny him although they were in such great mortal peril and although they had such great hope of pardon in prospect?

Death therefore is precious in the case of the saints, who had before them the precedent and pattern of Christ's death. Such was the grace that emanated from it that they did not hesitate to pay the price of their own death in order to gain him. Thus their death was proof that what had previously been ordained as punishment for sin was put to such good use that it became a means whereby the fruit of righteousness was more abundantly produced. Yet death should not on that account be considered a good thing, for it was turned into something so advantageous, not by its own virtue, but by the bounty of God. And so it is that, whereas death was once held up to us as a formidable threat to prevent the commission of sin, it is now held up to us as a requisite ordeal to prevent the commission of sin and to effect absolution of it if it is committed, as well as to assure the award of the palm of righteousness that is due to so great a victory.

[1] John 3.8.

VIII

Quod in sanctis primae mortis pro veritate susceptio
secundae sit mortis abolitio.

Si enim diligentius consideremus, etiam cum
quisque pro veritate fideliter et laudabiliter moritur,
mors cavetur. Ideo quippe aliquid eius suscipitur,
ne tota contingat et secunda insuper, quae numquam
finiatur, accedat. Suscipitur enim animae a corpore
separatio ne, Deo ab anima separato, etiam ipsa
separetur a corpore ac sic, totius hominis prima morte
completa, secunda excipiat sempiterna.

Quocirca mors quidem, ut dixi, cum eam morientes
patiuntur cumque in eis ut moriantur facit, nemini
bona est, sed laudabiliter toleratur pro tenendo vel
adipiscendo bono. Cum vero in ea sunt qui iam
mortui nuncupantur, non absurde dicitur et malis
mala et bonis bona. In requie sunt enim animae
piorum a corpore separatae, impiorum autem poenas
luunt, donec istarum ad aeternam vitam, illarum vero
ad aeternam mortem, quae secunda dicitur, corpora
revivescant.

VIII

That when the saints undergo the first death in the cause of truth they are thereby freed from the second death.

INDEED, a more careful consideration shows that, even when a person dies loyally and gloriously in the cause of truth, death is avoided. For he undergoes some part of it that he may not have the whole come to him, as well as the second, never-ending death besides. He accepts separation of soul from body to prevent separation of God from the soul before separation of soul from body; otherwise, when the first death of the entire man had run its course, it would be followed by the second death, which is eternal.

Therefore death, as I said,[1] is not good for anyone at the time when it is experienced by the dying and is causing them to die, but it is borne gloriously in order to keep or to obtain something that is good. But when those who are described as already dead are in the state of death, there is no mistake in saying that it is evil for the evil and good for the good. For the souls of the righteous that are separated from the body are at rest, whereas those of the wicked suffer punishment; and this situation obtains until the bodies of the righteous are resurrected to an eternal life and those of the wicked to an eternal or second death.

[1] See above, 13.6 (p. 153).

IX

*Tempus mortis, quo vitae sensus aufertur, in morienti-
bus an in mortuis esse dicendum sit.*

SED id tempus quo animae a corpore separatae aut
in bonis sunt aut in malis, utrum post mortem potius
an in morte dicendum est? Si enim post mortem
est, iam non ipsa mors, quae transacta atque praeterita est, sed post eam vita praesens animae bona
seu mala est. Mors autem tunc eis mala erat
quando erat, hoc est quando eam patiebantur cum
morerentur, quoniam gravis et molestus eius inerat
sensus; quo malo bene utuntur boni. Peracta autem
mors quonam modo vel bona vel mala est, quae iam
non est?

Porro si adhuc diligentius adtendamus, nec illa
mors esse apparebit cuius gravem ac molestum in
morientibus diximus sensum. Quamdiu enim sentiunt, adhuc utique vivunt; et si adhuc vivunt, ante
mortem quam in morte potius esse dicendi sunt, quia
illa, cum venerit, aufert omnem corporis sensum qui,
ea propinquante, molestus est. Ac per hoc quo
modo morientes dicamus eos qui nondum mortui
sunt, sed, inminente morte, iam extrema et mortifera
adflictione iactantur explicare difficile est, etiamsi
recte isti appellantur morientes quia, cum mors,

IX

*Whether the time of death, at which the feeling of
life is taken away, is properly said to be when
people are dying or when they are dead.*

BUT there arises the question whether the period
during which the souls, after separation from their
bodies, are in either a good or a bad state is better
referred to as after death or in death. If we say
after death, then it is no longer death itself, which
is over and past, that is good or evil, but the actual
life of the soul after it. Still, death was evil for
them at the time when it existed, that is, when they
were experiencing it as they were dying, since the
grievous, painful feeling of it was present in them;
and this is an evil which the good use to good advantage. But once death is completed, how can it
be good or evil if it no longer is?

Further, if we should observe still more carefully,
it will become clear that not even that process which
produced, as we said, a grievous and painful feeling
in the dying is actually death. For as long as they
experience feeling, they are certainly still alive; and
if they are still alive, we must speak of them as before
death rather than in death, because when death has
come it takes away all the physical sensation that
is so painful while death is approaching. And this
is why it is difficult to explain how we can describe
as dying those who are not yet dead, though, while
death threatens, they are already racked in a
final and fatal agony. Yet they are rightly called
dying because when death, which is already im-

161

quae iam inpendet, advenerit, non morientes, sed
mortui nuncupantur.

Nullus est ergo moriens nisi vivens, quoniam, cum
in tanta est extremitate vitae in quanta sunt quos
agere animam dicimus, profecto qui nondum anima
caruit adhuc vivit. Idem ipse igitur simul et moriens
est et vivens, sed morti accedens, vita cedens,[1] adhuc
tamen in vita quia inest anima corpori, nondum
autem in morte quia nondum abscessit a corpore.
Sed si, cum abscesserit, nec tunc in morte sed post
mortem potius erit, quando sit in morte quis dixerit?
Nam neque ullus moriens erit si moriens et vivens
simul esse nullus potest; quamdiu quippe anima in
corpore est, non possumus negare viventem. Aut si
moriens potius dicendus est in cuius iam corpore
agitur ut moriatur, nec simul quisquam potest esse
vivens et moriens, nescio quando sit vivens.

X

An vita mortalium mors potius quam vita dicenda sit.

Ex quo enim quisque in isto corpore morituro esse
coeperit, numquam in eo non agitur ut mors veniat.
Hoc enim agit eius mutabilitas toto tempore vitae
huius (si tamen vita dicenda est), ut veniatur in
mortem. Nemo quippe est qui non ei post annum

---

[1] recedens *or* decedens *some MSS.*

minent, has come, they are not termed dying but dead.

Accordingly, only a living person can be a dying one, for even when a man is as far gone in life as those who we say are giving up the ghost, surely he who has not yet been parted from it is still alive. The very same person then is at once both dying and living, but he is approaching death and withdrawing from life. Nevertheless, he is still in life because the soul is in his body, but not yet in death because he has not yet withdrawn from the body. But if, when he has withdrawn, he is not even then in death but rather after death, who could say when he is in death? Indeed, if no one can be at once dying and living, there will not even be anyone who is dying, since, as long as the soul is in the body, we cannot deny that he is living. Or if we must say rather that the person in whose body death is already in process of taking place is dying and if no one can be at once living and dying, then when in the world is he living?

X

Whether the life of mortals should be called death rather than life.

INDEED, from the very moment that a person begins his existence in this body that is destined to die, there is never a point when death is not coming on. For this advance of man into death is the effect of the change to which he is subject at every moment of our present life, if we can still call it life. Certainly there is no one who will not be nearer to death a year

sit quam ante annum fuit, et cras quam hodie, et
hodie quam heri, et paulo post quam nunc, et nunc
quam paulo ante propinquior, quoniam quidquid
temporis vivitur de spatio vivendi demitur, et cotidie
fit minus minusque quod restat, ut omnino nihil sit
aliud tempus vitae huius quam cursus ad mortem, in
quo nemo vel paululum stare vel aliquanto tardius ire
permittitur, sed urgentur omnes pari motu nec
diverso inpelluntur accessu.

Neque enim cui vita brevior fuit celerius diem
duxit quam ille cui longior; sed cum aequaliter et
aequalia momenta raperentur ambobus, alter habuit
propius, alter remotius quo non inpari velocitate
ambo currebant. Aliud est autem amplius viae
peregisse, aliud tardius ambulasse. Qui ergo usque
ad mortem productiora spatia temporis agit non
lentius pergit, sed plus itineris conficit.

Porro si ex illo quisque incipit mori, hoc est esse
in morte, ex quo in illo agi coeperit ipsa mors, id est
vitae detractio (quia, cum detrahendo finita fuerit,
post mortem iam erit, non in morte), profecto, ex
quo esse incipit in hoc corpore, in morte est. Quid
enim aliud diebus horis momentisque singulis agitur
donec, ea consumpta,[1] mors, quae agebatur, im-

---

[1] consummata *some MSS.*

later than he was a year before or will not be to-morrow than he is today or is not today than he was yesterday or will not be a little later than he is now or is not now than he was a little while ago. And the reason for this is as follows: whatever length of time our life goes on, all this is subtracted from our whole life-span, and what is left becomes less and less each day, so that our present life is nothing but a race toward the goal of death—a race in which no one is allowed either a brief pause or the slightest slackening of pace, but all are propelled with a uniform motion and driven along with no variation in the rate of progress.

Thus the person who had a shorter life did not complete a day more quickly than he who had a longer life; rather, since both had an equal number of moments taken from them at an equal rate, one was nearer and the other farther from the goal to which they both were racing with no difference of speed. It is one thing to have traversed a longer way and quite another to have proceeded at a slower pace. Hence the person who takes more time on the way to his death does not advance with less speed but covers a greater distance.

Further, if a person begins to die, that is, to be in a state of death from the time that the process of death itself commences in him, then surely he is in a state of death from the time that he begins to exist in this body. For death is the diminution of life because, once life has been ended by diminishing, he will then be past the time of death, not in death. Indeed, what else takes place but death every single day, hour and minute until, when life is used up, death,

pleatur et incipiat iam tempus esse post mortem,
quod, cum vita detraheretur, erat in morte? Numquam igitur in vita homo est ex quo est in isto corpore
moriente potius quam vivente, si et in vita et in
morte simul non potest esse.

An potius et in vita et in morte simul est, in vita
scilicet, in qua vivit donec tota detrahatur, in morte
autem quia iam moritur cum vita detrahitur? Si
enim non est in vita, quid est quod detrahitur donec
eius fiat perfecta consumptio?[1] Si autem non est
in morte, quid est vitae ipsa detractio? Non enim
frustra, cum vita fuerit corpori tota detracta, post
mortem iam dicitur, nisi quia mors erat cum detraheretur. Nam si, ea detracta, non est homo in
morte sed post mortem, quando, nisi cum detrahitur,
erit in morte?

XI

An quisquam simul et vivens esse possit et mortuus.

Si autem absurdum est ut hominem, antequam ad
mortem perveniat, iam esse dicamus in morte (cui
enim propinquat peragendo vitae suae tempora si
iam in illa est?), maxime quia nimis est insolens ut
simul et vivens esse dicatur et moriens cum vigilans

---

[1] consummatio *some MSS.*

which was going on, is complete and time, which comprised the period during death when life was being diminished, now enters upon the period after death? Accordingly, if man cannot be at one and the same time both in life and in death, he is never in life from the time he is in this body which is dying rather than living.

But perhaps man is at once both in life and in death, that is to say, he is in life, living it until it is wholly removed, but at the same time in death because he is dying from the moment that his life is diminished. For if he is not in life, what is it that suffers diminution until it is completely used up? On the other hand, if he is not in death, what is the diminution of life essentially? It is quite proper to speak of the time after death once life has been wholly removed from the body precisely because the time when life was being diminished was itself death. For if, after life has been removed, man finds himself not in death but past death, when will he be in death if not when life is being diminished?

XI

Whether anyone can at the same time be both living and dead.

On the other hand, to say that a man is already in death before he arrives at death is perhaps absurd, for what does he approach as he passes the moments of his life if he is already in death? And this would seem so especially since it is quite anomalous to speak of a person as both living and dying at the

et dormiens simul esse non possit, quaerendum est quando erit moriens. Etenim antequam mors veniat, non est moriens, sed vivens. Cum vero mors venerit, mortuus erit, non moriens. Illud ergo est adhuc ante mortem, hoc iam post mortem.

Quando ergo in morte? Tunc enim est moriens, ut, quem ad modum tria sunt cum dicimus 'ante mortem,' 'in morte,' 'post mortem,' ita tria singulis singula 'vivens,' 'moriens,' 'mortuusque' reddantur. Quando itaque sit moriens, id est in morte, ubi neque sit vivens, quod est ante mortem, neque mortuus, quod est post mortem, sed moriens, id est in morte, difficillime definitur. Quamdiu quippe est anima in corpore, maxime si etiam sensus adsit, procul dubio vivit homo, qui constat ex anima et corpore, ac per hoc adhuc ante mortem, non in morte esse dicendus est. Cum vero anima abscesserit omnemque abstulerit corporis sensum, iam post mortem mortuusque perhibetur.

Perit igitur inter utrumque quo moriens vel in morte sit, quoniam si adhuc vivit, ante mortem est, si vivere destitit, iam post mortem est. Numquam ergo moriens, id est in morte, esse conprehenditur. Ita etiam in transcursu temporum quaeritur praesens nec invenitur quia sine ullo spatio est per quod transitur ex futuro in praeteritum.

Nonne ergo videndum est ne ista ratione mors

---

[1] On this concept of the present see Augustine, *Confessions* 11.15.18–20.

same time, inasmuch as he cannot be awake and asleep at the same time. Hence we must ask when he will be a dying man. For before death comes, he is not dying, but living. But when death has come, he will be dead, not dying. Accordingly, the former state is still prior to death, the latter already subsequent to death.

When then is he in the state of death? For that is when he is dying, and thus there are three separate states, ' living,' ' dying,' and ' dead,' corresponding, respectively, to the three stages that we speak of, ' before death,' ' in death,' and ' after death.' It is therefore very hard to define when he is dying, that is, in death, a state in which he is neither living, which is prior to death, nor dead, which is subsequent to death, but dying, that is, in death. For as long as the soul is in the body, especially if sensation is also present, man, who consists of body and soul, doubtless lives, and for this reason he must be described as still being before death, not in death. When the soul, however, has departed and removed all bodily sensation, the man is spoken of as past death and dead.

There vanishes then between these two states the interval during which a person is dying or in process of death. For if he is still living, he is before death; if he has ceased to live, he is already past death. Accordingly, he is never conceived to be dying, that is, to be in the midst of death. So too, as time goes by, we seek the present moment without finding it because there is no duration of any length in the passage from future to past.[1]

We must surely then be careful lest, following this line of reasoning, we find ourselves saying that there

corporis nulla esse dicatur? Si enim est, quando est,
quae in ullo et in qua ullus esse non potest? Quando
quidem si vivitur, adhuc non est quia hoc ante mortem, non in morte. Si autem vivere iam cessatum
est, iam non est quia et hoc post mortem est, non in
morte. Sed rursus si nulla mors est ante quid vel
post, quid est quod dicitur ante mortem sive post
mortem? Nam et hoc inaniter dicitur si mors nulla
est. Atque utinam in paradiso bene vivendo egisse-
mus ut re vera nulla mors esset. Nunc autem non
solum est verum etiam tam molesta est ut nec ulla
explicari locutione possit nec ulla ratione vitari.

Loquamur ergo secundum consuetudinem (non
enim aliter debemus) et dicamus ' ante mortem '
priusquam mors accidat, sicut scriptum est: *Ante
mortem ne laudes hominem quemquam*.[1] Dicamus
etiam cum acciderit: Post mortem illius vel illius
factum est illud aut illud. Dicamus et de praesenti
tempore ut possumus, velut cum ita loquimur:
Moriens ille testatus est, et: Illis atque illis illud
atque illud moriens dereliquit, quamvis hoc nisi
vivens omnino facere non posset et potius hoc ante
mortem fecerit, non in morte.

Loquamur etiam sicut loquitur scriptura divina,
quae mortuos quoque non post mortem sed in morte

[1] ne glorifices quemquam *a few MSS.*

---

[1] Ecclesiasticus 11.28. This commonplace of ancient wisdom is attributed by Herodotus, 1.32.7, to Solon in his con-

is no death of the body. For if there is such a thing, when can it be? It cannot be in anyone nor can anyone be in it. If a person is alive, there is still no death because life is a state before death, not during death. On the other hand, if there has been a cessation of life, then there is no longer any death because here too is a state not during death, but after death. But, again, if there is no death before something or after something, what do we mean by the phrase ' before death ' or ' after death '? For these too are meaningless expressions if there is no death. Would that we had led such a good life in paradise that there really was no death! But, as things stand, death not only exists but is so trouble-some that it can neither be defined by any mode of speech nor be avoided by any device.

Let us then follow common usage in our speech, as indeed we ought, and say ' before death ' for the time before death occurs, just as we read in Scripture : " Praise no man before his death." [1] Let us also say, when it has occurred : " Such and such happened after the death of so and so." Let us speak too as best we can of contemporary time, as when, for example, we express ourselves thus : " Dying, he made his will," and : " Dying, he bequeathed such and such to so and so." And yet, unless he had been living, he could not have done this at all ; in fact, he did it rather before death, not in death.

Let us speak also in the same terms as the holy Scriptures, which do not scruple to say that the dead

versation with Croesus; cf. Juvenal, 10.274–275. It is examined critically by Aristotle, *Nicomachean Ethics* 1.10.11 (1100a10–1101b9).

esse non dubitat dicere. Hinc enim est illud:
Quoniam non est in morte qui memor sit tui. Donec
enim revivescant, recte esse dicuntur in morte, sicut
in somno esse quisque, donec evigilet, dicitur.
Quamvis in somno positos dicamus dormientes, nec
tamen eo modo possumus dicere eos qui iam sunt
mortui morientes. Non enim adhuc moriuntur qui,
quantum adtinet ad corporis mortem, de qua nunc
disserimus, iam sunt a corporibus separati.

Sed hoc est quod dixi explicari aliqua locutione
non posse, quonam modo vel morientes dicantur
vivere vel iam mortui etiam post mortem adhuc esse
dicantur in morte. Quo modo enim post mortem si
adhuc in morte, praesertim cum eos nec morientes
dicamus, sicuti eos qui in somno sunt dicimus dormientes, et qui in languore, languentes, et qui in
dolore, utique dolentes, et qui in vita, viventes? At
vero mortui, priusquam resurgant, esse dicuntur in
morte, nec tamen possunt appellari morientes.

Unde non inportune neque incongrue arbitror
accidisse, etsi non humana industria, iudicio fortasse
divino, ut hoc verbum quod est moritur in Latina
lingua nec grammatici declinare potuerint ea regula
qua cetera talia declinantur. Namque ab eo quod
est oritur fit verbum praeteriti temporis ' ortus est,'
et si qua similia sunt, per temporis praeteriti parti-

---

[1] Psalms 6.5.

too are not past death but in death. Hence indeed
comes the statement: " Since there is none in death
who is mindful of thee." [1] For until they are brought
to life again, they are rightly said to be in death, just
as every one is said to be in slumber until he wakes
up. Still, although we say that those who lie in
slumber are sleeping, we cannot similarly say that
those who are already dead are dying. For those
who are already separated from their bodies are not
still dying. These remarks, of course, concern only
the death of the body, which is the subject of our
present discussion.

But this is what I said could not be defined by any
mode of speech. How can either those who are
dying be said to be living or those who are already
dead be said, even after death, to be still in death?
For how can they be regarded as after death if they
are still in death, especially since we do not say that
they are dying then either, as we say that those who
are in slumber are sleeping and those who are in
weariness are weary and those who are in pain are
surely suffering pain and those who are in life are
living? But the dead, until they rise again, are said
to be in death and yet the term ' dying ' cannot be
used of them.

Hence I think that it is neither improper nor discordant that it has come about, though not by human
effort, yet perhaps by divine ordinance, that neither
were the grammarians able to conjugate in Latin the
verb *moritur* (' he dies ') according to the same rule as
the other verbs of this type. For from the verb *oritur*
(' he arises ') comes the past tense *ortus est* (' he has
arisen '), and all like verbs are conjugated with

cipia declinantur. Ab eo vero quod est moritur, si
quaeramus praeteriti temporis verbum, responderi
adsolet ' mortuus est,' u littera geminata. Sic enim
dicitur mortuus quo modo fatuus, arduus,[1] conspicuus et si qua similia, quae non sunt praeteriti
temporis, sed, quoniam nomina sunt, sine tempore
declinantur. Illud autem, quasi ut declinetur quod
declinari non potest, pro participio praeteriti temporis ponitur nomen. Convenienter itaque factum
est ut, quem ad modum id quod significat non potest
agendo, ita ipsum verbum non posset loquendo
declinari.

Agi tamen potest in adiutorio gratiae Redemptoris
nostri ut saltem secundam mortem declinare possimus. Illa est enim gravior et omnium malorum
pessima, quae non fit separatione animae et corporis,
sed in aeternam poenam potius utriusque complexu.
Ibi e contrario non erunt homines ante mortem atque
post mortem, sed semper in morte, ac per hoc numquam viventes, numquam mortui, sed sine fine
morientes. Numquam enim erit homini peius in
morte quam ubi erit mors ipsa sine morte.

XII

*Quam mortem primis hominibus Deus, si mandatum
eius transgrederentur, fuerit comminatus.*

Cum ergo requiritur quam mortem Deus primis hominibus fuerit comminatus si ab eo mandatum trans-

---

[1] arduus *is followed by a spurious adjective* carduus *in many
MSS.*

perfect participles. But if we ask for the past tense of the verb *moritur*, the regular answer is *mortuus est* ('he has died' or 'he is dead'), the letter *u* being doubled. For *mortuus* is used in the same way as *fatuus* ('foolish'), *arduus* ('steep'), *conspicuus* ('visible'), and any like words that do not imply past time, but, being adjectives, are declined without distinction of tense. That adjective, moreover, is employed in place of a past participle as if to make a tense where none can be. The result of this is, appropriately enough, that the verb itself can no more be declined by us in speech than can the act that it denotes in reality.[1]

Yet with the help of the grace of our Redeemer we may be enabled to decline, that is, evade, at least the second death. For the death that is effected, not by the separation of soul and body, but rather by the union of both for eternal punishment is more serious and the worst of all evils. There, conversely, men will not be in a state before death or after death but always in death, and for this reason never living, never dead, but endlessly dying. Indeed, man will never be worse off in death than where death itself will be deathless.

XII

On the death with which God threatened the first human beings if they should violate his commandment.

To the question then what kind of death it was with which God threatened the first human beings if

---

[1] Augustine is punning here on two senses of *declinare*, 'to decline,' that is, 'to inflect,' and 'to avoid.'

grederentur acceptum nec oboedientiam custodirent,
utrum animae an corporis an totius hominis an illam
quae appellatur secunda, respondendum est: Omnes.
Prima enim constat ex duabus, [secunda] [1] ex omnibus tota. Sicut enim universa terra ex multis terris
et universa ecclesia ex multis constat ecclesiis, sic
universa mors ex omnibus.

Quoniam prima constat ex duabus, una animae,
altera corporis, ut sit prima totius hominis mors cum
anima sine Deo et sine corpore ad tempus poenas
luit; secunda vero, ubi anima sine Deo cum corpore
poenas aeternas luit. Quando ergo dixit Deus
primo illi homini quem in paradiso constituerat de
cibo vetito: *Quacumque die ederitis ex illo*, *morte
moriemini*, non tantum primae mortis partem priorem,
ubi anima privatur Deo, nec tantum posteriorem, ubi
corpus privatur anima, nec solam [2] ipsam totam
primam, ubi anima et a Deo et a corpore separata
punitur, sed quidquid mortis est usque ad novissi-
mam, quae secunda dicitur, qua est nulla posterior,
comminatio illa complexa est.

---

[1] secunda *omitted in many MSS., and rightly bracketed by
editors as an interpolation arising from a misunderstanding of
the text.*
[2] solum *some MSS.*

they should violate the commandment received from him and should not observe obedience, whether it was death of the soul or of the body or of the whole man, or that which is called the second death, we must answer: " All of them." For the first death consists of two deaths, total death of all of them. Just as the whole earth consists of many lands and the whole church of many churches, so total death consists of all deaths.

The reason for this is as follows: the first death consists of two deaths, one of the soul and the other of the body, and thus the first death is that of the whole man when the soul without God and without the body suffers punishment for a certain length of time; the second death, on the other hand, occurs when the soul without God suffers eternal punishment along with the body. Accordingly, when God said concerning the forbidden food to that first man whom he had placed in paradise: " In the day that you eat of it you shall die," [1] his threat embraced not only the first part of the first death, when the soul is deprived of God, nor only the second part, when the body is deprived of the soul, nor even the entire first death alone, when the soul undergoes punishment after it is separated from both God and the body, but it included every kind of death down to the very last, which is called the second death and is followed by no other.

[1] Genesis 2.17.

SAINT AUGUSTINE

XIII

Praevaricatio primorum hominum quam primam senserit poenam.

Nam postea quam praecepti facta transgressio est, confestim, gratia deserente divina, de corporum suorum nuditate confusi sunt. Unde etiam foliis ficulneis, quae forte a perturbatis prima comperta sunt, pudenda texerunt, quae prius eadem membra erant, sed pudenda non erant. Senserunt ergo novum motum inoboedientis carnis suae, tamquam reciprocam poenam inoboedientiae suae.

Iam quippe anima libertate in perversum propria delectata et Deo dedignata servire pristino corporis servitio destituebatur, et quia superiorem dominum suo arbitrio deseruerat, inferiorem famulum ad suum arbitrium non tenebat, nec omni modo habebat subditam carnem, sicut semper habere potuisset si Deo subdita ipsa mansisset. Tunc ergo coepit caro concupiscere adversus spiritum, cum qua controversia nati sumus, trahentes originem mortis et in membris nostris vitiataque natura contentionem eius sive victoriam de prima praevaricatione gestantes.

XIII

*What the first punishment was that the first human
beings experienced for their transgression.*

For after God's command had been disobeyed, the
first human beings, as divine favour departed from
them, straightway became ashamed of the nakedness
of their bodies. Hence too they used fig leaves,
which perhaps were the first things they hit upon in
their embarrassment to cover their pudenda, that is,
shameful members.[1] These had been the same
organs before, but had not then been shameful.
Thus they experienced an unprecedented movement
of their own disobedient flesh as punishment in kind,
as it were, for their own disobedience.

The soul, in fact, delighting now in its own freedom
to do wickedness and scorning to serve God, was
stripped of the former subjection of the body, and
because it had wilfully deserted its own higher master,
no longer kept its lower servant responsive to its will.
It did not maintain its own flesh subject to it in all
respects, as it could have done for ever if it had itself
remained subject to God. Thus it was that the flesh
then began to " lust against the spirit." [2] This is our
congenital conflict. From the first transgression
come the beginning of death in us and the carnal
rebellion or even victory that we sustain in our limbs
and blighted being.

[1] Cf. Genesis 3.7–10.
[2] Galatians 5.17.

SAINT AUGUSTINE

XIV

Qualis homo sit factus a Deo et in quam sortem
deciderit suae voluntatis arbitrio.

DEUS enim creavit hominem rectum, naturarum
auctor, non utique vitiorum. Sed sponte depravatus
iusteque damnatus depravatos damnatosque genera-
vit. Omnes enim fuimus in illo uno quando omnes
fuimus ille unus qui per feminam lapsus est in peccatum, quae de illo facta est ante peccatum. Nondum
erat nobis singillatim creata et distributa forma in
qua singuli viveremus; sed iam erat natura seminalis
ex qua propagaremur. Qua scilicet propter peccatum vitiata et vinculo mortis obstricta iusteque
damnata, non alterius condicionis homo ex homine
nasceretur. Ac per hoc a[1] liberi arbitrii malo usu
series calamitatis huius exorta est, quae humanum
genus origine depravata, velut radice corrupta, usque
ad secundae mortis exitium, quae non habet finem,
solis eis exceptis qui per Dei gratiam liberantur,
miseriarum conexione perducit.

[1] a *omitted in some MSS.*

XIV

What man was like as created by God and into what condition he fell through the free exercise of his own will.

God created man upright, for He is the author of natural beings, not, surely, of their defects. Man, however, when he was willingly corrupted and justly condemned, engendered corrupt and condemned offspring. For we were all in that one man since all of us were that one man who fell into sin through the woman who was made from him before sin. We did not yet have individually created and apportioned shapes in which to live as individuals; what already existed was the seminal substance from which we were to be generated. Obviously, when this substance was debased through sin and shackled with the bond of death in just condemnation, no man could be born of man in any other condition. Thus from the abuse of free will has come the linked sequence of our disaster, by which the human race is conducted through an uninterrupted succession of miseries from that original depravity, as it were from a diseased root, all the way to the catastrophe of the second death that has no end. Only those who are freed through the grace of God are exempt from this fate.

SAINT AUGUSTINE

XV

Quod Adam peccaturus prius ipse reliquerit Deum quam relinqueretur a Deo, et primam fuisse animae mortem a Deo recessisse.

QUAM ob rem etiamsi in eo quod dictum est: *Morte moriemini*, quoniam non est dictum: Mortibus, eam solam intellegamus quae fit cum anima deseritur sua vita, quod illi Deus est (non enim deserta est ut desereret, sed ut desereretur deseruit; ad malum quippe eius prior est voluntas eius, ad bonum vero eius prior est voluntas Creatoris eius, sive ut eam faceret quae nulla erat sive ut reficiat quia[1] lapsa perierat)—etiamsi ergo hanc intellegamus Deum denuntiasse mortem in eo quod ait: *Qua die ederitis ex illo, morte moriemini*, tamquam diceret: Qua die me deserueritis per inoboedientiam, deseram vos per iustitiam, profecto in ea morte etiam ceterae denuntiatae sunt quae procul dubio fuerant secuturae.

Nam in eo quod inoboediens motus in carne animae inoboedientis exortus est, propter quem pudenda texerunt, sensa est mors una, in qua deseruit animam Deus. Ea significata est verbis eius quando timore dementi sese abscondenti homini dixit: *Adam, ubi es?* non utique ignorando quaerens, sed

---

[1] quae *a few MSS.*

---

[1] Genesis 2.17.   [2] *Ibid.*
[3] Genesis 3.9.

XV

*That, when Adam was about to sin, he himself
forsook God before he was forsaken by God,
and that his withdrawal from God was
the first death of the soul.*

Now, since in the words: " You shall die by
death," [1] it does not say ' by deaths,' let us understand here only that death which occurs when the
soul is forsaken by its own life, which in its case
means God. The soul was not first forsaken by God
and so then forsook him, but the soul first forsook
God and was then forsaken by him; for the will of
the soul acts first for its own evil, whereas it is the
will of the soul's creator that acts first for its good,
whether it be to create the soul which did not yet
exist or to recreate it because it had fallen and
perished. Accordingly, even though we understand
that it was this death of which God gave notice when
he said: " In the day that you eat of it you shall die
by death," [2] as if he had said: " In the day that you
forsake me with disobedience I shall forsake you with
justice," surely in this death he gave notice also of the
other deaths that doubtless were bound to follow.

For when in the flesh of the unruly soul there arose
an unruly movement, on account of which our first
parents covered up their shameful members, one
death was experienced, that in which the soul was
forsaken by God. This death was implied by his
words when he said to the man who was distraught
with fear and concealing himself: " Adam, where are
you ?" [3] For surely God did not ask this in ignorance

increpando admonens ut adtenderet ubi esset in quo
Deus non esset.

Cum vero corpus anima ipsa deseruit aetate cor
ruptum et senectute confectum, venit in experimentum mors altera, de qua Deus peccatum adhuc
puniens homini dixerat: *Terra es et in terram ibis*, ut
ex his duabus mors illa prima, quae totius est hominis,
compleretur, quam secunda in ultimo sequitur nisi
homo per gratiam liberetur. Neque enim corpus,
quod de terra est, rediret in terram nisi sua morte,
quae illi accidit cum deseritur sua vita, id est anima.
Unde constat inter Christianos veraciter catholicam
tenentes fidem etiam ipsam nobis corporis mortem
non lege naturae, qua nullam mortem homini [1] Deus
fecit, sed merito inflictam esse peccati quoniam
peccatum vindicans Deus dixit homini, in quo tunc
omnes eramus: *Terra es et in terram ibis.*

XVI

De philosophis qui animae separationem a corpore
non putant esse poenalem, cum Plato inducat
summum deum diis minoribus promittentem
quod numquam sint corporibus exuendi.

SED philosophi, contra quorum calumnias defendi-
mus civitatem Dei, hoc est eius ecclesiam, sapienter

[1] hominis *some MSS.*

[1] Genesis 3.19.

but to administer a rebuke that warned him to take heed where he was now that God was not in him.

When, however, the soul itself forsook the body, now broken down with length of years and worn out by old age, man experienced another death, about which God had said to him, when He was still punishing his sin: "You are earth and shall enter into earth."[1] Thus these two deaths made up that first death, which is that of the whole man; it is followed ultimately by the second death unless the man should be set free by grace. Indeed, neither would the body, which is made of earth, return into earth except for its own death; and that befalls it when it is forsaken by its own life, that is, by the soul. Hence Christians who truly hold the catholic faith are convinced that even the death of the body was imposed upon us not by a law of nature, since God did not create in nature any death for man, but as a retribution for sin; for God was avenging sin when he said to the man, in whom we were all included at that time: "You are earth and shall enter into earth."

XVI

On the philosophers who do not think that the separation of soul from body is a punishment, although Plato represents the supreme God as assuring the lesser deities that they are never to be stripped of their bodies.

But the philosophers, against whose slanders we are defending the City of God, that is to say, his

185

sibi videntur inridere quod dicimus animae a corpore
separationem inter poenas eius esse deputandam,
quia videlicet eius perfectam beatitudinem tunc illi
fieri existimant cum omni prorsus corpore exuta ad
Deum simplex et sola et quodam modo nuda redierit.

Ubi si nihil quo ista refelleretur opinio in eorum
litteris invenirem, operosius mihi disputandum esset
quo demonstrarem non corpus esse animae, sed corruptibile corpus onerosum. Unde illud est quod de
scripturis nostris in superiore libro commemoravimus:
Corpus enim corruptibile adgravat animam. Addendo
utique *corruptibile* non qualicumque corpore, sed
quale factum est ex peccato consequente vindicta,
animam perhibuit adgravari. Quod etiamsi non
addidisset, nihil aliud intellegere deberemus. Sed
cum apertissime Plato deos a summo Deo factos
habere inmortalia corpora praedicet eisque ipsum
Deum, a quo facti sunt, inducat pro magno beneficio
pollicentem quod in aeternum cum suis corporibus
permanebunt nec ab eis ulla morte solventur, quid
est quod isti ad exagitandam Christianam fidem
fingunt se nescire quod sciunt aut etiam sibi repug-
nantes adversum se ipsos malunt dicere, dum nobis
non desinant contradicere?

Nempe Platonis haec verba sunt, sicut ea Cicero
in Latinum vertit, quibus inducit summum deum

---

[1] Above, 12.16 (p. 69).   [2] Wisdom 9.15.
[3] Plato, *Timaeus* 41a–b.

church, are wise in their own eyes when they scoff at
our statement that the separation of soul from body
should be accounted among its punishments. The
reason for this is that they hold that the soul attains
its fullest bliss in the moment when, utterly stripped
of all body, it returns to God simple, alone and, in a
sense, naked.

In this matter, if I found nothing in their writings
to refute this belief, I should have to argue more
painstakingly to demonstrate that it is not the body
as such but a corruptible body that is burdensome to
the soul. This is what lies behind the following
statement that we quoted in the preceding book [1]
from our Scriptures: " For the corruptible body is
heavy upon the soul." [2] Surely, by adding ' corruptible ' the sage meant that the soul was weighed
down, not by just any sort of body, but by the body
such as it became as a result of sin and consequent
punishment. And even if he had not added this
term, we ought not to have understood anything else.
But Plato declares in the clearest manner that the
deities, who were made by the supreme God, have
immortal bodies, and he represents God himself,
their maker, as promising them a great boon in that
they will for ever remain united to their bodies and
never be severed from them by any death. Now, in
view of all this, why is it that those philosophers,
seeking to harry the Christian faith, pretend not to
know what they do know or even prefer to be at
odds with themselves and to speak against themselves, if only they may contradict us unremittingly ?

Here are the very words of Plato himself,[3] as translated by Cicero into Latin, in which he presents the

deos quos fecit adloquentem ac dicentem: " Vos qui
deorum satu orti estis, adtendite. Quorum operum
ego parens effectorque sum, haec sunt indissolubilia
me invito, quamquam omne conligatum solvi potest;
sed haudquaquam bonum [1] est ratione vinctum velle
dissolvere. Sed quoniam estis orti, inmortales vos
quidem esse et indissolubiles non potestis. Ne utiquam [2] tamen dissolvemini, neque vos ulla mortis
fata periment nec erunt valentiora quam consilium
meum, quod maius est vinculum ad perpetuitatem
vestram quam illa quibus estis [tum cum gigneba-
mini] [3] conligati." Ecce deos Plato dicit et corporis
animaeque conligatione mortales et tamen inmortales
dei a quo facti sunt voluntate atque consilio.

Si ergo animae poena est in qualicumque corpore
conligari, quid est quod eos adloquens deus tamquam
sollicitos ne forte moriantur, id est dissolvantur a
corpore, de sua facit inmortalitate securos, non
propter eorum naturam, quae sit compacta, non
simplex, sed propter suam invictissimam voluntatem,
qua potens est facere ut nec orta occidant nec conexa
solvantur, sed incorruptibiliter perseverent ?

[1] boni *one MS., Cicero.*

[2] ne utiquam *some MSS., Cicero, where* ne umquam *is also
attested:* nec umquam *or* numquam *or* nequaquam *other MSS.*

[3] tum cum gignebamini *found in some MSS., but omitted in
others and rightly bracketed by editors as an interpolation from
Cicero's text.*

[1] Cicero, *Timaeus* 11.40. Augustine's citations from Cicero
have been collected by M. Testard, *Saint Augustin et Cicéron*
(Paris, 1958), vol. 2: *Répertoire des Textes.*

[2] Plato does not in fact explicitly mention the bodies of

supreme God addressing the deities whom he made
and saying: "You who have sprung from the stock
of the gods, give heed. The works of which I am
parent and author are exempt from dissolution
against my will, although everything that is fastened
together can be sundered; but it is nowise good to
choose to undo what is bound together by reason.
But since you have had a beginning, you cannot be
immortal and indestructible. Yet you will by no
means be destroyed, nor will any necessity of death
annihilate you or be more powerful than my purpose,
which serves as a stronger bond for your continued
existence than those bonds by which you were
fastened together [at the time that you were
created]."[1] Thus Plato says both that the gods
are mortal because of the union of body and soul[2]
and that they are yet immortal because of the will
and purpose of God who made them.

If then it is punishment for the soul to be bound up
in any sort of body, why is it that God addresses
them as though they were anxious for fear that they
may die, that is, be detached from the body, and
why does he give them assurance of their immortality?
This assurance, moreover, is based, not on their
nature, which is composite rather than simple, but
on his own unconquerable will, by which he has
power to preserve such things as have a beginning
from perishing and such as have been joined together
from coming apart, and to make them endure without deterioration.

these gods. Still, without God's will and purpose, they are
mortal (and destructible) because they were created
(γεγένησθε, *orti estis*).

Et hoc quidem utrum Plato verum de sideribus dicat, alia quaestio est.   Neque enim ei continuo concedendum est globos istos luminum sive orbiculos luce corporea super terras seu die seu nocte fulgentes suis quibusdam propriis animis vivere eisque intellectualibus et beatis, quod etiam de ipso universo mundo, tamquam uno animali maximo quo cuncta cetera continerentur animalia, instanter adfirmat. Sed haec, ut dixi, alia quaestio est, quam nunc discutiendam non suscepimus.

Hoc tantum contra istos commemorandum putavi qui se Platonicos vocari vel esse gloriantur, cuius superbia nominis erubescunt esse Christiani ne commune illis cum vulgo vocabulum vilem faciat palliatorum tanto magis inflatam quanto magis exiguam paucitatem.   Et quaerentes quid in doctrina Christiana reprehendant, exagitant aeternitatem corporum, tamquam haec sint inter se contraria, ut et beatitudinem quaeramus animae et eam semper esse velimus in corpore, velut aerumnoso vinculo conligatam, cum eorum auctor et magister Plato donum a deo summo diis ab illo factis dicat esse concessum ne aliquando moriantur, id est a corporibus, quibus eos conexuit, separentur.

---

[1] Cf. Plato, *Timaeus* 41d–e.
[2] Cf. Plato, *Timaeus* 30c–31b; 92c.

But whether these words of Plato in reference to the stars [1] are true is another question. For it does not follow that we must grant him that those luminous globes or little disks that shine with physical light over the lands whether by day or by night are animated by souls of their own and that these souls are endowed with understanding and happiness. He emphatically makes this same statement about the universe as a whole, speaking of it as a single living thing of the greatest size that encloses all other living things.[2] But, as I said, this is another question, which I have not undertaken to discuss at the moment.

I have thought it best to bring up just this one point against those who plume themselves on being called or being Platonists and whose pride in this name makes them ashamed to be Christians. They fear that, if they share one designation with the common mass, it will detract for the wearers of the Greek cloak [3] from the prestige of their fewness, for they are puffed up in inverse proportion to their number. And so in their quest for something to censure in Christian doctrine they rail at the immortality of the body, as if there were any inconsistency in our seeking happiness for the soul and at the same time requiring it to exist for ever in a body, as if the bonds that bind them must be vexatious. Yet it is their founder and teacher Plato who says that the supreme God granted to the deities who were made by him the boon of never dying, that is, of never being separated from the bodies to which he joined them.

[3] The Greek *pallium* became the traditional costume of philosophers.

SAINT AUGUSTINE

XVII

Contra eos qui adserunt corpora terrena incor-
ruptibilia fieri et aeterna non posse.

CONTENDUNT etiam isti terrestria corpora sempiterna esse non posse, cum ipsam universam terram dei
sui, non quidem summi, sed tamen magni, id est
totius huius mundi, membrum in medio positum et
sempiternum esse non dubitent. Cum ergo deus ille
summus fecerit eis alterum quem putant deum, id est
istum mundum, ceteris diis, qui infra eum sunt,
praeferendum, eundemque esse existiment animan-
tem, anima scilicet, sicut asserunt, rationali vel in-
tellectuali in tam magna mole corporis eius inclusa,
ipsiusque corporis tamquam membra locis suis posita
atque digesta quattuor constituerit elementa, quorum iuncturam, ne umquam deus eorum tam magnus
moriatur, insolubilem ac sempiternam velint, quid
causae est ut in corpore maioris animantis tamquam
medium membrum aeterna sit terra, et aliorum
animantium terrestrium corpora, si Deus sicut illud
velit, aeterna esse non possint?

Sed terrae, inquiunt, terra reddenda est, unde
animalium terrestria sumpta sunt corpora; ex quo
fit, inquiunt, ut ea sit necesse dissolvi et emori et eo
modo terrae stabili ac sempiternae, unde fuerant

---

[1] On the concept of the universe as a divinity cf. Plato,
Timaeus 34a–b.
[2] Cf. Plato, *Timaeus* 30b.
[3] Cf. Plato, *Timaeus* 32c.

XVII

Against those who maintain that earthly bodies cannot become imperishable and eternal.

THESE philosophers also argue that earthly bodies cannot be everlasting, although they do not doubt that the entire earth itself constitutes a central and everlasting member of their god; by god they mean not the supreme God, but the great god that this whole universe is to them.[1] Well then, the supreme God created for them what they regard as another god, that is, this universe, with precedence over the other deities that are below him. Moreover, they think that this god is animate, possessing, that is, a soul which is, so they say, rational or intelligent and shut up within that massive body.[2] Further, according to them, God established the four elements like physical members of that same body, placed and arranged in their proper places; and to secure this great god of theirs from ever dying they would have it that the union of these elements is indissoluble and everlasting.[3] Granted all this, what reason is there, if the earth or central member, as it were, in the body of the larger animate being is eternal, why the bodies of other animate beings belonging to earth cannot be eternal if God were to will this as well as that?

Their contention is that earth, the source of the earthly bodies of living things, must be returned to earth; this, they say, is why these bodies must break up and perish and thus be restored to the steadfast and eternal earth from which they were derived.

193

sumpta, restitui. Si quis hoc etiam de igne similiter
adfirmet et dicat reddenda esse universo igni corpora
quae inde sumpta sunt ut caelestia fierent animalia,
nonne inmortalitas quam talibus diis, velut deo summo loquente, promisit Plato tamquam violentia dis-
putationis huius intercidet? An ibi propterea non
fit, quia Deus non vult, cuius voluntatem, ut ait
Plato, nulla vis vincit? Quid ergo prohibet ut hoc
etiam de terrestribus corporibus Deus possit efficere,
quandoquidem, ut nec ea quae orta sunt occidant nec
ea quae sunt vincta[1] solvantur nec ea quae sunt ex
elementis sumpta reddantur atque ut animae in
corporibus constitutae nec umquam ea deserant et
cum eis inmortalitate ac sempiterna beatitudine per-
fruantur, posse Deum facere confitetur Plato?

Cur ergo non possit ut nec terrestria moriantur?
An Deus non est potens quo usque Christiani credunt,
sed quo usque Platonici volunt? Nimirum quippe
consilium Dei et potestatem potuerunt philosophi,
nec potuerunt nosse prophetae, cum potius e contrario Dei prophetas ad enuntiandam eius, quantum
dignatus est, voluntatem Spiritus eius docuerit,
philosophos autem in ea cognoscenda coniectura
humana deceperit.

Verum non usque adeo decipi debuerunt, non
solum ignorantia verum[2] etiam pervicacia, ut et sibi

[1] iuncta *a few MSS.*
[2] sed magis *some MSS.*

[1] Cf. Plato, *Timaeus* 41a–b.

But suppose that a person made a similar assertion about fire and said that the bodies taken up from the universal fire for the creation of heavenly beings must be returned to it. On this hypothesis, will not the immortality which Plato,[1] speaking in the person of the supreme God, promised to such gods be rescinded by the violence, so to speak, of this line of argument? Or is this impossible in that region because God, whose will, as Plato says, no force can conquer, does not will it? What then is there to prevent God from having power to bring about the same thing in the case of earthly bodies too, especially since Plato acknowledges God's power to bring it about that what has a beginning need not perish nor need what has been bound come apart nor what has been taken from the elements be returned, and that souls established in bodies may not only never forsake them but even enjoy immortality and ever-lasting happiness together with them?

Why then should God not have power to bring it about that earthly things may not perish either? Is it that his power does not extend so far as Christians believe, but only so far as the Platonists hold? Those philosophers no doubt were in a position to know the purpose and power of God, whereas the prophets were not! No, quite the contrary; it was the prophets of God who were taught by his Spirit that they might reveal his will to the extent that he saw fit, while the philosophers were misled by human conjecture when they sought to discover it.

But neither ignorance nor obstinacy should have induced these philosophers to make such a mistake as to plead against themselves so patently. Yet this

apertissime refragentur magnis disputationum viribus
adserentes animae, ut beata esse possit, non terrenum
tantum sed omne corpus esse fugiendum et deos rursus dicentes habere beatissimas animas et tamen
aeternis corporibus inligatas, caelestes quidem igneis,
Iovis autem ipsius animam, quem mundum istum
volunt, omnibus omnino corporeis elementis quibus
haec tota moles a terra in caelum surgit inclusam.

Hanc enim animam Plato ab intimo terrae medio,
quod geometrae centron vocant, per omnes partes
eius usque ad caeli summa et extrema diffundi et
extendi per numeros musicos opinatur, ut sit iste
mundus animal maximum beatissimum sempiternum,
cuius anima et perfectam sapientiae felicitatem
teneret et corpus proprium non relinqueret cuiusque
corpus et in aeternum ex illa viveret et eam quamvis
non simplex sed tot corporibus tantisque conpactum
hebetare atque tardare non posset.

Cum igitur suspicionibus suis ista permittant, cur
nolunt credere divina voluntate atque potentia inmortalia corpora fieri posse terrena in quibus animae
nulla ab eis morte separatae, nullis eorum oneribus
adgravatae sempiterne ac feliciter vivant, quod deos
suos posse adserunt in corporibus igneis Iovemque
ipsum eorum regem in omnibus corporeis elementis?

---

[1] Cf. Plato, *Timaeus* 40a.
[2] Cf. Plato, *Timaeus* 34b.
[3] Cf. Plato, *Timaeus* 35c–36e.

is what they do. On the one hand, they maintain with great force of argument that the soul, in order to be happy, must keep clear not only of an earthly body but of every kind of body, and, on the other hand, they declare that the gods have souls which are supremely happy and yet bound up with eternal bodies, that is, celestial souls which are bound up with bodies of fire,[1] while the soul of Jupiter himself, whom they identify with the universe, is wholly contained in the sum total of material elements that constitute the entire structure which extends from earth to heaven.[2]

Plato holds the view that this soul of Jupiter spreads and extends by musical ratios from the earth's innermost core or centre, as it is called by geometricians, through all its parts to the highest and furthest reaches of heaven.[3] And thus, according to him, this universe is an everlasting living thing of the greatest magnitude and happiness; for its soul possesses the perfect bliss of wisdom and does not abandon its own body, while the body is for ever animated by the soul and, although it is not simple but composed of so many large bodies, has no power to make the soul sluggish or slothful.

Therefore, since these philosophers allow so much to their own speculations, why are they unwilling to believe that God's will and power can make earthly bodies immortal and that souls can live everlastingly and happily in them, inseparable from them by any death and undepressed by their weight? After all, they do maintain that such a life is possible for their gods in bodies of fire and for Jupiter himself, king of the gods, in the whole mass of material elements.

Nam si animae, ut beata sit, corpus est omne fugiendum, fugiant dii eorum de globis siderum, fugiat Iuppiter de caelo et terra; aut si non possunt, miseri iudicentur.

Sed neutrum isti volunt, qui neque a corporibus separationem audent dare diis suis, ne illos mortales colere videantur, nec beatitudinis privationem, ne infelices eos esse fateantur. Non ergo ad beatitudinem consequendam omnia fugienda sunt corpora, sed corruptibilia molesta, gravia moribunda, non qualia fecit primis hominibus bonitas Dei, sed qualia esse compulit poena peccati.

XVIII

De terrenis corporibus, quae philosophi adfirmant in caelestibus esse non posse quia quod terrenum est naturali pondere revocetur ad terram.[1]

SED necesse est, inquiunt, ut terrena corpora naturale pondus vel in terra teneat vel cogat ad terram et ideo in caelo esse non possint. Primi quidem illi

---

[1] *Two MSS. present a different tradition of titles in this and the remaining chapters of Book XIII; on the subject of chapter division and titles in Augustine's* City of God *see H.-I. Marrou, " La division en chapitres des livres de La Cité de Dieu," in Mélanges J. de Ghellinck (Gembloux, 1951), vol. 1, 235–249.*

---

[1] See above, 12.22 (p. 111 and note 1); 13.1 (p. 135); 13.3 (p. 141). In *De Genesi ad Litteram* 6.25.36, Augustine nicely distinguishes the natural mortality of the first human beings and their potential immortality, which they lost when they fell from grace through sin: *Illud* (sc. *corpus Adae*) *quippe ante peccatum et mortale secundum aliam et immortale*

For if a soul must shun every kind of body to be happy, let their gods flee from the starry globes and let their Jupiter flee from heaven and earth; or if they cannot do so, then let the verdict be that they are unhappy.

But these philosophers allow neither alternative, for they dare not attribute to their gods either a separation from bodies, lest they be found to worship gods who are but mortal, or a negation of bliss, lest it be shown by their own admission that their gods are unhappy. Accordingly, all bodies need not be shunned in order to attain bliss, but only such as are corruptible and vexatious, burdensome and moribund, that is, not such bodies as the bounty of God created for the first human beings,[1] but such as penalty for sin forced upon them.

XVIII

*On earthly bodies, which, according to the philosophers,
cannot exist in the heavenly region because anything
earthly is drawn back to earth by its natural
weight.*

BUT earthly bodies, these philosophers say, must either be held fast on earth or be forced earthward by their natural weight; and for that reason they cannot exist in heaven.[2] Those first human beings, it

---

*secundum aliam causam dici poterat: id est mortale quia poterat
mori, immortale quia poterat non mori. Aliud est enim non
posse mori, sicut quasdam naturas immortales creavit Deus;
aliud est autem posse non mori, secundum quem modum primus
creatus est homo immortalis.*

[2]   Augustine considers this problem also below, 22.11.

homines in terra erant nemorosa atque fructuosa, quae paradisi nomen obtinuit. Sed quia et ad hoc respondendum est vel propter Christi corpus cum quo ascendit in caelum vel propter sanctorum qualia in resurrectione futura sunt, intueantur paulo adtentius pondera ipsa terrena.

Si enim ars humana efficit ut ex metallis quae in aquis posita continuo submerguntur quibusdam modis vasa fabricata etiam natare possint, quanto credibilius et efficacius occultus aliquis modus operationis Dei, cuius omnipotentissima voluntate Plato dicit nec orta interire nec conligata posse dissolvi, cum multo mirabilius incorporea corporeis quam quaecumque corpora quibuscumque corporibus copulentur, potest molibus praestare terrenis ut nullo in ima pondere deprimantur, ipsisque animis perfectissime beatis ut quamvis terrena, tamen incorruptibilia iam corpora ubi volunt ponant et quo volunt agant situ motuque facillimo!

An vero si hoc angeli faciant et quaelibet animalia terrestria rapiant unde libet constituantque ubi libet, aut eos non posse aut onera sentire credendum est? Cur ergo sanctorum perfectos et beatos divino

---

[1] Cf. Plato, *Timaeus* 41a–b.
[2] Cf. *Bel and the Dragon* 36.

is true, did live on earth, which abounded in woods
and fruit and received the name ' paradise ' or park.
We must, however, find a reply to this argument to
account for the body with which Christ ascended into
heaven or for the sort of body that saints are destined
to have at resurrection. Let them therefore consider
a little more closely this matter of the earthly weights
in themselves.

Well now, we know that human skill can take metals
that immediately sink when placed in water and
fashion them by certain methods into vessels that
are even capable of floating. How much more
credible, how much more effective must God's skill
be, working in some mysterious way! His almighty
will, according to Plato, preserves both things that
had a beginning from perishing and things that were
bound together from disintegrating.[1] Moreover,
immaterial entities are much more marvellously
joined to material things than bodies are with bodies
of any sort whatsoever. Surely then God can not
only prevent earthly masses from being attracted to
the lowest region by any weight but also enable the
souls themselves to dwell in the most perfect bliss
with bodies which, though earthly, yet are also incorruptible and to set these bodies wherever they
wish and move them wherever they wish with the
utmost ease, be it of placement or movement.

Or if angels can do this and carry off any earthly
animals they please from wherever they please and
set them down wherever they please,[2] are we really
to believe that they cannot do this without feeling
the weight of the burdens? If not, then why should
we not believe that the spirits of the saints, made

munere spiritus sine ulla difficultate posse ferre quo
voluerint et sistere ubi voluerint sua corpora non
credamus? Nam cum terrenorum corporum, sicut
onera in gestando sentire consuevimus, quanto maior
est quantitas, tanto sit maior et gravitas ita ut plura
pondo quam pauciora plus premant, membra tamen
suae carnis leviora portat anima cum in sanitate
robusta sunt quam in languore cum macra sunt. Et
cum aliis gestantibus onerosior sit salvus et validus
quam exilis et morbidus, ipse tamen ad suum corpus
movendum atque portandum agilior est cum in bona
valetudine plus habet molis quam cum in peste vel
fame minimum roboris. Tantum valet in habendis
etiam terrenis corporibus, quamvis adhuc corrupti-
bilibus atque mortalibus, non quantitatis pondus, sed
temperationis modus. Et quis verbis explicat quantum distet inter praesentem quam dicimus sanitatem
et inmortalitatem futuram?

Non itaque nostram fidem redarguunt philosophi
de ponderibus corporum. Nolo enim quaerere cur
non credant terrenum esse posse corpus in caelo,
cum terra universa libretur in nihilo. Fortassis enim
de ipso medio mundi loco, eo quod in eum coeant
quaeque graviora, etiam argumentatio veri similior
habeatur. Illud dico: Si dii minores, quibus inter

---

[1] Cf. Job 26.7 (RSV): "He . . . hangs the earth upon
nothing."

perfect and happy by divine dispensation, can without any difficulty transport their bodies wherever they wish and set them wherever they wish? For granted that earthly bodies, like burdens whose weight we normally feel when we carry them, have their weight proportional to their mass, and thus the weight of a greater bodily mass is more oppressive than that of a smaller mass, nevertheless, the soul finds the organs of its flesh lighter to carry when they are sound and sturdy than when they are feeble and shrunken. And although a sound and healthy person is heavier for others to carry than a thin and sickly one, yet the person himself can move and carry his body with greater agility when he enjoys good health and has more weight than when through plague or starvation he has very little strength. Thus even when we have our earthly bodies, although they are still subject to putrefaction and death, it is not the weight of their mass, but the state of their constitution that makes all the difference. And who can find words to express the vast difference between the so-called health of our present state and the immortality of our future condition?

Our creed then is not refuted by the philosophers' argument about the weight of bodies. Now I will not put the question why they refuse to believe that there can be an earthly body in heaven, when the entire earth is balanced upon nothing.[1] For perhaps an even more probable argument against our view may be drawn from the very existence of a centre of the universe and from the fact that all heavier bodies converge upon it. What I do say is this: Let us suppose that the lesser gods, who were charged by

animalia terrestria cetera etiam hominem faciendum
commisit Plato, potuerunt, sicut dicit, ab igne removere urendi qualitatem, lucendi relinquere quae
per oculos emicaret, itane Deo summo concedere
dubitabimus, cuius ille voluntati potestatique con-
cessit ne moriantur quae orta sint et tam diversa,
tam dissimilia, id est corporea et incorporea, sibimet
conexa nulla possint dissolutione seiungi, ut de carne
hominis cui donat inmortalitatem corruptionem
auferat, naturam relinquat, congruentiam figurae
membrorumque detineat, detrahat ponderis tarditatem? Sed de fide resurrectionis mortuorum et de
corporibus eorum inmortalibus diligentius, si Deus
voluerit, in fine huius operis disserendum est.

XIX

*Contra eorum dogmata qui primos homines, si non
peccassent, inmortales futuros fuisse non
credunt, aeternitatem animarum volunt
carere corporibus.*

Nunc de corporibus primorum hominum quod in-
stituimus explicemus, quoniam nec mors ista, quae
bona perhibetur bonis nec tantum paucis intellegentibus sive credentibus sed omnibus nota est, qua fit
animae a corpore separatio, qua certe corpus animan-

---

[1] Cf. Plato, *Timaeus* 41c–d; 42d–e.
[2] Cf. Plato, *Timaeus* 45b.
[3] See below, 22.12–21 and 25–30.

Plato [1] with the creation of man as well as of the other terrestrial animals, were able, as he declares, to remove from fire the property of burning, while leaving that of brightness to flash through the eyes.[2] If then the will and power of the supreme God can, as Plato himself has allowed, preserve both things that had a beginning from perishing and the union of things so different and unlike as material and immaterial substances from the possibility of being parted by any means of disintegration, shall we hesitate to allow him to abolish putrefaction of the flesh of any man on whom he bestows immortality, while leaving its properties intact, and to retain the harmony of design among its members, while removing the sluggishness of its weight? But I intend to discuss both our belief in the resurrection of the dead and the immortality of their bodies more fully, God willing, at the end of this work.[3]

XIX

Against the views of those who do not believe that the first human beings would have been immortal if they had not sinned, but hold that the everlasting existence of souls is incorporeal.

LET us now resume our discussion about the bodies of the first human beings, for they could not have fallen victim even to that death which is said to be good for the good and which is known not only to the few that have understanding or faith but to all, had it not come as a just recompense in consequence of sin; this is the death by which the separation of the

tis, quod evidenter vivebat, evidenter emoritur, eis
potuisset accidere, nisi peccati meritum sequeretur.
Licet enim iustorum ac piorum animae defunctorum
quod in requie vivant dubitare fas non sit, usque
adeo tamen eis melius esset cum suis corporibus bene
valentibus vivere ut etiam illi qui omni modo esse
sine corpore beatissimum existimant hanc opinionem
suam sententia repugnante convincant.

Neque enim quisquam audebit illorum sapientes
homines, sive morituros sive iam mortuos, id est aut
carentes corporibus aut corpora relicturos, diis inmortalibus anteponere quibus Deus summus apud
Platonem munus ingens, indissolubilem scilicet vitam,
id est aeternum cum suis corporibus consortium,
pollicetur. Optime autem cum hominibus agi arbi-
tratur idem Plato, si tamen hanc vitam pie iusteque
peregerint, ut a suis corporibus separati in ipsorum
deorum qui sua corpora numquam deserunt re-
cipiantur sinum,

> Scilicet inmemores supera ut convexa revisant
> Rursus et incipiant in corpora velle reverti,

quod Vergilius ex Platonico dogmate dixisse laudatur.

Ita quippe animas mortalium nec in suis corporibus semper esse posse existimat, sed mortis necessitate dissolvi, nec sine corporibus durare perpetuo,
sed alternantibus vicibus indesinenter vivos ex

---

[1] Cf. Plato, *Timaeus* 41a–b.
[2] Cf. Plato, *Phaedo* 108c; *Phaedrus* 248c.
[3] Virgil, *Aeneid* 6.750–751.

soul from the body is effected and through which without question the body of a living being, which was visibly alive, visibly perishes. True, there can be no doubt that the souls of the just and holy who are deceased live in repose. Yet they would be so much better off living with their bodies in sound health that even those who think it perfect bliss to be completely disembodied refute their own belief by a conflicting tenet.

None of them will venture to rate wise men, whether yet to die or already dead (that is, men who either already are bodiless or presently will abandon their bodies) higher than the immortal gods to whom the supreme God, according to Plato, promises the immense privilege of an indissoluble life or, in other words, an everlasting union with their bodies.[1] But Plato also thinks that men, provided they have lived holy and just lives here on earth, receive the best reward that can be when they are separated from their bodies and received into the bosom of the very gods who never leave their bodies,[2]

> That, all forgetting, they may seek the vault
> On high again, and soon begin to have
> A will once more in bodies to reside,[3]

as Virgil so admirably expressed this view derived from Plato's creed.

Thus Plato does not believe that the souls of mortals can always remain in their bodies, but rather that they are released by an inevitable death. Nor does he think that these souls survive for ever without bodies; rather people live and die in ceaseless alternation as they pass from one state to the other.

mortuis et ex vivis mortuos fieri putat, ut a ceteris
hominibus hoc videantur differre sapientes, quod post
mortem feruntur ad sidera ut aliquanto diutius in
astro sibi congruo quisque requiescat atque inde
rursus miseriae pristinae oblitus et cupiditate habendi
corporis victus redeat ad labores aerumnasque mortalium, illi vero qui stultam duxerint vitam ad corpora suis meritis debita, sive hominum sive bestiarum,
de proximo revolvantur.

In hac itaque durissima condicione constituit etiam
bonas atque sapientes animas, quibus non talia corpora distributa sunt cum quibus semper atque in-
mortaliter viverent, ut neque in corporibus permanere
neque sine his possint in aeterna puritate durare.
De quo Platonico dogmate iam in libris superioribus
diximus Christiano tempori [1] erubuisse Porphyrium
et non solum ab animis humanis removisse corpora
bestiarum verum etiam sapientium animas ita
voluisse de corporeis nexibus liberari ut corpus omne
fugientes beatae apud Patrem sine fine teneantur.
Itaque ne a Christo vinci videretur vitam sanctis
pollicente perpetuam, etiam ipse purgatas animas
sine ullo ad miserias pristinas reditu in aeterna felicitate constituit. Et ut Christo adversaretur, resurrectionem incorruptibilium corporum negans non

---

[1] tempori *V and one other MS.:* tempore *most MSS.*

---

[1] Cf. Plato, *Phaedrus* 248a–249d.
[2] See above, 10.30.

Yet there seems to be a distinction between the fate of wise men and that of the rest of mankind. For, according to him, after death the former are borne to the starry heavens, and each of them reposes for a somewhat longer time on the star appropriate for him. From that star again, when he has forgotten his old misery and yielded to the desire for embodiment, he returns to the toils and troubles of mortals. On the other hand, those who have led stupid lives start on the cycle once more after a very short interval, occupying bodies, whether of man or beast, that are assigned to each according to his desert.[1]

This then is the exceedingly harsh fate to which Plato consigned even good and wise souls, for they were not provided with bodies with which they could live for ever free from death. This meant that they could neither occupy their bodies permanently nor survive without them in everlasting purity. As I have already said in a preceding book,[2] this Platonic tenet caused Porphyry embarrassment in the Christian era; he not only banned the bodies of beasts from union with human souls but also held that the souls of wise men were so completely released from the bonds of the body that they abandoned every sort of body and were preserved for ever happy in the Father's presence. Thus it was that, not to seem outdone by Christ, who promised an everlasting life to saints, Porphyry too assigned purified souls to a place of everlasting happiness without any return to former misery. On the other hand, in order also to oppose Christ, he denied the resurrection of incorruptible bodies and maintained that souls

solum sine terrenis sed sine ullis omnino corporibus eas adseruit in sempiternum esse victuras.

Nec tamen ista qualicumque opinione praecepit saltem ne diis corporatis religionis obsequio subderentur. Quid ita, nisi quia eas, quamvis nulli corpori sociatas, non credidit illis esse meliores? Quapropter, si non audebunt isti, sicut eos ausuros esse non arbitror, diis beatissimis et tamen in aeternis corporibus constitutis humanas animas anteponere, cur eis videtur absurdum quod fides Christiana praedicat, et primos homines ita fuisse conditos ut, si non peccassent, nulla morte a suis corporibus solverentur sed pro meritis oboedientiae custoditae inmortalitate donati cum eis viverent in aeternum, et talia sanctos in resurrectione habituros ea ipsa in quibus hic laboraverunt corpora ut nec eorum carni aliquid corruptionis vel difficultatis nec eorum beatitudini aliquid doloris et infelicitatis possit accidere?

XX

Quod caro sanctorum, quae nunc requiescit in spe, in meliorem reparanda sit qualitatem quam fuit primorum hominum ante peccatum.

PROINDE nunc sanctorum animae defunctorum ideo non habent gravem mortem, qua separatae sunt a cor-

---

[1] Cf. below, 22.27.

would live for ever not only without earthly bodies
but without any bodies at all.[1]

Yet, despite this belief, such as it was, Porphyry
did not go so far as to teach also that these souls
should not pay pious homage to gods with bodies.
Why so, unless because he did not believe that these
souls, although they were accompanied by no body,
were superior to those gods? Therefore, if those
philosophers will not venture, as I do not think they
will, to rank human souls above gods who are supremely happy and yet endowed with everlasting
bodies, why do they consider the message of Christi-
anity so absurd, when it declares that the first human
beings too were so created that, had they not
sinned, no death would have parted them from their
bodies? Rather they would have received as a
reward for maintaining obedience the gift of immortality and would have lived joined to their bodies
for ever. Moreover, the saints will possess at
resurrection those very bodies in which they toiled
in this life; and their bodies will be such that neither
shall any deterioration or handicap affect their flesh
nor any grief or misfortune their bliss.

XX

That the flesh of saints, which now reposes in hope,
will be restored to a higher condition than that
of the flesh of the first human beings before
they sinned.

LIKEWISE the souls of deceased saints even now
have no grief in death, though it has divorced them

poribus suis, quia caro eorum requiescit in spe, quaslibet sine ullo iam sensu contumelias accepisse videatur. Non enim, sicut Platoni visum est, corpora oblivione desiderant, sed potius, quia meminerunt quid sibi ab eo sit promissum qui neminem fallit, qui eis etiam de capillorum suorum integritate securitatem dedit, resurrectionem corporum, in quibus multa dura perpessi sunt, nihil in eis ulterius tale sensuri desiderabiliter et patienter expectant.

Si enim carnem suam non oderant quando eam suae menti infirmitate resistentem spiritali iure cohercebant, quanto magis eam diligunt etiam ipsam spiritalem futuram! Sicut enim spiritus carni serviens non incongrue carnalis, ita caro spiritui serviens recte appellabitur spiritalis, non quia in spiritum convertetur, sicut nonnulli putant ex eo quod scriptum est: *Seminatur corpus animale, surget* [1] *corpus spiritale,* sed quia spiritui summa et mirabili obtemperandi facilitate subdetur usque ad implendam inmortalitatis indissolubilis securissimam voluntatem, omni molestiae sensu, omni corruptibilitate et tarditate detracta.

Non solum enim non erit tale quale nunc est in quavis optima valetudine, sed nec tale quidem quale fuit in primis hominibus ante peccatum, qui licet

---

[1] surgit *or* resurget *some MSS. The Vulgate reading is uncertain here, but the Greek has the present tense,* ἐγείρεται.

---

[1] Cf. Psalms 16.9
[2] Cf. Luke 21.18.

from their bodies, because their flesh rests in hope,[1]
no matter what abuses it may seem to have received
after all sensation is gone. It is not because they
forget, as Plato thought, that they long for bodies.
On the contrary, it is because they remember what
they were promised by him who disappoints no one,
him who even gave them his warrant that their hairs
would remain intact,[2] that they longingly and patiently await the resurrection of their bodies, for,
though they endured much cruelty in them, they
will have no such pain in the future.

Indeed, if they did not hate their flesh [3] when it
sought in its weakness to oppose their purpose and
they had to constrain it by the law of the spirit, how
much more must they now love it since it too is to
become spiritual! For even as the spirit is with no
impropriety called carnal if it serves the flesh, so the
flesh will properly be called spiritual if it serves the
spirit. This will be, not because it will be changed
into spirit (some people draw this conclusion from the
scriptural statement: " It is sown an animal body, it
will rise a spiritual body "),[4] but because it will show
in its submission to the spirit a readiness to obey so
perfect and marvellous that it will carry out an unwavering resolve leading to indestructible immortality
without the least feeling of distress or the slightest
possibility of decay or sluggishness.

Not only will it not be such as it is now even in the
best of health, but it will not even be such as it was
in the case of the first human beings before they
sinned. For though they were not required to die

[3] Cf. Ephesians 5.29.
[4] 1 Corinthians 15.44.

morituri non essent nisi peccassent, alimentis tamen
ut homines utebantur, nondum spiritalia, sed adhuc
animalia corpora terrena gestantes.   Quae licet senio
non veterescerent ut necessitate perducerentur ad
mortem (qui status eis de ligno vitae, quod in medio
paradiso cum arbore vetita simul erat, mirabili Dei
gratia praestabatur), tamen et alios sumebant cibos
praeter unam arborem quae fuerat interdicta, non
quia ipsa erat malum, sed propter commendandum
purae et simplicis oboedientiae bonum, quae magna
virtus est rationalis creaturae sub Creatore Domino
constitutae.   Nam ubi nullum malum tangebatur,
profecto, si prohibitum tangeretur, sola inoboedientia
peccabatur.

Agebatur [1] ergo aliis quae sumebant ne animalia
corpora molestiae aliquid esuriendo ac sitiendo sen-
tirent.   De ligno autem vitae propterea gustabatur,
ne mors eis undecumque subreperet vel senectute
confecta, decursis temporum spatiis, interirent, tamquam cetera essent alimento, illud sacramento, ut sic
fuisse accipiatur lignum vitae in paradiso corporali,
sicut in spiritali, hoc est intellegibili, paradiso sapientia Dei, de qua scriptum est: *Lignum vitae est
amplectentibus eam.*

---

[1] alebantur *a few MSS.*

if they had not sinned, nevertheless, as human beings they took nourishment since their bodies were earthly —not yet spiritual but still animal. These bodies, it is true, did not grow old and decrepit and thus end of necessity in death; this privilege was afforded them by the wonderful grace of God from the tree of life that stood in the middle of paradise along with the forbidden tree. Nevertheless, they did take other nourishment also, except from the one tree that had been forbidden, not because it was itself an evil, but to teach the good of absolute and unqualified obedience. This is the great virtue of a rational being subordinate to the Lord his Creator. For where nothing evil, but only something forbidden, was touched, disobedience alone constituted the sin.

Therefore the purpose of the other nourishment that the first human beings took was to prevent their animal bodies from suffering any distress through hunger or thirst. On the other hand, they ate of the tree of life to avoid surprise by death from any quarter whatever or disintegration of their bodies through old age and exhaustion after they had run the full course of their years. One might say that all the other foods served as aliment, but the latter as a sort of sacrament. In this way the tree of life can be regarded as having played the same role in the material paradise as is played in the spiritual or intelligible paradise by the wisdom of God, of which we read in Scripture: " It is a tree of life to those who embrace it." [1]

[1] Proverbs 3.18.

SAINT AUGUSTINE

XXI

De paradiso, in quo primi homines fuerunt, quod
recte per significationem eius spiritale aliquid
intellegatur, salva veritate narrationis
historicae de corporali loco.

UNDE nonnulli totum ipsum paradisum, ubi primi
homines parentes generis humani sanctae scripturae
veritate fuisse narrantur, ad intellegibilia referunt
arboresque illas et ligna fructifera in virtutes vitae
moresque convertunt; tamquam visibilia et corporalia illa non fuerint, sed intellegibilium signi-
ficandorum causa eo modo dicta vel scripta sint.

Quasi propterea non potuerit esse paradisus corporalis, quia potest etiam spiritalis intellegi; tamquam ideo non fuerint duae mulieres, Agar et Sarra,
et ex eis duo filii Abrahae, unus de ancilla, alius de
libera, quia duo testamenta in eis figurata dicit
apostolus; aut ideo de nulla petra, Moyse percu-
tiente, aqua defluxerit, quia potest illic figurata
significatione etiam Christus intellegi, eodem apostolo
dicente: *Petra autem erat Christus.*

Nemo itaque prohibet intellegere paradisum vitam
beatorum, quattuor eius flumina quattuor virtutes,
prudentiam, fortitudinem, temperantiam atque iusti-

---

[1] Cf. Genesis 16.4; 21.2; Galatians 4.22–24.
[2] Cf. Exodus 17.6; Numbers 20.11.
[3] 1 Corinthians 10.4.

XXI

*That some spiritual symbolism may well be found in
the account of paradise, the abode of the first
human beings, without detracting from the
veracity of the historical narrative of its
existence in the material world.*

HENCE some people interpret symbolically the
entire episode of paradise itself, where, according to
the truthful account of holy Scripture, the first
human beings, parents of the human race, dwelt, and
they turn those trees and fruit-bearing plants into
virtues and ways of life. They assume that those
details were not visible and material objects but
were described as such in speech or writing for the
purpose of illustrating symbolically spiritual realities.

How absurd to maintain that there could not have
been a material paradise because it can be understood also in a spiritual sense; as if it were an argument that Abraham did not have two wives, Hagar
and Sarah, and from them two sons, one by the slave
and the other by the free woman, just because the
Apostle says that in them the two covenants were
illustrated; [1] or, again, that there was no rock from
which water flowed forth when Moses struck it [2]
because it can also be interpreted as a symbol of
Christ in that passage, for, in the words of the same
Apostle, " The rock, moreover, was Christ." [3]

No one therefore prevents us from understanding
paradise allegorically as the life of blessed men, its
four streams as the four virtues, namely, prudence,
courage, temperance and justice, its trees as all the

tiam, et ligna eius omnes utiles disciplinas et lig-
norum fructus mores piorum et lignum vitae, ipsam
bonorum omnium matrem, sapientiam et lignum
scientiae boni et mali transgressi mandati experimentum.   Poenam enim peccatoribus bene utique,
quoniam iuste, constituit Deus, sed non suo bono
experitur homo.

Possunt haec etiam in ecclesia intellegi, ut ea
melius accipiamus tamquam prophetica indicia prae-
cedentia futurorum, paradisum scilicet ipsam ecclesiam, sicut de illa legitur in cantico canticorum,
quattuor autem paradisi flumina quattuor evangelia,
ligna fructifera sanctos, fructus autem eorum opera
eorum, lignum vitae sanctum sanctorum utique
Christum, lignum scientiae boni et mali proprium
voluntatis arbitrium.

Nec se ipso quippe homo, divina voluntate contempta, nisi perniciose uti potest atque ita discit
quid intersit utrum inhaereat communi omnibus bono
an proprio delectetur. Se quippe amans donatur
sibi, ut inde timoribus maeroribusque completus
cantet in psalmo, si tamen mala sua sentit: *Ad me
ipsum*[1] *turbata est anima mea*, correctusque iam dicat:
Fortitudinem meam ad te custodiam. Haec et si qua

---

[1] ad me ipsum *most MSS., Vulg. (cf. Septuagint:* πρὸς
ἐμαυτόν): a me ipso *a few MSS.*

---

[1] Cf. Song of Songs 4.12–15.
[2] Psalms 42.6.
[3] Psalms 59.9.   The version in Augustine agrees with the
Vulgate. The Septuagint reads: τὸ κράτος μου, πρὸς σὲ
φυλάξω. The sense is altered by making τὸ κράτος μου a
vocative phrase, and the rendering of the RSV reflects this

useful studies, the fruits of the trees as the conduct of the righteous, the tree of life as wisdom, the very mother of all good things, and the tree of the knowledge of good and evil as experience that comes with the transgression of a commandment. For in ordaining punishment for those who sinned God certainly did something good because it was just, but it is not for his own good that man has this experience.

We may also interpret these objects in terms of the church and thus regard them better as prophetic prior indications of what was to come. Specifically, paradise may point to the church itself, as we read about it in the Song of Songs,[1] the four streams of paradise to the four gospels, the fruit-bearing trees to the saints and the fruits thereof to their works; the tree of life as Holy of Holies is surely Christ himself, and the tree of the knowledge of good and evil is personal control of one's own will.

For if man disdains the divine will, he can act only to his own detriment, and in this way he learns what a difference it makes whether he adheres to the good that is common to all or delights only in his own. If he loves himself, he is handed over to himself in order that, when he is thereby overwhelmed with fears and griefs, he may then sing with the psalmist, if only he is conscious of his own miseries: " My soul is troubled within me," [2] and that, when he is rehabilitated, he may then say: " I shall keep my strength for thee." [3] This is what may be said, and

difference: " O my Strength, I will sing praises to thee," according to the Syriac version, but according to the Hebrew of the consonantal Masoretic text: ". . . I will watch for thee."

alia commodius dici possunt de intellegendo spiritaliter paradiso, nemine prohibente, dicantur, dum tamen et illius historiae veritas fidelissima rerum gestarum narratione commendata credatur.

XXII

De corporibus sanctorum post resurrectionem, quae sic
spiritalia erunt ut non in spiritum caro vertatur.

CORPORA ergo iustorum quae in resurrectione futura sunt neque ullo ligno indigebunt quo fiat ut nullo morbo vel senectute inveterata moriantur neque ullis aliis corporalibus alimentis quibus esuriendi ac sitiendi qualiscumque molestia devitetur, quoniam certo et omni modo inviolabili munere inmortalitatis induentur, ut non nisi velint, possibilitate, non necessitate vescantur.

Quod angeli quoque visibiliter et tractabiliter adparentes, non quia indigebant, sed quia volebant et poterant, ut hominibus congruerent sui ministerii quadam humanitate, fecerunt. Neque enim in phantasmate angelos edisse credendum est quando eos homines hospitio susceperunt, quamvis utrum angeli essent ignorantibus simili [1] nobis indigentia vesci viderentur. Unde est quod ait angelus in libro

---

[1] cum simili *or* consimili *some MSS.*

---

[1] Cf. Genesis 18.8; 19.3.

there are possibly other more appropriate statements that may be made—no one forbids—in connexion with the allegorical interpretation of paradise. There is one condition, however: we must also believe in the actual truth of that story which is presented to us in a most faithful record of events.

XXII

That the bodies of saints after resurrection will be spiritual, yet their flesh will not be turned into spirit.

THE bodies then that the righteous will have at resurrection will need neither any tree to safeguard them against death from any disease or advance of old age nor any other material nourishment to keep them immune from suffering of any kind from hunger and thirst. The reason is that they will be endowed with a sure and absolutely inviolable gift of immortality, and hence they will eat only if they wish, having power, but no compulsion, to do so.

The angels, too, behaved similarly when they appeared in visible and tangible guise. Though they had no need to eat, yet they wished and were able to do so, in order that they might adapt themselves to life with human beings by introducing human qualities as they carried out their task. For we must not believe that the angels ate only in appearance when they were entertained by human beings.[1] To be sure, when it was not known whether they were angels, it was thought that they ate because of a need like ours. This is why the angel says in the

Tobiae: *Videbatis me manducare, sed visu vestro videbatis,* id est, necessitate reficiendi corporis, sicut vos facitis, me cibum sumere putabatis.

Sed si forte de angelis aliud credibilius disputari potest, certe fides Christiana de ipso Salvatore non dubitat, quod etiam post resurrectionem, iam quidem in spiritali carne, sed tamen vera, cibum ac potum cum discipulis sumpsit. Non enim potestas, sed egestas edendi ac bibendi talibus corporibus auferetur. Unde et spiritalia erunt, non quia corpora esse desistent, sed quia spiritu vivificante subsistent.

XXIII

Quid intellegendum sit de corpore animali et de corpore spiritali, et qui moriantur in Adam, qui vero vivificentur in Christo.

NAM sicut ista[1] quae habent animam viventem, nondum spiritum vivificantem[2] animalia dicuntur corpora nec tamen animae sunt, sed corpora, ita illa spiritalia vocantur corpora. Absit tamen ut spiritus ea credamus futura, sed corpora carnis habitura substantiam, sed nullam tarditatem corruptionemque

[1] ista corpora *or* corpora ista *some MSS.*
[2] spiritu vivificante *a few MSS.*

---

[1] Cf. Tobit 12.19. Augustine, quoting freely here, differs from the Vulgate and the Septuagint but is closer to the latter.
[2] Cf. Luke 24.42–43; Acts 10.41.

book of Tobias: " You saw me eating, but it was with your eyes that you saw," [1] that is, you thought that I, like you, took food because of the need to restore the body.

But at all events, though perhaps a more plausible view might be maintained concerning angels, the Christian faith has no doubt about the Saviour himself, that even after his resurrection, though he was now clothed in spiritual, albeit real, flesh, he partook of food and drink with his disciples.[2] For it is not the ability, but the need to eat and drink that will be removed from such bodies. Hence they will also be spiritual, not because they will cease to be bodies, but because they will have a life-giving spirit to sustain them.[3]

XXIII

*What we are to understand about the animal body
and the spiritual body, and who they are that
die in Adam but are brought to life in Christ.*

For just as those bodies that possess a living soul but not yet a life-giving spirit are called animal, that is, soul-endowed,[4] bodies though they are not souls but bodies, so the others that I have described are termed spiritual bodies. Yet far be it from us to believe that they will be spirits rather than bodies possessing the substance of flesh, though preserved

---

[3] Cf. 1 Corinthians 15.44–46.

[4] In his discussion Augustine plays on the derivation of 'animal' from *anima*, meaning 'wind,' 'breath,' 'vital principle,' and, especially in Christian writers, 'soul.'

carnalem spiritu vivificante passura. Tunc iam non terrenus, sed caelestis homo erit, non quia corpus, quod de terra factum est, non ipsum erit, sed quia dono caelesti iam tale erit ut etiam caelo incolendo, non amissa natura, sed mutata qualitate, conveniat.

Primus autem homo de terra terrenus in animam viventem factus est, non in spiritum vivificantem, quod ei post[1] oboedientiae meritum servabatur. Ideo corpus eius, quod cibo ac potu egebat ne fame adficeretur ac siti, et non inmortalitate illa absoluta atque indissolubili, sed ligno vitae a mortis necessitate prohibebatur atque in iuventutis flore tenebatur, non spiritale, sed animale fuisse non dubium est, nequaquam tamen moriturum nisi in Dei praedicentis minantisque sententiam delinquendo conruisset et, alimentis quidem etiam extra paradisum non negatis, a ligno tamen vitae prohibitus traditus[2] esset tempori vetustatique finiendus, in ea dumtaxat vita quam in corpore licet animali, donec spiritale oboedientiae merito fieret, posset in paradiso, nisi peccasset, habere perpetuam.

Quapropter, etiamsi mortem istam manifestam qua fit animae a corpore separatio intellegamus simul significatam in eo quod Deus dixerat: *Qua die ederitis ex illo, morte moriemini*, non ideo debet absurdum

---

[1] per *a few MSS.*
[2] traditus *omitted in* V *and one other MS. through homoeoteleuton.*

---

[1] Cf. 1 Corinthians 15.47.
[2] Cf. 1 Corinthians 15.45.
[3] Genesis 2.17.

by a life-giving spirit from all sluggishness and decay of flesh. Then man will no longer be earthly but heavenly, not because his body, which was fashioned of earth, will cease to be the same, but because the bounty of heaven will make it fit for dwelling even in heaven, with no loss of its substance but with a change in its quality.

The first human being, however, a man of the earth, earthly,[1] was formed as a living soul and not a life-giving spirit;[2] that state was reserved until he should earn it by obedience. Thus there is no doubt that his body was animal rather than spiritual: it stood in need of food and drink to avoid the pangs of hunger and thirst and was protected against the necessity of death and kept in the flower of youth, not by the final complete and indestructible immortality, but by the tree of life. Yet he would by no means have died if he had not fallen by sinning under the condemnation of which God had given notice and forewarning. Though he was not thereafter denied nourishment even outside of paradise, he was nevertheless barred from the tree of life and thus delivered to time and old age for an end to be made of him, at least in respect of the life that, if he had not sinned, he might have led in paradise continually renewed, though in a body merely animal until it should become spiritual as a reward for obedience.

Therefore, even if we were to understand that, when God spoke the words: " On the day that you eat of it you shall die,"[3] he meant to include the obvious form of death that brings separation of soul from body, still we need not find any inconsistency

225

videri, quia non eo prorsus die a corpore sunt soluti quo cibum interdictum mortiferumque sumpserunt. Eo quippe die, mutata in deterius vitiataque natura atque a ligno vitae separatione iustissima, mortis in eis etiam corporalis necessitas facta est, cum qua nos necessitate nati sumus. Propter quod apostolus non ait: Corpus quidem moriturum est propter peccatum, sed ait: *Corpus quidem mortuum est propter peccatum, spiritus autem vita est propter iustitiam.* Deinde subiunxit: *Si autem spiritus eius qui suscitavit Christum a mortuis habitat in vobis, qui suscitavit Christum a mortuis vivificabit et mortalia corpora vestra per inhabitantem spiritum eius in vobis.*

Tunc ergo erit corpus in spiritum vivificantem quod nunc est in animam viventem. Et tamen mortuum dicit apostolus quia iam moriendi necessitate constrictum est. Tunc autem ita[1] erat in animam viventem, quamvis non in spiritum vivificantem, ut tamen mortuum dici non recte posset, quia nisi perpetratione peccati necessitatem moriendi habere non posset.

Cum vero Deus et dicendo: *Adam, ubi es?* mortem significaverit animae, quae facta est illo deserente, et dicendo: *Terra es et in terram ibis* mortem significaverit corporis, quae illi fit anima discedente, propterea de morte secunda nihil dixisse credendus est, quia occultam esse voluit propter dispensationem

---

[1] ita *omitted in V and two other MSS.*

---

[1] Romans 8.10–11.   [2] Genesis 3.9.
[3] Genesis 3.19.

in the fact that the first human beings were not
parted forthwith from their bodies on the very day
that they took the forbidden and deadly food. It
was after all on that very day that they became
subject to the necessity of bodily death as well, a
necessity to which we are born. For this was a
consequence of the deterioration and blighting of
their natural bodies and the perfectly justified ban
that kept them from the tree of life. This is why
the Apostle does not say: " The body will die because of sin," but says rather: " The body is dead
because of sin, but the spirit is life because of
righteousness." He then added: " But if the Spirit
of him who raised Christ from the dead dwells in
you, he who raised Christ from the dead will give life
to your mortal bodies also through his Spirit which
dwells in you." [1]

Thus the body will then be to the life-giving spirit
what it is now to its living soul. And yet the
Apostle calls it dead because it is already held fast
by the necessity of dying. On the other hand, in
the past it existed for a living soul, though not for a
life-giving spirit, yet on such terms that it could not
properly be called dead, since it could not be subject
to inevitable death unless some sin were committed.

But when God said: " Adam, where are you? " [2]
he thus indicated the death of the soul, which took
place when he abandoned it; and when he said:
" You are earth and to earth shall you go," [3] he
referred to the death of the body, which takes place
when the soul departs from it. We must believe
that his reason for not mentioning the second death
was that he chose to keep it unrevealed for the sake

SAINT AUGUSTINE

testamenti novi, ubi secunda mors apertissime
declaratur, ut prius ista mors prima, quae communis
est omnibus, proderetur ex illo venisse peccato, quod
in uno commune factum est omnibus, mors vero
secunda non utique communis est omnibus propter
eos *qui secundum propositum vocati sunt, quos* ante
praescivit et praedestinavit, sicut ait apostolus, *con-*
formes imaginis filii sui, ut sit ipse primogenitus in multis
fratribus, quos a secunda morte per mediatorem Dei
gratia liberavit.

In corpore ergo animali primum hominem factum
sic apostolus loquitur. Volens enim ab spiritali,
quod in resurrectione futurum est, hoc quod nunc est
animale discernere: *Seminatur,* inquit, *in corruptione,*
surget[1] *in incorruptione; seminatur in contumelia,*
surget[1] *in gloria; seminatur in infirmitate, surget*[1] *in*
virtute; seminatur corpus animale, surget[1] *corpus*
spiritale. Deinde ut hoc probaret: *Si est,* inquit,
corpus animale, est et spiritale. Et ut quid esset
animale corpus ostenderet: *Sic,* inquit, [*et*][2] *scriptum*
est: Factus est primus homo in animam viventem. Isto
igitur modo voluit ostendere quid sit corpus animale,
quamvis scriptura non dixerit de homine primo, qui
est appellatus Adam, quando illi anima flatu Dei
creata est: Et factus est homo in corpore animali;

---

[1] surgit *some MSS. See above, p. 212, note 1.*
[2] et *omitted in most MSS., but cf. below, p. 234, note 1, and
p. 252, note 2, where it is well attested by the majority of the
MSS. The Vulgate is inconclusive here, but the Greek reads:*
οὕτως καὶ γέγραπται.

---

[1] See above, 13.2 (p. 137, note 1).
[2] Romans 8.28–29.

of his dispensation of the New Testament, where the second death is very plainly announced.[1] In this way it would first be published that the first death, which is common to all, came as a consequence of that sin which in one man became the joint act of all. The second death, however, is by no means common to all because an exception is made of those " who are called according to his purpose, whom he " earlier " foreknew and predestined," as the Apostle says, " to be conformed to the image of his Son, in order that he might be the first-born among many brethren." [2] These were delivered from the second death by the grace of God through the Mediator.

It was therefore in a merely animal body, as the Apostle tells us, that the first human being was created. For when he seeks to distinguish our present animal body from the spiritual one that will be ours at the resurrection, he says: " It is sown in corruption, it will rise in incorruption; it is sown in contempt, it will rise in glory; it is sown in weakness, it will rise in power; it is sown an animal body, it will rise a spiritual body." Then, to confirm this, he says: " If there is an animal body, there is also a spiritual body." [3] And to show what an animal body is, he says: " Thus it is also written: ' The first man was made into a living soul (anima).' " [4] He spoke in this way because he wanted to show what an animal body is, although Scripture did not say of the first man, who was called Adam, when his soul was created by the breath of God: " And man was made in an animal body," but rather: " Man was

[3] 1 Corinthians 15.42–44.
[4] 1 Corinthians 15.45. Cf. Genesis 2.7.

sed: *Factus est homo in animam viventem.* In eo ergo quod scriptum est: *Factus est primus homo in animam viventem*, voluit apostolus intellegi corpus hominis animale.

Spiritale autem quem ad modum intellegendum esset ostendit addendo: *Novissimus Adam in spiritum vivificantem*, procul dubio Christum significans, qui iam ex mortuis ita resurrexit ut mori deinceps omnino non possit. Denique sequitur et dicit: *Sed non primum quod spiritale est, sed quod animale, postea spiritale.* Ubi multo apertius declaravit se animale corpus insinuasse in eo quod scriptum est factum esse primum hominem in animam viventem, spiritale autem in eo quod ait: *Novissimus Adam in spiritum vivificantem.*

Prius est enim animale corpus, quale habuit primus Adam, quamvis non moriturum nisi peccasset, quale nunc habemus et nos, hactenus eius mutata vitiataque natura quatenus in illo, postea quam peccavit, effectum est, unde haberet iam moriendi necessitatem (tale [1] pro nobis etiam Christus primitus habere dignatus est, non quidem necessitate, sed potestate); postea vero spiritale, quale iam praecessit in Christo tamquam in capite nostro, secuturum est autem in membris eius ultima resurrectione mortuorum.

Adiungit deinde apostolus duorum istorum homi-

---

[1] quale *a few MSS.*

---

[1] 1 Corinthians 15.45.

made into a living soul." Accordingly, the Apostle intended us to understand that the animal body of man was implied in the scriptural words: " The first man was made into a living soul."

On the other hand, to indicate how we are to understand the term ' spiritual,' he added: " The last Adam was made into a life-giving spirit." [1] With these words he doubtless referred to Christ, who had already risen from the dead so as to be thereafter wholly immune to death.[2] Then he follows this up, saying: " But the spiritual does not come first; rather the animal, and later the spiritual." [3] Here he has far more openly revealed that he meant us to understand an animal body where Scripture says that the first man was made into a living soul, and a spiritual body where he says: " The last Adam was made into a life-giving spirit."

For first is the animal body, such as the first Adam had, though that would never have died, had he not sinned. Such too is the body that we now have, with its nature as much changed and decayed in our case as it was in Adam's after he sinned, whereby he was from then on doomed to die. Christ also deigned to assume originally such a body on our behalf, not indeed because he was obliged, but because he was able. But hereafter there will be a spiritual body, such as has already gone before us in the person of Christ as our head. This same kind of body will come later in the case of those who are his members at the final resurrection of the dead.

The Apostle then proceeds to state a very manifest

[2] Cf. Romans 6.9.
[3] 1 Corinthians 15.46.

num evidentissimam differentiam dicens: *Primus homo de terra terrenus, secundus homo de caelo.*[1] *Qualis terrenus, tales et terreni; qualis caelestis, tales et caelestes. Et quo modo induimus imaginem terreni, induamus et imaginem eius qui de caelo est.* Hoc apostolus ita posuit ut nunc quidem in nobis secundum sacramentum regenerationis fiat, sicut alibi dicit: *Quotquot in Christo baptizati estis Christum induistis.* Re autem ipsa tunc perficietur cum et in nobis quod est animale nascendo spiritale factum fuerit resurgendo. Ut enim eius itidem verbis utar: *Spe salvi facti sumus.*

Induimus autem imaginem terreni hominis propagatione praevaricationis et mortis, quam nobis intulit generatio; sed induemus [2] imaginem caelestis hominis gratia indulgentiae vitaeque perpetuae, quod nobis praestat regeneratio, non nisi per mediatorem Dei et hominum, hominem Christum Iesum, quem caelestem hominem vult intellegi quia de caelo venit ut terrenae mortalitatis corpore vestiretur quod caelesti inmortalitate vestiret. Caelestes vero ideo appellat et alios, quia fiunt per gratiam membra eius, ut cum illis sit unus Christus, velut caput et corpus.

---

[1] de caelo *V* (*cf. the corresponding Greek:* ἐξ οὐρανοῦ; *see also below, 13.24* [*p. 252, note* 3]; *18.11*): de caelo caelestis *most MSS., Vulg.*

[2] induemus *a few MSS.* (*cf. below, 13.24* [*p. 254, line* 9], induentur): induimus *most MSS.*

---

[1] 1 Corinthians 15.47–49.
[2] Galatians 3.27.

difference between these two men, saying: " The
first man is of the earth, earthly, the second man is
of heaven. As is the man of earth, so also are those
who are of the earth; as is the man of heaven, so also
are those who are of heaven. And even as we have
put on the image of the man of earth, let us also put
on the image of the man who is from heaven." [1]
The Apostle expressed himself in this way in order
that the sacrament of regeneration may even now
find fulfilment in us, just as he states elsewhere:
" As many of you as were baptized in the name of
Christ have put on Christ." [2] Actually, however,
this will be consummated only when in us too that
which is animal through birth has become spiritual
through resurrection. For, to quote his words
again: " In hope we were saved." [3]

We put on the image of the man of earth by lineal
transmission of sin and death, a legacy imposed on
us by birth; on the other hand, we shall put on
the image of the heavenly man by the grace of forgiveness and of eternal life. This we receive by
rebirth, but only through the Mediator between
God and men, the man Christ Jesus.[4] In him the
Apostle intends us to see the heavenly man because
he came from heaven to be clothed with a body of
earthly mortality in order that he might clothe it in
heavenly immortality. But his reason for using the
term ' heavenly ' of others too is that they become
His members through grace, and thus Christ is
united with them, even as a head with its body.[5]

[3] Romans 8.24.
[4] Cf. 1 Timothy 2.5.
[5] Cf. Romans 12.5; 1 Corinthians 12.27; Ephesians 5.30.

Hoc in eadem epistula evidentius ita ponit: *Per hominem mors et per hominem resurrectio mortuorum. Sicut enim in Adam omnes moriuntur, sic et in Christo omnes vivificabuntur*, iam utique in corpore spiritali quod erit in spiritum vivificantem, non quia omnes qui in Adam moriuntur membra erunt Christi (ex illis enim multo plures secunda in aeternum morte plectentur), sed ideo dictum est *omnes* atque *omnes*, quia, sicut nemo corpore animali nisi in Adam moritur, ita nemo corpore spiritali nisi in Christo vivificatur.

Proinde nequaquam putandum est nos in resurrectione tale corpus habituros quale habuit homo primus ante peccatum; nec illud quod dictum est: *Qualis terrenus, tales et terreni*, secundum id intellegendum quod factum est admissione peccati. Non enim existimandum est eum, priusquam peccasset, spiritale corpus habuisse et peccati merito in animale mutatum. Ut enim hoc putetur, parum adtenduntur tanti verba doctoris, qui ait: *Si est corpus animale, est et spiritale; sic et*[1] *scriptum est: Factus est primus homo Adam in animam viventem.* Numquid hoc post peccatum factum est, cum sit ista hominis prima conditio, de qua beatissimus Paulus ad corpus animale monstrandum hoc testimonium legis adsumpsit?

---

[1] sic et *most MSS.:* sicut *a few MSS. See above, p. 228, note 2.*

The Apostle puts this more plainly in the same letter as follows: " By a man came death and by a man has come also the resurrection of the dead. For as in Adam all die, so also in Christ shall all be made alive "[1]—and from that time surely in a spiritual body which will be for a life-giving spirit. Now, it does not follow that all those who die in Adam will be members of Christ, for a far greater number of them will be stricken with the second and everlasting death. Rather, the Apostle used the word ' all ' in both clauses because, just as no one dies with an animal body except in Adam, so no one is brought to life with a spiritual body except in Christ.

We must therefore by no means think that we shall have at resurrection the sort of body that the first man had before he sinned; neither should we interpret the words: " As was the man of earth, so also are those who are of the earth," in the light of what happened because sin was committed. For we must not imagine that the first man had a spiritual body before he had sinned and that it was changed into a merely animal one on account of sin. To think thus is to pay too little heed to the words of our great teacher, who says: " If there is an animal body, there is also a spiritual body. Thus too it is written: ' The first man Adam was made into a living soul.' " This surely did not happen after Adam had sinned since it is the first condition of man, in regard to which the blessed Paul adduced this testimony of the Law [2] to explain what the animal body is.

[1] 1 Corinthians 15.21–22.
[2] That is, Genesis 2.7.

XXIV

Qualiter accipienda sit vel illa insufflatio Dei qua
primus homo factus est in animam viventem
vel illa quam Dominus fecit dicens discipulis
suis: Accipite Spiritum sanctum.

UNDE et illud parum considerate quibusdam visum
est, in eo quod legitur: *Inspiravit Deus in faciem eius*
spiritum vitae, et factus est homo in animam viventem,
non tunc animam primo homini datam, sed eam quae
iam inerat Spiritu sancto vivificatam. Movet enim
eos quod Dominus Iesus, posteaquam resurrexit a
mortuis, insufflavit dicens discipulis suis: *Accipite*
Spiritum sanctum.

Unde tale aliquid factum existimant quale tunc
factum est, quasi et hic secutus evangelista dixerit:
Et facti sunt in animam viventem. Quod quidem si
dictum esset, hoc intellegeremus, quod animarum
quaedam vita sit Spiritus Dei, sine quo animae
rationales mortuae deputandae sunt, quamvis earum
praesentia vivere corpora videantur. Sed non ita
factum, quando est conditus homo, satis ipsa libri
verba testantur, quae ita se habent: *Et formavit Deus*
hominem pulverem de terra.

Quod quidam planius interpretandum putantes

---

[1] Genesis 2.7.
[2] A Manichaean heresy. Cf. Augustine, *De Genesi contra*
Manichaeos 2.8.11.
[3] John 20.22.
[4] Genesis 2.7.

XXIV

*In what sense we are to understand either God's
breathing into the first man by which he became
a living soul or the breathing upon the disciples
by the Lord when he said to them: " Receive
the Holy Spirit."*

In this connexion, certain thinkers have also given
too little thought to another point, namely, the significance of the passage that reads: " God breathed into
his face the breath (*spiritus*) of life, and man was made
into a living soul." [1]   They take this to mean, not that
a soul (*anima*) was then given to the first man, but that
the soul, which was already within him, was brought
to life by the Holy Spirit.[2]   Their reason is that, after
the Lord Jesus had risen from the dead, he breathed
on his disciples and said to them: " Receive the Holy
Spirit." [3]

This makes them think that the same sort of thing
happened here as in the earlier case, as if the evangelist had gone on to say in this case too: " And they
were made into a living soul."   If this statement had
really been made, we should understand it to mean
that the Spirit of God is in some sense the life of souls
and that without it rational souls must be considered
merely dead, although their presence seems to give
life to bodies.   But the very words of the Bible provide ample testimony that such was not the case
when man was created, for we are told: " And God
formed dust from the earth into man." [4]

Certain persons who thought that this should
be more clearly explained have said: " And God

dixerunt: *Et finxit Deus hominem de limo terrae,*
quoniam superius dictum fuerat: *Fons autem ascende-*
bat de terra et inrigabat omnem faciem terrae, ut ex hoc
limus intellegendus videretur, umore scilicet ter-
raque concretus. Ubi enim hoc dictum est, continuo
sequitur: *Et formavit Deus hominem pulverem de*
terra, sicut Graeci codices habent unde in Latinam
linguam scriptura ipsa conversa est. Sive autem
formavit sive *finxit* quis dicere voluerit, quod Graece
dicitur ἔπλασεν, ad rem nihil interest; magis tamen
proprie dicitur *finxit.* Sed ambiguitas visa est
devitanda eis qui *formavit* dicere maluerunt, eo quod
in Latina lingua illud magis obtinuit consuetudo,
ut hi dicantur fingere qui aliquid mendacio simulante
componunt.

Hunc igitur formatum hominem de terrae pulvere
sive limo (erat enim pulvis umectus)—hunc, inquam,
ut expressius dicam, sicut scriptura locuta est,
pulverem de terra animale corpus factum esse docet
apostolus cum animam accepit: *"Et factus est* iste
homo in animam viventem," id est, formatus iste pulvis
factus est in animam viventem.

Iam, inquiunt, habebat animam alioquin non appellaretur homo quoniam homo non est corpus solum
vel anima sola sed qui et [1] anima constat et corpore.

---

[1] ex *some MSS.*

---

[1] Genesis 2.6.
[2] Augustine's biblical quotation is, as generally in the case
of differences, closer to the text of the Septuagint than to that

fashioned man from the mud of the earth." For
just before came the statement: "But a spring went
up from the earth and watered the whole face of the
earth ";[1] and by this they decided mud should be
understood, because it is a mixture of moisture and
earth. For the words that immediately follow this
statement are: "And God formed dust from the
earth into man." This is the text found in the Greek
books from which the Bible itself was translated into
Latin.[2] It is immaterial whether you choose to
translate the Greek verb *eplasen* by *formavit* (he
formed) or *finxit* (he fashioned), though the latter
is the more appropriate term. Still the avoidance of
ambiguity seemed important to those who preferred
to say *formavit*, for it is commoner usage in Latin
to employ *fingere* in the case of those who contrive
something with false pretense.

Therefore this man who was formed from the
earth's dust or mud (for the dust was moistened)—or,
to put it more distinctly, in the words of Scripture,
this " dust from the earth " became an animal body,
as we learn from the Apostle,[3] when it received a
soul: "And this man was made into a living soul,"
that is, after it was shaped, this dust was made into a
living soul.

But, they retort, he already had a soul. Otherwise, he could not be called man since man is not
mere body or mere soul but an entity that consists of
body and soul both. This indeed is true. The soul

of the Vulgate. The Septuagint reads: καὶ ἔπλασεν ὁ θεὸς
τὸν ἄνθρωπον χοῦν ἀπὸ τῆς γῆς; the Vulgate text runs: *Formavit
igitur Dominus Deus hominem de limo terrae.*
[3] Cf. 1 Corinthians 15.44–45.

Hoc quidem verum est quod non totus homo sed pars
melior hominis anima est, nec totus homo corpus sed
inferior hominis pars est. Sed cum est utrumque
coniunctum simul, habet hominis nomen, quod tamen
et singula non amittunt etiam cum de singulis
loquimur. Quis enim dicere prohibetur cotidiani
quadam lege sermonis: Homo ille defunctus est et
nunc in requie est vel in poenis, cum de anima sola
possit hoc dici, et: Illo aut illo loco homo ille sepultus
est, cum hoc nisi de solo corpore non possit intellegi?

An dicturi sunt sic loqui scripturam non solere
divinam? Immo vero illa ita nobis in hoc adtestatur
ut etiam cum duo ista coniuncta sunt et vivit homo,
tamen etiam singula hominis vocabulo appellet,
animam scilicet interiorem hominem, corpus autem
exteriorem hominem vocans, tamquam duo sint
homines, cum simul utrumque sit homo unus. Sed
intellegendum est secundum quid dicatur homo ad
imaginem Dei et homo terra atque iturus in terram.
Illud enim secundum animam rationalem dicitur,
qualem Deus insufflando vel, si commodius dicitur,
inspirando indidit homini, id est hominis corpori;
hoc autem secundum corpus, qualem hominem Deus
finxit ex pulvere, cui data est anima ut fieret corpus
animale, id est homo in animam viventem.

Quapropter in eo quod Dominus fecit quando insufflavit dicens: *Accipite Spiritum sanctum*, nimirum

---

[1] Cf. 2 Corinthians 4.16 (AV): "But though our outward
man perish, yet the inward man is renewed day by day."
See also Augustine, *Contra Faustum Manichaeum* 24.2.

[2] John 20.22.

is not the entire man; it is the better part of him.
Nor is the body the entire man; it is the lower part
of him. Rather it is the union of both parts to which
the noun ' man ' is applied. Still the parts taken
singly do not lose their claim to the term, even when
we speak of them separately. For the law, as it
were, of colloquial speech does not stop anyone saying: " That man has died and is now in repose or in
punishment," though this statement can be made
only of the soul, or, again, saying: " That man lies
buried in this or that place," though the body alone
can properly be understood here.

Perhaps they will say that it is not usual for the
divine Scripture to express itself this way. Not so.
Scripture testifies on our side even to the point of
using the term ' man ' of the individual elements even
when the two are combined and man is still alive.
Note that it calls the soul the ' inner man ' and the
body the ' outer man,' as though they were two men,
whereas both together constitute but one man.[1]
But we must understand in what sense we speak of
" man as made in the image of God " and of " man as
earth and destined to return to earth." The former
statement refers to the rational soul—the thing that
God put into man, that is, into the body of man, by
blowing into him or, if the term is more convenient,
by breathing into him. On the other hand, the latter
statement refers to the body, man as fashioned by
God of dust—the thing that received a soul in order
that it might become an animal body, that is, that
man might be made into a living soul.

Therefore, when the Lord breathed upon his
disciples and said: " Receive the Holy Spirit," [2] he

hoc intellegi voluit, quod Spiritus sanctus non tantum
sit Patris verum etiam ipsius Unigeniti Spiritus.
Idem ipse quippe Spiritus et Patris et Filii, cum quo
est trinitas Pater et Filius et Spiritus sanctus,[1] non
creatura, sed Creator. Neque enim flatus ille cor-
poreus de carnis ore procedens substantia erat
Spiritus sancti atque natura, sed potius significatio
qua intellegeremus, ut dixi, Spiritum sanctum Patri
esse Filioque communem quia non sunt eis singulis
singuli, sed unus amborum est.

Semper autem iste Spiritus in scripturis sanctis
Graeco vocabulo πνεῦμα dicitur, sicut eum et hoc loco
Iesus appellavit, quando eum corporalis sui oris flatu
significans discipulis dedit. Et locis omnibus divinorum eloquiorum non mihi aliter umquam nuncupa-
tus occurrit. Hic vero ubi legitur: *Et finxit Deus
hominem pulverem de terra et insufflavit* (sive *inspiravit*)
in faciem eius spiritum vitae, non ait Graecus πνεῦμα,
quod solet dici Spiritus sanctus, sed πνοήν, quod
nomen in creatura quam in Creatore frequentius
legitur. Unde nonnulli etiam Latini propter differentiam hoc vocabulum non spiritum, sed flatum
appellare maluerunt.

Hoc enim est in Graeco etiam illo loco apud Esaiam
ubi Deus dicit: *Omnem flatum ego feci*, omnem ani-

---

[1] et Spiritus sanctus *perhaps to be deleted, according to*
Weyman.

---

[1] On the *Filioque* clause and the doctrine of the "Double
Procession" implied here and supported by Augustine, see

doubtless intended his action to imply that the Holy
Spirit is the spirit not only of the Father but also of
the only begotten Son himself.[1] For the spirit of
both the Father and the Son is one and the same.
It forms with them the Trinity of the Father and the
Son and the Holy Spirit, being not creature but
Creator. For actually the material breath that proceeded from the mouth of Christ's flesh was not the
substance and being of the Holy Spirit, but rather a
sign whereby we might understand that the Holy
Spirit, as I have said, is common to the Father and
the Son because they have not each his separate
spirit, but the one spirit belongs to both.

This spirit is regularly indicated in the holy
Scriptures by the Greek term *pneuma*, the word also
used by Jesus in the passage just cited, when he
expressed it symbolically in the breath of his material
mouth and bestowed it on his disciples. Nor do I
recall that it was ever otherwise named anywhere in
the holy Scriptures. But in the passage where we
read: " And God fashioned dust from the earth into
man and blew (or breathed) into his face the spirit of
life," the Greek text does not offer *pneuma*, the usual
designation for the Holy Spirit, but *pnoê*, a term more
often found in connexion with a created being than
with the creator. Hence, to make a distinction,
some Latin translators too have preferred to render
this word by *flatus* (breath) rather than by *spiritus*
(spirit).

The same thing occurs in Greek also in the passage
of Isaiah where God says: " I have made every

The *Oxford Dictionary of the Christian Church* (London, 1957),
edited by F. L. Cross, 504, *s.v.* " Filioque."

mam sine dubitatione significans. Quod itaque
Graece πνοή dicitur nostri aliquando flatum, aliquando spiritum, aliquando inspirationem vel aspira-
tionem, quando etiam Dei dicitur, interpretati sunt,
πνεῦμα vero numquam nisi spiritum, sive hominis (de
quo ait apostolus: *Quis enim scit hominum quae sunt
hominis nisi spiritus hominis qui in ipso est?*) sive pecoris
(sicut in Salomonis libro scriptum est: *Quis scit si
spiritus hominis ascendat susum* [1] *in caelum et spiritus
pecoris descendat deorsum in terram?*) sive istum cor-
poreum, qui etiam ventus dicitur, (nam eius hoc
nomen est ubi in psalmo canitur: *Ignis grando, nix
glacies, spiritus tempestatis*) sive iam non creatum, sed
Creatorem, sicut est de quo dicit Dominus in evangelio: *Accipite Spiritum sanctum,* eum corporei sui
oris flatu significans, et ubi ait: *Ite, baptizate* [*omnes*] [2]
gentes in nomine Patris et Filii et Spiritus sancti, ubi ipsa
trinitas excellentissime et evidentissime commendata
est, et ubi legitur: *Deus spiritus est,* et aliis plurimis
sacrarum litterarum locis.

In his quippe omnibus testimoniis scripturarum,
quantum ad Graecos adtinet, non πνοήν videmus
scriptum esse, sed πνεῦμα, quantum autem ad Latinos,
non flatum, sed spiritum. Quapropter in eo quod
scriptum est: *Inspiravit,* vel, si magis proprie dicen-

---

[1] susum *V and the second hand in one other MS.:* sursum
most MSS.

[2] omnes *omitted in V and most other MSS.*

---

[1] Isaiah 57.16 (Septuagint).   [2] 1 Corinthians 2.11.
[3] Ecclesiastes 3.21.   [4] Psalms 148.8.

breath," [1] meaning doubtless every soul. Thus, the Greek term *pnoê* is translated into Latin variously as *flatus* (breath), *spiritus* (spirit), *inspiratio* (breathing into) or *aspiratio* (breathing upon), even when used of God. *Pneuma*, on the other hand, is always rendered by *spiritus*. This holds true whether it is used of man (about whom the Apostle says: " For what man knows a man's thoughts except the spirit of the man which is in him? ") [2] or of beast (even as we read in the book of Solomon: " Who knows whether the spirit of man goes upward into heaven and the spirit of the beast goes downward into earth? ") [3] or of that material air in motion, which is also called wind (for this is the term used in the psalm where we sing: " Fire, hail, snow, ice, spirit of the tempest "),[4] or, finally, of the spirit that is not a thing created but is the creator (the same as that referred to in the Lord's words in the Gospel: " Receive the Holy Spirit," [5] as he expresses it symbolically in the breath of his material mouth). This last usage is also found not only where the Lord says: " Go and baptize all nations in the name of the Father and of the Son and of the Holy Spirit," [6] a passage in which the trinity itself is very eminently and manifestly denoted, but also where we read: " God is spirit," [7] and in very many other passages of sacred Scripture.

For in all these biblical citations we see that, so far as the Greek is concerned, the text offers *pneuma* rather than *pnoê*; and correspondingly in Latin it offers *spiritus* rather than *flatus*. Therefore, even if in the passage: " He breathed," or, to put it more

[5] John 20.22.   [6] Matthew 28.19.
[7] John 4.24.

245

SAINT AUGUSTINE

dum est, *Insufflavit in faciem eius spiritum vitae,* si Graecus non πνοήν, sicut ibi legitur, sed πνεῦμα posuisset, nec sic esset consequens ut Creatorem Spiritum, qui proprie dicitur in trinitate Spiritus sanctus, intellegere cogeremur, quando quidem πνεῦμα, ut dictum est, non solum de Creatore sed etiam de creatura dici solere manifestum est.

Sed cum dixisset, inquiunt, *spiritum,* non adderet *vitae* nisi illum sanctum Spiritum [1] vellet intellegi, et cum dixisset: *Factus est homo in animam,* non adderet *viventem* nisi animae vitam significaret, quae illi divinitus inpertitur dono Spiritus Dei. Cum enim vivat anima, inquiunt, proprio suae vitae modo, quid opus erat addere *viventem* nisi ut ea vita intellegeretur quae illi per sanctum Spiritum datur? Hoc quid est aliud nisi diligenter pro humana suspicione contendere et scripturas sanctas neglegenter adtendere? Quid enim magnum erat non ire longius, sed in eodem ipso libro paulo superius legere: *Producat terra animam viventem,* quando animalia terrestria cuncta creata sunt? Deinde, aliquantis interpositis, in eodem tamen ipso libro quid magnum erat advertere quod scriptum est: *Et omnia quae habent spiritum vitae et omnis qui erat super aridam mortuus est,*

[1] Spiritum *omitted in* V *and one other MS.*

[1] Genesis 2.7. Cf. Augustine, *De Genesi ad Litteram* 7.1.2: *Nonnulli . . . codices habent:* Spiravit *vel* Ispiravit in faciem

properly, " He blew into his face the spirit of life," [1]
the Greek had employed *pneuma* instead of *pnoê*, the
actual reading of the text, we should still not necessarily have to identify it with the Creator-Spirit,
who is properly called as a member of the trinity
the Holy Spirit; for, as I have said, it is clear that
pneuma is regularly used not only of the creator but
also of what is created.

But our opponents maintain that, when Scripture
said ' spirit,' it would not have added ' of life ' if it did
not intend it to be understood as the Holy Spirit and
that, when it said: " Man was made into a soul," it
would not have added the word ' living ' if it did not
mean us to understand the soul's life, which is
divinely imparted to it by grant of the spirit of God.
For since the soul lives, their argument runs, in a
manner belonging to its own life, what need was
there to add ' living ' if not to let us know that it
means the life that is given to it through the Holy
Spirit? What is this but diligence in defending
human conjecture and negligence in attending to
holy Scripture? For it would have been a simple
enough matter for them, without having to go further
afield, to read somewhat earlier in the very same
book: " Let the earth bring forth the living soul," [2]
at the point where the terrestrial animals were all
created. It would have been simple enough too, a
few pages later but still in the same book, to observe
the text of Scripture: " And all things that have the
spirit of life and everyone who was upon the dry land

eius. *Sed cum graeci habeant* ἐνεφύσησεν, *non dubitatur* flavit
vel sufflavit *esse dicendum.*

[2] Genesis 1.24.

cum insinuaret omnia quae vivebant in terra perisse diluvio?

Si ergo et animam viventem et spiritum vitae etiam in pecoribus invenimus, sicut loqui divina scriptura consuevit, et cum hoc quoque loco ubi legitur: *Omnia quae habent spiritum vitae*, non Graecus πνεῦμα, sed πνοὴν dixerit, cur non dicimus: Quid opus erat ut adderet *viventem* cum anima, nisi vivat, esse non possit? Aut quid opus erat ut adderet *vitae* cum dixisset *spiritum*? Sed intellegimus *animam viventem* et *spiritum vitae* scripturam suo more dixisse cum animalia, id est animata corpora, vellet intellegi quibus inesset per animam perspicuus iste etiam corporis sensus. In hominis autem conditione obliviscimur quem ad modum loqui scriptura consueverit, cum suo prorsus more locuta sit quo insinuaret hominem, etiam rationali anima accepta, quam non sicut aliarum carnium aquis et terra producentibus, sed Deo flante creatam voluit intellegi, sic tamen factum ut in corpore animali, quod fit anima in eo vivente, sicut illa animalia viveret, de quibus dixit: *Producat terra animam viventem*, et quae itidem dixit habuisse in se spiritum vitae, ubi etiam in Graeco non dixit πνεῦμα sed πνοήν, non utique Spiritum sanctum sed eorum animam tali exprimens nomine.

---

[1] Genesis 7.22 (Septuagint).

died," [1] a passage informing us that all things that lived on the earth perished in the flood.

Thus we find both a living soul and a spirit of life even in beasts, and this is the regular manner of expression in divine Scripture. Moreover, here too, in the passage just cited, where we read: "All things that have the spirit of life," the Greek term is *pnoê* rather than *pneuma*. Why then do we not ask: "Since a soul cannot exist without being alive, what need was there to add 'living'? Or what need was there to add 'of life' after saying 'spirit'? But we understand that Scripture has as usual employed the expressions 'living soul' and 'spirit of life' when it meant us to understand 'animals,' that is, animate bodies, such as might have in them through a soul the manifest sense perception that the body also possesses. On the other hand, when we come to the creation of man, we forget the usage that is found in Scripture. Yet it employed quite its normal style to instruct us that, even though man received a rational soul, which, as we are given to understand, was not brought forth like the souls of other fleshly creatures by the waters and the earth, but was created by the breath of God, he was nevertheless fashioned in such a way that, like those other animals, he lived in an animal body, which is created when a soul (*anima*) lives in it. Scripture refers to the other animals when it says: "Let the earth bring forth a living soul," and again when it says that they have in them a spirit of life. In their case too the Greek term is not *pneuma* but *pnoê*, and here surely Scripture does not use the noun to refer to the Holy Spirit but rather to their soul or life principle.

Sed enim Dei flatus, inquiunt, Dei ore exisse intellegitur, quem si animam crediderimus, consequens
erit ut eiusdem fateamur esse substantiae paremque [1]
illius sapientiae quae dicit: *Ego ex ore Altissimi prodii.*
Non quidem dixit sapientia ore Dei efflatam se
fuisse, sed ex eius ore prodisse. Sicut autem nos
possumus non de nostra natura, qua homines sumus,
sed de isto aere circumfuso, quem spirando ac
respirando ducimus ac reddimus,[2] flatum facere cum
sufflamus, ita omnipotens Deus non de sua natura
neque subiacenti creatura, sed etiam de nihilo potuit
facere flatum, quem corpori hominis inserendo in-
spirasse vel insufflasse convenientissime dictus est,
incorporeus incorporeum, sed inmutabilis mutabilem,
quia non creatus creatum. Verum tamen ut sciant
isti qui de scripturis loqui volunt et scripturarum
locutiones non advertunt non hoc solum dici exire ex
ore Dei quod est aequalis eiusdemque naturae,
audiant vel legant quod Deo dicente scriptum est:
*Quoniam tepidus es et neque calidus neque frigidus,
incipiam te reicere* [3] *ex ore meo.*
Nulla itaque causa est cur apertissime loquenti resi-
stamus apostolo ubi ab spiritali corpore corpus
animale discernens, id est ab illo in quo futuri sumus

[1] partemque *some MSS.*
[2] reducimus *V and a few other MSS.*
[3] eicere *some MSS.:* evomere *one MS., Vulg.*

---

[1] Ecclesiasticus 24.3.   [2] Revelation 3.16.

But in fact the breath of God, our opponents reply, is understood to have issued from the mouth of God, and if we identify it with the soul, we must logically admit that the soul is of the same substance as and on a par with that Wisdom which says: " I have come forth from the mouth of the Most High." [1] But Wisdom did not say that it had been breathed out of the mouth of God, but that it had come forth from his mouth. Moreover, reflect how, when we expel our breath, we can blow without taking from our own substance, whereby we are human beings; we may use the air enveloping us, that we draw in and return again as we inhale and exhale. Just so, God almighty had power to produce a breath that was not of his own substance or of some created thing inferior to him. He could even produce it out of nothing. Hence it was quite fittingly put, when he placed this breath in man's body, that he had breathed or blown it into him. This breath was incorporeal, even as God is incorporeal, but it was mutable, as he is not, because it was created by him who was not created. Nevertheless, in order that those who choose to discourse about Scripture without noting the idioms of Scripture may know that not only something of equal and identical substance with God's is said to come out of his mouth, let them but hear or read the recorded words of God: " Since you are lukewarm and neither hot nor cold, I shall proceed to spit you out of my mouth." [2]

There is therefore no reason to refuse our consent to the very lucid statement of the Apostle when, as he distinguishes the animal body from the spiritual body, that is, the body in which we now are from

hoc in quo nunc sumus, ait: *Seminatur corpus animale,
surget*[1] *corpus spiritale. Si est corpus animale, est et
spiritale. Sic et*[2] *scriptum est: Factus est primus homo
Adam in animam viventem, novissimus Adam in spiritum
vivificantem. Sed non primum quod spiritale est, sed
quod animale, postea spiritale. Primus homo de terra
terrenus, secundus homo de caelo.*[3] *Qualis terrenus,
tales et terreni; et qualis*[4] *caelestis, tales et caelestes.
Et quo modo induimus imaginem terreni, induamus et
imaginem eius qui de caelo est.* De quibus omnibus
apostolicis verbis superius locuti sumus.

Corpus igitur animale, in quo primum hominem
Adam factum esse dicit apostolus, sic erat factum,
non ut mori omnino non posset, sed ut non moreretur
nisi homo peccasset. Nam illud quod spiritu vivificante spiritale erit et inmortale mori omnino non
poterit, sicut anima creata est inmortalis, quae, licet
peccato mortua perhibeatur carens quadam vita sua,
hoc est dei Spiritu, quo etiam sapienter et beate
vivere poterat, tamen propria quadam, licet misera,
vita sua non desinit vivere quia inmortalis est creata;
sicut etiam desertores angeli, licet secundum quendam modum mortui sint peccando quia fontem vitae
deseruerunt qui Deus est, quem potando sapienter

---

[1] surgit *a few MSS. See above, p.* 212, *note* 1.
[2] sic et *most MSS.:* sicut *a few MSS. See above, p.* 228,
note 2.
[3] de caelo *V and two other MSS.:* de caelo caelestis *most
MSS., Vulg. See above, p.* 232, *note* 1.
[4] et qualis *most MSS., Vulg. (cf. the Greek:* καὶ οἷος*);* qualis
a few MSS. (cf. above, 13.23 [*p.* 232, *line* 3]).

that in which we are hereafter to be, he says: " It is sown an animal body, it will rise a spiritual body. If there is an animal body, there is also a spiritual body. Thus it is also written: ' The first man Adam was made into a living soul, the last Adam into a life-giving spirit.' But the spiritual does not come first; rather the animal, and later the spiritual. The first man is of the earth, earthly, the second man is of heaven. As is the man of earth, so also are those who are of the earth; as is the man of heaven, so also are those who are of heaven. And even as we have put on the image of the man of earth, let us also put on the image of the man who is from heaven." [1] Concerning all these words of the Apostle we have already spoken above.[2]

Accordingly, the animal body, with which, as the Apostle tells us, the first man Adam was made, was so made, not as to be wholly incapable of dying, but as not to suffer death if man had not sinned. For it is that body which will be spiritual and immortal through a life-giving spirit that will be wholly unable to die, like the soul, which was created immortal. True, the soul may be said to have died through sin when it loses a certain kind of life, that is, the spirit of God, whereby it might also have lived wisely and happily. Yet it does not cease to live a kind of life of its own, wretched though it be, since it was created immortal. The same is true of the rebellious angels. They died after a certain fashion by sinning because they forsook the fountain of life which is God; by imbibing of him they might have lived wisely and

[1] 1 Corinthians 15.44–49.
[2] See above, 13.23 (pp. 223–235).

et beate poterant vivere, tamen non sic mori potuerunt ut omni modo [1] desisterent vivere atque sentire
quoniam inmortales creati sunt, atque ita in secundam mortem post ultimum praecipitabuntur iudicium
ut nec illic vita careant, quando quidem etiam sensu,
cum in doloribus futuri sunt, non carebunt.

Sed homines ad Dei gratiam pertinentes, cives
sanctorum angelorum in beata vita manentium, ita
spiritalibus corporibus induentur ut neque peccent
amplius neque moriantur, ea tamen inmortalitate
vestiti quae, sicut angelorum, nec peccato possit
auferri, natura quidem manente carnis, sed nulla
omnino carnali corruptibilitate vel tarditate re-
manente.

Sequitur autem quaestio necessario pertractanda
et, Domino Deo veritatis adiuvante, solvenda: Si
libido membrorum inoboedientium ex peccato inoboedientiae in illis primis hominibus, cum illos divina
gratia deseruisset, exorta est, unde in suam nudi-
tatem oculos aperuerunt, id est eam curiosius adver-
terunt, et, quia inpudens motus voluntatis arbitrio
resistebat, pudenda texerunt, quo modo essent filios
propagaturi si, ut creati fuerant, sine praevaricatione
mansissent. Sed quia et liber iste claudendus est
nec tanta quaestio in sermonis angustias coartanda,
in eum qui sequitur commodiore dispositione [2]
differtur.

[1] omni modo *some MSS.*: omnino *other MSS.*
[2] disputatione *a few MSS.*

happily. Nevertheless, they could not die so as to be altogether quit of life and sensation since they were created immortal. Likewise, after the last judgement, when they are hurled headlong into the second death, they will not even there be devoid of life, for indeed they will not be devoid of feeling either when they are in torment.

But men who belong to the grace of God and are fellow-citizens of the holy angels who keep their happy life will be so endowed with spiritual bodies that they will thereafter neither sin any more nor die. For the immortality with which they are clothed will be such that, like the angels', it cannot be taken away through sin; and though their carnal substance will be kept, no vestige of carnal corruptibility or sluggishness will be left.

There next arises a problem which must of necessity be treated and, with the help of the Lord God of truth, be resolved. We know that the sensuality of our disobedient members arose in those first human beings as a result of the sin of disobedience, when they had been forsaken by divine grace; that it was as a consequence of this that they opened their eyes to their own nakedness, that is, observed it more narrowly; and that, because an indecent rising resisted the rule of their will, they covered up their indecent parts. All this being so, how would they have produced children if they had remained without sin, as they were created? But it is time to bring this book to a close; and besides, the discussion of so great a problem must not be squeezed into too short a space. Consequently, I postpone it to the following book for more convenient treatment.

BOOK XIV

LIBER XIV

I

*Per inoboedientiam primi hominis omnes in secundae
mortis perpetuitatem ruituros fuisse nisi multos
Dei gratia liberaret.*

Diximus iam superioribus libris ad humanum genus
non solum naturae similitudine sociandum verum
etiam quadam cognationis necessitudine in unitatem
concordem pacis vinculo conligandum ex homine uno
Deum voluisse homines instituere, neque hoc genus
fuisse in singulis quibusque moriturum nisi duo
primi, quorum creatus est unus ex nullo, altera ex
illo, id inoboedientia meruissent, a quibus admissum
est tam grande peccatum ut in deterius eo natura
mutaretur humana, etiam in posteros obligatione
peccati et mortis necessitate transmissa.

Mortis autem regnum in homines usque adeo
dominatum est ut omnes in secundam quoque mortem, cuius nullus est finis, poena debita praecipites
ageret nisi inde quosdam indebita Dei gratia liberaret. Ac per hoc factum est ut, cum tot tantaeque

---

[1] Cf. above, especially 12.22 (pp. 109–111); 12.28 (pp. 129–
131).

BOOK XIV

I

*That the disobedience of the first man would have
plunged all men into an everlasting second death
if many were not delivered by the grace
of God.*

As I have already stated in the preceding books,[1]
God's purpose in choosing to produce mankind from
but one man was not merely to unite the human race
in an alliance based on natural likeness but also to
bind it up by the tie of kinship, as it were, into a
single harmonious whole held together through the
bond of peace. Nor would this race have been subject to death in its individual members if the first
two human beings, of whom one was created from
no one and the other from the former, had not
brought mortality on themselves by their disobedience. Such was the enormity of their sin that man's
nature was adversely affected by it; even posterity
fell heir to a legacy of bondage to sin and of inevitable
death.

Moreover, the tyranny of death held such sway
over men that they would all have been swept headlong by merited punishment into the second and
endless death as well, were not some of them rescued
from it by God's unmerited grace. And thus, in
consequence, notwithstanding the many great

gentes per terrarum orbem diversis ritibus moribusque
viventes multiplici linguarum armorum vestium sint
varietate distinctae, non tamen amplius quam duo
quaedam genera humanae societatis existerent, quas
civitates duas secundum scripturas nostras merito
appellare possemus.[1] Una quippe est hominum
secundum carnem, altera secundum spiritum vivere
in sui cuiusque generis pace volentium et, cum id
quod expetunt adsequuntur, in sui cuiusque generis
pace viventium.

II

*De vita carnali, quae non ex corporis tantum sed
etiam ex animi intellegenda sit vitiis.*

Prius ergo videndum est quid sit secundum carnem, quid secundum spiritum vivere. Quisquis
enim hoc quod diximus prima fronte inspicit, vel non
recolens vel minus advertens quem ad modum
scripturae sanctae loquantur, potest putare philosophos quidem Epicureos secundum carnem vivere
quia summum bonum hominis in corporis voluptate
posuerunt, et si qui alii sunt qui quoquo modo corporis
bonum summum bonum esse hominis opinati sunt, et
eorum omne vulgus qui non aliquo dogmate vel eo
modo philosophantur, sed proclives ad libidinem nisi
ex voluptatibus, quas corporeis sensibus capiunt,

[1] possumus *or* possimus *some MSS.*

---

[1] Cf. Ephesians 2.19–22; Philippians 3.17–21.
[2] On pleasure as the *summum bonum* of Epicureans see
Cicero, *De Finibus Bonorum et Malorum* 1 and 2.

nations that live throughout the world with different religious and moral practices and are distinguished by a rich variety of languages, arms and dress, nevertheless there have arisen no more than two classes, as it were, of human society. Following our Scriptures,[1] we may well speak of them as two cities. For there is one city of men who choose to live carnally, and another of those who choose to live spiritually, each aiming at its own kind of peace, and when they achieve their respective purposes, they live such lives, each in its own kind of peace.

II

That the carnal life is to be understood as arising not only from the defects of the body but also from those of the mind.

WE must therefore first examine what it means to live according to the flesh and what to live according to the spirit. For someone who regards my statement but superficially, either not calling to mind or too little noting the mode of expression used in holy Scripture, may go astray. He may think that Epicurean philosophers do indeed live carnally because they have placed the highest good of man in bodily pleasure,[2] and that this is the case with any other philosophers who in one way or another have supposed that the bodily good is man's highest good, as well as with the entire mass of those who follow no philosophic creed or anything of that sort but in their propensity for lust know only the joy that comes from the pleasures that they feel in physical

gaudere nesciunt; Stoicos autem, qui summum bonum hominis in animo ponunt, secundum spiritum vivere quia et hominis animus quid est nisi spiritus? Sed sicut loquitur scriptura divina, secundum carnem vivere utrique monstrantur.

Carnem quippe appellat non solum corpus terreni atque mortalis animantis (veluti cum dicit: *Non omnis caro eadem caro; alia quidem hominis, alia autem caro pecoris, alia volucrum, alia piscium*) sed et aliis multis modis significatione huius nominis utitur, inter quos varios locutionis modos saepe etiam ipsum hominem, id est naturam hominis, carnem nuncupat, modo locutionis a parte totum, quale est: *Ex operibus legis non iustificabitur omnis caro.* Quid enim voluit intellegi nisi omnis homo? Quod apertius paulo post ait: *In lege nemo iustificatur,*[1] et ad Galatas: *Scientes autem quia non iustificatur*[1] *homo ex operibus legis.*

Secundum hoc intellegitur: *Et Verbum caro factum est,* id est homo. Quod non recte accipientes quidam putaverunt Christo humanam animam defuisse. Sicut enim a toto pars accipitur ubi Mariae Magdalenae verba in evangelio leguntur dicentis: *Tulerunt*

---

[1] iustificatur *some MSS., Vulg. (cf. the Greek: δικαιοῦται):* iustificabitur *other MSS.*

---

[1] On the *summum bonum* of the Stoics see Cicero, *De Finibus Bonorum et Malorum* 3 and 4.

[2] 1 Corinthians 15.39.

[3] Romans 3.20.

[4] Galatians 3.11. Augustine seems erroneously to attribute this quotation to St. Paul's Epistle to the Romans.

sensation. But the Stoics, he may suppose, who place man's highest good in the mind,[1] live according to the spirit. For what is man's mind if not spirit? But just as divine Scripture tells us, both groups manifestly live according to the flesh.

Scripture, in fact, does not use the term ' flesh ' only of the body of an earthly and mortal animate being, as when it says: " Not all flesh is alike, but there is one kind for man, another for animals, another for birds and another for fish." [2] There are, on the contrary, many other ways in which it employs the meaning of this noun, and among these different usages is that whereby man himself, that is, man's natural being, is often designated as flesh. We have here synecdoche, the figure of speech in which the whole is represented by a part, as, for example, in the passage: " All flesh will not be justified by works of the law." [3] For what was the intended meaning but ' every man.' This is more plainly stated a little further on: " No man is justified by the law," [4] and in the Epistle to the Galatians we read: " But knowing that a man is not justified by works of the law." [5]

It is on this principle that we understand the passage: " And the Word became flesh," [6] that is, man. But certain people, mistaking its meaning, have thought that Christ had no soul.[7] For just as, when we read in the Gospel these words of Mary Magdalene: " They have taken away my Lord, and

[5] Galatians 2.16.
[6] John 1.14.
[7] On this heresy associated with the Apollinarians and the Arians cf. Augustine, *De Haeresibus* 49 and especially 55.

Dominum meum et nescio ubi posuerunt eum, cum de sola
Christi carne loqueretur, quam sepultam de monu-
mento putabat ablatam, ita et a parte totum, carne
nominata, intellegitur homo, sicuti ea sunt quae
supra commemoravimus.

Cum igitur multis modis, quos perscrutari et col-
ligere longum est, divina scriptura nuncupet carnem,
quid sit secundum carnem vivere (quod profecto
malum est, cum ipsa carnis natura non sit malum) ut
indagare possimus, inspiciamus diligenter illum locum
epistulae Pauli apostoli quam scripsit ad Galatas, ubi
ait: *Manifesta autem sunt opera carnis, quae sunt fornicationes, inmunditiae, luxuria,*[1] *idolorum servitus,
veneficia, inimicitiae, contentiones, aemulationes, animositates, dissensiones, haereses, invidiae, ebrietates,
comisationes et his similia; quae praedico vobis, sicut*[2]
*praedixi, quoniam qui talia agunt regnum Dei non
possidebunt.*

Iste totus epistulae apostolicae locus, quantum ad
rem praesentem satis esse videbitur, consideratus
poterit hanc dissolvere quaestionem, quid sit secundum carnem vivere. In operibus namque carnis,
quae manifesta esse dixit eaque commemorata
damnavit, non illa tantum invenimus quae ad voluptatem pertinent carnis, sicuti sunt fornicationes, inmunditiae, luxuria,[3] ebrietates, comisationes, verum
etiam illa quibus animi vitia demonstrantur a voluptate carnis aliena. Quis enim servitutem quae idolis

[1] luxuria *V and two other MSS., Vulg.:* luxuriae *most
MSS.*

[2] sicut *many MSS., Vulg. (cf. the Greek:* καθώς); sicut et
other MSS.

[3] luxuriae *some MSS.*

I do not know where they have laid him,"[1] we understand a part from the whole, since she was speaking only of the flesh of Christ, which she thought had been carried away from the tomb where it had been buried, so, when flesh is mentioned, we may understand the whole from a part, that is, man, as in the passages cited above.

The ways then in which holy Scripture uses the term ' flesh ' are manifold, and it would be tedious to assemble and examine them all. Hence, to further our examination of the question what it means to live carnally, which is surely a bad thing, though the substance flesh itself is nothing bad, let us earnestly study the passage in St. Paul's Epistle to the Galatians where he says: " Now the works of the flesh are plain: fornication, impurity, licentiousness, idolatry, sorcery, enmity, strife, jealousy, anger, dissension, party spirit, envy, drunkenness, carousing, and the like; I warn you, as I warned you before, that those who do such things shall not inherit the kingdom of God."[2]

If we devote to this entire passage of the apostolic epistle such attention as the matter at hand is found to require, we shall be able to settle the question what it means to live according to the flesh. For in the works of the flesh, which he said were plain to see and which he enumerated and condemned, we find not only those that involve carnal pleasure, like fornication, impurity, licentiousness or carousing, but also those that display mental defects which have nothing to do with carnal pleasure. In the case of

[1] John 20.13.
[2] Galatians 5.19–21.

exhibetur, veneficia, inimicitias, contentiones, aemulationes, animositates, dissensiones, haereses, invidias
non potius intellegat animi vitia esse quam carnis?
Quando quidem fieri potest ut propter idololatriam
vel haeresis alicuius errorem a voluptatibus corporis
temperetur; et tamen etiam tunc homo, quamvis
carnis libidines continere atque cohibere videatur,
secundum carnem vivere hac apostolica auctoritate
convincitur, et in eo quod abstinet a voluptatibus
carnis damnabilia opera carnis agere demonstratur.

Quis inimicitias non in animo habeat? Aut quis
ita loquatur ut inimico suo vel quem putat inimicum
dicat: " Malam carnem," ac non potius: " Malum
animum habes adversus me "? Postremo, sicut
carnalitates, ut ita dicam, si quis audisset, non dubi-
taret carni tribuere, ita nemo dubitat animositates ad
animum pertinere. Cur ergo haec omnia et his
similia doctor gentium in fide et veritate opera carnis
appellat nisi quia eo locutionis modo quo totum
significatur a parte ipsum hominem vult nomine carnis intellegi?

idolatry, sorcery, enmity, strife, jealousy, anger, dissension, party spirit and envy, surely no one doubts that we have here defects of the mind rather than of the body. For it may happen that a person abstains from bodily pleasures because he worships idols or follows the mistaken doctrine of some sect; and yet even so, though such a person appears to check and curb his carnal desires, he stands convicted, on this same authority of the apostle, of living according to the flesh. In this case, his very abstention from the pleasures of the flesh proves that he is engaged in the damnable works of the flesh.

Does anyone who feels enmity not feel it in his mind? Or does anyone, in speaking to his enemy, real or imagined, say, " You are ill-disposed to me in your flesh," and not rather, " You are ill-disposed to me in your mind "? In fine, just as anyone who heard of ' carnalities,' if I may use this term, would attribute them to man's carnal nature, so no one doubts that ' animosities ' have to do with *animus* or mind. Why then does the instructor of the Gentiles in faith and truth [1] call all these and similar vices works of the flesh if not because he means the word ' flesh ' to be understood as meaning ' man ' by that figure of speech which uses a part to indicate the whole?

[1] Cf. 1 Timothy 2.7.

III

*Peccati causam ex anima, non ex carne prodisse, et
corruptionem ex peccato contractam non peccatum esse sed poenam.*

QUOD si quisquam dicit carnem causam esse in
malis moribus quorumcumque vitiorum eo quod
anima carne affecta sic vivit, profecto non universam
hominis naturam diligenter advertit. Nam *" corpus
quidem corruptibile adgravat animam."* Unde etiam
idem apostolus agens de hoc corruptibili corpore, de
quo paulo ante dixerat: *Etsi exterior homo noster corrumpitur: Scimus,* inquit, *quia si terrena nostra domus
habitationis* [1] *resolvatur, aedificationem habemus ex Deo,
domum non manu factam aeternam in caelis. Etenim in
hoc ingemescimus, habitaculum nostrum quod de caelo
est superindui cupientes, si tamen et induti non nudi in-
veniamur. Etenim qui sumus in hac habitatione ingemescimus gravati, in quo nolumus exspoliari, sed super-
vestiri, ut absorbeatur mortale a vita.*

Et adgravamur ergo corruptibili corpore, et ipsius
adgravationis causam non naturam substantiamque
corporis sed eius corruptionem scientes nolumus
corpore spoliari, sed eius inmortalitate vestiri. Et
tunc enim erit, sed quia corruptibile non erit, non

---

[1] habitationis *some MSS. (cf. the Greek:* τοῦ σκήνους):
huius habitationis *other MSS., Vulg.*

[1] Wisdom 9.15.
[2] 2 Corinthians 4.16.
[3] 2 Corinthians 5.1–4.

III

*That the cause of sin proceeded from the soul, not
from the flesh, and that the morbid condition
resulting from sin is not a sin but a punishment.*

Now someone may contend that the flesh is the
cause of every sort of vice in the case of bad morals
on the ground that it is the influence of the flesh on
the soul that makes the soul lead that kind of life.
But if he does, surely he has not seriously considered
the whole of man's natural being. For " the corruptible body is heavy upon the soul." [1]   Hence too,
our Apostle, who had just remarked in discussing this
corruptible body: " Though our outward man is in
decay," [2] went on to say: " We know that if the
earthly house which we occupy is destroyed, we have
a building from God, a house not made with hands,
eternal in the heavens.   In this one indeed we groan,
and long to have our heavenly dwelling put on over
it, in the hope that by thus putting it on we shall
not be found naked.   For while we are still in this
dwelling, we groan under our burden, not that we
would be stripped of our covering, but that we would
have the other covering put on over it, so that what
is mortal may be swallowed up by life." [3]

Consequently, we are burdened by the corruptible
body, and yet, knowing that the cause of our burden-
ing is not the true being and substance of the body
but its decay, we do not want to be stripped of the
body, but to be clothed with its immortality.   For
then too there will be a body, but because it will not

SAINT AUGUSTINE

gravabit. *Adgravat* ergo nunc *animam corpus corruptibile, et deprimit terrena inhabitatio sensum multa cogitantem.* Verum tamen qui omnia mala animae ex corpore putant accidisse in crrore sunt.

Quamvis enim Vergilius Platonicam videatur luculentis versibus explicare sententiam dicens:

> Igncus est ollis [1] vigor et caelestis origo
> Seminibus, quantum non noxia corpora tardant
> Terrenique hebetant artus moribundaque
> > membra,

omnesque illas notissimas quattuor animi perturbationes, cupiditatem timorem, laetitiam tristitiam, quasi origines omnium peccatorum atque vitiorum volens intellegi ex corpore accidere subiungat et dicat:

> Hinc metuunt cupiuntque, dolent gaudentque,
> > nec auras
> Suspiciunt,[2] clausae tenebris et carcere caeco,

tamen aliter se habet fides nostra. Nam corruptio corporis, quae adgravat animam, non peccati primi est causa, sed poena, nec caro corruptibilis animam peccatricem, sed anima peccatrix fecit esse corruptibilem carnem.

Ex qua corruptione carnis licet existant quaedam

[1] ollis *a few MSS.*, *Virgil:* illis *most MSS.*
[2] suscipiunt *some MSS. The better MSS. of Virgil read* despiciunt, *while others show a variant* respiciunt.

---

[1] Wisdom 9.15.
[2] Virgil, *Aeneid* 6.730–732.

be subject to decay, it will not be a burden. Accordingly, in our present life, " the corruptible body is heavy upon the soul, and the earthly dwelling presses down the mind that ponders many things." [1] Nevertheless, those who think that all evils of the soul arise from the body are in error.

Virgil, it is true, appears to be expounding Platonic doctrine in resplendent verse when he says:

> Fiery is the force and celestial the source
> Of those seeds, to the extent they are not
> By baleful bodies clogged nor by earthly limbs
> And mortal members numbed.[2]

He also intends us to regard the body as responsible for all four of the well-known emotions of the mind, namely, desire and fear, joy and grief,[3] which are the starting-point, as it were, of all sins and vices, for he adds to the above lines the following words:

> Hence come fear, desire, also gladness, pain
> To those who have no view of the sky above,
> Confined in gloom and sightless prison cave.[4]

Nevertheless, our faith is not quite the same. For the body's decay, which weighs down the soul, is not the cause of the first sin but the punishment for it, nor is it the flesh, which is subject to decay, that makes the soul sinful; it is the sinful soul that makes the flesh subject to decay.

Though this decay of the flesh may give rise to

---

[3] On these four emotions cf. Cicero, *Tusculanae Disputationes* 3.11.24–25; 4.6.11–12.

[4] Virgil, *Aeneid* 6.733–734.

incitamenta vitiorum et ipsa desideria vitiosa, non tamen omnia vitae iniquae vitia tribuenda sunt carni, ne ab his omnibus purgemus diabolum, qui non habet carnem. Etsi enim diabolus fornicator vel ebriosus vel si quid huius modi mali est, quod ad carnis pertinet voluptates, non potest dici, cum sit etiam talium peccatorum suasor et instigator occultus, est tamen maxime superbus atque invidus. Quae illum vitiositas sic obtinuit ut propter hanc esset in carceribus caliginosi huius aeris aeterno supplicio destinatus.

Haec autem vitia, quae tenent in diabolo principatum, carni tribuit apostolus, quam certum est diabolum non habere. Dicit enim inimicitias, contentiones, aemulationes, animositates, invidias opera esse carnis, quorum omnium malorum caput atque origo superbia est, quae sine carne regnat in diabolo. Quis autem illo est inimicior sanctis? Quis adversus eos contentiosior, animosior et magis aemulus atque invidus invenitur? At haec omnia cum habeat sine carne, quo modo sunt ista opera carnis nisi quia opera sunt hominis, quem, sicut dixi, nomine carnis appellat?

Non enim habendo carnem, quam non habet diabolus, sed vivendo secundum se ipsum, hoc est secundum hominem, factus est homo similis diabolo, quia et ille secundum se ipsum vivere voluit quando in veritate non stetit, ut non de Dei sed de suo mendacium loqueretur, qui non solum mendax verum etiam mendacii pater est. Primus est quippe men-

---

[1] Cf. Galatians 5.19–21.
[2] See above, 12.6 (p. 25 and note 1).

some incitements to vice and actual vicious desires,
yet we must not attribute all the faults of a wicked
life to the flesh; otherwise we exonerate the devil,
who has no flesh, from blame in all these cases. We
cannot, to be sure, maintain that the devil is guilty
of fornication or intoxication or any other such vice
involving carnal pleasures, though he is the hidden
persuader and prompter even of such sins. On the
other hand, he is exceedingly arrogant and envious,
and this depravity has so taken possession of him
that he is doomed for it to eternal punishment in the
prison house of our murky air.

The following vices, moreover, which have primacy
in the devil, are attributed by the Apostle to the
flesh, though we may be sure that the devil has none.
For the Apostle says that enmity, strife, jealousy,
anger and envy are works of the flesh.[1] But the
head and source of all these evils is pride,[2] and pride
reigns without flesh in the devil. Who indeed shows
more enmity than he to the saints? Who is found
guiltier of strife or anger against them, of jealousy
or envy toward them? But since he possesses all
these vices without flesh, how can they be works of
the flesh unless they are the works of man, to whom, as
I said before, the term ' flesh ' is applied as a designation?

It is not by having flesh, which the devil does not
have, but by living according to his own self, that is,
according to man, that man has become like the devil.
For the devil too chose to live according to his own
self when he did not adhere to the truth, and thus
the falsehood that he told had its source not in God
but in himself. The devil is not only a liar but also

titus, et a quo peccatum, ab illo coepit esse mendacium.

IV

Quid sit secundum hominem, quid autem secundum
Deum vivere.

CUM ergo vivit homo secundum hominem, non secundum Deum, similis est diabolo, quia nec angelo
secundum angelum, sed secundum Deum vivendum
fuit, ut staret in veritate et veritatem de illius, non
de suo mendacium loqueretur. Nam et de homine
alio loco idem apostolus ait: *Si autem veritas Dei in*
meo mendacio abundavit. Nostrum dixit mendacium,
veritatem Dei.

Cum itaque vivit homo secundum veritatem, non
vivit secundum se ipsum sed secundum Deum.
Deus est enim qui dixit: *Ego sum veritas.* Cum vero
vivit secundum se ipsum, hoc est secundum hominem,
non secundum Deum, profecto secundum mendacium
vivit, non quia homo ipse mendacium est, cum sit
eius auctor et creator Deus, qui non est utique auctor
creatorque mendacii, sed quia homo ita factus est
rectus ut non secundum se ipsum sed secundum eum
a quo factus est viveret, id est illius potius quam
suam faceret voluntatem. Non ita vivere quem ad
modum est factus ut viveret, hoc est mendacium.

Beatus quippe vult esse etiam non sic vivendo ut

---

[1] Cf. John 8.44.   [2] Romans 3.7.
[3] John 14.6.

father of lies,[1] for he was the first to lie, and falsehood began with him even as did sin.

IV

*What it means to live according to man and what to
live according to God.*

Therefore, when man lives according to man and
not according to God, he is like the devil, for even an
angel should have lived, not according to an angel,
but according to God if he was to adhere to the truth
and speak the truth that came from God and not the
falsehood that came from himself. For the Apostle
says elsewhere concerning man too: "But if through
my falsehood God's truthfulness has abounded."[2]
He speaks of falsehood as ours, but of truth as God's.

Consequently, when man lives according to truth,
he does not live according to his own self but according to God. For it was God who said: "I am the
truth."[3] On the other hand, when he lives according
to his own self, that is, according to man and not
according to God, assuredly he lives according to
falsehood. This does not mean that man himself is
falsehood, since his author and creator is God, and
God is certainly not the author and creator of falsehood. Rather it means that man was created right,
in the sense that he was to live not according to his
own self but according to his maker, that is, to do
the latter's will instead of his own. Not to live
after the fashion for which he was designed to live is
falsehood.

Man has indeed a will to be happy even when he

possit esse. Quid est ista voluntate mendacius?
Unde non frustra dici potest omne peccatum esse
mendacium. Non enim fit peccatum nisi ea voluntate qua volumus ut bene sit nobis vel nolumus ut
male sit nobis. Ergo mendacium est quod, cum fiat
ut bene sit nobis, hinc potius male est nobis, vel
cum fiat ut melius sit nobis, hinc potius peius est
nobis. Unde hoc nisi quia de Deo potest bene esse
homini, quem delinquendo deserit, non de se ipso,
secundum quem vivendo delinquit?

Quod itaque diximus hinc extitisse duas civitates
diversas inter se atque contrarias, quod alii secundum
carnem, alii secundum spiritum viverent, potest etiam
isto modo dici quod alii secundum hominem, alii
secundum Deum vivant. Apertissime quippe
[Paulus] [1] ad Corinthios dicit: *Cum enim sint* [2] *inter*
vos aemulatio et contentio, nonne carnales estis et secundum
hominem ambulatis? Quod ergo est ambulare secundum hominem, hoc est esse carnalem quod a carne,
id est a parte hominis, intellegitur homo.

Eosdem ipsos quippe dixit superius animales quos
postea carnales, ita loquens: *Quis enim scit,* inquit,
hominum quae sunt hominis nisi spiritus hominis qui in
ipso est? Sic et quae Dei sunt nemo scit nisi spiritus

---

[1] Paulus *omitted in most MSS.*
[2] sint *omitted in* V *and one other MS. following the Greek*
text: sit *one MS., Vulg.*

---

[1] See above, 14.1 (p. 261).
[2] 1 Corinthians 3.3.

does not live in a way that makes it possible for him to be so, but what is falser than a will of that sort? Hence we may say without impropriety that every sin is a falsehood. For when a sin is committed, it is committed only because of the will that we have to fare well or not to fare ill. Consequently, the falsehood is this, that a sin is committed in order that we may fare well and the result is rather that we fare ill, or that a sin is committed in order that we may fare better and the result is rather that we fare worse. What is the reason for this except that a man's welfare comes from God, not from himself? But he forsakes God by sinning and sins by living according to his own self.

Consequently, my former statement, that the existence of two different and opposing cities is due to the fact that some people live according to the flesh and others according to the spirit,[1] may also be put in this way, that some people live according to man and others according to God. Paul told the Corinthians very plainly: "For while there is jealousy and strife among you, are you not of the flesh and behaving according to man?"[2] Thus, whether we say that a man is of the flesh or that he behaves according to man, the sense is the same because the flesh, that is, a part of man, means man himself.

Those very same people, whom the Apostle here called carnal, were just previously referred to as animal when he said: "For what person knows a man's thoughts except the spirit of the man which is in him? So also no one knows the thoughts of God except the spirit of God. Now we have received

Dei. Nos autem, inquit, *non spiritum huius mundi accepimus, sed spiritum qui ex Deo est, ut sciamus quae a Deo donata sunt nobis; quae et loquimur non in sapientiae humanae doctis verbis, sed doctis spiritu,*[1] *spiritalibus spiritalia comparantes. Animalis autem homo non percipit quae sunt spiritus Dei; stultitia est enim illi.*

Talibus igitur, id est animalibus, paulo post dicit: *Et ego, fratres, non potui loqui vobis quasi spiritalibus, sed quasi carnalibus;* et illud et hoc eodem loquendi modo, id est a parte totum. Et ab anima namque et a carne, quae sunt partes hominis, potest totum significari quod est homo. Atque ita non est aliud animalis homo, aliud carnalis, sed idem ipsum est utrumque, id est secundum hominem vivens homo, sicut non aliud quam homines significantur sive ubi legitur: *Ex operibus legis non iustificabitur*[2] *omnis caro* sive quod scriptum est: *Septuaginta quinque animae descenderunt cum Iacob in Aegyptum.* Et ibi enim per omnem carnem omnis homo et ibi per septuaginta quinque animas septuaginta quinque homines intelleguntur.

---

[1] doctis spiritu *a few MSS.* (*cf. the Greek:* διδακτοῖς πνεύματος): docti spiritu *most MSS.:* doctrina spiritu *one MS., Vulg.*

[2] iustificabitur *some MSS., Vulg.* (*cf. the Greek:* δικαιωθήσεται): iustificatur *other MSS.*

---

[1] So the RSV for *spiritalibus spiritalia comparantes* (cf. the Greek: πνευματικοῖς πνευματικὰ συνκρίνοντες). But the precise meaning of the phrase is not certain, and alternative versions

not the spirit of this world, but the spirit which is from God, that we might understand the gifts bestowed on us by God. And we impart this in words not taught by human wisdom, but taught by the spirit, interpreting spiritual truths to those who possess the spirit.[1] The animal man does not receive the gifts of the spirit of God, for they are folly to him." [2]

It is to such people then, that is, to animal men, that he says a little later: " But I, brethren, could not address you as spiritual men, but as carnal men." [3] Both terms, animal and carnal, illustrate the same figure of speech, that is, the use of a part for the whole. For both the soul (*anima*) and the flesh, which are parts of man, can serve to indicate the whole which is man. And thus the animal man is not something different from the carnal man, but both are one and the same, that is, man living according to man. Similarly, the allusion is merely to men not only where we read: " No flesh will be justified by works of the law," [4] but also in the scriptural passage: " Seventy-five souls went down with Jacob into Egypt." [5] For in the former quotation, we take ' no flesh ' to mean ' no man,' and in the latter, ' seventy-five souls ' to mean ' seventy-five men.'

mentioned in the RSV are: "interpreting spiritual truths in spiritual language," and "comparing spiritual things with spiritual."
[2] 1 Corinthians 2.11–14.
[3] 1 Corinthians 3.1.
[4] Romans 3.20.
[5] Genesis 46.27.   As to the number of souls, the figure given here agrees with that of the Septuagint and Acts 7.14, but according to the Vulgate there were only seventy.

Et quod dictum est: *Non in sapientiae humanae doctis verbis*, potuit dici: "Non in sapientiae carnalis," sicut quod dictum est: *Secundum hominem ambulatis*, potuit dici: "Secundum carnem." Magis autem hoc apparuit in his quae subiunxit: *Cum enim quis dicat: Ego quidem sum Pauli, alius autem: Ego Apollo, nonne homines estis?* Quod dicebat: *Animales estis*, et: *Carnales estis*, expressius dixit: *Homines estis*, quod est: "Secundum hominem vivitis, non secundum Deum, secundum quem si viveretis, dii essetis."

V

Quod de corporis animaeque natura tolerabilior quidem Platonicorum quam Manichaeorum sit opinio, sed et ipsa reprobanda quoniam vitiorum omnium causas naturae carnis ascribit.[1]

Non igitur opus est in peccatis vitiisque nostris ad Creatoris iniuriam carnis accusare naturam, quae in genere atque ordine suo bona est. Sed, deserto Creatore bono, vivere secundum creatum bonum non est bonum, sive quisque secundum carnem sive secundum animam sive secundum totum hominem, qui ex anima constat et carne (unde et nomine solius animae et nomine solius carnis significari potest) eligat vivere. Nam qui velut summum bonum

---

[1] *ascribit conjectured by Dombart from* ascripti *in* V: adscribunt *other MSS.*

---

[1] 1 Corinthians 3.4.

Moreover, when the Apostle said: " In words not taught by human wisdom," he could equally well have used the phrase ' carnal wisdom,' just as when he said: " You behave according to man," he might have said: " According to the flesh." We see this more plainly in the words that he added: " For when one says, ' I belong to Paul,' and another, ' I belong to Apollos,' are you not merely men? " [1] When he states here: " You are men," he shows more explicitly what he intended by the phrases " You are animal " and " You are carnal." What he means is this: " You live according to man, not according to God, for if you lived according to him, you would be gods."

V

That although the view of the Platonists on the nature of the body and the soul is more tolerable than that of the Manichaeans, yet we must reject it too since it attributes the causes of all vices to the nature of the flesh.

IN the case of our sins and vices then we should not do an injustice to our creator by blaming the nature of the flesh, which is good in its own kind and order. But if a person abandons the good creator to live according to some created good, it is not good, whether he chooses to live according to the flesh or according to the soul or according to the whole man, who consists of soul and flesh and can therefore be designated by either term alone, that is, by soul or flesh. For when anyone approves the substance of

laudat animae naturam et tamquam malum naturam carnis accusat profecto et animam carnaliter adpetit et carnem carnaliter fugit quoniam id vanitate sentit humana, non veritate divina.

Non quidem Platonici sicut Manichaei desipiunt ut tamquam mali naturam terrena corpora detestentur, cum omnia elementa, quibus iste mundus visibilis contrectabilisque compactus est, qualitatesque eorum Deo artifici tribuant. Verum tamen ex terrenis artubus moribundisque membris sic affici animas opinantur ut hinc eis sint morbi cupiditatum et timorum et laetitiae sive tristitiae; quibus quattuor vel perturbationibus, ut Cicero appellat, vel passionibus, ut plerique verbum e verbo Graeco exprimunt, omnis humanorum morum vitiositas continetur.

Quod si ita est, quid est quod Aeneas apud Vergilium, cum audisset a patre apud inferos animas rursus ad corpora redituras, hanc opinionem miratur exclamans:

> O pater, anne aliquas ad caelum hinc ire putan-
> dum est
> Sublimes animas iterumque ad tarda reverti
> Corpora?   Quae lucis miseris tam dira cupido?

Numquidnam haec tam dira cupido ex terrenis artubus moribundisque membris adhuc inest animarum illi praedicatissimae puritati?   Nonne ab huius modi corporeis, ut dicit, pestibus omnibus eas asserit esse

---

[1] Cf. Augustine, *De Haeresibus* 46.
[2] Cf. Cicero, *Tusculanae Disputationes* 4.6.11.
[3] See above, 8.17.

the soul as the highest good and denounces the substance of the flesh as an evil, surely he is carnal both
in his pursuit of the soul and in his avoidance of the
flesh inasmuch as it is through human vanity and not
divine truth that he holds this view.

The Platonists, it is true, are not so foolish as the
Manichaeans, for they do not abominate earthly
bodies as the substance of evil [1] since all the elements
with their qualities that make up the framework of
this visible and tangible world are attributed by them
to their god as demiurge.   Nevertheless, they believe
that souls are so affected by their earthly limbs and
mortal members that they owe to them their infection with desires and fears, with joy or grief.   And
these four perturbations, as Cicero calls them, [2] or
passions, to use the common term translated literally
from the Greek, comprise the entire scope of depravity in human morals. [3]

But if this is the case, why in Virgil's poem does
Aeneas, after he hears his father in the world below
say that souls will again return to bodies, cry out in
wonderment at this belief:

> Oh father, can it be true that ever souls
> Rise hence on high and then once more return
> To sluggish frames?   What direful lust of life
> Does those poor fools possess? [4]

Does this so direful lust, derived from earthly limbs
and mortal members, still linger in that highly lauded
purity of souls?   Does Virgil not maintain that souls
have been cleansed of all such bodily plagues, as he

[4] Virgil, *Aeneid* 6.719–721.

purgatas cum rursus incipiunt in corpora velle
reverti?

Unde colligitur, etiamsi ita se haberet, quod est
omnino vanissimum, vicissim alternans incessabi-
liter euntium atque redeuntium animarum mundatio
et inquinatio, non potuisse veraciter dici omnes cul-
pabiles atque vitiosos motus animarum eis ex terrenis
corporibus inolescere, si quidem secundum ipsos illa,
ut locutor nobilis ait, dira cupido usque adeo non est
ex corpore ut ab omni corporea peste purgatam et
extra omne corpus animam constitutam ipsa [1] esse
compellat in corpore. Unde, etiam illis fatentibus,
non ex carne tantum afficitur anima ut cupiat metuat,
laetetur aegrescat, verum etiam ex se ipsa his potest
motibus agitari.

VI

*De qualitate voluntatis humanae, sub cuius iudicio
affectiones animi aut pravae habentur aut
rectae.*

INTEREST autem qualis sit voluntas hominis, quia si
perversa est, perversos habebit hos motus, si autem
recta est, non solum inculpabiles verum etiam lauda-
biles erunt. Voluntas est quippe in omnibus, immo
omnes nihil aliud quam voluntates sunt. Nam quid
est cupiditas et laetitia nisi voluntas in eorum con-
sensione quae volumus? Et quid est metus atque
tristitia nisi voluntas in dissensione ab his quae nolu-

[1] ipsam *some MSS.*

puts it, when the wish arises to return once more to
bodies?

Hence, even if souls (to make a completely baseless
supposition) actually underwent, as they come and
go, such endless alternation of purification and defile-
ment, we deduce that it cannot have been truthfully
said that all blameworthy and unwholesome emotions
of souls spring up in them from their earthly bodies.
For, according to the men themselves, that direful
lust, as their famous spokesman calls it, is so far from
having its source in the body that it of itself drives
the soul to exist in a body after it has been cleansed
of all bodily plague and situated outside all bodily
substance. Thus, even by their own admission, the
soul is not only so affected by the flesh that it feels
desire and fear, joy and grief, but it can also through
itself be stirred by these emotions.

VI

*On the character of the human will, whose judgement
determines whether the dispositions of the mind are
considered wrong or right.*

MOREOVER, the character of a man's will makes a
difference. For if it is wrong, these emotions will be
wrong; but if it is right, they will be not only not
blameworthy but even praiseworthy. The will is
indeed involved in them all, or rather, they are all
no more than acts of will. For what is desire or
joy but an act of will in sympathy with those things
that we wish, and what is fear or grief but an act of
will in disagreement with the things that we do not

mus? Sed cum consentimus appetendo ea quae
volumus, cupiditas, cum autem consentimus fruendo
his quae volumus, laetitia vocatur. Itemque cum
dissentimus ab eo quod accidere nolumus, talis
voluntas metus est, cum autem dissentimus ab eo
quod nolentibus accidit, talis voluntas tristitia est.
Et omnino pro varietate rerum quae appetuntur
atque fugiuntur, sicut allicitur vel offenditur voluntas
hominis, ita in hos vel illos affectus mutatur et ver-
titur.

Quapropter homo qui secundum Deum, non secundum hominem vivit oportet ut sit amator boni, unde
fit consequens ut malum oderit. Et quoniam nemo
natura, sed quisquis malus est vitio malus est, per-
fectum odium debet malis qui secundum Deum vivit,
ut nec propter vitium oderit hominem nec amet
vitium propter hominem, sed oderit vitium, amet
hominem. Sanato enim vitio, totum quod amare,
nihil autem quod debeat odisse remanebit.

VII

*Amorem et dilectionem indifferenter et in bono et in
malo apud sacras litteras inveniri.*

Nam cuius propositum est amare Deum et non secundum hominem, sed secundum Deum amare

---

[1] Cf. Psalms 139.22.
[2] Cf. Matthew 19.19.

wish? When our sympathy, however, is indicated by a pursuit of the things that we wish, it is called desire, but when it is indicated by an enjoyment of these things that we wish, it is called joy. Similarly, when we disagree with that which we do not wish to happen, such an act of will is fear, but when we disagree with that which happens to us against our will, such an act of will is grief. And generally, even as a man's will is attracted or repelled in accordance with the diverse character of the objects that are pursued or avoided, so it shifts and turns into emotions of one sort or the other.

Therefore, the man who lives according to God and not according to man is bound to be a lover of the good, and the consequence is that he hates evil. Moreover, since no one is evil by nature, but whosoever is evil is so because of some defect, the person who lives according to God owes to those who are evil a perfect hatred,[1] that is, he should neither hate a man because of his defect nor love a defect because of the man, but he should hate the defect and love the man. For once the defect is mended, only what he should love and nothing that he should hate will remain.

VII

That the terms ' love ' (amor) and ' attachment '
(dilectio) are found indiscriminately used in
holy Scripture with reference to both good
and evil.

IF a person's intention is to love God and also to love his neighbour even as himself,[2] not according to

287

proximum sicut etiam se ipsum, procul dubio propter
hunc amorem dicitur voluntatis bonae, quae usitatius
in scripturis sanctis caritas appellatur, sed amor
quoque secundum easdem sacras litteras dicitur.
Nam et amatorem boni apostolus dicit esse debere
quem regendo populo praecipit eligendum, et ipse
Dominus Petrum apostolum interrogans cum dixisset:
Diligis me plus his? ille respondit: *Domine, tu scis
quia amo te.* Et iterum Dominus quaesivit, non
utrum amaret, sed utrum diligeret eum Petrus; at
ille respondit iterum: *Domine, tu scis quia amo te.*
Tertia vero interrogatione et ipse Iesus non ait:
" Diligis me ? " sed: *Amas me?* ubi secutus ait evan-
gelista: *Contristatus est Petrus quia dixit ei tertio:
Amas me?* cum Dominus non tertio, sed semel dixerit:
Amas me? bis autem dixerit: *Diligis me?* Unde
intellegimus quod etiam cum dicebat Dominus:
Diligis me? nihil aliud dicebat quam: *Amas me?*
Petrus autem non mutavit huius unius rei verbum
sed etiam tertio: *Domine,* inquit, *tu omnia scis, tu
scis quia amo te.*

Hoc propterea commemorandum putavi, quia nonnulli arbitrantur aliud esse dilectionem sive caritatem, aliud amorem. Dicunt enim dilectionem

---

[1] Augustine appears to have in mind here Titus 1.8, where
it is said that a bishop should be φιλάγαθος, which is in-
adequately rendered *benignus* in the Vulgate.

[2] For the entire dialogue see John 21.15–17.

man, but according to God, he is beyond any doubt
called a man of good will because of this love. And
although this disposition is more commonly termed
' charity ' (*caritas*) in holy Scripture, yet it is also
designated as ' love ' (*amor*) according to the same
sacred writings. For the Apostle says that the
person whom he instructs the people to choose as
their ruler ought to be a lover of the good.[1] Moreover, when the Lord himself, speaking to the apostle
Peter, had asked: " Are you more attached (*diligis*)
to me than these? ", the latter replied: " Lord, you
know . that I love you." [2] And the Lord again
inquired, not whether Peter loved him, but whether
he was attached to him, and again he replied: " Lord,
you know that I love you." When, however, the question was put for the third time, even Jesus himself no
longer said: " Are you attached to me? " but: " Do
you love me? ", at which point the Evangelist then
comments: " Peter was grieved because he said to
him for the third time, ' Do you love me? ' " But
actually it was not thrice but only once that the Lord
said: " Do you love me? " For twice he had asked:
" Are you attached to me? " Hence we may infer
that even when the Lord said: " Are you attached
to me? " he meant simply: " Do you love me? "
Peter, on the other hand, did not change the word
used for this one thing but replied the third time
too: " Lord, you know everything; you know that
I love you."

I thought this matter worth mentioning because
some people are of the opinion that attachment or
charity is something different from love. They say
that attachment is to be taken in a good sense, but

289

accipiendam esse in bono, amorem in malo. Sic autem nec ipsos auctores saecularium litterarum locutos esse certissimum est. Sed viderint philosophi utrum vel qua ratione ista discernant. Amorem tamen eos in bonis rebus et erga ipsum Deum magni pendere libri eorum satis loquuntur. Sed scripturas religionis nostrae, quarum auctoritatem ceteris omnibus litteris anteponimus, non aliud dicere amorem, aliud dilectionem vel caritatem insinuandum fuit. Nam et amorem in bono dici iam ostendimus.

Sed ne quis existimet amorem quidem et in malo et in bono, dilectionem autem non nisi in bono esse dicendam, illud adtendat quod in psalmo scriptum est: *Qui autem diligit iniquitatem odit animam suam,* et illud apostoli Iohannis: *Si quis dilexerit mundum, non est dilectio Patris in illo.* Ecce uno loco dilectio et in bono et in malo. Amorem autem in malo (quia in bono iam ostendimus) ne quisquam flagitet, legat quod scriptum est: *Erunt enim homines se ipsos amantes, amatores pecuniae.*

Recta itaque voluntas est bonus amor et voluntas perversa malus amor. Amor ergo inhians habere quod amatur cupiditas est, id autem habens eoque fruens laetitia; fugiens quod ei adversatur timor est, idque, si acciderit, sentiens tristitia est. Proinde mala sunt ista si malus amor est, bona si bonus.

---

[1] Psalms 11.5.   [2] 1 John 2.15.
[3] 2 Timothy 3.2.

love in a bad sense. We can, however, be quite certain that this was not the usage even of writers of secular literature. But I leave it for the philosophers to determine whether and on what principle they make such a distinction. In any case their books bear witness enough that they do highly regard love when it is involved in good things and directed toward God himself. My concern has been to prove that the Scriptures of our religion, whose authority we set above that of all other writings, do not distinguish love from attachment or charity. For I have already demonstrated that love too is used in a good sense.

Lest anyone, however, imagine that whereas love can be used both in a good and in a bad sense, attachment is to be used only in a good sense, let him note what is written in the psalm: " He that is attached to iniquity hates his own soul," [1] and the statement of the apostle John who said: " If anyone has formed an attachment to the world, attachment to the Father is not in him." [2] Here in a single passage we have attachment used both in a good and in a bad sense. Further, in case anyone demands proof of the word love used in a bad sense, since I have already shown it used in a good sense, I would have him read these words of Scripture: " For men will be lovers of self, lovers of money." [3]

A right will therefore is good love and a wrong will is bad love. Hence the love that is bent on obtaining the object of its love is desire, while the love that possesses and enjoys its object is joy; the love that avoids what confronts it is fear, and the love that feels it when it strikes is grief. Accordingly, these emotions are bad if the love is bad, and good if it is good.

Quod dicimus de scripturis probemus. Concupiscit apostolus dissolvi et esse cum Christo; et: *Concupivit anima mea desiderare iudicia tua*, vel, si accommodatius dicitur: *Desideravit anima mea concupiscere iudicia tua;* et: *Concupiscentia sapientiae perducit ad regnum.* Hoc tamen loquendi obtinuit consuetudo, ut, si cupiditas vel concupiscentia dicatur nec addatur cuius rei sit, non nisi in malo possit intellegi. Laetitia in bono est: *Laetamini in Domino et exultate iusti;* et: *Dedisti laetitiam in cor meum;* et: *Adimplebis me laetitia cum vultu tuo.* Timor in bono est apud apostolum ubi ait: *Cum timore et tremore vestram ipsorum salutem operamini;* et: *Noli altum sapere, sed time;* et: *Timeo autem ne, sicut serpens Evam seduxit astutia sua, sic et vestrae mentes corrumpantur a castitate, quae est in Christo.* De tristitia vero, quam Cicero magis aegritudinem appellat, dolorem autem Vergilius ubi ait: "Dolent gaudentque," (sed ideo malui tristitiam dicere, quia aegritudo vel dolor usitatius in corporibus dicitur) scrupulosior quaestio est utrum inveniri possit in bono.

---

[1] Cf. Philippians 1.23.
[2] Psalms 119.20.
[3] Wisdom 6.20.
[4] Psalms 32.11.
[5] Psalms 4.7.
[6] Psalms 16.11.
[7] Philippians 2.12.

Let us now prove our point by the Scriptures. The Apostle " desires to depart and be with Christ ";[1] and, " My soul desired to long for thy judgements," or, to put it more appropriately, " My soul longed to desire thy judgements ";[2] and, " The desire for wisdom leads to a kingdom." [3] Nevertheless, idiomatic usage has brought it about that if the Latin terms for desire, *cupiditas* and *concupiscentia*, are used without any specification of the object desired, they can be taken only in a bad sense. The word for joy, *laetitia*, is used in a good sense: " Have joy in the Lord and exult, O righteous ";[4] and " Thou hast put joy in my heart ";[5] and, " Thou wilt fill me with joy by thy countenance." [6] The term for fear, *timor*, is used in a good sense in the passage where the Apostle says: " With fear and trembling work out your own salvation ";[7] and, " Do not feel proud, but fear ";[8] and, " But I fear that as the serpent deceived Eve by his cunning, so your minds will be led astray from the holiness which is in Christ." [9] But it is a more knotty problem to determine whether the word for grief, *tristitia*, can be found in a good sense. Cicero prefers to designate the emotion that it implies by the word for distress, *aegritudo*,[10] while Virgil uses the word for pain, *dolor*, when he says: " They feel pain and gladness." [11] But I have chosen to use the term ' grief ' because distress and pain are more commonly physical in their connotation.

[8] Romans 11.20.
[9] 2 Corinthians 11.3.
[10] Cf. Cicero, *Tusculanae Disputationes* 3.10.22–23.
[11] Virgil, *Aeneid* 6.733.

SAINT AUGUSTINE

VIII

De tribus perturbationibus, quas in animo sapientis
Stoici esse voluerunt, excluso dolore sive tristitia,
quam virtus animi sentire non debeat.

Quas enim Graeci appellant εὐπαθείας, Latine
autem Cicero constantias nominavit, Stoici tres esse
voluerunt pro tribus perturbationibus in animo
sapientis, pro cupiditate voluntatem, pro laetitia
gaudium, pro metu cautionem. Pro aegritudine vero
vel dolore, quam nos vitandae ambiguitatis gratia
tristitiam maluimus dicere, negaverunt esse posse
aliquid in animo sapientis.

Voluntas quippe, inquiunt, appetit bonum, quod
facit sapiens; gaudium de bono adepto est, quod
ubique adipiscitur sapiens; cautio devitat malum,
quod debet sapiens devitare. Tristitia porro quia
de malo est quod iam accidit, nullum autem malum
existimant posse accidere sapienti, nihil in eius
animo pro illa esse posse dixerunt. Sic ergo illi
loquuntur ut velle gaudere cavere negent nisi sapientem, stultum autem non nisi cupere laetari, metuere
contristari, et illas tres esse constantias, has autem
quattuor perturbationes secundum Ciceronem, secundum autem plurimos passiones. Graece autem

---

[1] Cf. Diogenes Laertius 7.116; Cicero, *Tusculanae Disputationes* 4.6.11–14.

294

VIII

*On the three disorders which, according to the Stoics,
exist in the mind of the wise man, pain or grief
being excluded since the virtuous mind ought
not to experience it.*

THE Stoics have replaced in their system the three
disorders by three corresponding well-ordered states
in the mind of the wise man; these states are called
eupatheiai in Greek and *constantiae* (' stable conditions ') by Cicero in Latin. [1] Thus for desire they
substitute will, for joy gladness, and for fear caution.
They have, however, denied the possibility of any
mental condition in the wise man corresponding to
distress or pain, which I have preferred to call grief
to avoid confusion.

Now will, they say, pursues the good, and this is
what the wise man does; gladness results from the
attainment of the good, which the wise man attains
wherever he may be; caution avoids evil, which the
wise man is bound to avoid. Grief, on the other
hand, arises from evil that has already happened;
hence, since they think that no evil can befall a wise
man, they have declared that there can be nothing
to correspond with grief in his mind. What they
say amounts then to this: only the wise man can
have will, gladness or caution, whereas the fool can
only have desire, joy, fear or grief, and the three
former conditions are well-ordered states while the
four latter are disordered states, which are called
perturbations by Cicero but are generally known as
passions. In Greek the three former dispositions,

illae tres, sicut dixi, appellantur εὐπάθειαι, istae autem quattuor πάθη.

Haec locutio utrum scripturis sanctis congruat cum quaererem quantum potui diligenter, illud inveni quod ait propheta: *Non est gaudere impiis, dicit Dominus*, tamquam impii laetari possint potius quam gaudere de malis quia gaudium proprie bonorum et piorum est. Item illud in evangelio: *Quaecumque vultis ut faciant vobis homines, haec et vos facite illis*, ita dictum videtur, tamquam nemo possit aliquid male vel turpiter velle sed cupere. Denique propter consuetudinem locutionis nonnulli interpretes addiderunt " bona " et ita interpretati sunt: " Quaecumque vultis ut faciant vobis homines bona." Cavendum enim putaverunt ne quisquam inhonesta velit sibi fieri ab hominibus, ut de turpioribus taceam, certe luxuriosa convivia, in quibus se, si et ipse illis faciat, hoc praeceptum existimet impleturum. Sed in Graeco evangelio, unde in Latinum translatum est, non legitur " bona," sed: *Quaecumque vultis ut faciant vobis homines, haec et vos facite illis;* credo propterea, quia in eo quod dixit *vultis* iam voluit intellegi " bona." Non enim ait " cupitis."

Non tamen semper his proprietatibus locutio nostra frenanda est, sed interdum his utendum est. Et

---

[1] Isaiah 57.21 (Septuagint). The Vulgate reads here: *non est pax impiis*.

[2] Matthew 7.12.

as I said before, are termed *eupatheiai*, the four latter *pathê*.

When I was investigating as thoroughly as I could the question whether these terms agree with the language of holy Scripture, I came upon this sentence of the prophet: "There is no gladness for the wicked, says the Lord."[1] This would imply that the wicked are able to feel only joy rather than gladness over evil things because gladness properly belongs to the good and the godly. Similarly, the text in the Gospel: "Whatever you will that men should do to you, do so also to them,"[2] seems to imply that no one can will something in an evil or base sense but may only desire it. Indeed, idiomatic usage has prompted some interpreters to add the expression ' good things ' to this statement, and they have explained it as follows: " Whatever good things you will that men should do to you." For they thought it necessary to guard against the case of someone wishing people to do discreditable things for him—such as extravagant banquets would certainly be, not to mention baser matters, and thinking in regard to such things that he would be carrying out the rule laid down if he too were to do the same for them. But in the Greek Gospel, from which the Latin version was made, we do not read ' good things ' but simply: " Whatever you will that men should do to you, do so also to them." The reason for this, I suppose, is that by his use of the verb ' will ' the writer had already intended that good things be understood, for he does not say ' you desire.'

Yet we must not always bridle our language by restricting it to such special meanings; rather we

cum legimus eos quorum auctoritati resultare fas non est, ibi sunt intellegendae [1] ubi rectus sensus alium exitum non potest invenire, sicut ista sunt quae exempli gratia partim ex propheta, partim ex evangelio commemoravimus. Quis enim nescit impios exultare laetitia? Et tamen: *Non est gaudere impiis, dicit Dominus.* Unde nisi quia gaudere aliud est quando proprie signateque hoc verbum ponitur? Item quis negaverit non recte praecipi hominibus ut quaecumque ab aliis sibi fieri cupiunt, haec eis et ipsi faciant, ne se invicem turpitudine inlicitae voluptatis oblectent? Et tamen saluberrimum verissimumque praeceptum est: *Quaecumque vultis ut faciant vobis homines, eadem et vos facite illis.* Et hoc unde nisi quia hoc loco modo quodam proprio voluntas posita est, quae in malo accipi non potest? Locutione vero usitatiore, quam frequentat maxime consuetudo sermonis, non utique diceretur: *Noli velle mentiri omne mendacium,* nisi esset et voluntas mala, a cuius pravitate illa distinguitur quam praedicaverunt angeli dicentes: *Pax in terra hominibus bonae voluntatis.* Nam ex abundanti additum est "bonae" si esse non potest nisi bona. Quid autem magnum in caritatis laudibus dixisset apostolus, quod non gaudeat super iniquitate, nisi quia ita malignitas gaudet?

[1] intellegendi *most MSS.*

---

[1] Ecclesiasticus 7.13.   [2] Luke 2.14.
[3] Cf. 1 Corinthians 13.6.

should use them only on occasion. And when we read those writers against whose authority it is wicked to rebel, these special meanings are to be understood only in places where the correct sense can find no alternative, as in those passages that I cited for illustration whether from the prophet or from the Gospel. For everyone knows that the wicked exult with joy, and yet, "There is no gladness for the wicked, says the Lord." Such differentiation is possible only because the verbal expression 'to be glad' has a different meaning when it is employed in a special and distinct sense. Similarly, who would deny that it is wrong to instruct men that they should also do to others whatever they desire others to do to them, lest they then regale one another with base and forbidden pleasures? And yet there cannot be a more wholesome or truer injunction than this: "Whatever you will that men should do to you, do so also to them." Why is this so? Only because in this passage the word 'will' is employed in a certain particular way and is not admissible in a bad sense. Yet no one certainly would have used the commoner idiom, to which customary usage especially resorts, to say: "Be it not your will to utter any lie," [1] unless there were also a bad will. A distinction is made between the perversity of the bad will and that other which the angels proclaimed when they said: "Peace on earth to men of good will." [2] For the addition of good was superfluous if will can only be good. Further, what great commendation of charity would it have been to say as the Apostle does, that it finds no gladness in iniquity,[3] if it were not that malice does find gladness thus?

Et apud auctores saecularium litterarum talis istorum verborum indifferentia reperitur. Ait enim Cicero orator amplissimus: " Cupio, patres conscripti, me esse clementem." Quia id verbum in bono posuit, quis tam perverse doctus existat qui non eum " Cupio," sed " Volo " potius dicere debuisse contendat? Porro apud Terentium flagitiosus adulescens insana flagrans cupidine:

> Nihil volo aliud, inquit, nisi Philumenam.

Quam voluntatem fuisse libidinem responsio quae ibi servi eius sanioris inducitur satis indicat. Ait namque domino suo:

> Quanto satius est
> Te id dare operam, qui [1] istum amorem ex animo
> amoveas tuo,
> Quam id loqui quo magis libido frustra accenda-
> tur tua?

Gaudium vero eos et in malo posuisse ille ipse Vergilianus testis est versus ubi has quattuor perturbationes summa brevitate complexus est:

> Hinc metuunt cupiuntque, dolent gaudentque.

Dixit etiam idem auctor:

> Mala mentis gaudia.

Proinde volunt cavent gaudent et boni et mali; atque ut eadem aliis verbis enuntiemus, cupiunt

---

[1] qui *some MSS.*, *Terence:* quo *other MSS.*

---

[1] Cicero, *In Catilinam* 1.2.4.

In authors of secular literature too we discover a
similar failure to differentiate these terms. For
example Cicero, a most accomplished orator, says:
" I have a desire, conscript fathers, to be merciful." [1]
But granted that he employed this word in a good
sense, would there be anyone so pedantically mis-
guided as to maintain that he ought not to have said
" I have a desire " but rather " I have a will "?
Again, in Terence the profligate youth who is hot
with mad desires says: " I have a will for nought
save Philumena." [2] But that this will was lust is
made amply clear by the reply of his more rational
slave, which is brought in at this point. He says to
his master:

> How much better it would be for you
> To make it your business to rid your mind of
> that love
> Than to chatter, uselessly inflaming your lust all
> the more!

Again, we have evidence of their use of gladness too
in a bad sense in that very verse in which Virgil listed
these four disorders with the utmost brevity:

Hence come fear, desire, also gladness, pain. [3]

The same poet also said:

The evil fits of gladness in the mind. [4]

Therefore will, caution and gladness are common
to both good men and bad; and, to express this same

---

[2] Terence, *Andria* 306–308.
[3] Virgil, *Aeneid* 6.733.
[4] Virgil, *Aeneid* 6.278–279.

timent laetantur et boni et mali. Sed illi bene, isti
male, sicut hominibus seu recta seu perversa voluntas
est. Ipsa quoque tristitia, pro qua Stoici nihil in
animo sapientis inveniri posse putaverunt, reperitur
in bono et maxime apud nostros. Nam laudat
apostolus Corinthios quod contristati fuerint secundum Deum. Sed fortasse quis dixerit illis apostolum
fuisse congratulatum quod contristati fuerint paenitendo, qualis tristitia, nisi eorum qui peccaverint,
esse non potest. Ita enim dicit: *Video quod epistula*
illa, etsi ad horam, contristavit vos; nunc gaudeo, non
quia contristati estis, sed quia contristati estis in paeni-
tentiam. Contristati enim estis secundum Deum, ut in
nullo detrimentum patiamini ex nobis. Quae enim se-
cundum Deum est tristitia paenitentiam in salutem in-
paenitendam operatur; mundi autem tristitia mortem
operatur. Ecce enim id ipsum secundum Deum contris-
tari quantam perfecit [1] *in vobis industriam.*

Ac per hoc possunt Stoici pro suis partibus re-
spondere ad hoc videri utilem esse tristitiam, ut
peccasse paeniteat, in animo autem sapientis ideo
esse non posse, quia nec peccatum in eum cadit cuius
paenitentia contristetur nec ullum aliud malum quod
perpetiendo et sentiendo sit tristis. Nam et Alci-
biadem ferunt (si me de nomine hominis memoria non
fallit), cum sibi beatus videretur, Socrate disputante
et ei quam miser esset quoniam stultus esset demon-

---

[1] perfecit *some MSS.* (*cf. the Greek:* κατειργάσατο): perficit
other MSS. (*cf. the Vulg.:* operatur).

---

[1] 2 Corinthians 7.8–11.

idea with other words, desire, fear and joy are emotions of good and bad alike. But the good feel these emotions in a good way, and the bad in a bad way, just as human acts of will are right or wrong. Even the term 'grief,' an emotion to which, as the Stoics held, there was nothing that could be found to correspond in the mind of the wise man, is seen used in a good sense, especially in our own writers. For the Apostle praises the Corinthians for having felt a godly grief. But perhaps someone may say that the Apostle congratulated them on the grief that they felt in repentance—such grief as there can be only on the part of those who have sinned. For here is what the Apostle says: "I see that that letter grieved you, though only for a while. As it is, I am glad, not because you were grieved, but because you were grieved into repenting. For you felt a godly grief, so that you suffered no loss through us. For godly grief produces a repentance that leads to salvation and brings no repentance; worldly grief produces death. For see what earnestness this godly grief has effected in you." [1]

This enables the Stoics to reply in support of their position that grief does indeed seem useful in so far as it represents repentance for sin, but it cannot exist in the mind of the wise man because he is liable neither to sin for which he may repent and be grieved nor to any other evil that may make him grieve as he endures or feels it. A story in point is related about Alcibiades, if I am not mistaken about the man's name. For though he considered himself happy, he burst into tears, we are told, when Socrates in a discussion proved to him how wretched he was

strante, flevisse. Huic ergo stultitia fuit causa
etiam huius utilis optandaeque tristitiae, qua homo
esse se dolet quod esse non debet. Stoici autem non
stultum, sed sapientem aiunt tristem esse non posse.

IX

De perturbationibus animi, quarum affectus rectos habet vita iustorum.

VERUM his philosophis, quod ad istam quaestionem
de animi perturbationibus adtinet, iam respondimus
in nono huius operis libro, ostendentes eos non tam
de rebus quam de verbis cupidiores esse conten-
tionis quam veritatis. Apud nos autem iuxta
scripturas sanctas sanamque doctrinam cives sanctae
civitatis Dei in huius vitae peregrinatione secundum
Deum viventes metuunt cupiuntque, dolent gaudentque, et quia rectus est amor eorum, istas omnes
affectiones rectas habent.

Metuunt poenam aeternam, cupiunt vitam aeternam. Dolent in re quia ipsi in semet ipsis adhuc
ingemescunt adoptionem expectantes, redemptionem
corporis sui; gaudent in spe quia fiet *sermo qui
scriptus est: Absorta est mors in victoriam.*[1] Item

---

[1] victoriam *some MSS. (cf. the Greek:* εἰς νῖκος): victoria
other MSS., Vulg.

---

[1] Cf. Cicero, *Tusculanae Disputationes* 3.32.77.
[2] See above, 9.4–5.

since he was foolish.[1] In his case then foolishness
was the cause of this useful and desirable grief, the
grief of a man who regrets that he is what he ought
not to be. But the Stoics maintain that the wise
man, not the fool, is exempt from grief.

IX

*On the mind's agitations and affections, of which only
such as are right are found in the lives of the
righteous.*

So far as this problem of mental agitations is concerned, however, I have already given my reply to
these philosophers in the ninth book of the present
work.[2] There I pointed out that they are interested
in words rather than in reality and more desirous of
dispute than of truth. Among us Christians, on the
other hand, in accordance with the holy Scriptures
and their sound doctrine, the citizens of the holy
City of God feel fear and desire, pain and gladness
while they live in God's fashion during the pilgrimage
of their present existence, and because their love
is right, all these feelings of theirs are right.

They fear eternal punishment and desire eternal
life. They feel pain over the present because they
are still groaning within themselves as they await
adoption, the ransom of their bodies;[3] they feel
gladness in hope because " there shall come to pass
the saying that is written: ' Death is swallowed up
in victory.' "[4] Again, they fear to sin and desire to

[3] Cf. Romans 8.23.
[4] 1 Corinthians 15.54.

SAINT AUGUSTINE

metuunt peccare, cupiunt perseverare; dolent in peccatis, gaudent in operibus bonis. Ut enim metuant peccare, audiunt: *Quoniam abundabit iniquitas, refrigescet*[1] *caritas multorum.* Ut cupiant perseverare, audiunt quod scriptum est: *Qui perseveraverit usque in finem, hic salvus erit.* Ut doleant in peccatis, audiunt: *Si dixerimus quia peccatum non habemus, nos ipsos seducimus, et veritas in nobis non est.* Ut gaudeant in operibus bonis, audiunt: *Hilarem datorem diligit Deus.*

Item, sicuti se infirmitas eorum firmitasque habuerit, metuunt temptari, cupiunt temptari, dolent in temptationibus, gaudent in temptationibus. Ut enim metuant temptari, audiunt: *Si quis praeoccupatus fuerit in aliquo delicto, vos, qui spiritales estis, instruite huius modi in spiritu mansuetudinis, intendens te ipsum, ne et tu tempteris.* Ut autem cupiant temptari, audiunt quendam virum fortem civitatis Dei dicentem: *Proba me, Domine, et tempta me; ure renes meos et cor meum.* Ut doleant in temptationibus, vident Petrum flentem. Ut gaudeant in temptationibus, audiunt Iacobum dicentem: *Omne gaudium existimate, fratres mei, cum in temptationes varias*[2] *incideritis.*

Non solum autem propter se ipsos his moventur affectibus verum etiam propter eos quos liberari cupiunt et ne pereant metuunt, et dolent si pereunt

[1] refrigescet *some MSS.*, Vulg. (*cf. the Greek:* ψυγήσεται): refrigescit *other MSS.*

[2] in temptationibus variis *a few MSS. The Vulgate is indecisive here, while the Greek reads:* πειρασμοῖς περιπέσητε ποικίλοις.

[1] Matthew 24.12.   [2] Matthew 10.22.

persevere; they feel pain over sins and gladness in good works. For motivation to fear sin they are told: "Because wickedness will be multiplied, the love of many will grow cold." [1] For motivation to desire to persevere they are told in the words of Scripture: "He who endures to the end will be saved." [2] For motivation to feel pain over sins they are told: "If we say we have no sin, we deceive ourselves, and the truth is not in us." [3] For motivation to feel gladness in good works they are told: "God loves a cheerful giver." [4]

Again, depending on their weakness or strength of character, they fear or desire to be tempted and feel pain or gladness amid temptations. For motivation to fear temptation they are told: "If a man is overtaken in any trespass, you who are spiritual should restore such a one in a spirit of gentleness. Look to yourself, each one of you, lest you too be tempted." [5] On the other hand, for motivation to desire temptation they hear a courageous man of the City of God saying: "Prove me, O Lord, and try me; burn my reins and my heart." [6] For motivation to feel pain amid temptations they see Peter weeping.[7] For motivation to feel gladness amid temptations they hear James saying: "Count it all gladness, my brethren, when you meet various temptations." [8]

Moreover, the citizens of the City of God are stirred by these feelings not only on their own account but also on account of those whom they desire to see set free and fear to see perish, whom

---

[3] 1 John 1.8.   [4] 2 Corinthians 9.7.
[5] Galatians 6.1.   [6] Psalms 26.2.
[7] Cf. Matthew 26.75.   [8] James 1.2.

et gaudent si liberantur. Illum quippe optimum et fortissimum virum qui in suis infirmitatibus gloriatur, ut eum potissimum commemoremus qui in ecclesiam Christi ex gentibus venimus, doctorem gentium in fide et veritate, qui et plus omnibus suis coapostolis laboravit et pluribus epistulis populos Dei, non eos tantum qui praesentes ab illo videbantur verum etiam illos qui futuri praevidebantur, instruxit— illum, inquam, virum, athletam Christi, doctum ab illo, unctum de illo, crucifixum cum illo, gloriosum in illo, in theatro huius mundi, cui spectaculum factus est et angelis et hominibus, legitime magnum ago- nem[1] certantem et palmam supernae vocationis in anteriora sectantem, oculis fidei libentissime spectant gaudere cum gaudentibus, flere cum flentibus, foris habentem pugnas, intus timores, cupientem dissolvi et esse cum Christo, desiderantem videre Romanos ut aliquem fructum habeat et in illis, sicut et in ceteris gentibus, aemulantem Corinthios et ipsa aemula- tione metuentem ne seducantur eorum mentes a castitate quae in Christo est, magnam tristitiam et continuum dolorem cordis de Israelitis habentem quod ignorantes Dei iustitiam et suam volentes

[1] magno agone *some MSS.*

---

[1] Cf. 2 Corinthians 12.5 and 9–10.
[2] Cf. 1 Timothy 2.7.
[3] Cf. 1 Corinthians 15.10.
[4] Cf. Galatians 1.12.
[5] Cf. 2 Corinthians 1.21.
[6] Cf. Galatians 2.20.
[7] Cf. 1 Corinthians 4.9.

they are pained to see perish and are glad to see set free. Let us who have come into the church of Christ from the Gentiles particularly call to mind that paragon of virtue and heroism who boasts of his own weaknesses,[1] the teacher of the Gentiles in faith and truth,[2] who worked harder than all his fellow apostles [3] and wrote numerous epistles to instruct not only the people of God who were seen by him at the time but also those whose future existence was foreseen—I refer to that man who was an athlete of Christ, who was taught by him,[4] anointed by him [5] and crucified with him,[6] who gloried in him and who in the theatre of this world, for which he was exhibited as a show before both angels and men,[7] fought a mighty fight according to the rules [8] and pressed forward for the prize of his heavenly calling.[9] With eyes of faith they very happily behold him rejoicing with those who rejoice and weeping with those who weep,[10] beset by fighting without and fear within,[11] desiring to depart and be with Christ,[12] and longing to see the Romans that he may reap some harvest among them too, as he has among the other Gentiles.[13] They behold him feeling jealousy for the Corinthians and in this very jealousy fearing that their minds may be led astray from the holiness which is in Christ.[14] They behold him grieving deeply and suffering constant heartache [15] for the Israelites because, being ignorant of the righteousness that comes from God, and wishing to establish

---

[8] Cf. 2 Timothy 2.5.
[9] Cf. Philippians 3.14.
[10] Cf. Romans 12.15.
[11] Cf. 2 Corinthians 7.5.
[12] Cf. Philippians 1.23.
[13] Cf. Romans 1.11–13.
[14] Cf. 2 Corinthians 11.2–3.
[15] Cf. Romans 9.2.

SAINT AUGUSTINE

constituere iustitiae Dei non essent subiecti, nec
solum dolorem verum etiam luctum suum denuntian-
tem quibusdam qui ante peccaverunt et non egerunt
paenitentiam super inmunditia et fornicationibus suis.

Hi motus, hi affectus de amore boni et de sancta
caritate venientes si vitia vocanda sunt, sinamus ut
ea quae vere vitia sunt virtutes vocentur. Sed cum
rectam rationem sequantur istae affectiones quando
ubi oportet adhibentur, quis eas tunc morbos seu
vitiosas passiones audeat dicere? Quam ob rem
etiam ipse Dominus in forma servi [1] agere vitam
dignatus humanam, sed nullum habens omnino peccatum adhibuit eas ubi adhibendas esse iudicavit.
Neque enim in quo verum erat hominis corpus et
verus hominis animus, falsus erat humanus affectus.
Cum ergo eius in evangelio ista referuntur: quod
super duritia [2] cordis Iudaeorum cum ira contristatus
sit; quod dixerit: *Gaudeo propter vos ut credatis;*
quod Lazarum suscitaturus etiam lacrimas fuderit;
quod concupiverit cum discipulis suis manducare
pascha; quod, propinquante passione, tristis fuerit
anima eius, non falso utique referuntur. Verum
ille hos motus certae dispensationis gratia ita, cum
voluit, suscepit animo humano ut, cum voluit, factus
est homo.

Proinde, quod fatendum est, etiam cum rectas et

[1] dei V, *Eugippius' Excerpts.*
[2] duritiam *some MSS.*

[1] Cf. Romans 10.3.   [2] Cf. 2 Corinthians 12.21.
[3] Cf. Philippians 2.7.   [4] Cf. Mark 3.5.

their own, they did not submit to God's righteous-ness.[1] Aye, and they behold him declaring not merely his pain but also his lamentation for certain persons who had sinned before and had not repented of their impurity and fornication.[2]

If these impulses and emotions that derive from love of the good and from holy charity are to be called vices, we may as well allow the real vices to be called virtues. But since these emotions attend upon right reason when they are shown under proper conditions, who would then dare to call them diseases or morbid passions? Hence, when the Lord deigned to lead a human life in the form of a slave,[3] yet keeping wholly free from sin, even he himself showed these emotions where he judged that they ought to be shown. For the human emotion in him who possessed a real human body and a real human mind was not feigned. Accordingly, when we read in the Gospel these things reported of him, namely, that he was grieved and angered at the Jews' hard-ness of heart;[4] that he said: " For your sake I am glad, so that you may believe ";[5] that as he was about to rouse Lazarus, he even shed tears;[6] that he earnestly desired to eat the Passover with his disciples;[7] that as his passion drew near, his soul was grieved,[8] there is certainly no falsehood in these reports. Rather, he assumed these emotions in his human mind for a definite providential purpose when he chose, just as he had become a man when he so chose.

Therefore, as we must admit, the emotions that we

[5] John 11.15.   [6] Cf. John 11.35.
[7] Cf. Luke 22.15.   [8] Cf. Matthew 26.38.

secundum Deum habemus has affectiones, huius vitae
sunt, non illius quam futuram speramus, et saepe illis
etiam inviti cedimus. Itaque aliquando, quamvis
non culpabili cupiditate, sed laudabili caritate move-
amur, etiam dum nolumus, flemus. Habemus ergo
eas ex humanae condicionis infirmitate; non autem
ita Dominus Iesus, cuius et infirmitas fuit ex potestate. Sed dum vitae huius infirmitatem gerimus,
si eas omnino nullas habeamus, tunc potius non recte
vivimus. Vituperabat enim et detestabatur apostolus quosdam quos etiam esse dixit sine affectione.
Culpavit etiam illos sacer psalmus de quibus ait:
Sustinui qui simul contristaretur, et non fuit. Nam
omnino non dolere, dum sumus in hoc loco miseriae,
profecto, sicut quidam etiam apud saeculi huius
litteratos sensit et dixit, ' non sine magna mercede
contingit inmanitatis in animo, stuporis in corpore.'

Quocirca illa quae ἀπάθεια Graece dicitur (quae, si
Latine posset, inpassibilitas diceretur), si ita intellegenda est (in animo quippe, non in corpore accipitur)
ut sine his affectionibus vivatur quae contra rationem
accidunt mentemque perturbant, bona plane et
maxime optanda est, sed nec ipsa huius est vitae.
Non enim qualiumcumque hominum vox est, sed
maxime piorum multumque iustorum atque sanctorum: *Si dixerimus quia* [1] *peccatum non habemus, nos*

---

[1] quoniam *some MSS., Vulg.*

---

[1] Cf. Romans 1.31.
[2] Psalms 69.20.
[3] Crantor, cited by Cicero, *Tusculanae Disputationes* 3.6.12.

have, even when they are right and godly, belong
to this present life, not to the one that we hope will
come, and we often yield to them even against our
will. Thus at times, though we may be stirred not by
blameworthy desire, but by praiseworthy charity, we
weep even while we would not. It follows then that
we possess these emotions by reason of the weakness
of our human condition; yet this was not so with the
Lord Jesus, whose very weakness derived from his
power. But if we were to feel no such emotions at
all while we still bear the weakness of our present life,
then rather should we not live a proper life. For
the Apostle berated and denounced certain persons
who, he also said, lacked natural affection.[1] The
holy Psalmist too censured those of whom he says:
" I looked for someone to share my grief, and there
was none." [2] For complete freedom from pain,
while we are in this place of misery, surely " befalls
us," as one of our worldly men of letters has said,
stating his opinion, " only at the great cost of
savagery of mind and torpor of body." [3]

In this connexion, let us consider the Greek concept of *apatheia*, ' impassivity ', which, if it could be
rendered in Latin, would be *impassibilitas*, ' impassi-
bility '. If, noting that the term applies to the mind
and not to the body, we are to take it to mean living
without those emotions which come contrary to
reason and agitate the mind, then it is clearly a good
and extremely desirable state; but this no more than
the other belongs to our present life. For the
Apostle speaks not for the common mass of men but
for such as are most godly and very righteous and
holy when he says: " If we say we have no sin, we

ipsos seducimus et veritas in nobis non est. Tunc itaque
ἀπάθεια ista erit quando peccatum in homine nullum
erit.

Nunc vero satis bene vivitur si[1] sine crimine.
Sine peccato autem qui se vivere existimat, non id
agit, ut peccatum non habeat, sed ut veniam non
accipiat. Porro, si ἀπάθεια illa dicenda est cum
animum contingere omnino non potest ullus affectus,
quis hunc stuporem non omnibus vitiis iudicet esse
peiorem? Potest ergo non absurde dici perfectam
beatitudinem sine stimulo timoris et sine ulla tristitia
futuram; non ibi autem futurum amorem gaudium-
que quis dixerit nisi omni modo a veritate seclusus?
Si autem ἀπάθεια illa est ubi nec metus ullus exterret
nec angit dolor, aversanda est in hac vita si recte,
hoc est secundum Deum, vivere volumus. In illa
vero beata quae sempiterna promittitur plane
speranda est.

Timor namque ille de quo dicit apostolus Iohannes:
*Timor non est in caritate, sed perfecta caritas foras mit-
tit timorem quia timor poenam habet; qui autem timet
non est perfectus in caritate,* non est eius generis timor
cuius ille quo timebat apostolus Paulus ne Corinthii
serpentina seducerentur astutia. Hunc enim timorem habet caritas, immo non habet nisi caritas.
Sed illius generis est timor qui non est in caritate de
quo ipse apostolus Paulus ait: *Non enim accepistis
spiritum servitutis iterum in timore.* Timor vero ille

[1] si *omitted in most MSS. by haplology.*

---

[1] 1 John 1.8. [2] 1 John 4.18.
[3] Cf. 2 Corinthians 11.3. [4] Romans 8.15.

deceive ourselves, and the truth is not in us." [1] Consequently, this condition of apathy will come to be only when man is without sin.

At the present time, however, we live well enough if we live without blame. But anyone who thinks that he lives without sin does not actually avoid sin but forfeits forgiveness. Further, if we are to define apathy as the condition that exists when the mind cannot be touched by any emotion at all, who would not consider this torpor worse than all the vices? We can then not unreasonably assert that consummate happiness will be free from the pangs of fear and from any grief; yet who but a person completely debarred from truth would assert that love and gladness will not be found there? Moreover, if apathy is that condition in which there is neither any fear to frighten nor pain to distress, we must avoid it in our present life if we wish to live in the right way, that is, according to God. But in that happy life which, as we are promised, will be everlasting, such a condition is clearly something for which we may properly hope.

The apostle John, it is true, says of fear: "There is no fear in love, but perfect love casts out fear. For fear has to do with punishment, and he who fears is not perfected in love." [2] But this fear is not the same as that which the apostle Paul felt when he feared that the Corinthians might be led astray by the serpent's cunning.[3] Such fear is felt by love and indeed can only be felt by love. But fear that is not a part of love is of that other sort; and the apostle Paul himself says of it: "For you did not receive the spirit of slavery to fall back into fear." [4] That holy

castus permanens in saeculum saeculi, si erit et in futuro saeculo, (nam quo alio modo potest intellegi permanere in saeculum saeculi?) non est timor exterrens a malo quod accidere potest, sed tenens in bono quod amitti non potest.

Ubi enim boni adepti amor inmutabilis est, profecto, si dici potest, mali cavendi timor securus est. Timoris quippe casti nomine ea voluntas significata est qua nos necesse erit nolle peccare, et non sollicitudine infirmitatis ne forte peccemus, sed tranquillitate caritatis cavere peccatum. Aut si nullius omnino generis timor esse poterit in illa certissima securitate perpetuorum feliciumque gaudiorum, sic est dictum: *Timor Domini castus permanens in saeculum saeculi*, quem ad modum dictum est: *Patientia pauperum non peribit in aeternum*. Neque enim aeterna erit ipsa patientia, quae necessaria non est nisi ubi toleranda sunt mala, sed aeternum erit quo per patientiam pervenitur. Ita fortasse timor castus in saeculum saeculi dictus est permanere, quia id permanebit quo timor ipse perducit.

Quae cum ita sint, quoniam recta vita ducenda est qua perveniendum sit ad beatam, omnes affectus istos vita recta rectos habet, perversa perversos. Beata vero eademque aeterna amorem habebit et gaudium non solum rectum verum etiam certum, timorem autem ac dolorem nullum. Unde iam apparet utcumque quales esse debeant in hac pere-

---

[1] Cf. Psalms 19.9.   [2] Psalms 19.9.
[3] Psalms 9. 18.

fear, however, that endures forever,[1] if it is to be present in the world to come (and how else can it be understood to endure for ever?) is not a fear that frightens a person away from an evil that may happen, but a fear that keeps him in a good that cannot be lost.

Where the love of a good thing attained is unchangeable, there surely, if the expression is possible, the fear of an evil to be avoided is carefree. For the words ' holy fear ' signify the act of will by which we shall inevitably refuse to sin and also guard against sin, not because of any anxiety about our weakness for fear that we may sin, but because of a calmness of mind that is the effect of love. Or if no kind of fear at all is to exist amid that absolute and carefree certainty of unending and blessed joys, then no more is implied by the saying: " The holy fear of the Lord that endures forever,"[2] than by the saying: " The patience of the poor shall not perish forever."[3] For patience itself will not be everlasting since it is unnecessary except where evils are to be endured, but the goal attained through patience will be everlasting. Perhaps it is in this sense that holy fear is said to endure for ever, that is, in the sense that the goal to which fear itself leads will so endure.

In the light of these considerations, since we must lead a right sort of life to arrive at a happy life, a right sort of life has all these emotions in a right way, and a wrong sort of life in a wrong way. Moreover, a happy and likewise everlasting life will know a love and gladness that are not only right but also assured, but of fear and pain it will be wholly free. This brings us in any case to a clear view of the kind of

grinatione cives civitatis Dei, viventes secundum spiritum, non secundum carnem, hoc est secundum Deum, non secundum hominem, et quales in illa quo tendunt inmortalitate futuri sint.

Civitas porro, id est societas, impiorum non secundum Deum sed secundum hominem viventium et in ipso cultu falsae contemptuque verae divinitatis doctrinas hominum daemonumve sectantium his affectibus pravis tamquam morbis et perturbationibus quatitur. Et si quos cives habet qui moderari talibus motibus et eos quasi temperare videantur, sic impietate superbi et elati sunt ut hoc ipso sint in eis maiores tumores quo minores dolores. Et si nonnulli tanto inmaniore quanto rariore vanitate hoc in se ipsis adamaverint ut nullo prorsus erigantur et excitentur, nullo flectantur atque inclinentur affectu, humanitatem totam potius amittunt quam veram adsequuntur tranquillitatem. Non enim quia durum aliquid, ideo rectum, aut quia stupidum est, ideo sanum.

X

An primos homines in paradiso constitutos ullis
perturbationibus priusquam delinquerent affectos
fuisse credendum sit.

SED utrum primus homo vel primi homines—duorum erat quippe coniugium—habebant istos

---

[1] That is, people like the Stoics.

life that citizens of the City of God must lead during their pilgrimage here—it is a life lived according to the spirit and not according to the flesh, that is, according to God and not according to man; and we can also see the kind of life that they will lead in that immortality toward which they are moving.

On the other hand, the city or community of the wicked is rocked by those emotions in their perverse form as if by diseases and convulsions. They live not according to God but according to man; and in their very worship of false divinity and scorn for the true divinity they follow the doctrines of men or demons. And if this city has any citizens who seem to control and, as it were, to moderate such emotions, they are so proud and arrogant in their irreligion that on this very account as their pain decreases their prideful swelling increases. And if because of a vanity as monstrous as it is rare some people [1] should be so enamoured of this restraint in themselves that they are not roused or stirred, moved or swayed by any emotion at all, they rather suffer a total loss of humanity than attain true tranquillity. For it does not follow that if a thing is hard, it must be right, or that if it is inert, it must be healthy.

X

Whether we are to believe that the first human beings who were placed in paradise were subject to agitations of any kind before they sinned.

BUT it is quite proper to inquire whether the first human being or rather human beings, since there

319

affectus in corpore animali ante peccatum quales in
corpore spiritali non habebimus, omni purgato
finitoque peccato, non inmerito quaeritur. Si enim
habebant, quo modo erant beati in illo memorabili
beatitudinis loco, id est paradiso? Quis tandem
absolute dici beatus potest qui timore afficitur vel
dolore? Quid autem timere aut dolere poterant illi
homines in tantorum tanta afluentia bonorum ubi
nec mors metuebatur nec ulla corporis mala valetudo,
nec aberat quicquam quod bona voluntas adipis-
ceretur nec inerat quod carnem animumve hominis
feliciter viventis offenderet?

Amor erat inperturbatus in Deum atque inter se
coniugum fida et sincera societate viventium, et ex
hoc amore grande gaudium, non desistente quod
amabatur ad fruendum. Erat devitatio tranquilla
peccati, qua manente, nullum omnino alicunde
malum quod contristaret inruebat. An forte cupiebant prohibitum lignum ad vescendum contingere
sed mori metuebant, ac per hoc et cupiditas et
metus iam tunc illos homines etiam in illo perturbabat
loco? Absit ut hoc existimemus fuisse ubi nullum
erat omnino peccatum. Neque enim nullum peccatum est ea quae lex Dei prohibet concupiscere atque
ab his abstinere timore poenae, non amore iustitiae.
Absit, inquam, ut ante omne peccatum iam ibi
fuerit tale peccatum ut hoc de ligno admitterent quod

was a union of two, felt these emotions in their animal
bodies before they sinned—I refer to the sort of
emotions from which we shall be free in our spiritual
bodies after all sin has been cleansed away and
ended. For if they did feel any such, how were they
happy in that never-to-be-forgotten place of happiness called paradise? Who indeed can be called
completely happy if he suffers fear or grief? On the
other hand, what could cause those people to fear
or grieve where everything was so abundant and so
good, where neither death nor bodily illness was
feared, where there was neither anything lacking
that a good will might want to attain nor anything
present to do hurt to the flesh or mind of a human
being as he lived his fortunate life?

Husband and wife lived in loyal and true partnership, and their love for God and for one another was
undisturbed. From this love sprang great gladness
since the object of their love was always present for
their enjoyment. There was a peaceful avoidance
of sin, and as long as this continued, no evil assailed
them from without to cause sorrow. Or could it be
that they desired to touch and eat of the forbidden
tree but feared to die and that for this reason both
desire and fear already then brought agitation upon
those two even in that place? Heaven forbid that
we should suppose it to have been so where no sin at
all existed! For it is surely sin to desire the things
that the law of God prohibits and to abstain from
them through fear of punishment and not through
love of righteousness. Heaven forbid, I say, that we
should think that before all sin there already existed
in paradise such sin as to cause them to commit in

de muliere Dominus ait: *Si quis viderit mulierem ad concupiscendum eam, iam moechatus est eam in corde suo.*

Quam igitur felices erant [1] et nullis agitabantur perturbationibus animorum, nullis corporum laedebantur incommodis, tam felix universa societas esset humana si nec illi malum quod etiam in posteros traicerent nec quisquam ex eorum stirpe iniquitate [2] committeret quod damnatione [3] reciperet. Atque, ista permanente felicitate donec per illam benedictionem qua dictum est: *Crescite et multiplicamini,* praedestinatorum sanctorum numerus compleretur, alia maior daretur, quae beatissimis angelis data est, ubi iam esset certa securitas peccaturum neminem neminemque moriturum et talis esset vita sanctorum post nullum laboris doloris mortis experimentum qualis erit post haec omnia in incorruptione corporum reddita resurrectione mortuorum.

XI

De lapsu primi hominis, in quo bene condita natura vitiata est nec potest nisi a suo auctore reparari.

SED quia Deus cuncta praescivit et ideo quoque hominem peccaturum ignorare non potuit, secundum

---

[1] erant *some MSS.:* erant primi homines *other MSS.*

[2] iniquitate *V and a few other MSS.:* iniquitatem *most MSS.*

[3] damnatione *V and a few other MSS.:* damnationem *most MSS.*

---

[1] Matthew 5.28.   [2] Genesis 1.28.

regard to the tree the very offence of which the Lord
says, referring to a woman: ' If anyone looks at a
woman lustfully, he has already committed adultery
with her in his heart." [1]

Just as fortunate, therefore, as were the first
human beings, who were neither troubled by any
agitations of mind nor distressed by any ailments of
body, would be the fellowship of all mankind if
neither had the first human beings done an evil which
was to be transmitted also to posterity nor had anyone of their stock sown in unrighteousness what he
must reap in damnation. Moreover, this happiness
would have continued until, through the blessing
granted in these words: " Be fruitful and multiply," [2]
the number of predestined saints was completed;
whereupon they would have received the still greater
gift of happiness that has been granted to the most
blessed angels, a happiness in which there would now
have been the certain assurance that no one would
sin and that no one would die, and in which the life
of the saints, without any previous experience of toil,
pain or death, would have been the same as it will be
after all these things, when the immunity of our bodies
to decay is restored at the resurrection of the dead.

XI

*On the fall of the first man in whom a well-created
natural state was impaired and can be restored
only by its creator.*

But God foreknew all things and must therefore
also have been aware that man would sin. For this

id quod praescivit atque disposuit civitatem sanctam [1] debemus adserere, non secundum illud quod in nostram cognitionem pervenire non potuit quia in Dei dispositione non fuit.   Neque enim homo peccato suo divinum potuit perturbare consilium, quasi Deum quod statuerat mutare conpulerit, cum Deus praesciendo utrumque praevenerit, id est, et homo, quem bonum ipse creavit, quam malus esset futurus et quid boni etiam sic de illo esset ipse facturus.

Deus enim etsi dicitur statuta mutare (unde tropica locutione in scripturis etiam paenituisse legitur Deum), iuxta id dicitur quod homo speraverat vel naturalium causarum ordo gestabat, non iuxta id quod se Omnipotens facturum esse praesciverat. Fecit itaque Deus, sicut scriptum est, hominem rectum ac per hoc voluntatis bonae.   Non enim rectus esset bonam non habens voluntatem.   Bona igitur voluntas opus est Dei, cum ea quippe ab illo factus est homo.

Mala vero voluntas prima, quoniam omnia opera mala praecessit in homine, defectus potius fuit quidam ab opere Dei ad sua opera quam opus ullum, et ideo mala opera, quia secundum se, non secundum Deum, ut eorum operum tamquam fructuum malorum voluntas ipsa esset velut arbor mala aut ipse homo in quantum malae voluntatis.   Porro mala

---

[1] sanctam *a few MSS.:* sanctam eam *most MSS.*

---

[1] Cf. Genesis 6.6; Exodus 32.14; 1 Samuel 15.11; 2 Samuel 24.16.

reason, we must base any doctrine of the holy city on his foreknowledge and dispensation and not on that which could not have come to our knowledge because it was not a part of God's dispensation. Man could not possibly upset the divine plan by his sin, as if he could have compelled God to change what he had decreed, for God through his foreknowledge had anticipated both the coming events, that is, both how bad the man whom he himself had created good would become and what good he himself would use him to effect even so.

God, it is true, is said to change his decrees, and hence we read in Scripture the statement in figurative speech even that God repented.[1] But such a statement is based on man's expectation or on the prospect implicit in the orderly course of natural causes, not on the Almighty's foreknowledge of what he will do. Thus, as Scripture tells us, God made man upright [2] and consequently of good will, for man would not have been upright without a good will. Good will then is the work of God, since man was created in possession of it by him.

On the other hand, the first evil act of will, preceding, as it did, all evil works in man, was rather a falling away from the work of God to the will's own works than any one work; and those works were evil because they followed the will's own pattern and not God's. Thus the will itself, or man himself in so far as he was possessed of an evil will, was the evil tree, as it were, that bore the evil fruit [3] that those works represented. Further, although an evil will is

[2] Cf. Ecclesiastes 7.29.
[3] Cf. Matthew 7.17–18.

325

voluntas quamvis non sit secundum naturam sed
contra naturam quia vitium est, tamen eius naturae
est cuius est vitium quod nisi in natura non potest
esse, sed in ea quam creavit ex nihilo, non quam
genuit Creator de semet ipso, sicut genuit Verbum
per quod facta sunt omnia, quia, etsi de terrae
pulvere Deus finxit hominem, eadem terra omnisque
terrena materies omnino de nihilo est animamque de
nihilo factam dedit corpori cum factus est homo.

Usque adeo autem mala vincuntur a bonis ut,
quamvis sinantur esse ad demonstrandum quam
possit et ipsis bene uti iustitia providentissima
Creatoris, bona tamen sine malis esse possint, sicut
Deus ipse verus et summus, sicut omnis super
istum caliginosum aerem caelestis invisibilis visi-
bilisque creatura; mala vero sine bonis esse non
possint quoniam naturae in quibus sunt, in quantum
naturae sunt, utique bonae sunt. Detrahitur porro
malum non aliqua natura quae accesserat vel ulla
eius parte sublata, sed ea quae vitiata ac depravata
fuerat sanata atque correcta.

Arbitrium igitur voluntatis tunc est vere liberum
cum vitiis peccatisque non servit. Tale datum est a
Deo, quod amissum proprio vitio nisi a quo dari
potuit reddi non potest. Unde Veritas dicit: *Si
vos Filius liberaverit, tunc vere liberi eritis.* Id ipsum

[1] Cf. John 1.3.   [2] Cf. Genesis 2.7.
[3] John 8.36.

not in accordance with nature but contrary to nature because it is a defect, nevertheless it belongs to the natural being of which it is a defect, for it can exist only in a natural substance. But it must exist in the natural substance that God created out of nothing, not in that which the Creator begot from himself, as he begot the Word through which all things were made.[1] For, although God fashioned man from the dust of the earth,[2] this very earth and all earthly matter are derived from nothing at all, and he gave to the body when man was created a soul that was made out of nothing.

But the good things prevail over the bad, so much so in fact that, although bad things are permitted to exist in order to show how the righteous Creator with his perfect foresight can make good use even of them, nevertheless good things can exist without bad, for example, the true and supreme God himself or again all visible and invisible creations in the heaven above our murky air. On the other hand, evil cannot exist without the good since the created things in which it is found are certainly good as created. Moreover, an evil is eliminated not by the removal of some substance, or any part of it, which had supervened, but by the healing and restoration of the substance that had become morbid and debased.

Accordingly, the decision of the will is truly free only when it is not a slave to faults and sins. It had that freedom when God first gave it, but, having lost such freedom by its own fault, it can regain it only from him in whose power it was to grant it originally. Truth says on this point: " If the Son sets you free, then you will be truly free."[3] This is tantamount

est autem ac si diceret: " Si vos Filius salvos fecerit,
tunc vere salvi eritis." Inde quippe liberator unde
salvator.

Vivebat itaque homo secundum Deum in paradiso
et corporali et spiritali. Neque enim erat paradisus
corporalis propter corporis bona et propter mentis
non erat spiritalis; aut vero erat spiritalis quo per
interiores et non erat corporalis quo per exteriores
sensus homo frueretur. Erat plane utrumque propter utrumque. Postea vero quam superbus ille
angelus ac per hoc invidus per eandem superbiam a
Deo ad semet ipsum conversus et quodam quasi
tyrannico fastu gaudere subditis quam esse subditus
eligens de spiritali paradiso cecidit (de cuius lapsu
sociorumque eius, qui ex angelis Dei angeli eius
effecti sunt, in libris undecimo et duodecimo huius
operis satis, quantum potui, disputavi), malesuada
versutia in hominis sensum serpere affectans, cui
utique stanti, quoniam ipse ceciderat, invidebat,
colubrum in paradiso corporali, ubi cum duobus illis
hominibus, masculo et femina, animalia etiam terrestria cetera subdita et innoxia versabantur, animal
scilicet lubricum et tortuosis anfractibus mobile,
operi suo congruum, per quem loqueretur elegit.
Eoque per angelicam praesentiam praestantioremque
naturam spiritali nequitia sibi subiecto et tamquam
instrumento abutens fallacia[1] sermocinatus est

---

[1] fallaciam *some MSS.*

---

[1] Cf. above, 13.21 (pp. 217–221).
[2] Cf. above, 11.13; 12.1 (pp. 3–8).

to saying: " If the Son saves you, then you will be truly saved." For the same act makes a saviour a deliverer too.

Thus man lived according to God in a paradise that was both corporeal and spiritual. This paradise was not merely corporeal to supply the good things of the body without also being spiritual to supply the good things of the mind;[1] nor was it merely spiritual for man to enjoy through his inner senses without also being corporeal for him to enjoy through his outer senses. It was clearly both for the good of both. Then, however, came that proud angel, whose very pride made him envious and also caused him to turn from God to follow himself. With the arrogance, as it were, of a tyrant he chose to rejoice over subjects rather than to be a subject himself; and consequently he fell from the spiritual paradise. I have discoursed as best I could in the eleventh and twelfth books of this work [2] on the fall of this angel and of those leagued with him, the former angels of God who became his angels. After his fall he sought by corrupting guile to work his way into the heart of man, whose unfallen state surely he envied since he himself had fallen. For this purpose he chose as his mouthpiece a serpent in the corporeal paradise, where along with those two human beings, male and female, there dwelt also all the other terrestrial animals, who were tame and harmless. This slippery animal, of course, which moves in twisting coils, was a suitable tool for his work. By his stature as an angel and his superior being he made it subject to him in spiritual wickedness, and misusing it as his instrument he conversed deceitfully with the woman. In so doing

feminae, a parte scilicet inferiore illius humanae copulae incipiens ut gradatim perveniret ad totum, non existimans virum facile credulum nec errando posse decipi, sed dum alieno credit errori.

Sicut enim Aaron erranti populo ad idolum fabricandum non consensit inductus sed cessit obstrictus, nec Salomonem credibile est errore putasse idolis esse serviendum, sed blanditiis femineis ad illa sacrilegia fuisse conpulsum, ita credendum est illum virum suae feminae, uni unum, hominem homini, coniugem coniugi, ad Dei legem transgrediendam non tamquam verum loquenti credidisse seductum sed sociali necessitudine paruisse. Non enim frustra dixit apostolus: *Et Adam*[1] *non est seductus, mulier autem seducta est*, nisi quia illa quod ei serpens locutus est tamquam verum esset accepit, ille autem ab unico noluit consortio dirimi nec in communione peccati; nec ideo minus reus, si sciens prudensque peccavit. Unde et apostolus non ait: " Non peccavit," sed: *Non est seductus*. Nam utique ipsum ostendit ubi dicit: *Per unum hominem peccatum intravit in mundum*, et paulo post apertius: *In similitudine*,[2] inquit, *praevaricationis Adae*.

Hos autem seductos intellegi voluit qui id quod

---

[1] Et Adam *Dombart, Vulg. (cf. the Greek:* καὶ ᾽Αδὰμ): sed Adam *most MSS.:* sed et Adam *or* Adam *a few MSS.*

[2] similitudine *most MSS. (cf. the Greek:* ἐπὶ τῷ ὁμοιώματι): similitudinem *V, Vulg.*

---

[1] Cf. Exodus 32.1–6.   [2] Cf. 1 Kings 11.4.
[3] 1 Timothy 2.14.   [4] Romans 5.12.
[5] Romans 5.14.

he no doubt began with the lower member of that human couple in order to arrive gradually at the whole. Presumably he did not think that the man was readily gullible or that he could be snared by his own mistake, but only if he gave way to the mistake of another.

So was it with Aaron, for he did not agree with the mistaken multitude to construct an idol because he was persuaded, but he yielded to it because he was under pressure.[1] Nor is it credible that Solomon mistakenly thought that he should serve idols; he was driven to such acts of irreligion by the blandishments of women.[2] Similarly, when we consider the situation of that first man and his woman, two fellow human beings all alone and married to each other, we must suppose that he was not led astray to transgress the law of God because he believed that she spoke the truth, but because he was brought to obey her by the close bond of their alliance. For the Apostle was not speaking idly when he said: " And Adam was not deceived, but the woman was deceived." [3] He must have meant that Eve had accepted what the serpent said to her as though it were true, while Adam refused to be separated from his sole companion even in a partnership of sin. Yet he was no less guilty if he sinned with knowledge and forethought. This also explains why the Apostle does not say: " He did not sin," but: " He was not deceived." For he surely refers to him where he states: " Sin came into the world through one man ";[4] and a little later when he says more explicitly: " Like the transgression of Adam." [5]

The Apostle meant us to understand the deceived

faciunt non putant esse peccatum. Ille autem scivit; alioquin quo modo verum erit: *Adam non est seductus?* Sed inexpertus divinae severitatis in eo falli potuit, ut veniale crederet esse commissum. Ac per hoc in eo quidem quo mulier seducta est non est ille seductus, sed eum fefellit quo modo fuerat iudicandum quod erat dicturus: *Mulier quam dedisti mecum* [1] *ipsa mihi dedit, et manducavi.* Quid ergo pluribus? Etsi credendo non sunt ambo decepti, peccando tamen ambo sunt capti et diaboli laqueis inplicati.

XII

De qualitate peccati a primis hominibus admissi.

Si quem vero movet cur aliis peccatis sic natura non mutetur humana quem ad modum illa duorum primorum hominum praevaricatione mutata est, ut tantae corruptioni quantam videmus atque sentimus et per hanc subiaceret et morti ac tot et tantis tamque inter se contrariis perturbaretur et fluctuaret affectibus, qualis in paradiso ante peccatum, licet in corpore animali esset, utique non fuit—si quis hoc movetur, ut dixi, non ideo debet existimare leve ac parvum illud fuisse commissum, quia in esca factum est, non quidem mala nec noxia nisi

---

[1] mecum *some MSS.* (*cf. Septuagint:* μετ' ἐμοῦ): mihi *other MSS.* (*cf. Vulg.:* mihi sociam).

---

[1] Genesis 3.12.

as being those who do not think that what they do is sin. Adam, however, knew; otherwise, how can it be true to say: "Adam was not deceived"? But since he was not yet acquainted with the strict justice of God, he might have been mistaken in believing that his offence was pardonable. Hence, though he did not suffer the same deception as the woman, yet he was mistaken about the verdict that would inevitably be pronounced on this plea that he would make: "The woman whom thou gavest to be with me, she gave it to me, and I ate." [1] To put it briefly then, we may say that although they were not both deceived by believing, yet both were taken captive by sinning and ensnared in the devil's toils.

XII

On the character of the sin committed by the first human beings.

SOMEONE may be moved to wonder why other sins do not change man's nature in the same way as the transgression of the first two human beings changed it. For as a result of that offence it was subjected to all the decay that we see and feel and consequently to death as well. Moreover, man became a prey to agitation and buffeting by many powerful and conflicting emotions and thus developed into something quite different from what he certainly was in paradise before sin in spite of his animal body. Someone, as I said, may be moved to wonder at this, but if so, he must not regard that offence as slight or trivial on the ground that it involved only food—a food not

quia prohibita. Neque enim quicquam mali Deus in illo tantae felicitatis loco crearet atque plantaret.

Sed oboedientia commendata est in praecepto, quae virtus in creatura rationali mater quodam modo est omnium custosque virtutum, quando quidem ita facta est ut ei subditam esse sit utile, perniciosum autem suam, non eius a quo creata est facere voluntatem. Hoc itaque de uno cibi genere non edendo ubi aliorum tanta copia subiacebat tam leve praeceptum ad observandum, tam breve ad memoria retinendum, ubi praesertim nondum voluntati cupiditas resistebat, quod de poena transgressionis postea subsecutum est, tanto maiore iniustitia violatum est quanto faciliore posset observantia custodiri.

XIII

Quod in praevaricatione Adae opus malum voluntas praecesserit mala.

In occulto autem mali esse coeperunt ut in apertam inoboedientiam laberentur. Non enim ad malum opus perveniretur nisi praecessisset voluntas mala. Porro, malae voluntatis initium quae[1] potuit esse nisi superbia? *Initium enim omnis peccati superbia est.* Quid est autem superbia nisi perversae celsitudinis appetitus? Perversa enim est celsitudo, deserto eo cui debet animus inhaerere principio, sibi

[1] quid *or* quod *some MSS.*

---

[1] Ecclesiasticus 10.13. See above, 12.6 (p. 25, note 1).

bad or harmful except that it was forbidden. Indeed, God would not have created and planted anything bad in that place of immense happiness.

But in God's command obedience was enjoined, and this virtue is, in a sense, the mother and guardian of all virtues in a rational creature, inasmuch as man has been naturally so created that it is advantageous for him to be submissive but ruinous to follow his own will and not the will of his creator. This command, which forbade the eating of one kind of food where a great abundance of other kinds lay close at hand, was as easy to observe as it was brief to remember, especially since the will was not yet then opposed by desire. Such opposition arose later as punishment for the transgression. Consequently, the crime of violating the command was all the greater in proportion to the ease with which it could have been heeded and upheld.

XIII

*That in Adam's transgression the evil act was
precededby an evil will.*

WHEN the first human beings began to be evil, they did so in secret, and this enabled them to fall into open disobedience. For the evil act could not have been arrived at if an evil will had not gone before. Further, what but pride can have been the start of an evil will? For " pride is the start of all sin." [1] Moreover, what is pride but a craving for perverse elevation? For it is perverse elevation to forsake the ground in which the mind ought to be

quodam modo fieri atque esse principium. Hoc fit cum sibi nimis placet. Sibi vero ita placet cum ab illo bono inmutabili deficit quod ei magis placere debuit quam ipse sibi. Spontaneus est autem iste defectus quoniam, si voluntas in amore superioris inmutabilis boni, a quo inlustrabatur ut videret et accendebatur ut amaret, stabilis permaneret, non inde ad sibi placendum averteretur et ex hoc tenebresceret et frigesceret, ut vel illa crederet verum dixisse serpentem vel ille Dei mandato uxoris praeponeret voluntatem putaretque se venialiter transgressorem esse praecepti si vitae suae sociam non desereret etiam in societate peccati.

Non ergo malum opus factum est, id est illa transgressio ut cibo prohibito vescerentur, nisi ab eis qui iam mali erant. Neque enim fieret ille fructus malus nisi ab arbore mala. Ut autem esset arbor mala contra naturam factum est quia nisi vitio voluntatis, quod contra naturam est, non utique fieret. Sed vitio depravari nisi ex nihilo facta natura non posset. Ac per hoc ut natura sit, ex eo habet quod a Deo facta est; ut autem ab eo quod est deficiat, ex hoc quod de nihilo facta est.

Nec sic defecit homo ut omnino nihil esset, sed ut inclinatus ad se ipsum minus esset quam erat cum ei

---

[1] Cf. Matthew 7.18.

rooted, and to become and be, in a sense, grounded in oneself. This happens when a man is too well pleased with himself, and such a one is thus pleased when he falls away from that unchangeable good with which he ought rather to have been pleased than with himself. Now this falling away is voluntary, for if the will had remained steadfast in love of the higher unchangeable good that provided it with light to see and kindled it with fire to love, it would not have been diverted from this love to follow its own pleasure. Nor would the will in consequence have grown so dark and cold as to allow either the first woman to believe that the serpent had spoken the truth or the first man to place his wife's will before God's injunction and to think that his transgression of the command could be pardoned if he did not forsake the partner of his life even when partnership in sin was involved.

Accordingly, the evil act, that is, the transgression that involved their eating of forbidden food, was committed only by those who were already evil. For only a bad tree could have produced that evil fruit.[1] Moreover, the badness of the tree was an event contrary to nature, because, except for a defect of will, which is contrary to nature, it could surely not have come to pass. But only a thing created out of nothing could be corrupted by a defect. And consequently, while it owes its existence as a being to its creation by God, yet it owes its lapse from its true being to its creation out of nothing.

Yet man did not lapse so completely as to lose all being, but by turning to himself he ended by having less true being than he had when he was rooted in

qui summe est inhaerebat. Relicto itaque Deo, esse
in semet ipso, hoc est sibi placere, non iam nihil esse
est sed nihilo propinquare. Unde superbi secundum
scripturas sanctas alio nomine appellantur sibi
placentes. Bonum est enim sursum habere cor, non
tamen ad se ipsum, quod est superbiae, sed ad
Dominum, quod est oboedientiae, quae nisi humilium
non potest esse.

Est igitur aliquid humilitatis miro modo quod
sursum faciat cor, et est aliquid elationis quod deorsum
faciat cor. Hoc quidem quasi contrarium videtur, ut
elatio sit deorsum et humilitas sursum. Sed pia
humilitas facit subditum superiori; nihil est autem
superius Deo, et ideo exaltat humilitas quae facit
subditum Deo. Elatio autem, quae in vitio est, eo
ipso respuit subiectionem et cadit ab illo quo non
est quicquam superius, et ex hoc erit inferius et fit
quod scriptum est: *Deiecisti eos cum extollerentur.*
Non enim ait: " Cum elati fuissent," ut prius extollerentur et postea deicerentur; sed cum extollerentur, tunc deiecti sunt. Ipsum quippe extolli iam
deici est.

Quapropter quod nunc in civitate Dei et civitati
Dei in hoc peregrinanti saeculo maxime commendatur
humilitas et in eius rege, qui est Christus, maxime

---

[1] Cf. 2 Peter 2.10.　　　[2] Psalms 73.18.
[3] Cf. Matthew 11.29.

him who has the highest being. Therefore, to leave God and to have being in oneself, that is, to follow one's own pleasure, is not to be nothing already but to come nearer to being nothing. This is why in scriptural language the proud are also called self-pleasers.[1] It is indeed a good thing to have an aspiring mind, yet aspiring not to oneself, which belongs to pride, but to God, which belongs to obedience, and obedience can belong only to the humble.

Accordingly, strange as it may seem, there is something in humility to uplift the mind, and there is something in exaltation to abase the mind. It does indeed appear somewhat of a paradox that exaltation abases and humility uplifts. But religious humility makes the mind submissive to what is superior; hence, since nothing is superior to God, humility elevates the mind in making it submissive to God. On the other hand, exaltation that is connected with a fault automatically scorns subordination and lapses from him who is supreme. This will bring it lower, and the words of Scripture come to pass: "Thou hast cast them down when they were being exalted."[2] Scripture does not say: "When they had been exalted," and thus imply that they were first exalted and afterwards cast down; but at the very moment that they were being exalted, then were they cast down. For the very act of being exalted is already an act of being cast down.

At this time, as we know, in the City of God and for the City of God during its pilgrimage in this world humility is most highly recommended[3] and is also most emphasized in the case of Christ, its

praedicatur contrariumque huic virtuti elationis vitium in eius adversario, qui est diabolus, maxime dominari sacris litteris edocetur, profecto ista est magna differentia qua civitas, unde loquimur, utraque discernitur, una scilicet societas piorum hominum, altera impiorum, singula quaeque cum angelis ad se pertinentibus, in quibus praecessit hac amor Dei, hac amor sui.

Manifesto ergo apertoque peccato ubi factum est quod Deus fieri prohibuerat diabolus hominem non cepisset nisi iam ille sibi ipsi placere coepisset. Hinc enim et delectavit quod dictum est: *Eritis sicut dii.* Quod melius esse possent summo veroque principio cohaerendo per oboedientiam, non suum sibi existendo principium per superbiam. Dii enim creati non sua veritate sed Dei veri participatione sunt dii. Plus autem appetendo minus est qui, dum sibi sufficere deligit,[1] ab illo qui ei vere sufficit deficit.

Illud itaque malum quo, cum sibi homo placet, tamquam sit et ipse lumen, avertitur ab eo lumine quod ei si placeat et ipse fit lumen—illud, inquam, malum praecessit in abdito ut sequeretur hoc malum quod perpetratum est in aperto. Verum est enim quod scriptum est: *Ante ruinam exaltatur cor et ante gloriam humiliatur.* Illa prorsus ruina quae fit in

---

[1] deligit *V and a few other MSS.*: diligit *most MSS.*

[1] Cf. Philippians 2.8–11.
[2] See below, 14.28 (pp. 405–407).
[3] Genesis 3.5.
[4] See above, 9.23. Cf. Psalms 82.6; John 10.34.
[5] Proverbs 18.12; cf. Proverbs 16.18.

king.[1] From the sacred Scriptures we learn also that the fault of exaltation, which is the antithesis of this virtue, reigns supreme in his adversary, the devil. This is surely the great difference that sets apart the two cities of which we are speaking, the one being a community of religious men, the other of irreligious men, each with the angels that belong to it. In one city love of God came first; in the other, love of self.[2]

Accordingly, the devil would not have trapped man by the overt and manifest sin of doing what God had forbidden to be done if man had not already begun to be pleased with himself. This is why he was also delighted with the words: "You will be as gods."[3] But they could better have come to be such if they had through obedience adhered to their highest and true ground and not through pride set themselves up as their own ground. For created gods are gods not by any true being of their own but by participation in the true God.[4] Striving for more diminishes a person, who by choosing to be sufficient unto himself suffers a deficiency in lapsing from the one who is truly sufficient for him.

The initial wrong therefore was that whereby, when man is pleased with himself, as if he were in himself a light, he is diverted from that light through which, if he would but choose it, he himself also becomes a light. This wrong, I repeat, came first in secret and prepared the way for the other wrong that was committed openly. For the words of Scripture are true: "Before a fall the mind is exalted but is humbled before honour."[5] In short, the fall that takes place in secret precedes the fall that

341

occulto praecedit ruinam quae fit in manifesto, dum
illa ruina esse non putatur.   Quis enim exaltationem
ruinam putat, cum iam ibi sit defectus quo est
relictus Excelsus?   Quis autem ruinam esse non
videat quando fit mandati evidens atque indubitata
transgressio?

Propter hoc Deus illud prohibuit quod, cum esset
admissum, nulla defendi posset imaginatione iustitiae.   Et audeo dicere superbis esse utile cadere in
aliquod apertum manifestumque peccatum unde sibi
displiceant qui iam sibi placendo ceciderant.   Salu-
brius enim Petrus sibi displicuit quando flevit quam
sibi placuit quando praesumpsit.   Hoc dicit et sacer
psalmus: *Imple facies eorum ignominia, et quaerent
nomen tuum, Domine,* id est, ut tu eis placeas quarenti-
bus nomen tuum qui sibi placuerant quaerendo
suum.

XIV

*De superbia transgressoris, quae ipsa fuit
transgressione deterior.*

SED est peior damnabiliorque superbia qua etiam
in peccatis manifestis suffugium excusationis in-
quiritur, sicut illi primi homines, quorum et illa dixit:
Serpens seduxit me, et manducavi, et ille dixit: *Mulier
quam dedisti mecum,[1] haec mihi dedit a ligno, et edi.*

---

[1] mecum *some MSS.* (*cf. Septuagint:* μετ᾽ ἐμοῦ): mihi
other MSS. (*cf. Vulg.:* mihi sociam).

---

[1] Cf. Matthew 26.33 and 75.   [2] Psalms 83.16.
[3] Genesis 3.13.

takes place in full view, but the former fall is not regarded as such. For who considers exaltation a fall, though there is already present in it the lapse whereby the Most High is deserted? On the other hand, who could fail to see that there is a fall when a manifest and unquestionable transgression of some command takes place?

This explains why God forbade that act which, when it was performed, could not be defended under any pretext of righteousness. I dare say too that it is useful for the proud to fall into some patent and obvious sin by which they may become displeased with themselves after they had already fallen by being pleased with themselves. Peter was in a healthier state when he was displeased with himself and wept than when he was pleased with himself and too confident.[1] This idea is also expressed in a holy psalm: " Fill their faces with shame, and they will seek thy name, O Lord," [2] that is: " Let those who had pleased themselves when they sought their own name be pleased with thee as they seek thine."

XIV

On the transgressor's pride, which was worse than the transgression itself.

But worse and more damnable is the pride that prompts a man to seek refuge in an excuse even when sins are clear to see. Thus, in the case of the first human beings, the woman said: " The serpent beguiled me, and I ate," [3] and the man said: " The woman whom thou gavest to be with me, she gave

SAINT AUGUSTINE

Nusquam hic sonat petitio veniae, nusquam in-
ploratio medicinae. Nam licet isti non, sicut Cain,
quod commiserunt negent, adhuc tamen superbia in
aliud quaerit referre quod perperam fecit, superbia
mulieris in serpentem, superbia viri in mulierem.
Sed accusatio potius quam excusatio vera est ubi
mandati divini est aperta transgressio. Neque enim
hoc propterea non fecerunt, quia id mulier serpente
suadente, vir muliere inpertiente commisit, quasi
quicquam Deo, cui vel crederetur vel cederetur,
anteponendum fuit.

XV

De iustitia retributionis quam primi homines pro sua
inoboedientia receperunt.

QUIA ergo contemptus est Deus iubens, qui
creaverat, qui ad suam imaginem fecerat, qui ceteris
animalibus praeposuerat, qui in paradiso constituerat,
qui rerum omnium copiam salutisque praestiterat,
qui praeceptis nec pluribus nec grandibus nec
difficilibus oneraverat sed uno brevissimo atque
levissimo ad oboedientiae salubritatem adminicula-
verat, quo eam creaturam cui libera servitus ex-
pediret se esse Dominum commonebat, iusta dam-

---

[1] Genesis 3.12.
[2] Cf. Genesis 4.9.

me fruit of the tree, and I ate." [1]   In these words nowhere do we hear of any entreaty for pardon, nowhere
of any supplication for healing.   For though they do
not deny the offence that they committed, as did
Cain,[2] yet their pride still seeks to lay the blame for
its wrong act on another, the pride of the woman on
the serpent, the pride of the man on the woman.
But where the transgression of a divine command is
manifest, such a pretext is really to accuse rather
than to excuse oneself.   For indeed this transgression was no less their act merely because the woman
committed the offence on the advice of the serpent
or because the man did it when the woman offered
him the fruit, as if there were something that should
take precedence of God when it is a question of
reliance or compliance.

XV

On the justice of the retribution that was meted out to
the first human beings for their disobedience.

MAN, as we know, scorned the bidding of God who
had created him, who had made him in his own image,
who had placed him above the other animals, who
had established him in paradise, who had provided
him with an abundance of all things and of security,
and who had not laden him with commands that were
numerous or onerous or difficult but had propped him
up for wholesome obedience with one very brief and
easy command, whereby he sought to impress upon
this creature, for whom free service was expedient,
that he was the Lord.   Therefore, as a consequence,

345

natio subsecuta est, talisque damnatio ut homo, qui
custodiendo mandatum futurus fuerat etiam carne
spiritalis, fieret etiam mente carnalis et, qui sua
superbia sibi placuerat, Dei iustitia sibi donaretur,
nec sic ut in sua esset omnimodis potestate, sed a se
ipse quoque dissentiens sub illo cui peccando consensit pro libertate quam concupivit duram mise-
ramque ageret servitutem, mortuus spiritu volens et
corpore moriturus invitus, desertor aeternae vitae
etiam aeterna, nisi gratia liberaret,[1] morte damnatus.
Quisquis huius modi damnationem vel nimiam vel
iniustam putat metiri profecto nescit quanta fuerit
iniquitas in peccando ubi tanta erat non peccandi
facilitas.[2]

Sicut enim Abrahae non inmerito magna oboedientia praedicatur quia, ut occideret filium, res
difficillima est imperata, ita in paradiso tanto maior
inoboedientia fuit quanto id quod praeceptum est
nullius difficultatis fuit. Et sicut oboedientia secundi
hominis eo praedicabilior quo factus est oboediens
usque ad mortem, ita inoboedientia primi hominis eo
detestabilior quo factus est inoboediens usque ad
mortem. Ubi enim magna est inoboedientiae
poena proposita et res a Creatore facilis imperata,
quisnam satis explicet quantum malum sit non

[1] liberet *the first hand of V and a few other MSS.*
[2] in non peccando felicitas *V* (in *deleted*) *and one other MS.*

---

[1] Cf. Genesis 22.2; Hebrews 11.17; James 2.21; Wisdom of Solomon 10.5; Ecclesiasticus 44.20.
[2] Philippians 2.8.

just condemnation followed, and this condemnation was such that man, who would have been spiritual even in flesh if he had observed the order, became carnal in mind as well. Moreover, this man who had pleased himself in his pride was then granted to himself by God's justice; yet this was not done in such a way that he was completely in his own power, but that he disagreed with himself and so led, under the rule of the one with whom he agreed when he sinned, a life of cruel and wretched slavery in place of the freedom for which he had conceived a desire. He was willingly dead in spirit and unwillingly destined to die in body; a deserter of the eternal life, he was doomed also to eternal death, unless he were freed by grace. Whoever thinks that condemnation of this sort is either excessive or unjust surely does not know how to gauge the magnitude of wickedness in sinning when the opportunity for not sinning was so ample.

Just as Abraham's obedience is not undeservedly celebrated as great because he was ordered to do a very difficult thing, namely, to slay his son,[1] so in paradise disobedience was all the greater because the command that was given would have involved no difficulty. And just as the obedience of the Second Man is the more laudable because " he became obedient unto death," [2] so the disobedience of the first man is the more abominable because he became disobedient unto death. For where the proposed punishment for disobedience is great and the command of the Creator is easy to obey, who can adequately expound how grave an evil it is not to obey when an easy matter has been ordered by so mighty

SAINT AUGUSTINE

oboedire in re facili et tantae potestatis imperio et tanto terrente [1] supplicio?

Denique, ut breviter dicatur, in illius peccati poena quid inoboedientiae nisi inoboedientia retributa est? Nam quae hominis est alia miseria nisi adversus eum ipsum inoboedientia eius ipsius, ut, quoniam noluit quod potuit, quod non potest velit? In paradiso enim etiamsi non omnia poterat ante peccatum, quidquid tamen non poterat, non volebat, et ideo poterat omnia quae volebat. Nunc vero, sicut in eius stirpe cognoscimus et divina scriptura testatur, *homo vanitati similis factus est.* Quis enim enumerat quam multa quae non potest velit dum sibi ipse, id est voluntati eius ipse animus eius eoque inferior caro eius, non obtemperat? Ipso namque invito, et animus plerumque turbatur et caro dolet et veterescit et moritur, et quidquid aliud patimur, quod non pateremur inviti si voluntati nostrae nostra natura omni modo atque ex omnibus partibus oboediret.

At enim aliquid caro patitur quo servire non sinitur. Quid interest unde, dum tamen per iustitiam dominantis Dei, cui subditi servire noluimus, caro nostra nobis, quae subdita fuerat, non serviendo molesta sit, quamvis nos Deo non serviendo molesti nobis potuerimus esse, non illi? Neque enim sic ille nostro ut nos servitio corporis indigemus, et ideo

[1] terrente *V and two other MSS.:* terrentis *or* terrenti *other MSS.*

[1] Cf. Terence, *Andria* 305–306, quoted by Augustine below, 14.25 (p. 395).
[2] Psalms 144.4.

a power and is attended by the terror of such awful punishment?

To put it briefly then, in the punishment of that sin the requital for disobedience was no other than disobedience. For man's wretchedness consists only in his own disobedience to himself, wherefore, since he would not do what he then could, he now has a will to do what he cannot.[1] In paradise, to be sure, man could not do everything whatsoever even before he sinned, yet, whatever he could not do, he did not have a will to do, and in that way he could do everything that he would. Now, however, as we recognize in his offspring and as holy Scripture attests, "Man has become like vanity."[2] For who can count up all the things that man has a will to do but cannot as long as he is disobedient to himself, that is, as long as his very mind and even his flesh, which is lower, are disobedient to his will? For even against his will his mind is very often agitated and his flesh feels pain, grows old, dies and suffers whatever else we suffer; but we should not suffer all this against our will if our being in every way and in every part gave obedience to our will.

Someone may perhaps protest that the flesh is unable to serve us because of what it suffers. But what difference does it make how this happens? It only matters that through the justice of God, who is our master and to whom we his subjects refused service, our flesh, which had been subject to us, is troublesome by its insubordination, though we by our insubordination to God have succeeded only in being troublesome to ourselves and not to him. For he does not need our service as we need that of the

nostra est quod recipimus, non illius poena quod
fecimus. Dolores porro qui dicuntur carnis animae
sunt in carne et ex carne. Quid enim caro per se
ipsam sine anima vel dolet vel concupiscit?

Sed quod concupiscere caro dicitur vel dolere, aut
ipse homo est, sicut disseruimus, aut aliquid animae
quod carnis afficit passio, vel aspera, ut faciat dolorem, vel lenis, ut voluptatem. Sed dolor carnis
tantum modo offensio est animae ex carne et quaedam ab eius passione dissensio, sicut animi [1] dolor,
quae tristitia nuncupatur, dissensio est ab his rebus
quae nobis nolentibus acciderunt. Sed tristitiam plerumque praecedit metus, qui et ipse in anima est,
non in carne. Dolorem autem carnis non praecedit
ullus quasi metus carnis qui ante dolorem in carne
sentiatur. Voluptatem vero praecedit appetitus
quidam qui sentitur in carne quasi cupiditas eius,
sicut fames et sitis et ea quae in genitalibus usitatius
libido nominatur, cum hoc sit generale vocabulum
omnis cupiditatis.

Nam et ipsam iram nihil aliud esse quam ulciscendi
libidinem veteres definierunt, quamvis nonnumquam
homo, ubi vindictae nullus est sensus, etiam rebus
inanimis irascatur et male scribentem stilum conlidat
vel calamum frangat iratus. Verum et ista, licet
inrationabilior, tamen quaedam ulciscendi libido est
et nescio qua, ut ita dixerim, quasi umbra retri-

[1] animae *some MSS.*

---

[1] See above, 14.2 (pp. 263–267).
[2] Cf. Cicero, *Tusculanae Disputationes* 3.5.11; 4.9.21.

350

body; so that what we get is punishment for us, but what we did was none for him. Further, the so-called pains of the flesh are pains of the soul that exist in and proceed from the flesh. For what pain or desire does the flesh experience by itself apart from a soul?

When we say that the flesh feels desire or pain, we mean that it is either man himself, as I have argued,[1] or some part of the soul affected by what the flesh experiences, whether it be harsh and painful or gentle and pleasant. Pain of the flesh is only a vexation of the soul arising from the flesh and a sort of disagreement with what is done to the flesh, just as the pain of the mind that we call grief is a disagreement with the things that have happened to us against our will. But grief is generally preceded by fear, which is also something in the soul and not in the flesh. Pain of the flesh, on the other hand, is not preceded by anything like fear on the part of the flesh that is felt in the flesh before the pain. Pleasure, however, is preceded by a certain craving that is felt in the flesh as its own desire, such as hunger, thirst and the desire that is mostly called lust when it affects the sex organs, though this is a general term applicable to any kind of desire.

Even anger itself, so the ancients defined it,[2] is nothing but a lust for revenge, although at times a man vents his anger even upon inanimate objects, where no effect of vengeance can be felt, and in his rage smashes his style or breaks his reed pen when it writes badly. But even this lust, though rather irrational, is a sort of lust for revenge and something like a shadowy reflection, as it were, of the principle

351

butionis, ut qui male faciunt mala patiantur. Est igitur libido ulciscendi, quae ira dicitur; est libido habendi pecuniam, quae avaritia; est libido quomodocumque vincendi, quae pervicacia; est libido gloriandi, quae iactantia nuncupatur. Sunt multae variaeque libidines, quarum nonnullae habent etiam vocabula propria, quaedam vero non habent. Quis enim facile dixerit quid vocetur libido dominandi, quam tamen plurimum valere in tyrannorum animis etiam civilia bella testantur?

XVI

De libidinis malo, cuius nomen, cum multis vitiis
congruat, proprie tamen motibus obsceni caloris
ascribitur.

Cum igitur sint multarum libidines rerum, tamen, cum libido dicitur neque cuius rei libido sit additur, non fere adsolet animo occurrere nisi illa qua obscenae partes corporis excitantur. Haec autem sibi non solum totum corpus nec solum extrinsecus verum etiam intrinsecus vindicat totumque commovet hominem, animi simul affectu cum carnis appetitu coniuncto atque permixto, ut ea voluptas sequatur qua maior in corporis voluptatibus nulla est, ita ut momento ipso temporis quo ad eius pervenitur extremum paene omnis acies et quasi vigilia cogitationis obruatur. Quis autem amicus sapientiae sanctorumque gaudiorum, coniugalem agens vitam

---

[1] Cf. Cicero, *Tusculanae Disputationes* 4.9.20.

of retribution whereby they who do evil must suffer
evil. There is then a lust for revenge, which is
called anger; there is a lust for possessing money,
which is termed greed; there is a lust for winning
at any price, which is termed obstinacy; and there
is a lust for bragging, which is termed vainglory.[1]
There are many different kinds of lust, of which some
have special designations also while others have none.
No one, for example, would find it easy to say what
the lust to be overlord is called, though, as even civil
wars attest, it exercises a very powerful influence in
the minds of tyrants.

XVI

*On the evil of lust, a term which, though it is appli-
cable to many vices, is especially ascribed to the
stirrings of obscene heat.*

THEREFORE, although there are lusts for many
things, yet when the term lust is employed without the
mention of any object, nothing comes to mind usually
but the lust that excites the shameful parts of the
body. Moreover, this lust asserts its power not only
over the entire body, nor only externally, but also
from within. It convulses all of a man when the
emotion in his mind combines and mingles with the
carnal drive to produce a pleasure unsurpassed among
those of the body. The effect of this is that at the
very moment of its climax there is an almost total
eclipse of acumen and, as it were, sentinel alertness.
But surely any friend of wisdom and holy joys, who
lives in wedlock but knows, as the Apostle admon-

353

sed, sicut apostolus monuit, *sciens suum vas possidere in sanctificatione et honore, non in morbo desiderii, sicut et gentes quae ignorant Deum*, non mallet, si posset, sine hac libidine filios procreare, ut etiam in hoc serendae prolis officio sic eius menti ea quae ad hoc opus creata sunt quem ad modum cetera suis quaeque operibus distributa membra servirent, nutu voluntatis acta, non aestu libidinis incitata?

Sed neque ipsi amatores huius voluptatis sive ad concubitus coniugales sive ad inmunditias flagitiorum, cum voluerint, commoventur. Sed aliquando inportunus est ille motus poscente nullo, aliquando autem destituit inhiantem, et cum in animo concupiscentia ferveat, friget in corpore. Atque ita mirum in modum non solum generandi voluntati verum etiam lasciviendi libidini libido non servit; et cum tota plerumque menti cohibenti adversetur, nonnumquam et adversus se ipsa [1] dividitur, commotoque animo, in commovendo corpore se ipsa non sequitur.

XVII

De nuditate primorum hominum, quam post peccatum turpem pudendamque viderunt.

Merito huius libidinis maxime pudet, merito et ipsa membra quae suo quodam, ut ita dixerim, iure,

---

[1] ipsam *some MSS.*

---

[1] 1 Thessalonians 4.4–5.

ished, " how to possess his bodily vessel in holiness
and honour, not in the disease of lust like the gentiles
who do not know God," [1] would prefer, if he could,
to beget children without this kind of lust. For he
would want his mind to be served, even in this function of engendering offspring, by the parts created for
this kind of work, just as it is served by the other
members, each assigned to its own kind of work.
They would be set in motion when the will urged,
not stirred to action when hot lust surged.

But not even those who are enamoured of this
pleasure are aroused whether to marital intercourse
or to the uncleanness of outrageous vice just when
it is their will. At times the urge intrudes uninvited;
at other times it deserts the panting lover, and although desire is ablaze in the mind, the body is
frigid. In this strange fashion lust refuses service
not only to the will to procreate but also to the lust
for wantonness; and though for the most part it
solidly opposes the mind's restraint, there are times
when it is divided even against itself and, having
aroused the mind, inconsistently fails to arouse the
body.

XVII

*On the nakedness of the first human beings, which
seemed to them base and shameful after they
sinned.*

It is reasonable then that we should feel very much
ashamed of such lust, and reasonable too that those
members which it moves or does not move by its own

non omni modo ad arbitrium nostrum movet aut non
movet, pudenda dicuntur, quod ante peccatum
hominis non fuerunt; nam sicut scriptum est: *Nudi
erant, et non confundebantur*, non quod eis sua nuditas
esset incognita, sed turpis nuditas nondum erat quia
nondum libido membra illa praeter arbitrium com-
movebat, nondum ad hominis inoboedientiam redar-
guendam sua inoboedientia caro quodam modo
testimonium perhibebat.

Neque enim caeci creati erant, ut inperitum vulgus
opinatur, quando quidem et ille vidit animalia
quibus nomina inposuit, et de illa legitur: *Vidit mulier
quia bonum lignum in escam*[1] *et quia placet oculis ad
videndum.* Patebant ergo oculi eorum, sed ad hoc
non erant aperti, hoc est non adtenti, ut cognoscerent
quid eis indumento gratiae praestaretur, quando
membra eorum voluntati repugnare nesciebant.
Qua gratia remota, ut poena reciproca inoboedientia
plecteretur, extitit in motu corporis quaedam inpudens novitas, unde esset indecens nuditas, et fecit
adtentos reddiditque confusos.

Hinc est quod, postea quam mandatum Dei aperta
transgressione violarunt, scriptum est de illis: *Et
aperti sunt oculi amborum et agnoverunt quia nudi erant,
et consuerunt folia fici et fecerunt sibi campestria.*

---

[1] escam *most MSS. (cf. Septuagint:* εἰς βρῶσιν; *Vulg.:* ad
vescendum): (a)esca *V and two other MSS.*

---

[1] Genesis 2.25.
[2] Cf. Genesis 2.20. The notion of their blindness derives
from Genesis 3.7, cited below.

right, so to speak, and not in full subjection to our will, should be called pudenda or shameful parts as they were not before man sinned; for we read in Scripture: "They were naked, and not embarrassed." [1] And the reason for this is not that they were unaware of their nakedness, but that their nakedness was not yet base because lust did not yet arouse those members apart from their will, and the flesh did not yet bear witness, so to speak, through its own disobedience against the disobedience of man.

For the first human beings had not been created blind, as the ignorant multitude think, since Adam saw the animals upon which he bestowed names, [2] and of Eve we read: "The woman saw that the tree was good for food and that it was a delight for the eyes to behold." [3] Accordingly, their eyes were not closed, but they were not open, that is, attentive so as to recognize what a boon the cloak of grace afforded them, in that their bodily members did not know how to oppose their will. When this grace was lost and punishment in kind for their disobedience was inflicted, there came to be in the action of the body a certain shameless novelty, and thereafter nudity was indecent. It drew their attention and made them embarrassed.

This is why Scripture says of them, after they had violated God's command in open transgression: "And the eyes of both were opened, and they discovered that they were naked, and they sewed fig leaves together and made themselves aprons." [4]

[3] Genesis 3.6.
[4] Genesis 3.7.

Aperti sunt, inquit, *oculi amborum*, non ad videndum, nam et antea videbant, sed ad discernendum inter bonum quod amiserant et malum quo ceciderant. Unde et ipsum lignum, eo quod istam faceret dinoscentiam si ad vescendum contra vetitum tangeretur, ex ea re nomen accepit, ut appellaretur lignum sciendi boni et mali. Experta enim morbi molestia, evidentior fit etiam iucunditas sanitatis.

Cognoverunt ergo *quia nudi erant*, nudati scilicet ea gratia qua fiebat ut nuditas corporis nulla eos, lege peccati menti eorum repugnante, confunderet. Hoc itaque cognoverunt quod felicius ignorarent si Deo credentes et oboedientes non committerent quod eos cogeret experiri infidelitas et inoboedientia quid noceret. Proinde confusi inoboedientia carnis suae, tamquam teste poena inoboedientiae suae, *consuerunt folia fici et fecerunt sibi campestria*, id est succinctoria genitalium, nam quidam interpretes " succinctoria " posuerunt. Porro autem " campestria " Latinum quidem verbum est, sed ex eo dictum quod iuvenes qui nudi exercebantur in campo pudenda operiebant. Unde qui ita succincti sunt, campestratos vulgus appellat. Quod itaque adversus damnatam culpa inoboedientiae voluntatem libido inoboedienter movebat, verecundia pudenter tegebat.

" The eyes of both," we are told, " were opened,"
yet not that they might see, since they could see
already, but that they might distinguish between the
good that they had lost and the evil into which they
had fallen. This also explains why the tree itself,
which was to enable them to make such a distinction
if they laid hands on it to eat its fruit in spite of the
prohibition, was named for that fact and called the
tree of the knowledge of good and evil. For experience of discomfort in sickness gives a clearer insight
into the joys of health as well.

Accordingly, "they realized that they were naked,"
stripped naked, that is, of the grace that kept nakedness of body from embarrassing them before the law
of sin came into opposition with their minds. Thus
they learned what they would more fortunately not
have known if through belief in God and obedience
to his word they had refrained from an act that
would compel them to find out by experience what
harm unbelief and disobedience could do. Therefore, embarrassed by their flesh's disobedience, a
punishment that bore witness to their own disobedience, " they sewed fig leaves together and made
themselves aprons (campestria)," that is, loin-cloths,
a term employed by certain translators. (Moreover,
though campestria is a Latin word, it derives its origin
from the practice of young men who used to cover
up their pudenda while they exercised in the nude
on the so-called campus or field. Hence, those who
are so girt are commonly designated as campestrati.)
Thus modesty, prompted by a sense of shame, covered
what was disobediently aroused by lust against a
will condemned for disobedience.

359

SAINT AUGUSTINE

Ex hoc omnes gentes, quoniam ab illa stirpe pro-
creatae sunt, usque adeo tenent insitum pudenda
velare ut quidam barbari illas corporis partes nec in
balneis nudas habeant sed cum earum tegimentis
lavent. Per opacas quoque Indiae solitudines, cum
quidam nudi philosophentur, unde gymnosophistae
nominantur, adhibent tamen genitalibus tegmina,
quibus per cetera membrorum carent.

XVIII

De pudore concubitus non solum vulgaris sed etiam
coniugalis.

Opus vero ipsum quod libidine tali peragitur non
solum in quibusque stupris, ubi latebrae ad subter-
fugienda humana iudicia requiruntur, verum etiam in
usu scortorum, quam terrena civitas licitam turpitudinem fecit, quamvis id agatur quod eius civitatis
nulla lex vindicat, devitat tamen publicum etiam
permissa atque inpunita libido conspectum, et
verecundia naturali habent provisum lupanaria ipsa
secretum faciliusque potuit inpudicitia non habere
vincla prohibitionis quam inpudentia removere lati-
bula illius foeditatis.

Sed hanc etiam ipsi turpes turpitudinem vocant,
cuius licet sint amatores, ostentatores esse non audent.

---

[1] Cf. Herodotus 1.10; Plato, *Republic* 452c.

Ever since that time, this habit of concealing the pudenda has been deeply ingrained in all peoples, descended, as they are, from the original stock. In fact, certain barbarians do not expose those parts of the body even in the bath but wash with their coverings on.[1] In the dark retreats of India too certain men who practice philosophy in the nude (and hence are called gymnosophists) nevertheless use coverings for their genitals, though they have none for the other parts of the body.

XVIII

On the sense of shame in sexual intercourse, whether promiscuous or marital.

LET us consider the act itself that is accomplished by such lust, not only in every kind of licentious intercourse, for which hiding-places are prerequisite to avoid judgement before human tribunals, but also in the practice of harlotry, a base vice that has been legalized by the earthly city. Although in the latter case the practice is not under the ban of any law of this city, nevertheless even the lust that is allowed and free of penalty shuns the public gaze. Because of an innate sense of shame even brothels have made provision for privacy, and unchastity found it easier to do without the fetters of legal prohibition than shamelessness did to eliminate the secret nooks of that foul business.

But this harlotry is called a base matter even by those who are base themselves, and although they are enamoured of it, they dare not make public dis-

Quid, concubitus coniugalis, qui secundum matri-
monialium praescripta tabularum procreandorum fit
causa liberorum, nonne et ipse, quamquam sit licitus
et honestus, remotum ab arbitris cubile conquirit?[1]
Nonne omnes famulos atque ipsos etiam paranym-
phos et quoscumque ingredi quaelibet necessitudo
permiserat ante mittit foras quam vel blandiri
coniux coniugi incipiat? Et quoniam, sicut ait
etiam quidam "Romani maximus auctor eloquii,"
omnia recte facta in luce se conlocari volunt, id est
appetunt sciri, hoc recte factum sic appetit sciri ut
tamen erubescat videri. Quis enim nescit, ut filii
procreentur, quid inter se coniuges agant, quando
quidem ut id agatur tanta celebritate ducuntur
uxores? Et tamen, cum agitur unde filii nascantur,
nec ipsi filii, si qui inde iam nati sunt, testes fieri
permittuntur. Sic enim hoc recte factum ad sui
notitiam lucem appetit animorum ut tamen refugiat
oculorum. Unde hoc nisi quia sic geritur quod
deceat ex natura ut etiam quod pudeat comitetur ex
poena?

[1] requirit *some MSS.*

play of it. What of marital intercourse, which has
for its purpose, according to the terms of the marriage
contract, the procreation of children? Lawful and
respectable though it is, does it not seek a chamber
secluded from witnesses? Before the bridegroom
begins even to caress his bride, does he not first send
outside all servants and even his own groomsmen as
well as any who had been permitted to enter for
kinship's sake, whatever the tie? And since, as a
certain " supreme master of Roman eloquence " [1]
also maintains, all right actions wish to be placed in
the light of day,[2] that is, are eager to become known,
this right action also desires to become known, though
it still blushes to be seen. For who does not know
what goes on between husband and wife for the
procreation of children? Indeed, it is for the
achievement of this purpose that wives are married
with such ceremony. And yet, when the act for the
birth of children is being consummated, not even the
children that may already have been born from the
union are allowed to witness it. For this right action
does indeed seek mental light for recognition of it,
but it shrinks from visual light. What is the reason
for this if not that something by nature fitting and
proper is carried out in such a way as to be accompanied also by something of shame as punishment?

[1] Cf. Lucan 7.62–63.
[2] Cicero, *Tusculanae Disputationes* 2.26.64.

SAINT AUGUSTINE

XIX

*Quod partes irae atque libidinis quae in homine tam
vitiose moventur ut eas necesse sit frenis sapientiae cohiberi in illa ante peccatum naturae
sanitate non fuerint.*

HINC est quod et illi philosophi qui veritati propius
accesserunt iram atque libidinem vitiosas animi
partes esse confessi sunt, eo quod turbide atque
inordinate moverentur ad ea etiam quae sapientia
perpetrari vetat, ac per hoc opus habere moderatrice
mente atque ratione. Quam partem animi tertiam
velut in arce quadam ad istas regendas perhibent
conlocatam ut illa imperante, istis servientibus possit
in homine iustitia ex omni animi parte servari.

Hae igitur partes, quas et in homine sapiente ac
temperante fatentur esse vitiosas, ut eas ab his
rebus ad quas iniuste moventur mens conpescendo et
cohibendo refrenet ac revocet atque ad ea permittat
quae sapientiae lege concessa sunt (sicut iram ad
exerendam [1] iustam cohercitionem, sicut libidinem
ad propagandae prolis officium)—hae, inquam, partes
in paradiso ante peccatum vitiosae non erant. Non
enim contra rectam voluntatem ad aliquid movebantur unde necesse esset eas rationis tamquam
frenis regentibus abstinere.

Nam quod nunc ita moventur et ab eis qui tem-

---

[1] exercendam *some MSS.*

---

[1] That is, the Neoplatonists.
[2] Cf. Plato, *Republic* 586d–e.

XIX

*That anger and lust, parts that are stirred in man with
such harmful effect that they must be checked and
curbed by wisdom, did not exist in that sound
state of his being before he sinned.*

HERE we have the reason why those philosophers [1]
too who came closer to the truth admitted that
anger and lust are faulty divisions of the soul. They
reasoned that these emotions proceed in a confused
and disorderly way to engage even in acts that
wisdom forbids and that consequently they stand in
need of a controlling and rational mind. This third
part of the soul,[2] according to them, resides in a
sort of citadel to rule the other two parts in order
that, as it commands and they serve, justice in man
may be preserved among all the parts of the soul.

Now as for these two divisions of the soul, those
philosophers confess that they are vicious even in a
wise and temperate man. It is for this reason that
the mind by repression and restraint curbs and re-
calls them from things that they are wrongly moved
to do, but allows them to follow any course that the
law of wisdom has sanctioned. Anger, for example,
is permitted for the display of a just compulsion,
and lust for the duty of propagating offspring. But
these divisions, I maintain, were not vicious in paradise before man sinned, for they were not set going
against a right will in pursuit of anything that made
it necessary to check them with the guiding reins, as
it were, of reason.

For in so far as these emotions are now set going

365

peranter et iuste et pie vivunt, alias facilius, alias
difficilius, tamen cohibendo et repugnando modi-
ficantur, non est utique sanitas ex natura, sed
languor ex culpa. Quod autem irae opera aliarumque affectionum in quibusque dictis atque factis non
sic abscondit verecundia ut opera libidinis quae fiunt
genitalibus membris, quid causae est nisi quia in
ceteris membra corporis non ipsae affectiones sed,
cum eis consenserit, voluntas movet, quae in usu
eorum omnino dominatur? Nam quisquis verbum
emittit iratus vel etiam quemquam percutit non
posset hoc facere nisi lingua et manus iubente
quodam modo voluntate moverentur; quae membra,
etiam cum ira nulla est, moventur eadem voluntate.
At vero genitales corporis partes ita libido suo iuri
quodam modo mancipavit ut moveri non valeant si
ipsa defuerit et nisi ipsa vel ultro vel excitata sur-
rexerit. Hoc est quod pudet, hoc est quod intuen-
tium oculos erubescendo devitat; magisque fert
homo spectantium multitudinem quando iniuste
irascitur homini quam vel unius aspectum et quando
iuste miscetur uxori.

in this way and controlled with more or less ease or
difficulty, yet still controlled, by restraint and opposition on the part of those who lead temperate, just
and holy lives, this is by no means a healthy state
due to nature; it is a morbid condition due to guilt.
Moreover, if modesty does not conceal the actions
prompted by anger and the other emotions in every
word and deed as it does those of lust in which the
sexual organs are used, the reason is simply that in
other cases the members of the body are not put
into operation by the emotions themselves but by the
will, after it has consented to them, for it has complete
control in the employment of such members. No
one who utters a word in anger or even strikes a
person could do so if his tongue or hand were not
set in motion at the command, so to speak, of his
will; and these members can also be set in motion
by the same will even when there is no anger. But
in the case of the sexual organs, lust has somehow
brought them so completely under its rule that they
are incapable of activity if this one emotion is lacking
and has not sprung up spontaneously or in answer to
a stimulus. Here is the cause of shame, here is
what blushingly avoids the eye of onlookers; and a
man would sooner put up with a crowd of spectators
when he is wrongly venting his anger upon another
than with the gaze of a single individual even when
he is rightly having intercourse with his wife.

SAINT AUGUSTINE

XX

De vanissima turpitudine Cynicorum.

Hoc illi canini philosophi, hoc est Cynici, non viderunt, proferentes contra humanam verecundiam quid aliud quam caninam, hoc est inmundam inpudentemque sententiam, ut scilicet, quoniam iustum est quod fit in uxore, palam non pudeat id agere nec in vico aut platea qualibet coniugalem concubitum devitare? Vicit tamen pudor naturalis opinionem huius erroris. Nam etsi perhibent hoc aliquando gloriabundum fecisse Diogenem, ita putantem sectam suam nobiliorem futuram, si in hominum memoria insignior eius inpudentia figeretur, postea tamen a Cynicis fieri cessatum est, plusque valuit pudor, ut erubescerent homines hominibus, quam error, ut homines canibus esse similes affectarent.

Unde et illum vel illos qui hoc fecisse referuntur potius arbitror concumbentium motus dedisse oculis hominum nescientium quid sub pallio gereretur quam humano premente conspectu potuisse illam peragi voluptatem. Ibi enim philosophi non erubescebant videri se velle concumbere ubi libido ipsa erubesceret surgere. Et nunc videmus adhuc esse philosophos

---

[1] The term is derived from the Greek κύων meaning ' dog.'

[2] Cf. Diogenes Laertius 6.69; Athenaeus 4.48; Plutarch, *De Stoicorum Repugnantiis* 21 (= *Moralia* 1044b); Apuleius, *Florida* 14.

XX

On the utterly absurd indecency of the Cynics.

THOSE canine philosophers, or Cynics,[1] were not aware of this fact when they expounded a view offensive to human modesty, a view that can only be termed canine, that is, base and shameless. They held that since the act is lawful when it is done with a wife, no one should feel ashamed to do it openly and engage in marital intercourse on any street or square. Nevertheless, our natural sense of shame has been victorious over this heretical notion. There is, to be sure, a tradition that Diogenes once ostentatiously performed such an act because he thought that his school would win more publicity in this way, that is, if its shamelessness was more sensationally impressed upon the memory of mankind.[2] The later Cynics, however, have abandoned any such practice, and modesty has prevailed over error, that is, the instinct among men to feel ashamed before other men has prevailed over the doctrine that men should make it their aim to be like dogs.

Hence I prefer to think that Diogenes and others who reputedly did such a thing rather acted out the motions of lying together before the eyes of men who really did not know what was done under the cloak. I do not believe that there could have been any achievement of such pleasure under the glare of human gaze. For those philosophers did not blush to seem willing to lie together in a place where lust itself would have blushed to rear its head. Even now we see that there are still Cynic philosophers

369

Cynicos. Hi enim sunt qui non solum amiciuntur
pallio verum etiam clavam ferunt. Nemo tamen
eorum audet hoc facere quod si aliqui ausi essent, ut
non dicam ictibus lapidantium, certe conspuentium
salivis obruerentur.

Pudet igitur huius libidinis humanam sine ulla
dubitatione naturam, et merito pudet. In eius
quippe inoboedientia, quae genitalia corporis membra solis suis motibus subdidit et potestati voluntatis
eripuit, satis ostenditur quid sit hominis illi primae
inoboedientiae retributum, quod in ea parte maxime
oportuit apparere qua generatur ipsa natura quae illo
primo et magno in deterius est mutata peccato; a
cuius nexu nullus eruitur nisi id quod, cum omnes in
uno essent, in communem perniciem perpetratum
est et Dei iustitia vindicatum Dei gratia in singulis
expietur.

XXI

*De benedictione multiplicandae fecunditatis humanae
ante peccatum data, quam praevaricatio non
ademerit et cui libidinis morbus accesserit.*

ABSIT itaque ut credamus illos coniuges in paradiso
constitutos per hanc libidinem, de qua erubescendo
eadem membra texerunt, impleturos fuisse quod in
sua benedictione Deus dixit: *Crescite et multiplica-*

---

[1] Their club is thought to recall a traditional attribute of
Hercules, who was their favourite model.
[2] Genesis 1.28.

among us. They are the ones who not only wrap themselves in a cloak but also carry a club.[1] Yet none of them dares to behave so, for it would bring down upon any who had dared a shower, if not of stones, at any rate of spittle from the outraged public.

Human nature then doubtless feels shame at this lust, and rightly so. For its disobedience, which subjected the sexual organs to its impulses exclusively and wrested them from control by the will, is a sufficient demonstration of the punishment that was meted out to man for that first disobedience. And it was fitting that this punishment should show itself particularly in that part of the body which engenders the very creature that was changed for the worse through that first great sin. No one can be delivered from the meshes of that sin unless the offence that was committed to the common disaster of all and punished by the justice of God when all men existed in but one, is expiated in each man singly by the grace of God.

XXI

That the blessing of increase in human fertility given before sin was not forfeited through transgression but alloyed with the disease of lust.

FAR be it then from us to believe that the couple that were placed in paradise would have fulfilled through this lust, which shamed them into covering those organs, the words pronounced by God in his blessing: " Increase and multiply and fill the earth." [2]

mini et replete terram. Post peccatum quippe orta
est haec libido; post peccatum eam natura non
inpudens, amissa potestate cui corpus ex omni parte
serviebat, sensit adtendit, erubuit operuit. Illa vero
benedictio nuptiarum, ut coniugati crescerent et
multiplicarentur et implerent terram, quamvis et in
delinquentibus manserit, tamen antequam delinquerent data est ut cognosceretur procreationem filiorum
ad gloriam conubii, non ad poenam pertinere peccati.

Sed nunc homines, profecto illius quae in paradiso
fuit felicitatis ignari, nisi per hoc quod experti sunt,
id est per libidinem, de qua videmus etiam ipsam
honestatem erubescere nuptiarum, non potuisse
gigni filios opinantur, alii scripturas divinas, ubi
legitur post peccatum puduisse nuditatis et pudenda
esse contecta, prorsus non accipientes sed infideliter
inridentes; alii vero, quamvis eas accipiant et
honorent, illud tamen quod dictum est: *Crescite et
multiplicamini,* non secundum carnalem fecunditatem
volunt intellegi quia et secundum animam legitur
tale aliquid dictum: *Multiplicabis me* [1] *in anima mea
in virtute,* [2] ut id quod in genesi sequitur: *Et implete
terram et dominamini eius,* terram intellegant carnem,
quam praesentia sua implet anima eiusque maxime

---

[1] me *omitted in a few MSS., Vulg.*
[2] in virtute *some MSS.* (*cf. Septuagint:* ἐν δυνάμει): virtutem
a few MSS., Vulg.: in virtute tua *or* virtute *other MSS.*

---

[1] Augustine has the Manichaeans in mind here.
[2] Psalms 138.3.
[3] Genesis 1.28.

For it was only after man sinned that this lust arose; it was after man sinned that his natural being, retaining the sense of shame but losing that dominance to which the body was subject in every part, felt and noticed, then blushed at and concealed that lust. The nuptial blessing, however, whereby the pair, joined in marriage, were to increase and multiply and fill the earth, remained in force even when they sinned, yet it was given before they sinned, for its purpose was to make it clear that the procreation of children is a part of the glory of marriage and not of the punishment of sin.

There are, nevertheless, in our own day men who must surely lack knowledge of that former happiness in paradise, for they believe that children could only have been engendered by the means with which they are personally acquainted, that is, by lust, which, as we see, causes embarrassment even to the honourable state of marriage. Some of these men [1] not merely reject outright but unbelievingly deride the holy Scriptures, in which we read that after sin nakedness caused shame and the organs of shame were covered. Others among them, on the other hand, accept and honour the Scriptures but hold that the words ' Increase and multiply ' are not to be taken as referring to carnal fertility because some similar statement is also found with reference to the soul: " Thou wilt multiply me with strength in my soul." [2] Relying on this passage, they interpret allegorically the words that follow in *Genesis:* " Both fill the earth and be masters of it." [3] By earth they understand the flesh which the soul fills with its presence and over which it has greatest mastery when it is multi-

dominatur cum in virtute multiplicatur; carnales
autem fetus sine libidine, quae post peccatum exorta
inspecta, confusa, velata est, nec tunc nasci potuisse,
sicut neque nunc possunt, nec in paradiso futuros
fuisse, sed foris, sicut et factum est. Nam postea
quam inde dimissi sunt, ad gignendos filios coierunt
eosque genuerunt.

XXII

*De copula coniugali a Deo primitus instituta atque
benedicta.*

Nos autem nullo modo dubitamus secundum benedictionem Dei crescere et multiplicari et implere
terram donum esse nuptiarum, quas Deus ante peccatum hominis ab initio constituit, creando masculum
et feminam, qui sexus evidens utique in carne est.
Huic quippe operi Dei etiam benedictio ipsa sub-
iuncta est. Nam cum scriptura dixisset: *Masculum
et feminam fecit eos*, continuo subdidit: *Et benedixit
eos Deus dicens: Crescite et multiplicamini et implete
terram et dominamini eius*, et cetera.

Quae omnia quamquam non inconvenienter possint etiam ad intellectum spiritalem referri, masculum tamen et feminam non sicut simile aliquid etiam
in homine uno intellegi potest quia videlicet in eo
aliud est quod regit, aliud quod regitur. Sed sicut

---

[1] Genesis 1.27–28.

plied in inner strength, or virtue. But carnal offspring, they maintain, could no more have been
born then than now without lust, which arose after
man sinned, was observed with embarrassment and
concealed, and they would not have been born in
paradise but only outside it, as in fact happened.
For it was after the first couple had been sent away
from there that they united to beget children and
did beget them.

XXII

*On the matrimonial bond as originally established and
blessed by God.*

I MYSELF, however, have no doubt at all that to
increase, multiply and fill the earth in accordance
with the blessing of God is a gift of marriage and that
God established this institution from the beginning
before man's fall by the creation of male and female;
the difference in sex is in any case clear enough in
the flesh. It was also with this work of God that the
blessing itself was connected, for immediately after
the scriptural words: " Male and female he created
them," there was added: " And God blessed them,
and God said to them: ' Increase and multiply and
fill the earth and be masters of it,' "[1] and so on.

Granted that all this can without impropriety be
taken in a spiritual sense, yet we cannot understand
' male ' and ' female ' as figurative terms referring
to any analogy in a single human being on the ground
that in him, as we know, there is one element that
rules and another that is ruled. As the bodies of

evidentissime apparet in diversi sexus corporibus, masculum et feminam ita creatos ut prolem generando crescerent et multiplicarentur et implerent terram magnae absurditatis est reluctari. Neque enim de spiritu qui imperat et carne quae obtemperat, aut de animo rationali qui regit et inrationali cupiditate quae regitur, aut de virtute contemplativa quae excellit et de activa quae subditur, aut de intellectu mentis et sensu corporis, sed aperte de vinculo coniugali quo invicem sibi uterque sexus obstringitur, Dominus interrogatus utrum liceret quacumque causa dimittere uxorem, quoniam propter duritiam cordis Israelitarum Moyses dari permisit libellum repudii, respondit atque ait: *Non legistis quia qui fecit ab initio masculum et feminam fecit eos et dixit: Propter hoc dimittet homo patrem et matrem et adhaerebit uxori suae, et erunt duo in carne una? Itaque iam non sunt duo, sed una caro. Quod ergo Deus coniunxit, homo non separet.*

Certum est igitur masculum et feminam ita primitus institutos ut nunc homines duos diversi sexus videmus et novimus, unum autem dici vel propter coniunctionem vel propter originem feminae, quae de masculi latere creata est. Nam et apostolus per hoc primum, quod Deo instituente praecessit, exemplum singulos quosque admonet ut viri uxores suas diligant.

---

[1] Matthew 19.4–6.
[2] Cf. Ephesians 5.25–33; Colossians 3.19.

different sex make abundantly clear, it is the height of absurdity to deny that male and female were created as they were to increase, multiply and fill the earth by begetting offspring. For when the Lord was asked whether it was permitted to divorce one's wife on any grounds whatever, since Moses allowed the Israelites to give a bill of divorcement on account of their hardness of heart, his reply did not concern the spirit which commands and the flesh which obeys, or the rational mind which rules and the irrational desire which is ruled, or the contemplative virtue which is superior and the active virtue which is subordinate, or the understanding of the mind and the sensation of the body, but it plainly referred to the marriage tie which binds both sexes to one another. In this answer he said: " Have you not read that he who made them from the beginning made them male and female, and said, ' For this reason a man shall leave his father and mother and be joined to his wife, and the two shall become one flesh '? So they are no longer two but one flesh. What therefore God has joined together, let not man put asunder." [1]

There is no doubt then that from the very beginning male and female were fashioned in quite the same way as we see and know two human beings of different sex to be now and that they are called ' one ' either because of their union or because of the origin of the female, who was created from the side of the male. For the Apostle too invoked this first example, which God instituted as a precedent, to admonish each and every one that husbands should love their wives.[2]

XXIII

An etiam in paradiso generandum fuisset si nemo
peccasset, vel utrum contra aestum libidinis
pugnatura illic fuisset ratio castitatis.

QUISQUIS autem dicit non fuisse coituros nec genera-
turos nisi peccassent, quid dicit nisi propter numerosi-
tatem sanctorum necessarium hominis fuisse peccatum? Si enim non peccando soli remanerent quia,
sicut putant, nisi peccassent, generare non possent,
profecto ut non soli duo iusti homines possent esse
sed multi, necessarium peccatum fuit. Quod si
credere absurdum est, illud potius est credendum,
quod sanctorum numerus quantus conplendae illi
sufficit beatissimae civitati, tantus existeret etsi
nemo peccasset, quantus nunc per Dei gratiam de
multitudine colligitur peccatorum, quo usque filii
saeculi huius generant et generantur.

Et ideo illae nuptiae dignae felicitate paradisi, si
peccatum non fuisset, et diligendam prolem gig-
nerent et pudendam libidinem non haberent. Sed
quo modo id fieri posset, nunc non est quo demonstretur exemplo. Nec ideo tamen incredibile debet
videri etiam illud unum sine ista libidine voluntati
potuisse servire, cui tot membra nunc serviunt. An

---

[1] Cf. Luke 20.34.

XXIII

Whether procreation would have been allowed even in paradise if no one had sinned, or whether the principle of chastity would have fought there against the ardour of lust.

WHEN anyone says that there would have been no copulation or generation if the first human beings had not sinned, does he not imply that man's sin was required to complete the number of saints? For if by not sinning they would have continued to be solitary because, so some think, they could not have produced offspring if they had not sinned, then surely sin was required before there could be not just two but many righteous persons. But if that is too absurd to believe, we must rather believe that even if no one had sinned, a sufficiently large number of saints would have come into existence to populate that supremely happy city—as large a number, that is, as are now being gathered through the grace of God from the multitude of sinners, and as will be, so long as " the children of this world " beget and are begotten.[1]

This leads to the conclusion that if no sin had been committed, that marriage, being worthy of the happiness of paradise, would have produced offspring to be loved, yet no lust to cause shame. But there is now no example with which to illustrate how this could have been effected. Nevertheless, that is no reason why it should seem incredible that the will, which is now obeyed by so many members, might also have been obeyed in the absence of this lust by

vero manus et pedes movemus, cum volumus, ad ea quae his membris agenda sunt sine ullo renisu, tanta facilitate quanta et in nobis et in aliis videmus, maxime in artificibus quorumque operum corporalium ubi ad exercendam infirmiorem tardioremque naturam agilior accessit industria, et non credimus ad opus generationis filiorum, si libido non fuisset, quae peccato inoboedientiae retributa est, oboedienter hominibus ad voluntatis nutum similiter ut cetera potuisse illa membra servire?

Nonne [1] Cicero in libris de re publica, cum de imperiorum differentia disputaret et huius rei similitudinem ex natura hominis adsumeret, ut filiis dixit imperari corporis membris propter oboediendi facilitatem, vitiosas vero animi partes ut servos asperiore imperio coherceri? Et utique ordine naturali animus anteponitur corpori, et tamen ipse animus imperat corpori facilius quam sibi. Verum tamen haec libido, de qua nunc disserimus, eo magis erubescenda extitit [2] quod animus in ea nec sibi efficaciter imperat ut omnino non libeat nec omni modo corpori ut pudenda membra voluntas potius quam libido commoveat. Quod si ita esset, pudenda non essent.

Nunc vero pudet animum resisti sibi a corpore, quod ei natura inferiore subiectum est. In aliis

[1] nonne hoc *some MSS.*
[2] existit *some MSS.*

---

[1] Cf. Cicero, *De Re Publica* 3.25.37.

that one part as well. Consider how, when we choose, we set our hands and feet in motion to do the things that are theirs to do, how we manage this without any conflict and with all the facility that we see both in our own case and in that of others, especially among workers in all kinds of physical tasks, where a natural capacity that is too weak and slow is fitted for its employment by the application of greater dexterity and effort. May we not similarly believe that those organs of procreation could, like the others, have served mankind by obedience to the decision of the will for the generation of children even if there had been no lust inflicted as punishment for the sin of disobedience?

When in his discussion of the different forms of rule in his work entitled *On the Commonwealth* Cicero drew an analogy for his purpose from human nature, did he not say that the members of the body are ruled like children because of their readiness to obey, whereas the depraved parts of the soul are constrained like slaves by a harsher rule?[1] No doubt, in the order of nature, the soul ranks above the body, yet the soul itself finds it easier to rule the body than to rule itself. Nevertheless, this lust that we are now discussing is something all the more shameful because under its effect the soul neither succeeds in ruling itself so as to have no lust at all nor controls the body completely in such a way that the organs of shame are set in motion by the will rather than by lust. Indeed, if such were the case, they would no be organs of shame.

As things now stand, the soul is ashamed of the body's opposition to it, for the body is subject to it

quippe affectionibus cum sibi resistit, ideo minus
pudet, quia, cum a se ipso vincitur, ipse se vincit;
etsi inordinate atque vitiose quia ex his partibus quae
rationi subici debent, tamen a partibus suis ac per
hoc, ut dictum est, a se ipso vincitur. Nam cum
ordinate se animus vincit, ut inrationabiles [1] motus
eius menti rationique subdantur, si tamen et illa Deo
subdita est, laudis atque virtutis est. Minus tamen
pudet cum sibi animus ex vitiosis suis partibus non
obtemperat quam cum ei corpus, quod alterum ab
illo est atque infra illum est et cuius sine illo natura
non vivit, volenti iubentique non cedit.

Sed cum alia membra retinentur voluntatis imperio, sine quibus illa quae contra voluntatem libidine
concitantur id quod appetunt implere non possunt,
pudicitia custoditur, non amissa sed non permissa
delectatione peccati. Hunc renisum, hanc repug-
nantiam, hanc voluntatis et libidinis rixam vel certe
ad voluntatis sufficientiam libidinis indigentiam procul dubio, nisi culpabilis inoboedientia poenali
inoboedientia plecteretur, in paradiso nuptiae non
haberent, sed voluntati membra, ut cetera, ita cuncta
servirent.

Ita genitale arvum vas in hoc opus creatum seminaret, ut nunc terram manus, et quod modo de hac

---

[1] inrationabiles *one late MS., Dombart, as elsewhere preferred by* Augustine: inrationales *most MSS.*

because of its lower nature. When the soul opposes itself in the case of other emotions, it feels less ashamed because when it is vanquished by itself, the soul is its own vanquisher. Although this victory of soul over soul is disorderly and morbid because it is a victory of constituents that should be subject to reason, yet it is a victory of its own constituents and therefore, as was said, a self-conquest. For when the soul vanquishes itself in an orderly fashion and thus subordinates its irrational emotions to the rule of a rational purpose, such a victory is laudable and virtuous, provided that its purpose in turn is subordinate to God. Still, the soul feels less ashamed when it is not obeyed by its own depraved constituents than when its will and bidding are not heeded by the body, which is different from it and inferior to it and has a substance that has no life without it.

But when a curb is imposed by the will's authority on the body's other members, without which those organs that are excited by lust in defiance of the will cannot fulfil their craving, chastity is safeguarded, not because the pleasure of sinning has disappeared, but because it is not allowed to appear. If culpable disobedience had not been punished with disobedience in retribution, then doubtless the marriage in paradise would not have experienced this resistance, this opposition, this conflict of will and lust or, at any rate, the deficiency of lust as against the sufficiency of will; rather, the will would have been obeyed not only by other members of the body but by all alike.

Under those circumstances, the organ created for this work would have sown its seed upon the field of

383

re nobis volentibus diligentius disputare verecundia
resistit et compellit veniam, honore praefato, a
pudicis auribus poscere, cur id fieret nulla causa esset,
sed in omnia quae de huius modi membris sensum
cogitantis adtingerent sine ullo timore obscenitatis
liber sermo ferretur, nec ipsa verba essent quae
vocarentur obscena, sed quidquid inde diceretur tam
honestum esset quam de aliis cum loquimur corporis
partibus. Quisquis ergo ad has litteras inpudicus
accedit culpam refugiat, non naturam. Facta deno-
tet suae turpitudinis, non verba nostrae necessitatis,
in quibus mihi facillime pudicus et religiosus lector
vel auditor ignoscit donec infidelitatem refellam, non
de fide rerum inexpertarum, sed de sensu exper-
tarum argumentantem. Legit enim haec sine
offensione qui non exhorret apostolum horrenda
feminarum flagitia reprehendentem, quae *inmutaverunt naturalem usum in eum usum qui est contra
naturam*, praecipue quia nos non damnabilem obsceni-
tatem nunc, sicut ille, commemoramus atque repre-
hendimus, sed in explicandis, quantum possumus,
humanae generationis effectibus verba tamen, sicut
ille, obscena vitamus.

generation,[1] as the hand does now upon the earth. And though I am now hampered by modesty when I wish to treat this subject in greater detail, and am compelled to apologize to chaste ears and to ask their pardon, there would then have been no reason for this to happen. Discussion, free and unencumbered by any fear of obscenity, would range over every aspect that might occur to the thought of anyone who reflected on bodily parts of this sort. There would not even be words that could be called obscene, but all our talk on this subject would be as decent as what we say in speaking about the other members of the body. Accordingly, if anyone approaches in a wanton spirit what I have written here, let him shun any guilt on his own part, not the natural facts. Let him censure the deeds of his own depravity, not the words of my necessity. Herein I shall very readily be pardoned by the chaste and devout reader or listener as long as I refute the scepticism which relies for argument not on the faith in things unexperienced, but on the perception of things experienced. For these words of mine will give no offence to the reader who is not appalled by the Apostle's censure of the appalling immoralities of the women who " exchanged natural relations for unnatural," [2] especially since I am not, like the Apostle, now bringing up and censuring damnable lewdness. Still, in explaining, as best I can, the working of human generation I try, like him, to avoid the use of lewd terms.

[1] Cf. Virgil, *Georgica* 3.136.
[2] Romans 1.26.

XXIV

*Quod insontes homines et merito oboedientiae in
paradiso permanentes ita genitalibus membris
usuri fuissent ad generationem prolis sicut
ceteris, ad arbitrium voluntatis.*

SEMINARET igitur prolem vir, susciperet femina
genitalibus membris quando id opus esset et quantum opus esset, voluntate motis, non libidine con-
citatis. Neque enim ea sola membra movemus ad
nutum quae conpactis articulata sunt ossibus, sicut
manus et pedes et digitos, verum etiam illa quae
mollibus remissa sunt nervis, cum volumus, movemus
agitando et porrigendo producimus et torquendo
flectimus et constringendo duramus, sicut ea sunt
quae in ore ac facie, quantum potest, voluntas movet.
Pulmones denique ipsi, omnium, nisi medullarum,
mollissimi viscerum et ob hoc antro pectoris com-
muniti, ad spiritum ducendum ac remittendum
vocemque emittendam seu modificandam, sicut folles
fabrorum vel organorum, flantis, respirantis, lo-
quentis, clamantis, cantantis serviunt voluntati.

Omitto quod animalibus quibusdam naturaliter
inditum est, ut tegmen, quo corpus omne vestitur,
si quid in quocumque loco eius senserint abigendum,

386

XXIV

*That if human beings had remained innocent and had
earned the right to stay in paradise by their
obedience, they would have used their genital
organs for the procreation of offspring in
the same way as they used the rest, that
is, at the discretion of the will.*

THE seed of offspring then would have been sown
by the man and received by the woman at such time
and in such amount as was needed, their genital
organs being directed by the will and not excited by
lust. For we move at our bidding not only those
members which have joints and solid bones, like
hands, feet and fingers, but we can at will shake and
move, stretch and extend, twist and bend or contract
and stiffen even the parts that are slackly composed
of soft muscular tissue, like those which the will
moves, as far as it can, in the mouth and face. Indeed, even the lungs, which, except for the marrows,
are the most delicate of all the internal organs and for
that reason are sheltered in the cavity of the chest,
are made to function in this way for the purpose of
drawing in and expelling the breath and uttering
or modulating a sound; for just as bellows serve the
will of blacksmiths or organists, so lungs serve the
will of anyone who blows out or draws in his breath
or speaks or shouts or sings.

I shall not dwell on the natural endowment of
certain animals in connexion with the covering that
clothes their entire body; suffice it to say that if in
any part of it they feel anything that should be driven

ibi tantum moveant ubi sentiunt, nec solum insi-
dentes muscas verum etiam haerentes hastas cutis
tremore discutiant. Numquid quia id non potest
homo, ideo Creator quibus voluit animantibus donare
non potuit? Sic ergo et ipse homo potuit oboedientiam etiam inferiorum habere membrorum, quam
sua inoboedientia perdidit. Neque enim Deo difficile fuit sic illum condere ut in eius carne etiam illud
non nisi eius voluntate moveretur quod nunc nisi
libidine non movetur.

Nam et hominum quorundam naturas novimus
multum ceteris dispares et ipsa raritate mirabiles
nonnulla ut volunt de corpore facientium quae alii
nullo modo possunt et audita vix credunt. Sunt
enim qui et aures moveant vel singulas vel ambas
simul. Sunt qui totam caesariem, capite inmoto,
quantum capilli occupant, deponunt ad frontem
revocantque cum volunt. Sunt qui eorum quae
voraverint incredibiliter plurima et varia, paululum
praecordiis contrectatis, tamquam de sacculo quod
placuerit integerrimum proferunt. Quidam voces
avium pecorumque et aliorum quorumlibet hominum
sic imitantur atque exprimunt ut, nisi videantur,
discerni omnino non possint. Nonnulli ab imo sine
paedore ullo ita numerosos pro arbitrio sonitus edunt

off, they are able to make it move just at the point
where they feel the object and to dislodge with a
quiver of their hide not only flies settled upon them
but also spears sticking in them. Granted that man
does not have this faculty, yet surely it does not
follow that the creator was unable to grant it to such
animate beings as he chose. Hence man himself
too may once have commanded even from his lower
members an obedience that by his own disobedience
he has lost. For it was not difficult for God to design
him in such a way that even what now is moved in
his flesh only by lust was then moved only by his
will.

Certain human beings too, as we know, have
natural endowments that are quite different from
those of others and remarkable for their very rarity.
They can at will do with their bodies some things
that others find utterly impossible to imitate and
scarcely credible to hear. For some people can
actually move their ears, either one at a time or both
together. Other people, without moving their head,
can bring all the scalp that is covered with hair to
the forefront and then draw it back again at will.
Others can swallow an astonishing number of different
objects and then, with a very slight contraction of
their diaphragm, bring forth, as though from a bag,
whatever item they please in perfect condition.
Certain people mimic and render so expertly the
utterances of birds and beasts, as well as of any other
human beings, that it is impossible to tell the difference unless they are seen. Some people produce
at will without any stench such rhythmical sounds
from their fundament that they appear to be making

ut ex illa etiam parte cantare videantur. Ipse sum
expertus sudare hominem solere cum vellet. Notum
est quosdam flere cum volunt atque ubertim lacrimas
fundere.

Iam illud multo est incredibilius quod plerique
fratres memoria recentissima experti sunt. Presbyter fuit quidam, Restitutus nomine, in paroecia
Calamensis ecclesiae. Quando [1] ei placebat (roga-
batur autem ut hoc faceret ab eis qui rem mirabilem
coram scire cupiebant), ad imitatas quasi lamentantis
cuiuslibet hominis voces ita se auferebat a sensibus et
iacebat simillimus mortuo ut non solum vellicantes
atque pungentes minime sentiret sed aliquando etiam
igne ureretur admoto sine ullo doloris sensu nisi
postmodum ex vulnere. Non autem obnitendo, sed
non sentiendo non movere corpus eo probabatur
quod tamquam in defuncto nullus inveniebatur
anhelitus. Hominum tamen voces, si clarius lo-
querentur, tamquam de longinquo se audire postea
referebat.

Cum itaque corpus etiam nunc quibusdam, licet in
carne corruptibili hanc aerumnosam ducentibus
vitam, ita in plerisque motionibus et affectionibus
extra usitatum naturae modum mirabiliter serviat,
quid causae est ut non credamus ante inoboedientiae
peccatum corruptionisque supplicium ad propagan-
dam prolem sine ulla libidine servire voluntati
humanae humana membra potuisse? Donatus est

---

[1] qui quando *some MSS.*

---

[1] A Numidian city located south of Hippo and east of Cirta.

music even from that quarter. From my own experience I know of a man who used to perspire at
will. Certain people are known to weep at will and
to shed a flood of tears.

But here is something far more incredible, a
spectacle that a large number of our own brethren
very recently witnessed. There was a certain
presbyter, Restitutus by name, in the parish of the
church of Calama.[1] Whenever he pleased (and he
used to be asked to do it by those who desired to
have a firsthand knowledge of the amazing phenomenon), he would withdraw from his senses to an
accompaniment of cries as of some person in distress
and lie still exactly like a dead man. In this state
he not only was completely insensitive to pinching
and pricking but at times was even burned by the
application of fire and yet felt no pain except afterwards from the wound. Proof that his body remained motionless, not through deliberate effort, but
through absence of feeling was provided by the fact
that, like someone deceased, he showed no sign of
breathing. Nevertheless, he later reported that he
could hear people talking, as though from a distance,
if they spoke distinctly enough.

The body then, as we have seen, even now remark-
ably serves certain people beyond the ordinary limits
of nature in many kinds of movement and feeling
although they are living our present wretched life
in perishable flesh. That being so, what is there
to keep us from believing that human members may
have served the human will without lust for the procreation of offspring before the sin of disobedience
and the consequent punishment of deterioration?

itaque homo sibi quia deseruit Deum placendo sibi,
et non oboediens Deo non potuit oboedire nec sibi.
Hinc evidentior miseria qua homo non vivit ut vult.
Nam si ut vellet viveret, beatum se putaret; sed nec
sic tamen esset si turpiter viveret.

XXV

*De vera beatitudine, quam temporalis vita non
obtinet.*

Quamquam si diligentius adtendamus, nisi beatus
non vivit ut vult, et nullus beatus nisi iustus. Sed
etiam ipse iustus non vivet [1] ut vult nisi eo pervenerit
ubi mori falli offendi omnino non possit eique sit
certum ita semper futurum. Hoc enim natura
expetit, nec plene atque perfecte beata erit nisi
adepta quod expetit. Nunc vero quis hominum
potest ut vult vivere quando ipsum vivere non est in
potestate? Vivere enim vult, mori cogitur. Quo
modo ergo vivit ut vult qui non vivit quamdiu vult?
Quod si mori voluerit, quo modo potest ut vult vivere
qui non vult vivere? Et si ideo mori velit, non quo
nolit vivere, sed ut post mortem melius vivat, nondum ergo ut vult vivit, sed cum ad id quod vult
moriendo pervenerit.

---

[1] vivit *some MSS.*

Man therefore was handed over to himself because he forsook God in his self-satisfaction, and since he did not obey God, he could not obey even himself. From this springs the more obvious wretchedness whereby man does not live as he chooses. For if he lived as he chose, he would deem himself happy; but yet he would not be happy even so if he lived an indecent life.

XXV

On the true happiness, which our present life does not possess.

Yet, if we are to regard the matter more closely, only a happy man lives as he chooses, and only a righteous man is happy. But even the righteous man himself will not live as he chooses until he arrives where he both is wholly free from death, deception and injury and is assured that he will always so remain. For this is what our nature seeks, and it will not be fully and perfectly happy unless it attains what it seeks. But who among us now can live as he chooses when the very matter of living is not in his power? For he chooses to live but is compelled to die. How then does he live as he chooses if he does not live as long as he chooses? But if he should choose to die, how can he live as he chooses when he does not choose to live? And if a person should choose to die, not because he does not choose to live, but in order to have a better life after death, then he does not yet live as he chooses, but will so live when by dying he has attained to what he chooses.

Verum ecce vivat ut vult, quoniam sibi extorsit sibique imperavit non velle quod non potest atque hoc velle quod potest, sicut ait Terentius:

> Quoniam non potest id fieri quod vis,
> Id velis quod possis,

num ideo beatus est, quia patienter miser est? Beata quippe vita si non amatur, non habetur. Porro si amatur et habetur, ceteris omnibus rebus excellentius necesse est ametur quoniam propter hanc amandum est quidquid aliud amatur. Porro si tantum amatur quantum amari digna est (non enim beatus est a quo ipsa beata vita non amatur ut digna est), fieri non potest ut eam qui sic amat non aeternam velit. Tunc igitur beata erit quando aeterna erit.

XXVI

Quod felicitas in paradiso viventium sine erubescendo appetitu generandi officium credenda sit implere potuisse.

Vivebat itaque homo in paradiso sicut volebat quamdiu hoc volebat quod Deus iusserat. Vivebat fruens Deo, ex quo bono erat bonus. Vivebat sine ulla egestate, ita semper vivere habens in potestate. Cibus aderat ne esuriret, potus ne sitiret, lignum vitae ne illum senecta dissolveret. Nihil corrup-

---

[1] Terence, *Andria* 305–306.

But, presto, let him live as he chooses, since he has dragooned and ordered himself not to choose what he cannot have, but to choose what he can have, just as we read in Terence:

> Since what you will you cannot do,
> Then will to do what you can do.[1]

Is such a person happy because he is wretched patiently? No, indeed, for the happy life belongs to no one who does not love it. Moreover, if a man does love it and have it, he must love it above all other things since whatever else is loved must be loved for the sake of this happy life. Further, if it is loved as much as it deserves to be loved—and unless a person loves the happy life itself as it deserves, he is not happy—the man who so loves it cannot help but wish it to be eternal. Life therefore will be happy when it is eternal.

XXVI

That we must believe that the happy pair who lived in paradise could have fulfilled the function of generation without shameful desire.

Accordingly, man lived in paradise just as he chose for as long a time as his choice coincided with God's command. He lived in the enjoyment of God, whose goodness ensured his goodness. He lived without any want and had it in his power always to live such a life. He had food at hand against hunger, drink against thirst and the tree of life against the decay of old age. There was no deterioration in the

395

tionis in corpore vel ex corpore ullas molestias ullis
eius sensibus ingerebat. Nullus intrinsecus morbus,
nullus ictus metuebatur extrinsecus. Summa in
carne sanitas, in animo tota tranquillitas.

Sicut in paradiso nullus aestus aut frigus, sic [1] in
eius habitatore nulla ex cupiditate vel timore acci-
debat [2] bonae voluntatis offensio. Nihil omnino
triste, nihil erat inaniter laetum. Gaudium verum
perpetuabatur ex Deo, in quem flagrabat *caritas de
corde puro et conscientia bona et fide non ficta*, atque
inter se coniugum fida ex honesto amore societas,
concors mentis corporisque vigilia et mandati sine
labore custodia. Non lassitudo fatigabat otiosum,
non somnus premebat invitum.

In tanta facilitate rerum et felicitate hominum,
absit ut suspicemur non potuisse prolem seri sine
libidinis morbo; sed eo voluntatis nutu moverentur
membra illa quo cetera, et sine ardoris inlecebroso
stimulo cum tranquillitate animi et corporis nulla
corruptione integritatis infunderetur gremio maritus uxoris. Neque enim quia experientia probari
non potest, ideo credendum non est, quando illas
corporis partes non ageret turbidus calor sed spon-
tanea potestas, sicut opus esset, adhiberet, ita tunc
potuisse utero coniugis salva integritate feminei

---

[1] sic *V and one other MS.:* ita *most MSS.*
[2] accedebat *some MSS.*

---

[1] 1 Timothy 1.5.
[2] Cf. Virgil, *Aeneid* 8.406.

body or arising from it to cause any discomfort to any of his senses. There was no fear of disease from within or of injury from without. He had perfect health in his flesh and complete tranquillity in his soul.

Just as in paradise it was neither too hot nor too cold, so in its occupant there was no interference from desire or fear to thwart his good will. There was no depressing gloom at all, no unreal gaiety. True joy emanated continuously from God, for whom there glowed " love from a pure heart and a good conscience and sincere faith." [1] Between husband and wife there was a loyal partnership springing from honest love; there was a harmonious alertness of mind and body and an effortless observance of God's command. No one suffered from weariness in his leisure, no one was overcome with sleep against his will.

In such facility of living and such felicity of mankind, far be it from us to suspect that it was impossible for the seed of offspring to be sown without the infection of lust; rather, the sexual organs could have been set in motion by the same authority of the will as the other bodily members. The husband, exempt from all seductive goading of passion, could have come to rest on his wife's bosom [2] with peace of mind undisturbed and pristine state of body intact. Granted that we cannot prove this by actual experiment, yet that is no reason why we should refuse to believe that when those parts of the body were not impelled by turbulent ardour but brought into play by a voluntary exercise of capacity as the need arose, the male seed could then be introduced into the

genitalis virile semen inmitti, sicut nunc potest
eadem integritate salva ex utero virginis fluxus
menstrui cruoris emitti. Eadem quippe via posset
illud inici qua hoc potest eici. Ut enim ad parien-
dum non doloris gemitus, sed maturitatis inpulsus
feminea viscera relaxaret, sic ad fetandum et con-
cipiendum non libidinis appetitus, sed voluntarius
usus naturam utramque coniungeret.

De rebus loquimur nunc pudendis et ideo, quamvis,
antequam earum puderet, quales esse potuissent
coniciamus ut possumus, tamen necesse est ut nostra
disputatio magis frenetur ea quae nos revocat
verecundia quam eloquentia, quae nobis parum sup-
petit, adiuvetur. Nam cum id quod dico nec ipsi
experti fuerint qui experiri potuerunt—quoniam,
praeoccupante peccato, exilium de paradiso ante
meruerunt quam sibi in opere serendae propaginis
tranquillo arbitrio convenirent—quo modo nunc, cum
ista commemorantur, sensibus occurrit humanis nisi
experientia libidinis turbidae, non coniectura placi-
dae voluntatis?

Hinc est quod inpedit loquentem pudor, etsi non
deficiat ratio cogitantem. Verum tamen omni-
potenti Deo, summo ac summe bono creatori omnium naturarum, voluntatum autem bonarum adiu-
tori et remuneratori, malarum autem relictori et

wife's uterus without damage to her maidenhead, even as now the menstrual flow can issue from a maiden's uterus without any such damage. For the seed could be injected through the same passage as that by which the menses can be ejected. Just as for parturition the womb of the female would not have been unclosed by any groan of travail but by some impulse when the time was ripe, so for impregnation and conception the two sexes would have been brought together not by lustful appetite but by exercise of the will.

The matters of which I am speaking now provoke shame. I am, to be sure, trying to conceive, as best I can, what they might have been like before they became a cause for shame; yet, for the reason stated, my discussion must rather be curbed by modesty that calls me back than further advanced by my eloquence, inadequate as it is. Not even those who were in a position to experience what I am describing did experience it, since their sin came first and thus they incurred exile from paradise before they could unite with one another dispassionately and deliberately in the work of propagating their kind. Hence it is impossible that when this subject is mentioned, it should now bring before our imagination anything but our own experience of turbulent lust rather than any speculative notion of a calm act of will.

Consequently, a sense of shame impedes my speech, though my mind is not at a loss for matter. Nevertheless, God almighty, who is the supreme and supremely good creator of all things, who supports and rewards all good will but abandons and condemns all bad will and orders both alike, surely did not lack

damnatori, utrarumque ordinatori, non defuit utique
consilium quo certum numerum civium in sua sapientia praedestinatum etiam ex damnato genere humano
suae civitatis impleret, non eos iam meritis, quando
quidem universa massa tamquam in vitiata radice
damnata est, sed gratia discernens et liberatis non
solum de ipsis verum etiam de non liberatis quid eis
largiatur ostendens. Non enim debita, sed gratuita
bonitate tunc se quisque agnoscit erutum malis
cum ab eorum hominum consortio fit inmunis cum
quibus illi iusta[1] esset poena communis. Cur ergo
non crearet Deus quos peccaturos esse praescivit,
quando quidem in eis et ex eis et quid eorum culpa
mereretur et quid sua gratia donaretur posset
ostendere, nec sub illo creatore ac dispositore perversa inordinatio delinquentium rectum perverteret
ordinem rerum?

XXVII

*De peccatoribus, et angelis et hominibus, quorum
perversitas non perturbat providentiam.*

PROINDE peccatores, et angeli et homines, nihil
agunt quo inpediantur *magna opera Domini, exquisita
in omnes voluntates eius*, quoniam qui providenter
atque omnipotenter sua cuique distribuit non solum

---

[1] iuste *one MS.*, *Dombart.*

---

[1] Psalms 111.2. Augustine's text reflects that of the
Septuagint and agrees with the Vulgate, but cf. the RSV:

a plan by which he could complete the set number of citizens foreordained in his wisdom for his city even from among the condemned human race. Since the entire mass of mankind has been condemned from its diseased root, as it were, he does not now select them by their deserts but by his grace, and he manifests his bounty to those who have been delivered not only in his treatment of them but also in his dealing with those who have not been delivered. For each one can see that he has been rescued from evils by a kindness that is not owed to him but freely given when he becomes exempt from participation in the fate of those in whose just punishment he had shared. There was no reason then why God should not have created men of whom he had foreknowledge that they would sin. For that enabled him to exhibit in them and through them both the due reward of their guilt and the gift of his grace, and as long as he was creator and disposer, the perverse disorder of transgressors could not pervert the right order of creation.

XXVII

That the wickedness of sinners, whether angels or men, does not disrupt the course of Providence.

SINNERS therefore, whether angels or men, do nothing that can encumber the " great works of the Lord sought out to suit his every will," [1] since he who providently and omnipotently bestows on each his own knows how to make good use not only of the

" Great are the works of the Lord, studied by all who have pleasure in them."

bonis verum etiam malis bene uti novit. Ac per hoc
propter meritum primae malae voluntatis ita damnato
atque obdurato angelo malo ut iam bonam voluntatem ulterius non haberet bene utens Deus cur non
permitteret ut ab illo primus homo, qui rectus, hoc
est bonae voluntatis, creatus fuerat, temptaretur?
Quando quidem sic erat institutus ut, si de adiutorio
Dei fideret bonus homo, malum angelum vinceret, si
autem creatorem atque adiutorem Deum superbe
sibi placendo desereret, vinceretur, meritum bonum
habens in adiuta divinitus voluntate recta, malum
vero in deserente Deum voluntate perversa.

Quia et ipsum fidere de adiutorio Dei non quidem
posset sine adiutorio Dei, nec tamen ideo ab his
divinae gratiae beneficiis sibi placendo recedere non
habebat in potestate. Nam sicut in hac carne
vivere sine adiumentis alimentorum in potestate non
est, non autem in ea vivere in potestate est, quod
faciunt qui se ipsos necant, ita bene vivere sine
adiutorio Dei etiam in paradiso non erat in potestate,
erat autem in potestate male vivere, sed beatitudine
non permansura et poena iustissima secutura. Cum
igitur huius futuri casus humani Deus non esset
ignarus, cur eum non sineret invidi angeli malig-
nitate temptari, nullo modo quidem quod vinceretur
incertus, sed nihilo minus praescius quod ab eius
semine adiuto sua gratia idem ipse diabolus fuerat
sanctorum gloria maiore vincendus?

good but also of the evil. Hence, although the evil
angel had been condemned to such obduracy in retribution for his first evil will that he could no longer
have a good will, why should God not have made
good use of him and allowed him to tempt the first
human being, who had been created upright, that is,
with a good will? For man had been so constituted
that if as a good human being he trusted in God's
help, he would defeat the evil angel, but if in proud
self-satisfaction he abandoned God, his creator and
helper, he would be defeated; and thus with a right
will that was divinely helped he would earn a good
recompense, but with a wrong will that abandoned
God, an evil recompense.

Even to trust in the help of God was impossible
without the help of God, though this did not prevent
man from having it in his power to fall back from the
benefits of divine grace through self-satisfaction.
For just as it is not in our power to live in this flesh
without the help of food, yet it is in our power not
to live in it at all, as we see in the case of those who
commit suicide, so it was not in man's power to live
a good life without God's help even in paradise,
although it was in his power to live an evil life; but
in this case his happiness would not endure and a very
just punishment would follow. Therefore, since God
was not unaware of this imminent fall of man, why
should he not have allowed him to be tempted by the
spiteful and envious angel? He was indeed perfectly well aware that man would be defeated, but
he equally well foresaw that this selfsame devil was
destined to be defeated by man's seed with the help
of divine grace to the greater glory of the saints.

SAINT AUGUSTINE

Ita factum est ut nec Deum aliquid futurorum
lateret nec praesciendo quemquam peccare con-
pelleret et quid interesset inter propriam cuiusque
praesumptionem et suam tuitionem angelicae et
humanae rationali creaturae consequenti experientia
demonstraret. Quis enim audeat credere aut dicere
ut neque angelus neque homo caderet in Dei
potestate non fuisse? Sed hoc eorum potestati
maluit non auferre atque ita et quantum mali
eorum superbia et quantum boni sua gratia valeret
ostendere.

XXVIII

De qualitate duarum civitatum, terrenae atque caelestis.

FECERUNT itaque civitates duas amores duo, terrenam scilicet amor sui usque ad contemptum Dei,
caelestem vero amor Dei usque ad contemptum sui.
Denique illa in se ipsa, haec in Domino gloriatur.
Illa enim quaerit ab hominibus gloriam, huic autem
Deus conscientiae testis maxima est gloria. Illa in
gloria sua exaltat caput suum; haec dicit Deo suo:
Gloria mea et exaltans caput meum. Illi in principibus
eius vel in eis quas subiugat [1] nationibus dominandi
libido dominatur; in hac serviunt invicem in caritate
et praepositi consulendo et subditi obtemperando.

---

[1] subiugat *most MSS.:* subiungat *one MS.:* subiugant
should perhaps be read with principes *understood as subject.*

---

[1] Cf. 2 Corinthians 10.17.
[2] Psalms 3.3.

Thus God neither overlooked any event of the future nor compelled anyone through his prescience to sin, yet he showed by the actual consequences of experience to angels and men, the rational beings of creation, the difference between an individual's private self-assertion and his own divine protection. Who would dare to believe or say that it was not in God's power to arrange that neither angel nor man should fall? But God preferred to allow this matter to remain within their power and thus to demonstrate what great evil their pride could bring and what great good his grace could effect.

XXVIII

On the character of the two cities, the earthly and the heavenly.

The two cities then were created by two kinds of love: the earthly city by a love of self carried even to the point of contempt for God, the heavenly city by a love of God carried even to the point of contempt for self. Consequently, the earthly city glories in itself while the other glories in the Lord.[1] For the former seeks glory from men, but the latter finds its greatest glory in God, the witness of our conscience. The earthly city lifts up its head in its own glory; the heavenly city says to its God: " My glory and the lifter of my head." [2] In the one, the lust for dominion has dominion over its princes as well as over the nations that it subdues; in the other, both those put in charge and those placed under them serve one another in love, the former by their counsel,

Illa in suis potentibus diligit virtutem suam; haec dicit Deo suo: *Diligam te, Domine, virtus mea.*

Ideoque in illa sapientes eius secundum hominem viventes aut corporis aut animi sui bona aut utriusque sectati sunt; aut qui potuerunt cognoscere Deum *non ut Deum honoraverunt aut gratias egerunt, sed evanuerunt in cogitationibus suis, et obscuratum est insipiens cor eorum; dicentes se esse sapientes* (id est, dominante sibi superbia, in sua sapientia sese extollentes) *stulti facti sunt et inmutaverunt gloriam incorruptibilis Dei in similitudinem* [1] *imaginis corruptibilis hominis et volucrum et quadrupedum et serpentium* (ad huiusce modi enim simulacra adoranda vel duces populorum vel sectatores fuerunt), *et coluerunt atque servierunt creaturae potius quam Creatori, qui est benedictus in saecula.* In hac autem nulla est hominis sapientia nisi pietas qua recte colitur verus Deus, id expectans praemium in societate sanctorum non solum hominum verum etiam angelorum, *ut sit Deus omnia in omnibus.*

---

[1] similitudinem *most MSS., Vulg., as also above, 8.10 and 23:* similitudine *V* (*cf. the Greek:* ἐν ὁμοιώματι).

the latter by their obedience. The earthly city loves
its own strength as revealed in its men of power; the
heavenly city says to its God: " I will love thee, O
Lord, my strength." [1]

Thus in the earthly city its wise men who live
according to man have pursued the goods either of
the body or of their own mind or of both together;
or if any of them were able to know God, " they did
not honour him as God or give thanks to him, but
they became futile in their thinking and their sense-
less minds were darkened; claiming to be wise,"
that is, exalting themselves in their own wisdom
under the dominion of pride, " they became fools,
and exchanged the glory of the immortal God for
images resembling mortal man or birds or beasts or
reptiles," for in the adoration of idols of this sort
they were either leaders or followers of the populace,
" and worshipped and served the creature rather than
the creator, who is blessed forever." [2] In the heavenly
city, on the other hand, man's only wisdom is the
religion that guides him rightly to worship the true
God and awaits as its reward in the fellowship of
saints, not only human but also angelic, this goal,
" that God may be all in all." [3]

[1] Psalms 18.1.
[2] Romans 1.21–23 and 25.
[3] 1 Corinthians 15.28.

BOOK XV

LIBER XV

I

*De duobus ordinibus generationis humanae in
diversos fines ab initio procurrentis.*

DE felicitate paradisi vel de ipso paradiso et de vita
ibi primorum hominum eorumque peccato atque
supplicio multi multa senserunt, multa dixerunt,
multa litteris mandaverunt. Nos quoque secundum
scripturas sanctas, vel quod in eis legimus vel quod
ex eis intellegere potuimus earum congruentes
auctoritati, de his rebus in superioribus libris diximus.
Enucleatius autem si ista quaerantur, multiplices
atque multimodas pariunt disputationes, quae pluribus intexendae sint [1] voluminibus quam hoc opus
tempusque deposcit, quod non ita largum habemus
ut in omnibus quae possunt requirere otiosi et
scrupulosi, paratiores ad interrogandum quam capa-
ciores ad intellegendum, nos oporteat inmorari.

Arbitror tamen satis nos iam fecisse magnis et
difficillimis quaestionibus de initio vel mundi vel
animae vel ipsius generis humani, quod in duo genera
distribuimus, unum eorum qui secundum hominem,

---

[1] sunt *some MSS*.

---

[1] Particularly in Book XIV.

BOOK XV

I

*On the two branches of the human race and the
different ends towards which they run their
course from the beginning.*

THE happiness of paradise or paradise itself and
the life there of the first human beings with their
sin and punishment have given rise to many opinions,
many discussions and many volumes. I too have
expressed myself on these matters in the preceding
books,[1] following in my discussion the authority of
the holy Scriptures and guided either by what I read
in them or by what I was able to deduce from them.
A more detailed consideration of this subject would
engender a great number and variety of discussions,
which could not be elaborated without filling more
volumes than my time allows or this project demands.
Limitations of time forbid me to dwell on all the
questions that may seem requisite to men who have
leisure and hanker for precision. Their readiness to
raise questions exceeds the capacity of their minds
to understand the answers.

Nevertheless, I think that I have already done
justice to the great and intricate problems relating
to the beginning whether of the world or of the soul
or of the human race itself. I distinguish two
branches of mankind: one made up of those who

alterum eorum qui secundum Deum vivunt; quas
etiam mystice appellamus civitates duas, hoc est duas
societates hominum, quarum est una quae prae-
destinata est in aeternum regnare cum Deo, altera
aeternum supplicium subire cum diabolo. Sed iste
finis est earum, de quo post loquendum est. Nunc
autem quoniam de exortu earum sive in angelis,
quorum numerus ignoratur a nobis, sive in duobus
primis hominibus satis dictum est, iam mihi videtur
earum adgrediendus excursus ex quo illi duo generare
coeperunt donec homines generare cessabunt. Hoc
enim universum tempus sive saeculum, in quo cedunt
morientes succeduntque nascentes, istarum duarum
civitatum de quibus disputamus excursus est.

Natus est igitur prior Cain ex illis duobus generis
humani parentibus, pertinens ad hominum civitatem,
posterior Abel, ad civitatem Dei. Sicut enim in uno
homine, quod dixit apostolus, experimur quia *non
primum quod spiritale est, sed quod animale, postea
spiritale* (unde unusquisque, quoniam ex damnata
propagine exoritur, primo sit necesse est ex Adam
malus atque carnalis; quod si in Christum renascendo
profecerit, post erit bonus et spiritalis), sic in universo genere humano, cum primum duae istae coeperunt nascendo atque moriendo procurrere civitates, prior est natus civis huius saeculi, posterius
autem isto peregrinus in saeculo et pertinens ad
civitatem Dei, gratia praedestinatus, gratia electus,

---

[1] Books XIX–XXII.
[2] Cf. Genesis 4.1–2.
[3] 1 Corinthians 15.46.

live according to man, the other of those who live according to God. I speak of these branches also allegorically as two cities, that is, two societies of human beings, of which one is predestined to reign eternally with God and the other to undergo eternal punishment with the devil. But this is their final state, which is to be treated later.[1] At this juncture, inasmuch as I have said enough about origins, that of the angels, whose number we do not know, and that of the first two human beings, I should, I think, undertake to trace the careers of the two cities from the moment when the two human beings first produced offspring up to the time when procreation will come to an end. For the history of the aforesaid two cities that are my subject extends through this entire period or era, during which those who die make room for the new-born who take their place.

Cain then was the first-born of those two parents of the human race, one who belonged to the city of men; Abel was born later and belonged to the City of God.[2] Now we know by experience that where the individual is concerned, as the Apostle has remarked, " it is not the spiritual which is first but the animal and then the spiritual "[3]—hence everyone, arising as he does from a condemned stock, is first inevitably evil and carnal through Adam; but if he starts to progress through rebirth in Christ, he will later be good and spiritual. The same thing is true of the entire human race. For at the very start, when the two cities began their history through birth and death, the first to be born was the citizen of this world, and only after him came the alien in this world who is a member of the City of God, one predestined

gratia peregrinus deorsum, gratia civis sursum. Nam quantum ad ipsum adtinet, ex eadem massa oritur quae originaliter est tota damnata, sed tamquam figulus Deus—hanc enim similitudinem non inpudenter [1] sed prudenter introducit apostolus—ex eadem massa fecit aliud vas in honorem, aliud in contumeliam. Prius autem factum est vas in contumeliam, post vero alterum in honorem, quia et in ipso uno, sicut iam dixi, homine prius est reprobum, unde necesse est incipiamus et ubi non est necesse ut remaneamus, posterius vero probum, quo proficientes veniamus et quo pervenientes maneamus. Proinde non quidem omnis homo malus erit bonus, nemo tamen erit bonus qui non erat malus; sed quanto quisque citius mutatur in melius, hoc in se facit nominari quod adprehendit celerius et posteriore cooperit vocabulum prius.

Scriptum est itaque de Cain quod condiderit civitatem; Abel autem tamquam peregrinus non condidit. Superna est enim sanctorum civitas, quamvis hic pariat cives, in quibus peregrinatur donec regni eius tempus adveniat, cum congregatura est omnes in suis corporibus resurgentes, quando eis promissum dabitur regnum, ubi cum suo principe, rege saeculorum, sine ullo temporis fine regnabunt.

[1] inprudenter *some MSS.*

by grace and chosen by grace, one by grace an alien below and by grace a citizen above. In himself he has his origin in the same lump that was condemned in its entirety at the beginning, but God, like a potter, to use the figure that the Apostle not impudently but prudently introduces, made " out of the same lump one vessel to be honoured and another to be despised." [1] But first to be made was the vessel for dishonour, then later the other for honour; for the individual too, as I have already indicated, begins with the inferior, which must be our starting-point, but need not be our permanent abode, and later comes to the superior, toward which we may advance as we move forward and in which we may abide when we have reached it. Consequently, though not every evil man will later be good, yet no one will be good who was not evil earlier; but the sooner a particular man changes for the better, the more speedily he may receive the name belonging to his new status and hide his former name under the later one.

Thus we read in Scripture that Cain founded a city,[2] but Abel, being a sojourner, founded none. For the city of the saints is above, though it brings forth citizens here below, in whose persons it sojourns as an alien until the time of its kingdom shall come. On that day it will assemble them all as they rise again in their bodies, and they will receive their promised kingdom, where with their Prince, who is king of the ages,[3] they will reign for all eternity.

[1] Romans 9.21.   [2] Cf. Genesis 4.17.
[3] Cf. 1 Timothy 1.17.

SAINT AUGUSTINE

II

De filiis carnis et filiis promissionis.

Umbra sane quaedam civitatis huius et imago prophetica ei significandae potius quam praesentandae
servivit in terris quo eam tempore demonstrari
oportebat. Et dicta est etiam ipsa civitas sancta
merito significantis imaginis, non expressae, sicut
futura est, veritatis. De hac imagine serviente et de
illa quam significat libera civitate sic apostolus ad
Galatas loquitur: *Dicite mihi,* inquit, *sub lege volentes
esse legem non audistis? Scriptum est enim quod
Abraham duos filios habuit, unum de ancilla et unum de
libera. Sed ille quidem qui de ancilla secundum carnem
natus est; qui autem de libera, per repromissionem.
Quae sunt in allegoria. Haec enim sunt duo testamenta, unum quidem a monte Sina in servitutem generans,
quod est Agar. Sina enim mons est in Arabia, quae
coniuncta* [1] *est huic quae nunc est Hierusalem; servit
enim cum filiis suis. Quae autem sursum est Hierusalem
libera est, quae est mater nostra. Scriptum est enim:
Laetare, sterilis quae non paris, erumpe et exclama,* [2]
*quae non parturis, quoniam multi filii desertae, magis
quam eius quae habet virum. Nos autem, fratres,
secundum Isaac promissionis filii sumus. Sed sicut tunc*

[1] qui coniunctus *a few MSS.,* Vulg.
[2] clama *some MSS.,* Vulg. (*but* exclama *in cod.* Fuldensis).

---

[1] On the sense of allegory here cf. Augustine, *De Trinitate*
15.9.15.

II

On the children of the flesh and the children of the promise.

THERE was indeed a kind of shadow and prophetic likeness of this city of God that served rather as a sign pointing to it than as a representation of its reality on earth when the time for its manifestation was due. The image too was called a holy city, a name which it earned by serving as a symbol, not showing directly the reality which is still to come. It is of this image in its serving role and of the free city that it foreshadows that the Apostle speaks when he says to the Galatians: " Tell me, you who desire to be under the law, have you not heard the law? For it is written that Abraham had two sons, one by a slave and one by a free woman. But the son of the slave was born according to the flesh, the son of the free woman through promise. Now this is an allegory.[1] These women are two covenants. One is from Mount Sinai, bearing children for slavery; this is Hagar. Now Sinai is a mountain in Arabia and corresponds to the present Jerusalem, for she is in slavery with her children. But the Jerusalem above is free, and she is our mother. For it is written: ' Rejoice, O barren one that dost not bear; break forth and shout, thou who art not in travail; for the desolate hath more children than she who hath a husband.' [2] Now we, brethren, like Isaac, are children of promise. But as at that time he who

---

[2] Isaiah 54.1.

qui secundum carnem natus fuerat persequebatur eum qui secundum spiritum, ita et nunc. Sed quid dicit scriptura? Eice ancillam et filium eius; non enim heres erit filius ancillae cum filio liberae. Nos autem, fratres, non sumus ancillae filii sed liberae qua libertate Christus nos liberavit.

Haec forma intellegendi de apostolica auctoritate descendens locum nobis aperit quem ad modum scripturas duorum testamentorum, veteris et novi, accipere debeamus. Pars enim quaedam terrenae civitatis imago caelestis civitatis effecta est, non se significando, sed alteram, et ideo serviens. Non enim propter se ipsam sed propter aliam significandam est instituta, et, praecedente alia significatione, et ipsa praefigurans praefigurata est. Namque Agar, ancilla Sarrae, eiusque filius imago quaedam huius imaginis fuit; et quoniam transiturae erant umbrae luce veniente, ideo dixit libera Sarra, quae significabat liberam civitatem, cui rursus alio modo significandae etiam illa umbra serviebat: *Eice ancillam et filium eius; non enim heres erit filius ancillae cum filio meo Isaac,* quod ait apostolus: *Cum filio liberae.*

Invenimus ergo in terrena civitate duas formas, unam suam praesentiam demonstrantem, alteram caelesti civitati significandae sua praesentia servientem. Parit autem cives terrenae civitatis peccato vitiata natura, caelestis vero civitatis cives parit a

---

[1] Genesis 21.10.

[2] Galatians 4.21–5.1.

[3] Hagar, a slave, foreshadowed the earthly Jerusalem, which, being itself enslaved, was also regarded as *serving* to foreshadow the Jerusalem above, the free city symbolized by Sarah.

was born according to the flesh persecuted him who was born according to the spirit, so it is now. But what does Scripture say? 'Cast out the slave and her son; for the son of the slave shall not inherit with the son of the free woman.'[1] So we, brethren, are not children of the slave but of the free woman by virtue of the freedom with which Christ has set us free."[2]

This method of interpretation, which comes down to us with apostolic authority, opens the way for us to understand the writing of the two covenants, the old and the new. A certain part of the earthly city has been used to make an image of the heavenly city, and since it thus symbolizes not itself but the other, it is in servitude. For it was established not for its own sake but to symbolize another city, and since it too was anticipated by another symbol, the foreshadowing image itself was also foreshadowed.[3] Hagar, who was Sarah's slave, represented together with her son an image of this image; and since the shadows were to vanish with the coming of light, Sarah, who was free and symbolized the free city, which in turn the shadow, Hagar, served to prefigure in another way, said: "Cast out the slave and her son; for the son of the slave shall not inherit with my son Isaac," or, as the Apostle puts it, "with the son of the free woman."

We find then in the earthly city two aspects: in one it manifests its own presence and in the other it serves by its presence to point to the heavenly city. Moreover, citizens of the earthly city are brought forth by a natural being that is corrupted by sin, whereas the citizens of the heavenly city are brought

peccato naturam liberans gratia. Unde illa vocantur vasa irae, ista vasa misericordiae. Significatum est hoc etiam in duobus filiis Abrahae, quod unus de ancilla, quae dicebatur Agar, secundum carnem natus est Ismael, alter est autem de Sarra libera secundum repromissionem natus Isaac. Uterque quidem de semine Abrahae, sed illum genuit demonstrans consuetudo naturam, illum[1] vero dedit promissio significans gratiam. Ibi humanus usus ostenditur, hic divinum beneficium commendatur.

III

De sterilitate-Sarrae, quam Dei gratia fecundavit.

SARRA quippe sterilis erat et desperatione prolis saltem de ancilla sua concupiscens habere quod de se ipsa non se posse cernebat, dedit eam fetandam viro, de quo parere voluerat nec potuerat. Exegit itaque etiam sic debitum de marito utens iure suo in utero alieno. Natus est ergo Ismael sicut nascuntur homines, permixtione sexus utriusque usitata lege naturae. Ideo dictum est: *Secundum carnem*[2] non quod ista beneficia Dei non sint aut non illa operetur Deus, cuius opifex sapientia *adtingit*, sicut

---

[1] istum *a few MSS.*   [2] hominem *a few MSS.*

---

[1] Cf. Romans 9.22–23.   [2] Cf. Genesis 16.1–3.
[3] Galatians 4.23.

forth by a grace that frees nature from sin. Hence the former are called ' vessels of wrath,' the latter ' vessels of mercy.' [1] This distinction was symbolized also in the two sons of Abraham; for one, Ishmael, the son of the slave called Hagar, was born according to the flesh, the other, Isaac, the son of the free woman Sarah, was born according to the promise. Both sons, to be sure, sprang from the seed of Abraham, but the one was produced by ordinary practice showing nature's way, the other came as a gift of the promise pointing to grace. In one case man's wont is presented, in the other God's beneficence is commended.

III

On the barrenness of Sarah, who was made fertile through the grace of God.

SARAH was barren and, despairing of progeny, desired to have at least from her slave what she saw that she could not have from herself. Therefore she gave this woman to be made pregnant to her husband, by whom she herself had vainly wished to have children.[2] Even so, accordingly, she exacted her due from her husband, exercising her right by another's womb. Hence Ishmael was born like other human beings in accordance with the ordinary law of nature through sexual intercourse. This explains the expression, " according to the flesh ";[3] it is not because such bounties are not the gift of God or because matters like these are not included in the activity of God, whose craftsmanlike wisdom "ranges,"

SAINT AUGUSTINE

scriptum est, *a fine usque ad* [1] *finem fortiter et disponit omnia suaviter*, sed ubi significandum fuerat Dei donum quod indebitum hominibus gratis gratia largiretur, sic oportuit dari filium quem ad modum naturae non debebatur excursibus. Negat enim natura iam filios tali commixtioni maris et feminae qualis esse poterat Abrahae et Sarrae in illa iam aetate, etiam mulieris accedente sterilitate, quae nec tunc parere potuit quando non aetas fecunditati sed aetati fecunditas defuit.

Quod ergo naturae sic affectae fructus posteritatis non debebatur significat quod natura generis humani peccato vitiata ac per hoc iure damnata nihil verae felicitatis in posterum merebatur. Recte igitur significat Isaac, per repromissionem natus, filios gratiae, cives civitatis liberae, socios pacis aeternae, ubi sit non amor propriae ac privatae quodam modo voluntatis sed communi eodemque inmutabili bono gaudens atque ex multis unum cor faciens, id est perfecte concors oboedientia caritatis.

IV

De terrenae civitatis vel concertatione vel pace.

TERRENA porro civitas, quae sempiterna non erit (neque enim, cum extremo supplicio damnata fuerit, iam civitas erit), hic habet bonum suum, cuius

[1] ad *most MSS.*, *Vulg.* (*cf. Septuagint:* ἐπὶ πέρας): in *V and two other MSS.*

---

[1] Wisdom 8.1.   [2] Cf. Acts 4.32.

as it is written, "mightily from one end to the other and orders all things agreeably." [1] But where there was a need to convey the meaning of a divine gift not in payment of a debt, but freely bestowed by grace upon men, the gift of a son had to be made by means that were not due to any course of nature. For nature denies children to the sort of sexual union that Abraham and Sarah could have had at their advanced age. Besides, the woman had been barren and unable to bear offspring even when her age was not deficient for fertility; but fertility then was deficient for her age.

Now the implication conveyed by the fact that a natural creature in this condition could not claim any fruit of posterity is this: human nature depraved by sin and justly condemned for it did not merit true happiness for the future. Isaac, therefore, son of the promise, is rightly regarded as a symbol of the children of grace, citizens of the free city and partners in eternal peace, a state where there exists no love of a will that is personal or, so to speak, private, but a love that rejoices in a common and unchangeable good and makes a single mind out of many, [2] that is a completely harmonious response to the voice of Christian love.

IV

On strife and peace in the earthly city.

Now the earthly city will not be everlasting, for when it is condemned to final punishment, it will no longer be a city. It has its good here on earth and

societate laetatur qualis esse de talibus laetitia rebus
potest. Et quoniam non est tale bonum ut nullas
angustias faciat amatoribus suis, ideo civitas ista
adversus se ipsam plerumque dividitur litigando,
bellando atque pugnando et aut mortiferas aut certe
mortales victorias requirendo. Nam ex quacumque
sui parte adversus alteram sui partem bellando sur-
rexerit, quaerit esse victrix gentium cum sit captiva
vitiorum; et si quidem, cum vicerit, superbius ex-
tollitur, etiam mortifera. Si vero condicionem cogi-
tans casusque communes magis quae accidere possunt
adversis angitur quam eis quae provenerunt secundis
rebus inflatur, tantummodo mortalis est ista victoria.
Neque enim semper dominari poterit permanendo eis
quos potuerit subiugare vincendo.

Non autem recte dicitur ea bona non esse quae
concupiscit haec civitas, quando est et ipsa [1] in suo
humano genere melior. Concupiscit enim terrenam
quandam pro rebus infimis pacem; ad eam namque
desiderat pervenire bellando, quoniam, si vicerit et
qui resistat non fuerit, pax erit, quam non habebant
partes in vicem adversantes et pro his rebus quas
simul habere non poterant infelici egestate certantes.
Hanc pacem requirunt laboriosa bella, hanc adipiscitur quae putatur gloriosa victoria.

Quando autem vincunt qui causa iustiore pug-

---

[1] *After* ipsa *perhaps* per ea (*sc.* bona) *should be added.*

rejoices to partake of it with the sort of joy that can be derived from things of this sort. And since this good is not of the sort to cause no difficulties for those who love it, the earthly city is generally divided against itself. There are litigations; there are wars and battles; there is pursuit of victories that either cut lives short or at any rate are short-lived. For whatever part of it has risen up in war against the other part, it seeks to be victorious over other nations though it is itself the slave of vices; and if, when it is victorious, it becomes exceedingly proud and haughty, its victory also cuts lives short. But if it reflects upon the common vicissitudes of the human lot and is more distressed by possible misfortunes than puffed up by that favourable course of events, that victory is merely short-lived. For it will not be able to rule lastingly over those whom it was able to subjugate victoriously.

It is incorrect, however, to say that the goods that this city covets are not good, since through them even the city itself is better after its own human fashion. Thus to gain the lowest kind of goods it covets an earthly peace, one that it seeks to attain by warfare; for if it is victorious and no one remains to resist it, there will be peace, which the conflicting parts of the city did not have while they opposed one another and struggled in their wretched poverty for the things that both could not enjoy at the same time. Such is the peace that the toilsome wars are waged to gain; such is the peace that the reputedly glorious victory achieves.

When, however, the victors are those who were champions of the more righteous cause, who can

nabant, quis dubitet gratulandam esse victoriam et
provenisse optabilem pacem? Haec bona sunt et
sine dubio Dei dona sunt. Sed si, neglectis melioribus quae ad supernam pertinent civitatem, ubi erit
victoria in aeterna et summa pace secura, bona ista
sic concupiscuntur ut vel sola esse credantur vel his
quae meliora creduntur amplius diligantur, necesse
est miseria consequatur et quae inerat augeatur.

V

*De primo terrenae civitatis auctore, fratricida cuius
impietati Romanae urbis conditor germani caede
responderit.*

Primus itaque fuit terrenae civitatis conditor
fratricida; nam suum fratrem, civem civitatis aeternae in hac terra peregrinantem, invidentia victus
occidit. Unde mirandum non est quod tanto post
in ea civitate condenda quae fuerat huius terrenae
civitatis, de qua loquimur, caput futura et tam multis
gentibus regnatura huic primo exemplo et, ut Graeci
appellant, ἀρχετύπῳ quaedam sui generis imago
respondit. Nam et illic, sicut ipsum facinus quidam
poeta commemoravit illorum,

> Fraterno primi maduerunt sanguine muri.

Sic enim condita est Roma quando occisum Remum
a fratre Romulo Romana testatur historia, nisi quod

---

[1] Cf. below, 19.17 (vol. 6, 193–199).   [2] Lucan 1.95.
[3] On Romulus' slaying of Remus cf. above, 3.6 (vol. 1,
281–283).

doubt that the victory in that case justifies joyous
celebration and that the peace that resulted is
desirable? These things are goods and certainly
gifts of God. But there are higher goods that belong
to the city above, in which victory will be untroubled
in everlasting and ultimate peace.[1] If these goods
are neglected while others are so coveted that they
either are believed to be the only goods or are
cherished more than the goods that are believed to
be higher, then the inevitable consequence will be
new misery and more and more added to the old.

V

On the first founder of the earthly city, the fratricide
whose wickedness was repeated by the founder of
Rome when he slew his own brother.

THE first founder of the earthly city was consequently a fratricide; for, overcome by envy, he slew
his own brother, who was a citizen of the eternal city
sojourning upon this earth. No wonder then that this
first example or, as the Greeks call it, archetype was
followed by a copy of its own likeness long afterwards
at the foundation of the city that was destined to be
the capital of this earthly city, our present topic, and
to rule over so many nations. For here too, as one
of their poets put it when he recorded this crime,

In blood fraternal were the first walls steeped.[2]

This is indeed the way that Rome was founded
when Remus, as the history of Rome tells us, was
slain by his brother Romulus.[3] These two brothers,

isti terrenae civitatis ambo cives erant. Ambo gloriam de Romanae rei publicae institutione quaerebant, sed ambo eam tantam quantam si unus esset habere non poterant. Qui enim volebat dominando gloriari minus utique dominaretur si eius potestas vivo consorte minueretur. Ut ergo totam dominationem haberet unus, ablatus est socius; et scelere crevit in peius quod innocentia minus esset et melius.

Hi autem fratres Cain et Abel non habebant ambo inter se similem rerum terrenarum cupiditatem; nec in hoc alter alteri invidit, quod eius dominatus fieret angustior qui alterum occidit si ambo dominarentur (Abel quippe non quaerebat dominationem in ea civitate quae condebatur a fratre), sed invidentia illa diabolica qua invident bonis mali nulla alia causa nisi quia illi boni sunt, illi mali. Nullo enim modo fit minor accedente seu permanente consorte possessio bonitatis, immo possessio bonitas, quam tanto latius quanto concordius individua sociorum possidet caritas. Non habebit denique istam possessionem qui eam noluerit habere communem; et tanto eam reperiet ampliorem quanto amplius ibi potuerit amare consortem.

Illud igitur quod inter Remum et Romulum exortum est quem ad modum adversus se ipsam terrena civitas dividatur ostendit, quod autem inter Cain et

however, were both citizens of the earthly city.
Both sought the glory of founding the Roman State,
but both could not have as much glory each for himself as either could have if there were but one founder.
For if the goal was to boast of power, there would of
course be less power if sovereignty was limited by an
existing partner. Accordingly, in order that all
power might accrue to one single person, his fellow
was removed; and what innocence would have kept
smaller and better grew through crime into something larger and inferior.

The brothers Cain and Abel, on the other hand,
were not moved by the same desire for earthly
things; nor did envy arise in the one who slew the
other because his power would be restricted if both
held it, for Abel did not want power in the city that
was being founded by his brother. Cain's envy was
rather of that diabolical sort that the wicked feel for
the good just because they *are* good, not wicked like
themselves. The goodness that a person possesses
is, in fact, not at all diminished if it comes to be or
continues to be shared with another. On the contrary, goodness is a possession of the undifferentiated
love of fellow-members; and the more harmony
there is among men, the further that possession
extends. Consequently, anyone who refuses to
share this possession with another will not have it at
all; and he will find that the extent of his possession
of it is in proportion to his success in loving a partner
in it.

The conflict, therefore, that arose between Remus
and Romulus showed how the earthly city is divided
against itself, but the dispute between Cain and

Abel inter duas ipsas civitates, Dei et hominum,
inimicitias demonstravit. Pugnant ergo inter se
mali et mali. Item pugnant inter se mali et boni.
Boni vero et boni, si perfecti sunt, inter se pugnare
non possunt. Proficientes autem nondumque perfecti ita possunt ut bonus quisque ex ea parte pugnet
contra alterum qua etiam contra semet ipsum. Et
in uno quippe homine *caro concupiscit adversus spiritum
et spiritus adversus carnem.* Concupiscentia ergo
spiritalis contra alterius potest pugnare carnalem vel
concupiscentia carnalis contra alterius spiritalem,
sicut inter se pugnant boni et mali; vel certe ipsae
concupiscentiae carnales inter se duorum bonorum,
nondum utique perfectorum, sicut inter se pugnant
mali et mali, donec eorum qui curantur ad ultimam
victoriam sanitas perducatur.

VI

*De languoribus quos ex poena peccati etiam cives
civitatis Dei in huius vitae peregrinatione
patiuntur et a quibus Deo medente
sanantur.*

LANGUOR est quippe iste, id est illa inoboedientia de
qua in libro quarto decimo disseruimus, primae inoboedientiae supplicium et ideo non natura sed

---

[1] Galatians 5.17.
[2] *E.g.*, 14.1 (pp. 259–261); 14.11 (pp. 323–333).

Abel proved that there is enmity between the two cities themselves, the City of God and the city of men. Accordingly, there are battles of wicked against wicked. There are also battles of wicked against good and good against wicked. But the good, if they have achieved perfection, cannot fight among themselves. If, however, they are advancing toward perfection but have not yet attained it, fighting among them is possible to the extent that each good man may fight against another through that part of him with which he also fights against himself. Even in a single person " the desires of the flesh are against the spirit, and the desires of the spirit are against the flesh." [1] Thus spiritual desire can fight against the carnal desire of another, or carnal desire against the spiritual desire of another, just as the good and the wicked fight with one another; or again, where there are two good, but certainly not yet perfect men, their carnal desires can assuredly fight with one another, just as the wicked fight among themselves, until the health of those who are on the path of recovery is guided to its final triumph.

VI

On the infirmities from which even citizens of the City of God suffer as punishment for sin during their sojourn in this life and from which they are restored by God's healing hand.

Now infirmity of this sort, that is, the disobedience which we discussed in Book XIV,[2] is our punishment for the first disobedience and so is not an element in

vitium, propter quod dicitur proficientibus bonis et ex
fide in hac peregrinatione viventibus: *In vicem onera
vestra portate, et sic adimplebitis legem Christi.* Item
alibi dicitur: *Corripite inquietos, consolamini pusil-
lanimes, suscipite infirmos, patientes estote ad omnes.
Videte ne quis malum pro malo alicui reddat.* Item
alio loco: *Si praeoccupatus fuerit homo in aliquo delicto,
vos qui spiritales estis, instruite huius modi in spiritu
mansuetudinis, intendens te ipsum, ne et tu tempteris;* et
alibi: *Sol non occidat super iracundiam vestram;* et in
evangelio: *Si peccaverit in te frater tuus, corripe eum
inter te et ipsum.*[1] Item de peccatis, in quibus multorum cavetur offensio, apostolus dicit: *Peccantes
coram omnibus argue, ut ceteri timorem habeant.*

Propter hoc et de venia in vicem danda multa
praecipiuntur et magna cura propter tenendam pacem, sine qua nemo poterit videre Deum, ubi ille
terror quando iubetur servus decem milium talen-
torum reddere debita, quae illi fuerant relaxata,
quoniam debitum denariorum centum conservo suo
non relaxavit. Qua similitudine proposita, Dominus
Iesus adiecit atque ait: *Sic et vobis faciet Pater vester
caelestis, si non dimiseritis unusquisque fratri suo de
cordibus vestris.* Hoc modo curantur cives civitatis
Dei in hac terra peregrinantes et paci supernae
patriae suspirantes. Spiritus autem sanctus opera-

---

[1] ipsum solum *a few MSS., Vulg.* (*cf. the Greek:* αὐτοῦ μόνου).

---

[1] Galatians 6.2.
[2] 1 Thessalonians 5.14–15.
[3] Galatians 6.1.
[4] Ephesians 4.26.
[5] Matthew 18.15.
[6] 1 Timothy 5.20.
[7] Cf. Hebrews 12.14.
[8] Cf. Matthew 18.23–34.
[9] Matthew 18.35.

nature but a defect. This is why the good who are
progressing toward perfection and living by faith
during their sojourn on earth are admonished: " Bear
one another's burdens, and thus you will fulfil the
law of Christ." [1] So too elsewhere: " Admonish the
unruly, encourage the fainthearted, help the weak,
be patient with all. See that none of you repays
evil for evil." [2] Again, in another passage: " If a
man is overtaken in any trespass, you who are spiritual should instruct such a one in a spirit of gentleness. Look to yourself, lest you too be tempted "; [3]
and in yet another passage: " Do not let the sun go
down on your anger "; [4] and in the Gospel: " If your
brother sins against you, tell him his fault, between
you and him." [5] Similarly, on the subject of sins, the
Apostle, being heedful lest they become widespread,
says: " As for those who sin, rebuke them in the
presence of all, so that the rest may stand in fear." [6]

It is on this account that numerous precepts are
enjoined upon us concerning mutual forgiveness and
the great care requisite for maintaining peace, without which no one will be able to see God. [7] The
frightening experience of a slave bears upon this:
he was ordered to repay debts of ten thousand
talents, though they had already been forgiven him,
because he did not forgive his fellow slave a debt of
a hundred denarii. [8] After the Lord Jesus had
delivered this parable, he added: " So also your
heavenly Father will do to every one of you, if you
do not forgive your brother from your heart." [9]
This is the way that the citizens of the City of God
are nursed while they sojourn here on earth and sigh
for the peace of their heavenly fatherland. But the

433

tur intrinsecus ut valeat aliquid medicina quae adhibetur extrinsecus. Alioquin, etiamsi Deus ipse
utens creatura sibi subdita in aliqua specie humana
sensus adloquatur humanos, sive istos corporis sive
illos quos istis simillimos habemus in somnis, nec
interiore gratia mentem regat atque agat, nihil
prodest homini omnis praedicatio veritatis.

Facit autem hoc Deus a vasis misericordiae irae
vasa discernens dispensatione qua ipse novit multum
occulta sed tamen iusta. Ipso quippe adiuvante
mirabilibus et latentibus modis, cum peccatum quod
habitat in membris nostris, quae potius iam poena
peccati est, sicut apostolus praecipit, non regnat in
nostro mortali corpore ad oboediendum desideriis
eius nec ei membra nostra velut iniquitatis arma
exhibemus, convertitur ad mentem non sibi ad
mala, Deo regente, consentientem et eam regentem
tranquillius nunc habebit, postea, sanitate perfecta
atque inmortalitate percepta, homo sine ullo peccato
in aeterna pace regnabit.

VII

*De causa et pertinacia sceleris Cain, quem a facinore
concepto nec Dei sermo revocavit.*

SED hoc ipsum quod, sicut potuimus, exposuimus,
cum Deus locutus esset ad Cain eo more quo cum

---

[1] Cf. Romans 9.22–23.
[2] Cf. Romans 6.12–13.

Holy Spirit works internally to make the medicine that is applied externally effective. Otherwise, even if God himself employs a creature subject to him to address in some human form the human senses, whether those of the body or the ones that we possess very much like them when we sleep, and yet does not rule and move our minds with his inner grace, no preaching of the truth is of any avail to man.

But God does do this, distinguishing the vessels of wrath from the vessels of mercy by the profoundly hidden yet just dispensation that is known to him alone.[1] For he helps in wonderful and secret ways, and when the sin that dwells in our members, or rather the punishment for sin, in the words of the Apostle's injunction,[2] no longer reigns in our mortal bodies to make us obey the desires of the body, and when we no longer present our members to the body as instruments of wickedness, we undergo a change of heart so that, under God's rule, man does not agree with himself to do evil, but will find in this new mind and heart in our age a more peaceful ruler; later, when he gains perfect health and obtains his immortality, he will reign free from all sin in eternal peace.

VII

On the cause of Cain's crime and his stubborn determination to commit the deed, from which, once conceived, not even the words of God recalled him.

But this very matter of admonition that I have been discussing as best I could, what good did it do Cain when God spoke with him in his customary way

primis hominibus per creaturam subiectam velut
eorum socius forma congrua loquebatur, quid ei
profuit? Nonne conceptum scelus in necando fratre
etiam post verbum divinae admonitionis implevit?
Nam cum sacrificia discrevisset amborum, in illius
respiciens, huius despiciens, quod non dubitandum
est potuisse cognosci signo aliquo adtestante visibili,
et hoc ideo fecisset Deus, quia mala erant opera
huius, fratris vero eius bona, contristatus est Cain
valde et concidit facies eius. Sic enim scriptum est:
*Et dixit Dominus ad Cain: Quare tristis factus es et
quare concidit facies tua? Nonne si recte offeras, recte
autem non dividas, peccasti? Quiesce; ad te enim
conversio eius, et tu dominaberis illius.*

In hac admonitione vel monitu quem Deus protulit
ad Cain, illud quidem quod dictum est: *Nonne si
recte offeras, recte autem non dividas, peccasti?* quia non
elucet cur vel unde sit dictum, multos sensus peperit
eius obscuritas cum divinarum scripturarum quisque
tractator secundum fidei regulam id conatur ex-
ponere. Recte quippe offertur sacrificium cum

---

[1] From Genesis 4.6 ff. it would appear that God addressed
Cain directly, but on God's manner of speaking to man cf.
Augustine, *De Genesi ad Litteram* 8.18.37; 9.2.3–4.

[2] Genesis 4.6–7. Augustine's text differs markedly from
the Vulgate but is close to the Septuagint. The sense is not
clear, and, to make his point, Augustine exploits the ambiguity
of the language in the passage. The Latin for ' it is to come
back to you ' is *ad te . . . conversio eius,* which means literally:
' the turning of it (*or* him) to you.' The phrase lacks a verb
and *eius* can mean in the context either ' of it ' or ' of him.'
Similarly, in ' you are to master it ' the Latin allows ' him ' to
be understood for ' it.' The passage is rendered in the RSV

of conversing with the first human beings through a creature subject to him, that is, by assuming an appropriate form as though he were one of their number?[1] Did he not carry out the crime of fratricide that he had conceived, even after God had admonished him against it? For God had discriminated between the sacrifices of the two brothers by showing regard for the offering of the one but not for that of the other, a preference which, we must not doubt, could be ascertained by the evidence of some visible sign; and God must have done as he did because the works of Cain were evil whereas those of his brother were good. But Cain then became exceedingly grim and his countenance fell. For in Scripture we read: " And the Lord said to Cain: ' Why have you turned grim, and why has your countenance fallen? If your offering is rightly made, but is not rightly allotted, have you not committed a sin? Calm down, for it is to come back to you, and you are to master it.' "[2]

In this admonition or warning that God imparted to Cain, the reason or ground for the statement made: " If your offering is rightly made, but is not rightly allotted, have you not committed a sin? " is not clear; and its obscurity has given rise to many interpretations whenever a commentator on the holy Scriptures attempts to explain the words according to the canon of faith. Certainly a sacrifice is rightly offered when

as follows: " The Lord said to Cain, ' Why are you angry, and why has your countenance fallen? If you do well, will you not be accepted? And if you do not do well, sin is couching at the door; its desire is for you, but you must master it.' "

offertur Deo vero, cui uni tantummodo sacrificandum
est. Non autem recte dividitur dum non discernuntur recte vel loca vel tempora vel res ipsae quae
offeruntur vel qui offert et cui offertur vel hi quibus
ad vescendum distribuitur quod oblatum est, ut
divisionem hic discretionem intellegamus, sive cum
offertur ubi non oportet aut quod non ibi sed alibi
oportet, sive cum offertur quando non oportet aut
quod non tunc sed alias oportet, sive cum [1] offertur
quod nusquam et numquam penitus debuit, sive cum
electiora sibi eiusdem generis rerum tenet homo
quam sunt ea quae offert Deo, sive eius rei quae
fit particeps profanus aut quilibet quem
fas non est fieri.

In quo autem horum Deo displicuerit Cain facile
non potest inveniri. Sed quoniam Iohannes apostolus, cum de his fratribus loqueretur: *Non sicut Cain*,
inquit, *ex maligno* [2] *erat et occidit fratrem suum. Et
cuius rei gratia occidit? Quia opera illius maligna
fuerunt, fratris autem eius* [3] *iusta*, datur intellegi
propterea Deum non respexisse in munus eius, quia
hoc ipso male dividebat, dans Deo aliquid suum,
sibi autem se ipsum. Quod omnes faciunt qui non
Dei sed suam sectantes voluntatem, id est non recto
sed perverso corde viventes, offerunt tamen Deo
munus, quo putant eum redimi ut eorum non opitu-

---

[1] cum *V* (*before correction*) *and a few other MSS.:* cum id
most MSS.

[2] ex maligno *some MSS.* (*cf. the Greek:* ἐκ τοῦ πονηροῦ): qui
ex maligno *other MSS., Vulg.* (*but* qui *omitted by first hand of
cod. Fuldensis*).

[3] ipsius *or* illius *a few MSS.*

---

[1] 1 John 3.12.

it is offered to the true God, to whom alone we
should sacrifice. But it is not rightly allotted if
we do not rightly discriminate either the places or
the times or the objects of sacrifice or the giver
and the recipient of the offering or those to whom
the animal offered in sacrifice is distributed for eating.
In other words, we interpret allotment in this context to mean discrimination. An offering may be
made at the wrong place, that is, the thing offered
may be forbidden there but elsewhere acceptable;
or it may be made at the wrong time, that is, the
thing offered may be forbidden at one time but
acceptable at another. It may be an offering of
something that ought absolutely not to have been
offered anywhere or at any time, or a man may keep
for himself the choicer parts of the same sort of
thing that he offers to God, or it may be that the
offering provided is partaken of by a profane person
or anyone else who may not lawfully partake of it.

It is, however, no easy matter to discover in which
of these ways Cain displeased God. But the apostle
John, in speaking of these brothers, said: " Be not
like Cain who was of the evil one and murdered his
brother. And why did he murder him? Because
his own deeds were evil and his brother's righteous." [1]
Thus we are given to understand that God had no
regard for his gift because it was ill-allotted in this
respect, that he gave something of his to God but
gave himself only to himself, as is done by all who do
not pursue God's will but their own, that is, who live
with a heart not upright but perverted, and yet offer
a gift to God. With this gift they think that he is
being bribed to help them, not in curing their wicked

439

letur sanandis pravis cupiditatibus sed explendis. Et
hoc est terrenae proprium civitatis, deum vel deos
colere quibus adiuvantibus regnet in victoriis et pace
terrena, non caritate consulendi, sed dominandi
cupiditate. Boni quippe ad hoc utuntur mundo, ut
fruantur Deo; mali autem contra ut fruantur mundo
uti volunt Deo, qui tamen eum vel esse vel res
humanas curare iam credunt. Sunt enim multo
deteriores qui ne hoc quidem credunt. Cognito
itaque Cain quod super eius germani sacrificium nec
super suum respexerat Deus, utique fratrem bonum
mutatus imitari, non elatus debuit aemulari. Sed
contristatus est et concidit facies eius. Hoc peccatum maxime arguit Deus, tristitiam de alterius
bonitate, et hoc fratris. Hoc quippe arguendo in-
terrogavit dicens: *Quare contristatus es, et quare concidit facies tua?* Quia enim fratri invidebat Deus
videbat et hoc arguebat.

Nam hominibus, quibus absconditum est cor
alterius, esse posset ambiguum et prorsus incertum
utrum illa tristitia malignitatem suam, in qua se
Deo displicuisse didicerat, an fratris doluerit boni-
tatem, quae Deo placuit, cum in sacrificium eius
aspexit. Sed rationem reddens Deus cur eius
oblationem accipere noluerit ut sibi ipse potius
merito quam ei frater inmerito displiceret, cum esset

desires, but in satisfying them. This is, in fact, characteristic of the earthly city, namely, to worship a god or gods by whose aid it may reign victoriously in earthly peace, moved not by love to provide for others, but by lust to lord it over them. For whereas the good make use of the world in order to enjoy God, the wicked would like to make use of God in order to enjoy the world—at least those among them who still believe that he exists or concerns himself with human affairs; for those who do not believe even so much are in a far worse state. Thus when Cain learned that God had shown regard for his brother's sacrifice and not for his own, he ought surely to have mended his ways and imitated his good brother instead of becoming prideful and showing rivalry. But he turned grim, and his countenance fell. This is a sin that God especially reproves, namely, turning grim over another's goodness, and a brother's at that. And it was, in fact, to reprove this that God asked: "Why have you turned grim, and why has your countenance fallen?" For God saw that he envied his brother, and for that he reproved him.

Now human beings, whose hearts are hidden from each other, might be in doubt and quite uncertain whether Cain turned grim because he grieved over his own wickedness, by which, as he learned, he had displeased God, or because he grieved over his brother's goodness, which found favour with God, when God had regard for his sacrifice. God, however, explained why he refused to accept Cain's offering in order to make him rightly displeased with himself rather than wrongly displeased with his

iniustus non recte dividendo, hoc est non recte
vivendo, et indignus cuius adprobaretur oblatio,
quam esset iniustior quod fratrem iustum gratis
odisset ostendit. Non tamen eum dimittens sine
mandato sancto, iusto et bono: *Quiesce*, inquit; *ad
te enim conversio eius, et tu dominaberis illius.* Numquid fratris? Absit. Cuius igitur nisi peccati?
Dixerat enim: *Peccasti*, tum deinde addidit: *Quiesce;
ad te enim conversio eius, et tu dominaberis illius.*
Potest quidem ita intellegi ad ipsum hominem con-
versionem esse debere peccati ut nulli alii quam sibi
sciat tribuere debere quod peccat.

Haec est enim salubris paenitentiae medicina et
veniae petitio non incongrua, ut, ubi ait: *Ad te enim
conversio eius*, non subaudiatur " erit " sed " sit,"
praecipientis videlicet, non praedicentis modo.
Tunc enim dominabitur quisque peccato, si id sibi
non defendendo praeposuerit sed paenitendo subie-
cerit. Alioquin, et illi serviet dominanti si patro-
cinium adhibuerit accidenti.[1]

Sed ut peccatum intellegatur concupiscentia ipsa
carnalis, de qua dicit apostolus: *Caro concupiscit
adversus spiritum*, in cuius carnis fructibus et invidiam
commemorat, qua utique Cain stimulabatur et ac-

---

[1] accedenti *some MSS.*

---

[1] Galatians 5.17.

brother. For though Cain was already wrong in not allotting rightly, that is, in not living rightly, and hence did not deserve to have his offering approved, God showed how much more wrong he was to hate his righteous brother for no good reason. Yet God did not send him away without a holy, righteous and kind exhortation, for he said: " Calm down, for it is to come back to you, and you are to master it." Might it mean ' master him,' that is, his brother? Heaven forbid! Master what then if not his sin? For after God had said: " You have committed a sin," he then at once added: " Calm down, for it is to come back to you, and you are to master it." Certainly the expression that something, that is, sin should come back to the man himself can be taken to mean that he must know that he should put the blame for his sinning on none other than himself.

This is a wholesome medicine of repentance and an entreaty for pardon that is not inappropriate. Consequently, when God says: " For it is to come back to you," we should understand the verb not as ' will come ' but as ' should come,' that is, we should take the speaker to be prescribing, not predicting. For each one will master his sin only when he does not put it over himself by defending it but makes it subject to himself by repenting it. Otherwise, he will also be its slave while it is master if he lends it his support at its incidence.

But sin may also mean carnal desire itself, about which the Apostle says: " The desires of the flesh are against the spirit." [1] Among the fruits of the flesh he includes envy, and it was envy certainly that goaded and kindled Cain to destroy his brother.

cendebatur in fratris exitium, bene subauditur
" erit," id est: *Ad te enim conversio eius erit, et tu
dominaberis illius.* Cum enim commota fuerit pars
ipsa carnalis quam peccatum appellat apostolus ubi
dicit: *Non ego operor illud, sed quod habitat in me peccatum* (quam partem animi etiam philosophi dicunt
esse vitiosam, non quae mentem debeat trahere, sed
cui mens debeat imperare eamque ab inlicitis operibus ratione cohibere)—cum ergo commota fuerit ad
aliquid perperam committendum, si quiescatur et
obtemperetur dicenti apostolo: *Nec exhibueritis
membra vestra arma iniquitatis peccato*, ad mentem
domita et victa convertitur, ut subditae ratio
dominetur.

Hoc praecepit Deus huic qui facibus invidiae in-
flammabatur in fratrem et quem debuerat imitari
cupiebat auferri. *Quiesce*, inquit, manus ab scelere
contine, non regnet peccatum in tuo mortali corpore
ad oboediendum desideriis eius, nec exhibeas membra tua iniquitatis arma peccato. *Ad te enim conversio eius*, dum non adiuvatur relaxando sed quies-
cendo frenatur, *et tu dominaberis illius*, ut, cum
forinsecus non permittitur operari, sub potestate
mentis regentis et benevolentis adsuescat etiam
intrinsecus non moveri.

Dictum est tale aliquid in eodem divino libro et de
muliere quando post peccatum, Deo interrogante

---

[1] Romans 7.17.
[2] Romans 6.13.
[3] Cf. Romans 6.12.

For that interpretation the simple future is to be understood, as follows: " For it will come back to you, and you will master it." Such is the situation when man's carnal part itself is aroused. This part is labelled sin by the Apostle in the passage where he says: " I do not do it, but sin which dwells within me."[1] There are philosophers too who say that this part of the soul is depraved and thus should not drag the mind after it but should be ruled by the mind and forced by reason to abstain from forbidden deeds. Accordingly, if, when it is aroused to commit some wrong act, we calm down and obey the words of the Apostle: " Do not yield your members to sin as instruments of wickedness,"[2] it comes back, subdued and vanquished, to the mind and subjects itself to the mastery of reason.

This was God's injunction to Cain, who was so inflamed by the firebrands of envy against his own brother that he was eager to see eliminated the very one whom he should have imitated. " Calm down," God said, withhold your hands from crime, let not sin reign in your mortal body to make you obey its desires,[3] and do not yield your members to sin as instruments of wickedness. " For it will come back to you," as long as you do not assist it by slackness but curb it by calmness, " and you will master it." In this way, if it is not allowed to act outwardly, it will become accustomed, under the benevolent authority and control of the mind, to rest quiet inwardly as well.

Something like this was said of the woman too in the same divinely inspired book, when, after the sin had been committed, God asked questions and gave

atque iudicante, damnationis sententias acceperunt, in serpente diabolus et in se ipsis illa et maritus. Cum enim dixisset ei: *Multiplicans multiplicabo tristitias tuas et gemitum tuum*, et *in tristitiis paries filios*, deinde addidit: *Et ad virum tuum conversio tua, et ipse tui dominabitur.* Quod dictum est ad Cain de peccato vel de vitiosa carnis concupiscentia, hoc isto loco de peccatrice femina, ubi intellegendum est virum ad regendam uxorem animo carnem regenti similem esse oportere. Propter quod dicit apostolus: *Qui diligit uxorem suam se ipsum diligit. Nemo enim umquam carnem suam odio habuit.*

Sananda sunt enim haec sicut nostra, non sicut aliena damnanda. Sed illud Dei praeceptum Cain sicut praevaricator accepit. Invalescente quippe invidentiae vitio, fratrem insidiatus occidit. Talis erat terrenae conditor civitatis. Quo modo autem significaverit etiam Iudaeos, a quibus Christus occisus est pastor ovium hominum, quem pastor ovium pecorum praefigurabat Abel, quia in allegoria prophetica res est, parco nunc dicere, et quaedam hinc adversus Faustum Manichaeum dixisse me recolo.

---

[1] Genesis 3.16. Augustine's text is close to the sense of the Septuagint, but cf. the RSV for the latter part of the quotation: " Yet your desire shall be for your husband, and he shall rule over you."

judgement. Found guilty, the devil received his sentence in the person of the serpent, while the woman and her husband received theirs in their own persons. For when God had said to her: " I shall greatly multiply your sorrows and your groaning, and with sorrow shall you bring forth children," he added next: " And you shall ever come to your husband, and he shall be your master."[1] The same words spoken to Cain about sin or the depraved desire of the flesh are here used of the sinful woman; and in this instance we are to understand that man, in order to rule his wife, should resemble the mind that rules the flesh. This is why the Apostle says: " He who loves his wife loves himself. For no man ever hated his own flesh."[2]

We should, therefore, seek to cure such faults of the flesh as being our own, not merely condemn them as though they were foreign to us. But Cain received that admonition of God like a transgressor. For as the fault of envy grew strong within him, he lay in wait for his brother and slew him. Such was the founder of the earthly city. He also was a symbol of the Jews who slew Christ, shepherd of the flock of men, who was foreshadowed in Abel, shepherd of the flock of sheep. But since a prophetic allegory is involved here, I say no more on this subject for the present. Besides, I recall having already said something on it in my work *Against Faustus the Manichaean*.[3]

[2] Ephesians 5.28–29.
[3] Cf. *Contra Faustum Manichaeum* 12.9.

SAINT AUGUSTINE

VIII

*Quae ratio fuerit ut Cain inter principia generis
humani conderet civitatem.*

Nunc autem defendenda mihi videtur historia ne
sit scriptura incredibilis, quae dicit aedificatam ab
uno homine civitatem eo tempore quo non [1] plus
quam viri quattuor vel potius tres, postea quam
fratrem frater occidit, fuisse videntur in terra, id est
primus homo pater omnium et ipse Cain et eius
filius Enoch, ex cuius nomine ipsa civitas nuncupata
est. Sed hoc quos movet parum considerant non
omnes homines qui tunc esse potuerunt scriptorem
sacrae huius historiae necesse habuisse nominare,
sed eos solos quos operis suscepti ratio postulabat.
Propositum quippe scriptoris illius fuit per quem
sanctus Spiritus id agebat per successiones certarum
generationum ex uno homine propagatarum pervenire ad Abraham ac deinde ex eius semine ad
populum Dei, in quo distincto a ceteris gentibus
praefigurarentur et praenuntiarentur omnia quae de
civitate cuius aeternum erit regnum et de rege eius
eodemque conditore Christo in Spiritu praevidebantur esse ventura, ita ut nec de altera societate
hominum taceretur, quam terrenam dicimus civitatem, quantum ei commemorandae satis esset ut
civitas Dei etiam suae adversariae conparatione
clarescat.

[1] non *omitted in V and several other MSS.*

VIII

*How it was that Cain founded a city amid the first
beginnings of the human race.*

My task at this time, I think, is to uphold the
historical account. Otherwise Scripture may not
seem credible when it states that a city was built by
one man at a time when the earth was populated
apparently by not more than four men or rather by
only three after the act of fratricide. These three
were presumably the first man, who was the father
of all, Cain himself and his son Enoch, after whose
name the city itself was called.[1] But those who are
troubled here overlook the fact that the writer of this
sacred history was under no obligation to name all
the people who may then have existed but only the
few required by the plan of the work undertaken.
For the aim of that writer, through whom the Holy
Spirit was operating, was to arrive at Abraham
through a succession of certain generations descended
from a single man, and then to proceed from the seed
of Abraham to God's people, which was set apart
from the other nations and would serve to foreshadow
and foretell all things that relate to the city whose
kingdom will be eternal and to its king and founder
Christ, as they were foreseen by inspiration of the
Spirit as destined to come. In this connexion, moreover, the other society of men, which we call the
earthly city, was likewise mentioned and described
to an extent sufficient for the City of God to stand
out in brilliant relief by contrast with its opposite.

---

[1] Cf. Genesis 4.17.

449

Cum igitur scriptura divina, ubi et numerum annorum quos illi homines vixerunt commemorat, ita
concludat ut dicat de illo de quo loquebatur: *Et
genuit filios et filias, et fuerunt omnes dies* illius vel
illius quos vixit anni tot, *et mortuus est*, numquid quia
eosdem filios et filias non nominat, ideo intellegere
non debemus per tam multos annos quibus tunc in
saeculi huius prima aetate vivebant nasci potuisse
plurimos homines, quorum coetibus condi possent
etiam plurimae civitates? Sed pertinuit ad Deum,
quo ista inspirante conscripta sunt, has duas societates
suis diversis generationibus primitus digerere atque
distinguere, ut seorsum hominum, hoc est secundum
hominem viventium, seorsum autem filiorum Dei, id
est hominum secundum Deum viventium, generationes contexerentur usque [1] diluvium, ubi ambarum
societatum discretio concretioque narratur—discretio
quidem quod ambarum separatim generationes commemorantur, unius fratricidae Cain, alterius autem
qui vocabatur Seth (natus quippe fuerat et ipse de
Adam pro illo quem frater occidit); concretio autem
quia, bonis in deterius declinantibus, tales universi
facti fuerant ut diluvio delerentur, excepto uno iusto,
cui [2] nomen erat Noe, et eius coniuge et tribus
filiis totidemque nuribus, qui homines octo ex illa

[1] usque ad *some MSS.*
[2] cui *V and two other MSS.:* cuius *most MSS.*

---

[1] Cf., *e.g.*, Genesis 5.4–5.

Now in passages where the number of years that those first men lived is recorded, holy Scripture ends by saying about the man of whom it was speaking: " And he had sons and daughters, and all the days " that this one or that lived " were " so and so many years, " and he died." [1] But the fact that these sons and daughters are not named surely does not prevent us from inferring that during the many years that people lived in that youth of our world, large numbers of men might have been born and large numbers of cities might have been founded by their congregating. But it was the concern of God, by whose inspiration these accounts were written, to arrange and distinguish from the beginning these two societies in their respective generations. Thus, on the one hand, the generations of men, that is, of those who lived according to man, and, on the other hand, the generations of the children of God, that is, of men who lived according to God, were interwoven in the narrative until the flood, where the separation and coalescence of the two societies are related. They are treated as separate because separate accounts are given of the generations of the two societies, one sprung from the fratricide Cain, the other from his brother called Seth; for the latter too was born to Adam, to take the place of the son who was slain by his brother. But they are also described as having coalesced because, as the good changed increasingly for the worse, they all became equally worthy of destruction in the flood, with the exception of only one righteous man called Noah, his wife, his three sons and his three daughters-in-law. These eight human beings alone deserved

451

omnium vastatione mortalium per arcam evadere meruerunt.

Quod igitur scriptum est: *Et cognovit Cain uxorem suam, et concipiens peperit Enoch; et erat aedificans civitatem in nomine filii sui Enoch*, non est quidem consequens ut istum primum filium genuisse credatur. Neque enim hoc ex eo putandum est, quia dictus est cognovisse uxorem suam, quasi tunc se illi primitus concumbendo miscuisset. Nam et de ipso patre omnium Adam non tunc solum hoc dictum est quando conceptus est Cain, quem primogenitum videtur habuisse, verum etiam posterius eadem scriptura: *Cognovit*, inquit, *Adam Evam uxorem suam, et concepit et peperit filium, et nominavit nomen illius Seth*. Unde intellegitur ita solere illam scripturam loqui, quamvis non semper, cum in ea legitur factos hominum fuisse conceptus, non tamen solum cum primum sibi sexus uterque miscetur. Nec illud necessario est argumento ut primogenitum patri existimemus Enoch, quod eius nomine illa civitas nuncupata est. Non enim ab re est ut propter aliquam causam, cum et alios haberet, diligeret eum pater ceteris amplius. Neque enim et Iudas primogenitus fuit, a quo Iudaea cognominata est et Iudaei.

Sed etiamsi conditori civitatis illius iste filius primus est natus, non ideo putandum est tunc a patre conditae civitati nomen eius inpositum quando natus est, quia nec constitui tunc ab uno poterat civitas, quae nihil est aliud quam hominum multitudo

---

[1] Genesis 4.17.
[2] Genesis 4.25.

to escape in the ark from that annihilation of all mortals.

Therefore, though we read in Scripture: " And Cain knew his wife, and she conceived and bore Enoch; and he built a city in the name of his son Enoch," [1] we need not necessarily believe that this was the first son that he had. For no such inference should be drawn from the statement that he knew his wife, as though he had only then for the first time had sexual intercourse with her. Not only were these words used of Adam himself, the father of all men at the time when Cain, who seems to have been his first-born offspring, was conceived, but later too the same Scripture tells us: " Adam knew his wife Eve, and she conceived and bore a son, and called his name Seth." [2] From this we may conclude that Scripture usually, though not always, uses these words when we read in it that men were conceived. But their use is not limited to the case when a couple have sexual intercourse for the first time. Nor is the fact that this city was called after Enoch's name cogent proof that we should regard him as his father's first-born. For it is quite possible that, though the father also had other sons, he loved him for some reason beyond the rest. Judah, as we know, was not a first-born son either, yet Judaea and the Jews were named after him.

But even if Enoch was the first-born son of the founder of that city, we must not infer that his father founded the city and bestowed his name upon it at the time of his birth, for a city, which is nothing but a group of men united by some bond of fellowship, could not have been established at that time by just

SAINT AUGUSTINE

aliquo societatis vinculo conligata. Sed cum illius
hominis familia tanta numerositate cresceret ut
haberet iam populi quantitatem, tunc potuit utique
fieri ut et constitueret et nomen primogeniti sui
constitutae inponeret civitati. Tam longa quippe
vita illorum hominum fuit ut illic memoratorum
quorum et anni taciti non sunt, qui vixit minimum
ante diluvium ad septingentos quinquaginta tres
perveniret. Nam plures nongentos annos etiam
transierunt, quamvis nemo ad mille pervenerit.

Quis itaque dubitaverit per unius hominis aetatem
tantum multiplicari potuisse genus humanum ut
esset unde constituerentur non una sed plurimae civitates? Quod ex hoc conici facillime potest, quia
ex uno Abraham non multo amplius quadringentis
annis numerositas Hebraeae gentis tanta procreata
est ut in exitu eiusdem populi ex Aegypto sescenta
hominum milia fuisse referantur bellicae iuventutis,
ut omittamus gentem Idumaeorum non pertinentem
ad populum Israel, quam genuit frater eius Esau,
nepos Abrahae, et alias natas ex semine ipsius
Abrahae non per Sarram coniugem procreato.[1]

[1] procreatas *some MSS.*

---

[1] Cf. Genesis 5.31. Augustine follows the Septuagint in
setting the age of Lamech at 753 years, but according to the
Vulgate he was 777 years old when he died. Enoch, according
to Genesis 5.23, reached only 365 years, but his passing was
not regarded as a natural death; cf. Genesis 5.24; Hebrews
11.5; also below, 15.10 (pp. 461–465).

454

one person. When, however, that man's family grew so numerous that it had a multitude of people, then it was certainly possible for him to establish a city and to bestow the name of his first-born son upon the city so established. For the men of those days had such long lives that, among those mentioned in that account with their years also given, even the one who had the shortest life before the flood reached the age of seven hundred and fifty-three.[1] Several, in fact, even exceeded nine hundred years, though no one reached a thousand.

Who then can doubt that it was possible for the human race to multiply so greatly during the span of one man's life that there was a sufficient population for the establishment of not just one but many cities? We can quite readily work this out from the case of Abraham. For from that one man the Hebrew nation reproduced so prolifically in a little more than four hundred years [2] that there were, as we are told, six hundred thousand young men of military age in the exodus of that people from Egypt,[3] not to mention the nation of the Idumaeans which, descending from Israel's brother Esau, Abraham's grandson,[4] does not belong to the people of Israel, or the other nations sprung from the seed of Abraham himself yet not through his wife Sarah.[5]

[2] Cf. Exodus 12.40. Unlike the Vulgate, the Septuagint, whose tradition Augustine follows, includes in this number the years passed by the patriarchs in Canaan.

[3] Cf. Exodus 12.37.

[4] For the descendants of Esau see Genesis 36.

[5] For Abraham's descendants by Keturah and Hagar see Genesis 25.1–4 and 12–15.

SAINT AUGUSTINE

IX

De longa vita hominum quae fuit ante diluvium et de ampliore humanorum corporum forma.

Quam ob rem nullus prudens rerum existimator dubitaverit Cain non solum aliquam verum etiam magnam potuisse condere civitatem, quando in tam longum tempus protendebatur vita mortalium, nisi forte infidelium quispiam ex ipsa numerositate annorum nobis ingerat quaestionem qua vixisse tunc homines scriptum est in auctoritatibus [1] nostris, et hoc neget esse credendum. Ita quippe non credunt etiam magnitudines corporum longe ampliores tunc fuisse quam nunc sunt. Unde et nobilissimus eorum poeta Vergilius de ingenti lapide quem in agrorum limite infixum vir fortis illorum temporum pugnans et rapuit et cucurrit et intorsit et misit:

Vix illum (inquit) lecti bis sex cervice subirent,
Qualia nunc hominum producit corpora tellus,

significans maiora tunc corpora producere solere tellurem. Quanto magis igitur temporibus recentioribus mundi ante illud nobile diffamatumque diluvium! Sed de corporum magnitudine plerumque incredulos nudata per vetustatem sive per vim fluminum variosque casus sepulcra convincunt, ubi apparuerunt vel unde ceciderunt incredibilis magnitudinis ossa

---

[1] auctoribus *some MSS.*

---

[1] Cf. Pliny the Elder, *Naturalis Historia* 7.48.153–49.164.

IX

*On the longevity of men before the flood and on the
larger stature of human bodies.*

HENCE no intelligent judge could doubt that it was
possible for Cain to found not only a city of some
sort but even a large one, since the lives of mortals
were prolonged for so great a span.[1] But some
unbeliever might perhaps dispute with us the many
centuries that, as we read in our authorities, the men
of that age lived, and might argue that this is incredible. In the same way some people refuse to believe
that men's bodies were of much larger size then than
they are now. It was this point that prompted their
most distinguished poet Virgil to say of an enormous
boundary-stone that a brave warrior of those early
times caught up and, as he ran, swung around and
hurled:

> Scarce could that stone twice six picked men
>   upraise
> With bodies such as now the earth displays.[2]

The implication is that in those days the earth used
to produce larger bodies. How much more so then
was that true before that celebrated and far-famed
flood when the world was younger!

As far as the size of bodies is concerned, however,
sceptics are generally persuaded by the evidence in
tombs uncovered through the ravages of time, the
violence of streams or various other occurrences. For
incredibly large bones of the dead have been found

[2] Virgil, *Aeneid* 12.899–900.

mortuorum. Vidi ipse, non solus sed aliquot mecum, in Uticensi litore molarem hominis dentem tam ingentem ut, si in nostrorum dentium modulos minutatim concideretur, centum nobis videretur facere potuisse. Sed illum gigantis alicuius fuisse crediderim. Nam praeter quod erant omnium multo quam nostra maiora tunc corpora, gigantes longe ceteris anteibant, sicut aliis deinde nostrisque temporibus rara quidem, sed numquam ferme defuerunt quae modum aliorum plurimum excederent. Plinius Secundus, doctissimus homo, quanto magis magisque praeterit saeculi excursus, minora corpora naturam ferre testatur; quod etiam Homerum commemorat saepe carmine fuisse conquestum, non haec velut poetica figmenta deridens, sed in historicam fidem tamquam miraculorum naturalium scriptor adsumens. Verum, ut dixi, antiquorum magnitudines corporum inventa plerumque ossa, quoniam diuturna sunt, etiam multo posterioribus saeculis produnt.

Annorum autem numerositas cuiusque hominis quae temporibus illis fuit nullis nunc talibus documentis venire in experimentum potest. Nec tamen ideo fides sacrae huic[1] historiae deroganda est, cuius tanto inpudentius narrata non credimus quanto impleri certius praenuntiata conspicimus. Dicit tamen etiam idem Plinius esse adhuc gentem ubi ducentos annos vivitur. Si ergo humanarum vitarum

---

[1] huius *some MSS.*

---

[1] An African city S.E. of Hippo on the Gulf of Carthage.
[2] Cf. Pliny the Elder, *Naturalis Historia* 7.16.73–75.
[3] Cf. Homer, *Iliad* 5.302–304.

in them or dislodged from them. On the shoré of Utica[1] I myself, not alone but with several others, saw a human molar so enormous that, if it were divided up into pieces to the dimensions of our teeth, it would, so it seemed to us, have made a hundred of them. But that molar, I should suppose, belonged to some giant. For not only were bodies in general much larger then than our own, but the giants towered far above the rest, even as in subsequent times, including our own, there have almost always been bodies which, though few in number, far surpassed the size of the others. Pliny the Elder, a man of great learning, declares that, as the world advances more and more in age, nature bears smaller and smaller bodies;[2] and when he mentions that even Homer often regretted this in his poetry,[3] he does not ridicule such statements as poetic fictions but, speaking as a recorder of the wonders of nature, assumes their historicity. But, as I have said, the size of ancient bodies is disclosed even to much later ages by the frequent discovery of bones, for bones are long-lasting.

On the other hand, the longevity of individuals in those days cannot now be demonstrated by any such tangible evidence. Yet we should not on that account question the reliability of this sacred history; our refusal to believe what it relates would be as shameless as our evidence of the fulfilment of its prophecies is certain. Moreover, the same Pliny also says that there is still a tribe where people live to be two hundred years old.[4] Accordingly, if we

---

[4] Pliny the Elder, *Naturalis Historia* 7.48.154, where the Greek historian Hellanicus is cited as authority.

diuturnitates quas experti non sumus hodie habere
creduntur incognita nobis loca, cur non habuisse
credantur et tempora? An vero credibile est alicubi
esse quod hic non est, et incredibile est aliquando
fuisse quod nunc non est?

X

*De differentia qua inter Hebraeos et nostros codices
videntur annorum numeri dissonare.*

Quocirca, etsi inter Hebraeos et nostros codices de
ipso numero annorum nonnulla videtur esse distantia,
quod ignoro qua ratione sit factum, non tamen tanta
est ut illos homines tam longaevos fuisse dissentiant.
Nam ipse homo primus Adam, antequam gigneret
filium qui est appellatus Seth ducentos triginta
vixisse annos reperitur in codicibus nostris, in
Hebraeis autem centum triginta perhibetur. Sed
postea quam eum genuit, septingentos vixisse legitur
in nostris, octingentos vero in illis; atque ita in
utrisque universitatis summa concordat.

Ac deinde per consequentes generationes antequam
gignatur qui gigni commemoratur, minus vixisse
apud Hebraeos pater eius invenitur centum annos;

---

[1] Augustine's knowledge of the Hebrew version came, not
from the Hebrew itself, but from Jerome's Latin translation
of it, which was already available to him before he began to
compose the *City of God* in 413. By 'our own' version Augustine means an Old Latin version made from the Greek text of
the Septuagint; cf. *The Oxford Dictionary of the Christian*

460

believe that places unknown to us show in our own
day such human longevity as we have not experienced, why should we not believe the same of times
in the distant past? Or if it is possible to believe
that something that does not exist here does exist
somewhere, is it impossible to believe that something
that does not exist now did exist at some time?

X

*On the difference and discrepancy that we see between the
Hebrew version and our own in the number of years.*

Now we see here, to be sure, some discrepancy
between the Hebrew version and our own [1] in regard
to the precise number of years (and I do not know
how this came about), but they are not so far apart
that there is any disagreement about the longevity
of those first men. Thus we find in our version that
Adam, the father of all men, was two hundred and
thirty years old before he had the son called Seth,
but in the Hebrew text we read that he was a hundred
and thirty. On the other hand, after the birth of
his son, he lived, according to our version, for seven
hundred years, but, according to the other, for
eight hundred years; [2] thus both texts are in agreement on the total sum.

We find this same variation in the generations that
followed: in the Hebrew version, before the birth of
each son whose birth is mentioned, the age of his

Church (London, 1957), edited by F. L. Cross, 980, *s.v.* " Old
Latin Versions "; also 1431, *s.v.* " Vulgate."
  [2] Cf. Genesis 5.3–4.

sed postea quam est genitus idem ipse, centum
minus quam in Hebraeis inveniuntur in nostris.
Atque ita et[1] hinc et inde numeri universitas con-
sonat. In sexta autem generatione nusquam utrique
codices discrepant. In septima vero, ubi ille qui
natus est Enoch non mortuus, sed, quod Deo placuerit, translatus esse narratur, eadem dissonantia est,
quae in superioribus quinque de centum annis antequam gigneret eum qui ibi commemoratus est
filium, atque[2] in summa similis consonantia. Vixit
enim annos, antequam transferretur, secundum
utrosque codices trecentos sexaginta quinque.

Octava generatio habet quidem nonnullam di-
versitatem, sed minorem ac dissimilem ceteris.
Mathusalam quippe, quem genuit Enoch, antequam
gigneret eum qui in ipso ordine sequitur, secundum
Hebraeos non centum minus sed viginti amplius
vixit annos; qui rursus in nostris, postea quam eum
genuit, reperiuntur additi, et in utrisque sibi summa
universi numeri occurrit. In sola nona generatione,
id est in annis Lamech, filii Mathusalae, patris autem
Noe, summa universitatis discrepat, sed non plurimum. Viginti enim et quattuor annos plus vixisse
in Hebraeis quam in nostris codicibus invenitur.
Namque antequam gigneret filium qui vocatus est

---

[1] et *omitted in V and several other MSS.*
[2] atque ita *some MSS.*

---

[1] Cf. Genesis 5.21–24. Augustine's *placuerit*, 'he pleased,'
reflects the Septuagint εὐηρέστησεν; cf. Hebrews 11.5–6. The

father is a hundred years less than in ours, but after the birth of this son, the number of years given in our text is a hundred less than in the Hebrew. Thus there is agreement on the total when the numbers in both cases are added. In the sixth generation, however, there is no discrepancy anywhere between the two versions. But in the seventh, in which, as we are told, Enoch, born though he was, did not die but was translated because he pleased God,[1] there is the same disagreement of a hundred years as in the first five generations about his age before he had the son mentioned there, and a like agreement about the total. For, according to the texts of both groups, he was three hundred and sixty-five years old before he was translated.

In the eighth generation some divergence does indeed appear, but it is smaller than the others and different. For before Methuselah, Enoch's son, engendered the one who comes next in order, he was not a hundred years younger but twenty years older according to the Hebrew version.[2] But these years, in turn, are found added in our text after he had this son, and in both versions the total sums tally. Only in the ninth generation, that is, in the age attained by Lamech, son of Methuselah and father of Noah, is there a discrepancy in the total sum, but it is not very large.[3] For he lived twenty-four years longer according to the Hebrew version than according to our own. Before the birth of his son called

Vulgate reads: *ambulavit ... cum Deo,* 'he walked with God.' See above, 15.8 (p. 455, note 1).

[2] Cf. Genesis 5.25-27.
[3] Cf. Genesis 5.28-31.

Noe, sex minus habet in Hebraeis quam in nostris; postea vero quam eum genuit, triginta amplius in eisdem quam in nostris. Unde, sex illis detractis, restant viginti quattuor, ut dictum est.

XI

De annis Mathusalae, cuius aetas quattuordecim annis diluvium videtur excedere.

PER hanc autem discrepantiam Hebraeorum codicum atque nostrorum exoritur illa famosissima quaestio ubi Mathusalam quattuordecim annos vixisse post diluvium conputatur, cum scriptura ex omnibus qui in terra tunc fuerant solos octo homines in arca exitium commemoret evasisse diluvii, in quibus Mathusalam non fuit. Secundum codices enim nostros Mathusalam, priusquam gigneret illum quem vocavit Lamech, vixit annos centum sexaginta septem; deinde ipse Lamech, antequam ex illo natus esset Noe, vixit annos centum octoginta octo, qui fiunt simul trecenti quinquaginta quinque. His adduntur sescenti Noe, quoto eius anno diluvium factum est, qui fiunt nongenti quinquaginta quinque ex quo Mathusalam natus est usque ad annum diluvii.

---

[1] This question is similarly characterized by Jerome in his *Liber Hebraicarum Quaestionum in Genesim*, on Genesis 5.25. The matter is taken up again by Augustine in *Quaestiones in Heptateuchum* 1.2, where the difficulty is regarded as due to a textual error in the Hebrew manuscripts.

[2] Cf. Genesis 5.25, where the Vulgate puts the age at 187 years.

Noah he is six years younger in the Hebrew version than in our own; but after the birth of this son he lived thirty years longer by the former account than by the latter. If those six years are subtracted from the thirty, the difference is the above-mentioned twenty-four.

XI

On the age of Methuselah, whose life-span seems to extend fourteen years beyond the time of the flood.

THIS discrepancy between the Hebrew text and our own gives rise to that very celebrated problem [1] concerning the fourteen years that Methuselah, according to our calculation, lived after the flood. For Scripture relates that of all those who were then on earth only eight people escaped destruction by the flood in an ark, and Methuselah was not among them. According to our text, Methuselah was a hundred and sixty-seven years old before the birth of the son whom he called Lamech; [2] then Lamech himself was a hundred and eighty-eight years old before he became the father of Noah, [3] and these two ages combined come to three hundred and fifty-five years. If we add to this sum the six hundred years of Noah's age at the time of the flood, [4] the total becomes nine hundred and fifty-five, [5] and this is the number of years that elapsed from the birth of Methuselah to the year of the flood.

[3] Cf. Genesis 5.28, where the Vulgate puts the age at 182 years.
[4] Cf. Genesis 7.6.
[5] But 969 according to the figures given in the Vulgate.

Omnes autem [1] anni vitae Mathusalam nongenti sexaginta novem conputantur, quia, cum vixisset annos centum sexaginta septem et genuisset filium qui est appellatus Lamech, post eum genitum vixit annos octingentos duo, qui omnes, ut diximus, nongenti sexaginta novem fiunt. Unde detractis nongentis quinquaginta quinque, ab ortu Mathusalae usque ad diluvium remanent quattuordecim, quibus vixisse creditur post diluvium. Propter quod eum nonnulli, etsi non in terra, ubi omnem carnem quam vivere in aquis natura non sinit constat fuisse deletam, cum patre suo qui translatus fuerat aliquantum fuisse atque ibi, donec diluvium praeteriret, vixisse arbitrantur, nolentes derogare fidem codicibus quos in auctoritatem celebriorem suscepit ecclesia et credentes Iudaeorum potius quam istos non habere quod verum est.

Non enim admittunt quod magis hic esse potuerit error interpretum quam in ea lingua esse falsum unde in nostram per Graecam scriptura ipsa translata est, sed inquiunt non esse credibile septuaginta interpretes, qui uno simul tempore unoque sensu interpretati sunt, errare potuisse aut ubi nihil eorum intererat voluisse mentiri, Iudaeos vero, dum nobis invident quod lex et prophetae ad nos inter-

[1] enim *V and one other MS.*

---

[1] Cf. Genesis 5.26, where the Vulgate says that he lived for 782 years after the birth of Lamech.

Now all the years of Methuselah's life add up to nine hundred and sixty-nine, for he was a hundred and sixty-seven years old at the birth of his son called Lamech and lived for eight hundred and two years more after the birth.[1] And, as I said before, all these years come to nine hundred and sixty-nine. If the nine hundred and fifty-five years that intervened between the birth of Methuselah and the flood are subtracted from that total, there remain fourteen years, which he presumably lived beyond the time of the flood. Hence some people suppose that he was indeed alive then but not on earth, where, as we know, all flesh that nature does not allow to live in water was destroyed. They think that he was for some time in the company of his father, who had been translated, and that he lived there until the flood was over. They are reluctant to withhold credence from the text whose acceptance by the Church has accorded it more general authority, and prefer to believe that it is the version of the Jews, rather than the other, that is deficient in the truth.

These people refuse to allow that a mistake of the translators might be involved here; instead, they prefer to think that there is a misstatement in that language from which Scripture itself was translated into our own tongue through the Greek. They maintain that it is beyond belief that the seventy translators, who made their versions at one and the same time and with one and the same meaning, could have erred or would have wished to pervert the truth in a matter where it made no difference to them. In their view it was the Jews, who begrudging us the acquisition of the Law and Prophets

467

pretando transierint, mutasse quaedam in codicibus
suis ut nostris minueretur auctoritas.

Hanc opinionem vel suspicionem accipiat quisque
ut putaverit. Certum est tamen non vixisse Mathusalam post diluvium sed eodem anno fuisse defunc-
tum, si verum est quod de numero annorum in
Hebraeis codicibus invenitur. De illis autem septuaginta interpretibus quid mihi videatur suo loco
diligentius inserendum est, cum ad ipsa tempora,
quantum necessitas huius operis postulat, com-
memoranda, adiuvante Domino, venerimus. Praesenti enim sufficit quaestioni secundum utrosque
codices tam longas habuisse vitas illius aevi homines
ut posset aetate unius, qui de duobus quos solos terra
tunc habuit parentibus primus est natus, ad con-
stituendam etiam civitatem multiplicari genus
humanum.

XII

*De opinione eorum qui primorum temporum homines
tam longaevos quam scribitur fuisse non
credunt.*

NEQUE enim ullo modo audiendi sunt qui putant aliter annos illis temporibus conputatos, id est tantae
brevitatis ut unus annus noster decem illos habuisse
credatur. Quapropter, inquiunt, cum audierit quisque vel legerit nongentos annos quemque vixisse,
debet intellegere nonaginta; decem quippe illi anni
unus est noster et decem nostri centum illi fuerunt.

---

[1] See below, 18.42–44 (vol. 6, 27–39).

through translation, made certain alterations in their version to diminish the authority of ours.

Everyone is free to accept this belief or suspicion as he sees fit. Yet it is certain that Methuselah did not live beyond the time of the flood but died in the same year, if what we find in the Hebrew text about the number of years is true. As for those seventy translators, I intend to include a more detailed account of my views about them in its proper place,[1] when, with God's help, I come to treat of their times to the extent required by the scope of this work. For our present inquiry it suffices to know that, according to both versions, the people of that period enjoyed such longevity that the human race could multiply enough even to establish a city within the lifetime of a single individual, the first offspring of the two parents who were then alone on earth.

XII

On the view of those who do not believe that the earliest human beings lived as long as Scripture records.

No heed whatsoever should be paid to those who think that years were differently calculated in those early days, that is, were of such brief duration that one of our years comprises ten of those others. Thus, according to them, whenever anyone hears or reads that a person has lived for nine hundred years, he should understand that ninety is meant, for one of our years is equal to ten of those others and a hundred of the latter were equal to ten of ours.

Ac per hoc, ut putant, viginti trium annorum fuit Adam quando genuit Seth, et ipse Seth viginti agebat et sex menses quando ex illo natus est Enos, quos appellat scriptura ducentos et quinque annos, quoniam, sicut isti suspicantur quorum exponimus opinionem, unum annum qualem nunc habemus in decem partes illi dividebant et easdem partes annos vocabant. Quarum partium habet una quadratum senarium eo quod sex diebus Deus perfecerit opera sua ut in septimo requiesceret (de qua re in libro undecimo, sicut potui, disputavi). Sexiens autem seni, qui numerus quadratum senarium facit, triginta sex dies sunt, qui multiplicati deciens ad trecentos sexaginta perveniunt, id est duodecim menses lunares. Propter quinque dies enim reliquos quibus solaris annus impletur et diei quadrantem, propter quem quater ductum eo anno quo bissextum vocant unus dies adicitur, addebantur a veteribus postea dies ut occurreret numerus annorum, quos dies Romani intercalares vocabant.

Proinde etiam Enos, quem genuit Seth, decem et novem agebat annos quando ex illo natus est filius eius Cainan, quos annos dicit scriptura centum nonaginta. Et deinceps per omnes generationes, in quibus hominum anni commemorantur ante diluvium, nullus fere in nostris codicibus invenitur qui, cum esset centum annorum vel infra vel etiam cen-

---

[1] See above, 11.8.
[2] This added day was called thus because in the Roman calendar February 24, the day repeated every fourth year, was designated as *ante diem sextum Kalendas Martias* or, more

Hence, by their reckoning, Adam was in his twenty-third year when he became the father of Seth, and Seth himself was twenty years and six months old when his son Enos was born. But in Scripture Seth's age is said to be two hundred and five years, for, according to the surmise of those whose view we are presenting, one of our own years used to be divided into ten parts, and these parts were called years. Each of these parts comprises the square of six because God completed his works in six days that he might rest on the seventh (a subject which I have discussed as best I could in Book XI).[1] Now six times six, or the square of six, makes thirty-six days, which, multiplied by ten, comes to three hundred and sixty days or twelve lunar months. The solar year requires five more days for its completion, plus a quarter of a day, which is the reason why one day, called *bissextus*,[2] is added every fourth year. Hence the ancients later added days to make the years come out right in number, and the Romans labelled them intercalary days.

Thus on this theory too Enos, the son of Seth, was nineteen years old when his son Cainan was born, but according to Scripture his age was a hundred and ninety.[3] And so through all subsequent generations where mention is made of men's ages before the flood, we find in our text [4] no one who had a son when he was a hundred years old or less or even a

briefly, a.d. vi Kal. Mart., and hence the intercalary day was the 'twice-sixth' day before the Kalends of March.

[3] Cf. Genesis 5.9 (Septuagint).

[4] That is, according to the ages given in the Latin version based upon the Septuagint.

tum viginti aut non multo amplius, genuerit filium.
Sed qui minima aetate genuerunt centum sexaginta
et quod excurrit fuisse referuntur, quia nemo, inquiunt, decem annorum homo potest gignere filios,
qui numerus centum appellabantur anni ab illis
hominibus. Sed in annis sedecim est matura pubertas et proli iam idonea procreandae, quos centum et
sexaginta annos illa tempora nuncupabant.

Ut autem aliter annum tunc fuisse conputatum
non sit incredibile, adiciunt quod apud plerosque
scriptores historiae reperitur Aegyptios habuisse
annum quattuor mensum,[1] Acarnanas sex mensum,
Lavinios tredecim mensum. Plinius Secundus cum
commemorasset relatum fuisse in litteras [2] quendam
vixisse centum quinquaginta duos, alium decem
amplius, alios ducentorum annorum habuisse vitam,
alios trecentorum, quosdam ad quingentos, alios ad
sescentos, nonnullos ad octingentos etiam pervenisse,
haec omnia inscitia [3] temporum accidisse arbitratus
est. "Alii quippe," inquit, "aestate determinabant
annum et alterum hieme, alii quadripertitis temporibus, sicut Arcades, inquit, quorum anni tri-
menstres fuerunt." Adiecit etiam aliquando Aegyptios, quorum parvos annos quaternorum mensum
fuisse supra diximus, lunae fine limitasse annum.

---

[1] mensum *V and a few other MSS.:* mensium *many MSS.
So also below.*

[2] litteris *some MSS.*

[3] inscitia *some MSS., Pliny:* inscientia *other MSS.*

hundred and twenty or somewhat more. But the earliest age at which men had children then is reported to have been a hundred and sixty and above. For no person, it is maintained, can have children at the age of ten, that is, according to the calculation of those people, a hundred. Puberty is developed and capable of procreation in the sixteenth year, which, by ancient reckoning, was called the hundred and sixtieth year.

To lend credibility to the theory that the year was differently calculated in those early times, the proponents of this view add as evidence from the works of a good many historians the fact that the Egyptians had a year of four months,[1] the Acarnanians of six months and the Lavinians of thirteen months. Pliny the Elder mentioned[2] that, according to the testimony of written sources, one person lived for a hundred and fifty-two years and another for ten years longer, that some people lived to be two hundred years old and others to be three hundred years old and that some people even attained the age of five hundred, others of six hundred and still others of eight hundred. But, in his judgement, all this was due to ignorance of chronology. For, as he said, " some people counted the summer as one year and the winter as a second year, others counted each of the four seasons as a year, like the Arcadians whose years were three months long." The Egyptians, he added, whose short years, as I mentioned above, were each four months long, at times even made the end of a year coincide with the waning of the moon.

---

[1] Cf. above, 12.11 (p. 51).
[2] Pliny the Elder, *Naturalis Historia* 7.48.154–155.

"Itaque apud eos," inquit, "et singula milia annorum vixisse produntur."

His velut probabilibus argumentis quidam non destruentes fidem sacrae huius historiae, sed astruere nitentes, ne sit incredibile quod tam multos annos vixisse referuntur antiqui, persuaserunt sibi nec se suadere inpudenter existimant tam exiguum spatium temporis tunc annum vocatum ut illi decem sint unus noster et decem nostri centum illorum. Hoc autem esse falsissimum documento evidentissimo ostenditur. Quod antequam faciam, non mihi tacendum videtur quae credibilior possit esse suspicio.

Poteramus certe hanc adseverationem ex Hebraeis codicibus redarguere atque convincere, ubi Adam non ducentorum triginta sed centum triginta annorum fuisse reperitur quando tertium genuit filium.[1] Qui anni si tredecim nostri sunt, procul dubio, primum quando genuit, undecim vel non multo amplius annorum fuit. Quis potest hac aetate generare usitata ista nobisque notissima lege naturae?

Sed hunc omittamus, qui fortasse etiam quando creatus est potuit; non enim eum tam parvum quam infantes nostri sunt factum fuisse credibile est. Seth filius eius non ducentorum quinque, sicut nos legimus, sed centum quinque fuit quando genuit Enos;[2] ac per hoc secundum istos nondum habebat

---

[1] See below, 15.14 (pp. 487–493).
[2] Cf. Genesis 5.3.
[3] Cf. Genesis 5.6.

" Thus," he remarked, " among them some people are reported to have lived even for a thousand years."

Certain individuals regard these arguments as plausible and attempt by use of them not to weaken but to strengthen the trustworthiness of our sacred history and thus to lend credibility to the tradition that the ancients lived for so many years. Hence they have persuaded themselves and deem it no shame to persuade others that the period of time then called a year was so brief that ten of those years are equal to one of ours and ten of ours to a hundred of the former. The utter falsity of such reasoning, however, can be demonstrated by the clearest evidence.[1] But before I prove this, I think that I should mention the possibility of a more credible view.

We could surely have disproved and refuted this assertion by evidence from the Hebrew text, where we find that Adam was not two hundred and thirty but a hundred and thirty years old when he became the father of a third son.[2] For if this number of years is equal to thirteen of ours, he must obviously have been eleven years old or only slightly more when he had his first son. Now who can engender children at such an age in accordance with that ordinary law of nature so well known to us all?

But let us pass over Adam. He could perhaps have engendered children even when he was created, for it is unlikely that he was made as small as our babies are at birth. His son Seth was not two hundred and five, as our text tells us, but a hundred and five when he became the father of Enos;[3] and consequently he was not yet eleven years old accord-

undecim annos aetatis. Quid dicam de Cainan eius filio, qui, cum apud nos centum septuaginta reperiatur, apud Hebraeos septuaginta legitur fuisse quando genuit Maleleel? Quis generat homo septennis si tunc anni septuaginta nuncupabantur qui septem fuerunt?

XIII

An in dinumeratione annorum Hebraeorum magis quam septuaginta interpretum sit sequenda auctoritas.

SED cum hoc dixero, continuo referetur illud Iudaeorum esse mendacium, de quo superius satis actum est; nam septuaginta interpretes, laudabiliter celebratos viros, non potuisse mentiri. Ubi si quaeram quid sit credibilius, Iudaeorum gentem tam longe lateque diffusam in hoc conscribendum mendacium uno consilio conspirare potuisse et, dum aliis invident auctoritatem, sibi abstulisse veritatem, an septuaginta homines, qui etiam ipsi Iudaei erant, uno in loco positos, quoniam rex Aegyptius Ptolomaeus eos ad hoc opus asciverat, ipsam veritatem gentibus alienigenis invidisse et communicato [1]

---

[1] communia *V and a few other MSS.*

---

[1] Cf. Genesis 5.12.
[2] See above, 15.11 (p. 467).

ing to those others. What should I say of his son
Cainan? Though in our text we find that he was a
hundred and seventy, we read in the Hebrew text
that he was seventy when he became the father of
Mahalaleel.[1] Now, if we assume that they then
called seven actual years seventy, what person of
that age engenders children?

XIII

*Whether in the calculation of years we should follow
the authority of the Hebrew version rather than that
of the Septuagint.*

But when I speak thus, some people will at once
retort that this falsehood emanates from the Jews—
a subject on which I have sufficiently touched above.[2]
Their reasoning is that the seventy translators, who
were laudably distinguished men, could not have
told lies. Here then are the alternatives: either the
Jewish people, though scattered so far and wide,
were able to conspire unanimously to write such
falsehood and so deprived themselves of the truth
by their reluctance to share scriptural authority with
others, or when the seventy men, who were also Jews
themselves, had been assembled in one place, since
the Egyptian king Ptolemy had summoned them for
this work,[3] they were reluctant to share the scriptural
truth with foreign nations and accomplished their
purpose by joint agreement. Now if I should ask

[3] Concerning the composition of the Septuagint version cf.
The Oxford Dictionary of the Christian Church (London, 1957),
edited by F. L. Cross, 1240, *s.v.* " Septuagint."

istuc [1] fecisse consilio, quis non videat quid proclivius faciliusque credatur ?

Sed absit ut prudens quispiam vel Iudaeos cuiuslibet perversitatis atque malitiae tantum potuisse credat in codicibus tam multis et tam longe lateque dispersis vel septuaginta illos memorabiles viros hoc de invidenda gentibus veritate unum communicasse consilium. Credibilius ergo quis dixerit, cum primum de bibliotheca Ptolomaei describi ista coeperunt, tunc aliquid tale fieri potuisse in codice uno, sed primitus inde descripto, unde iam latius emanaret, ubi potuit quidem accidere etiam scriptoris error.

Sed hoc in illa quaestione de vita Mathusalae non absurdum est suspicari et in illo alio ubi, superantibus viginti quattuor annis, summa non convenit. In his autem in quibus continuatur ipsius mendositatis similitudo ita ut ante genitum filium qui ordini inseritur alibi supersint centum anni, alibi desint, post genitum autem ubi deerant supersint, ubi supererant desint ut summa conveniat (et hoc in prima, secunda, tertia, quarta, quinta,[2] septima generatione invenitur), videtur habere quandam, si dici potest, error ipse constantiam nec casum redolet, sed industriam.

Itaque illa diversitas numerorum aliter se haben-

---

[1] istud *some MSS.*
[2] quinta sexta *V and two other MSS.*

---

[1] That is, in the case of Lamech; see above, 15.10 (p. 463).

which alternative is more plausible, who would fail to see what can more easily and readily be believed?

But I would not have any intelligent person think either that the Jews, no matter how great their depravity and spite, could have effected all this in so many and so widely scattered codices or that those celebrated seventy men unanimously agreed on this common plan to withhold through envy the truth from the gentiles. Accordingly, some one might more plausibly propose that when this text was transcribed for the first time in Ptolemy's library, some such distortion could then have occurred in a single codex, which, however, was the first copy and source from which the mistake spread more widely. A mere scribal error might originally have been involved here.

Now this is a reasonable enough surmise in the problem concerning Methuselah's life-span and in that other case [1] where an extra twenty-four years makes a difference in the total. On the other hand, there are cases where the same error consistently appears, so that a difference of a hundred years occurs in the two corresponding versions before the birth of a son included in the succession, but after the birth a like number of years are added or subtracted as required to make up the difference in the total; and this is the situation we find in the first, second, third, fourth, fifth and seventh generations. In such cases the error itself seems to conform, if I may say so, to a certain pattern and gives the impression not of chance but of design.

Therefore, except where this uniformity in the addition and subtraction of a hundred years over so

tium in codicibus Graecis et Latinis, aliter in Hebraeis,
ubi non est ista de centum annis prius additis et
postea detractis per tot generationes continuata
parilitas, nec malitiae Iudaeorum nec diligentiae vel
prudentiae septuaginta interpretum, sed scriptoris
tribuatur errori qui de bibliotheca supradicti regis
codicem describendum primus accepit. Nam etiam
nunc, ubi numeri non faciunt intentum ad aliquid
quod facile possit intellegi vel quod appareat utiliter
disci, et neglegenter describuntur et neglegentius
emendantur. Quis enim sibi existimet esse di-
scendum quot milia hominum tribus Israel singillatim
habere potuerunt quoniam prodesse aliquid non
putatur? Et quotus quisque hominum est cui
profunditas utilitatis huius appareat?

Hic vero, ubi per tot contextas generationes centum anni alibi adsunt, alibi desunt, et post natum
qui commemorandus fuerat filium desunt ubi ad-
fuerunt, adsunt ubi defuerunt ut summa concordet,
nimirum cum vellet persuadere qui hoc fecit ideo
numerosissimos annos vixisse antiquos, quod eos
brevissimos nuncupabant, et hoc de maturitate
pubertatis, qua idonea filii gignerentur, conaretur
ostendere, atque ideo in illis centum annis decem

many successive generations is involved, that disparity of numbers as they appear in Greek and Latin
texts, on the one hand, and in Hebrew texts, on the
other, is to be attributed neither to any spitefulness
on the part of the Jews nor to any deliberate design
on the part of the seventy translators, but to the
error of the scribe who first received the original
codex from the library of King Ptolemy to transcribe.
For even nowadays, when numbers do not call attention to something that can be readily understood
or appears useful to learn, they are carelessly copied
and more carelessly corrected. Who indeed would
think that he ought to learn how many thousands of
people each of the tribes of Israel might have had?
For such knowledge is not thought to afford any
advantage, and only a small percentage of people are
aware of its profound usefulness.

The case, however, is different where for so many
successive generations there are a hundred years
more in one version and a hundred years less in the
corresponding part of the other version, and after
the birth of the son who was next to be mentioned
there is a deficiency of a hundred years where there
was first an excess and *vice versa*, so that the total
tallies. The person who was responsible for these
variations wished to persuade us that the very large
number of years that the ancients reportedly lived
was due to the extreme brevity of their so-called
years. Moreover, he attempted to demonstrate this
point by reference to the sexual maturity requisite
for the procreation of children, and thought that if
sceptics were told that ten of our years comprised a
hundred of those others, they might not be unwilling

nostros insinuandos putaret incredulis, ne homines
tamdiu vixisse recipere in fidem nollent, addidit
centum ubi gignendis filiis habilem non invenit
aetatem, eosdemque post genitos filios, ut congrueret summa, detraxit. Sic quippe voluit credibiles
facere idonearum generandae proli convenientias
aetatum ut tamen numero non fraudaret universas
aetates viventium singulorum.

Quod autem id [1] in sexta generatione non fecit,
hoc ipsum est quod magis monet [2] ideo illum fecisse
cum res quam dicimus postulavit, quia non fecit ubi
non postulavit. Invenit namque in eadem generatione apud Hebraeos vixisse Iared, antequam
genuisset Enoch, centum sexaginta duos, qui secundum illam rationem brevium annorum fiunt anni
sedecim et aliquid minus quam menses duo; quae
iam aetas apta est ad gignendum, et ideo addere
centum annos breves, ut nostri viginti sex fierent,
necesse non fuit, nec post natum Enoch eos detrahere
quos non addiderat ante natum. Sic factum est ut
hic nulla esset inter codices utrosque varietas.

Sed rursus movet cur in octava generatione, antequam de Mathusalam nasceretur Lamech, cum apud
Hebraeos legantur centum octoginta duo anni,
viginti minus inveniuntur in codicibus nostris, ubi

---

[1] id *omitted in some MSS.*
[2] monet *adopted by Dombart from one MS.:* movet *most
MSS.*

to give credence to that longevity of early people. It was doubtless for these reasons that he added a hundred years in the cases where he did not find the age suitable for engendering children, and after their birth subtracted a like number to make the total tally. For he sought to lend plausibility and propriety to the age suitable for producing offspring, yet without cheating the individual in the total number of years of his life-span.

The fact that he did not do this in the sixth generation prompts us all the more to think that he did it when it was required for the reason that I mentioned, since he did not do it where it was not required. For he found that in the sixth generation, according to the Hebrew text,[1] Jared was a hundred and sixty-two years old before he became the father of Enoch, and this age becomes, on that theory of short years, sixteen plus something under two months. Since this age is already suitable for engendering children, it was not necessary to add a hundred short years to make it twenty-six of ours, or to subtract them after the birth of Enoch, as they had not been added before his birth. Thus it happened that in this case there was no discrepancy between the two versions.

On the other hand, we are puzzled by the situation in the eighth generation. For before Methuselah became the father of Lamech, he was a hundred and eighty-two years old according to the Hebrew text,[2] but in our version, where a hundred years are usually

[1] Cf. Genesis 5.18.
[2] Cf. Genesis 5.25, where the Hebrew text actually gives 187 years, which, in view of what follows, is probably what Augustine wrote.

potius addi centum solent, et post genitum Lamech
conplendam restituuntur ad summam, quae in codicibus utrisque non discrepat. Si enim centum septuaginta annos propter pubertatis maturitatem decem
et septem volebat intellegi, sicut nihil addere, ita
nihil detrahere iam debebat quia invenerat aetatem
idoneam generationi filiorum, propter quam in aliis
centum illos annos, ubi eam non inveniebat, addebat.
Hoc autem de viginti annis merito putaremus casu
mendositatis accidere potuisse nisi eos, sicut prius
detraxerat, restituere postea curaret ut summae
conveniret integritas. An forte astutius factum
existimandum est, ut illa qua centum anni prius
solent adici et postea detrahi occultaretur industria,
cum et illic ubi necesse non fuerat, non quidem de
centum annis, verum tamen de quantulocumque
numero prius detracto, post reddito tale aliquid
fieret?

Sed quomodolibet istuc [1] accipiatur, sive credatur
ita esse factum sive non credatur, sive postremo ita
sive non ita sit, recte fieri nullo modo dubitaverim ut,
cum diversum aliquid in utrisque codicibus invenitur,
quando quidem ad fidem rerum gestarum utrumque
esse non potest verum, ei linguae potius credatur
unde est in aliam per interpretes facta translatio.

[1] istud *some MSS.*

---

[1] The Septuagint, which served as the basis of Augustine's
version, gives 167 years; see above, 15.11 (p. 467).

added, we find instead twenty years less;[1] these twenty years are restored after Lamech's birth to complete the total, which agrees in both versions. Now if by a hundred and seventy years the proponent of the short-year theory meant us to understand seventeen for the requisite sexual maturity, there was no need for him either to add or to subtract anything here because he had found an age suitable for the procreation of children. It was this consideration that prompted him to add those hundred years in the other cases where he did not find it. Now we might properly suppose that this matter of twenty years could have been due to an accidental error, were it not for the fact that he took the trouble to restore them, after he had subtracted them, to make the total sum tally. Or are we perhaps to think that this was done for the more subtle purpose of concealing the deliberate practice of first adding and then subtracting a hundred years since something similar was done even where it had not been necessary? In this case it was not a question, to be sure, of a hundred years, but still of a certain number of years which, however small, was first subtracted and then restored.

But it does not really matter what explanation we adopt. For whether or not we believe that it happened as I suggested, or whether, in fine, this is or is not the case, the fact is that when some divergence appears in the two texts, it is impossible for both versions to be true and historically accurate; and I myself should in no way doubt that credence is rightly given rather to the original language from which a rendering was made by translators into

Nam in quibusdam etiam codicibus Graecis tribus et uno Latino et uno etiam Syro inter se consentientibus inventus est Mathusalam sex annis ante diluvium fuisse defunctus.

XIV

De parilitate annorum, qui eisdem quibus nunc spatiis et in prioribus saeculis cucurrerunt.

Nunc iam videamus quonam modo evidenter possit ostendi non tam breves ut illi decem unus esset noster, sed tantae prolixitatis annos quantae nunc habemus, quos utique circuitus conficit solis, in illorum hominum vita prolixissima conputatos. Sescentensimo nempe anno vitae Noe scriptum est factum esse diluvium. Cur ergo ibi legitur: *Et aqua diluvii facta est super terram sescentensimo anno in vita* [1] *Noe, secundi mensis, septima et vicensima mensis,* si annus ille minimus, quales decem faciunt unum nostrum, triginta sex habebat dies? Tantillus quippe annus, si antiquo more hoc nomen accepit, aut non habet menses, aut mensis eius est triduum ut habeat duodecim menses.

Quo modo igitur hic dictum est: *Sescentensimo anno, secundi mensis, septima et vicensima* [2] *mensis,* nisi quia tales quales nunc sunt etiam tunc erant menses?

---

[1] in vita *V and a few other MSS.* (cf. Septuagint: ἐν τῇ ζωῇ): vitae *many MSS., Vulg.*
[2] vicesima die *some MSS.*

another tongue. As it happens, there are certain codices—three in Greek, one in Latin and one also in Syriac, all in agreement with one another—according to which Methuselah perished six years before the flood.[1]

XIV

On the equal length of years, which were of the same duration in earlier ages as they are now.

LET us now consider how it can be plainly shown that the years calculated in the very long lives of those early people were not so brief that ten of them represented one of ours, but were equal in length to our own years, as defined, of course, by solar revolutions. According to Scripture, it was in the six hundredth year of Noah's life that the flood occurred. Why then do we read there: " And the water of the flood came upon the earth in the six hundredth year of Noah's life, in the second month, on the twenty-seventh day of the month," [2] if that very short year, which is only one tenth as long as our own, had thirty-six days? For so small a year, if indeed this was the name it was given in ancient practice, either has no months at all or has months of three days' duration if it is to have twelve of them.

How then can it be said in this passage: " In the six hundredth year, in the second month, on the twenty-seventh day of the month," unless the months even then were the same as they are now? How

---

[1] Cf. Augustine, *Quaestiones in Heptateuch* 1.2.
[2] Genesis 7.10–11.

SAINT AUGUSTINE

Nam quo pacto aliter vicensimo et septimo die secundi mensis diceretur coeptum esse diluvium? Deinde postea in fine diluvii ita legitur: *Et sedit arca in mense septimo, septima et vicensima* [1] *mensis, super montes Ararat. Aqua autem minuebatur usque ad undecimum mensem; in undecimo autem mense, prima die mensis, paruerunt capita montium.*

Si igitur tales menses erant, tales profecto et anni erant quales nunc habemus. Menses quippe illi triduani viginti et septem dies habere non poterant. Aut si pars tricensima tridui tunc appellabatur dies, ut omnia proportione minuantur, ergo nec toto quadriduo nostro factum est illud tam grande diluvium quod memoratur factum quadraginta diebus et noctibus. Quis hanc absurditatem et vanitatem ferat? Proinde removeatur hic error qui coniectura falsa ita vult astruere scripturarum nostrarum fidem ut alibi destruat. Prorsus tantus etiam tunc dies fuit quantus et nunc est, quem viginti quattuor [2] horae diurno curriculo nocturnoque determinant; tantus mensis quantus et nunc est, quem luna coepta et finita concludit; tantus annus quantus et nunc est, quem duodecim menses lunares, additis propter cursum solarem quinque diebus et quadrante, consummant, quanti anni sescentensimi vitae Noe secundus erat mensis eiusque mensis vicensimus et septimus dies quando coepit esse diluvium, in quo dies quadraginta continuatae ingentes pluviae memorantur, qui dies non binas ac paulo amplius

---

[1] vicesima die *some MSS.*   [2] et quattuor *some MSS.*

---

[1] Genesis 8.4–5.   [2] Cf. Genesis 7.12.

could it otherwise have been said that the flood had
begun on the twenty-seventh day of the second
month? Then later, at the end of the flood, we
read the following: "And in the seventh month, on
the twenty-seventh day of the month, the ark came
to rest upon the mountains of Ararat. And the water
continued to abate until the eleventh month; in the
eleventh month, on the first day of the month, the
tops of the mountains were seen." [1]

If then those months were like ours, the years too
were surely like those we now have. For those
three-day months could not have had twenty-seven
days. Or if, to reduce everything proportionally,
a thirtieth part of the three-day period was at that
time designated as a day, then that vast flood which
is reported to have lasted for forty days and nights [2]
did not last even for four entire days according to
our reckoning. Now who could tolerate such idle
nonsense? Away then with this error that seeks to
base the credibility of our Scriptures on false conjecture only to undermine it elsewhere. For the
day even then was just as long as it is now, a period
defined by twenty-four hours in the course of a day
and a night; the month was as long as it is now, a
period marked by the waxing and waning of the
moon; the year too was as long as it is now, a period
completed by twelve lunar months plus five and a
quarter days to square it with the sun's revolution;
and such was the length of the six hundredth year
of Noah's life when, in the second month and on the
twenty-seventh day of this month, the flood began.
During this flood, we are told, it rained heavily and
incessantly for forty days, each of which comprised

horas habebant, sed vicenas et quaternas die noctuque transactas. Ac per hoc tam magnos annos vixerunt illi antiqui usque amplius quam nongentos quantos postea vixit Abraham centum septuaginta et post eum filius eius Isaac centum octoginta et filius eius Iacob prope centum quinquaginta, et quantos, interposita aliquanta aetate, Moyses centum viginti, et quantos etiam nunc vivunt homines septuaginta vel octoginta vel non multo amplius, de quibus dictum est: *Et amplius eis labor et dolor.*

Illa vero numerorum varietas quae inter codices Hebraeos invenitur et nostros neque de hac antiquorum longaevitate dissentit; et si quid habet ita diversum ut verum esse utrumque non possit, rerum gestarum fides ab ea lingua repetenda est ex qua interpretatum est quod habemus. Quae facultas cum volentibus ubique gentium praesto sit, non tamen vacat quod septuaginta interpretes in plurimis quae diversa dicere videntur ex Hebraeis codicibus emendare ausus est nemo. Non enim est illa diversitas putata mendositas, nec ego ullo modo putandam existimo. Sed ubi non est scriptoris error, aliquid eos divino spiritu, ubi sensus esset consentaneus veritati et praedicans veritatem, non interpretantium munere, sed prophetantium libertate aliter dicere voluisse credendum est.

---

[1] Cf. Genesis 25.7.   [2] Cf. Genesis 35.28.
[3] Cf. Genesis 47.28.   [4] Cf. Deuteronomy 34.7.
[5] Psalms 90.10.

not just a little above two hours but twenty-four hours, encompassing a day and a night. And hence the years of those early people who lived even to ages over nine hundred were as long as those of Abraham who later lived to the age of one hundred and seventy [1] and after him, of his son Isaac who lived to the age of a hundred and eighty,[2] and of Isaac's son Jacob who lived to the age of almost a hundred and fifty,[3] and after an interval of some time, of Moses who lived to the age of a hundred and twenty,[4] and of people even nowadays who live to the age of seventy or eighty or not much more; of which it is said: "And more than these are toil and pain."[5]

Moreover, the difference in numbers that we find between the Hebrew text and our own constitutes no disagreement about this longevity of the ancients; and if any discrepancy is such that the two versions cannot both be true, we must seek the authentic account of events in that language from which our text was translated. Though this opportunity is universally available to those who wish to take it, yet, significantly enough, no one has ventured to correct the Septuagint version from the Hebrew text in the very many places where it seems to offer something different. The reason is that those differences were not considered falsifications, nor do I think that they should be in any way. Rather, where no scribal error is involved, and where the sense would be harmonious with the truth and would proclaim the truth, we should believe that they were moved by the divine Spirit to say something differently, not as part of the service that they did as translators, but exercising the freedom that they enjoyed as prophets.

Unde merito non solum Hebraeis verum etiam ipsis, cum adhibet testimonia de scripturis, uti apostolica invenitur auctoritas. Sed hinc me opportuniore loco, si Deus adiuverit, promisi diligentius locuturum. Nunc quod instat expediam. Non enim ambigendum est ab homine qui ex primo homine primus est natus, quando tamdiu vivebant, potuisse constitui civitatem, sane terrenam, non illam quae dicitur civitas Dei, de qua ut scriberemus laborem tanti huius operis in manus sumpsimus.

XV

An credibile sit primi saeculi viros usque ad eam aetatem qua filios generasse referuntur a concubitu continuisse.

DICET ergo aliquis: "Itane credendum est hominem filios generaturum nec habentem propositum continentiae centum et amplius vel, secundum Hebraeos, non multo minus, id est octoginta, septuaginta, sexaginta annos a concumbendi opere vacuisse,[1] aut si non vacaret, nihil prolis gignere potuisse?" Haec quaestio duobus modis solvitur. Aut enim tanto serior fuit proportione pubertas quanto vitae totius maior annositas, aut, quod magis video esse credibile, non hic primogeniti filii com-

---

[1] vacavisse *or* vacasse *some MSS.*

---

[1] See above, 15.11 (p. 469).
[2] See below, 18.42–44 (vol. 6, 27–39).

Hence apostolic authority, we find, rightly employs not only the Hebrew text but also that of the Septuagint in citing scriptural proofs. But, as I have promised,[1] I shall, with God's help, discuss this matter more thoroughly in a more appropriate place.[2] At the present time, I shall concentrate on the subject at hand, and my point is this: it should not be doubted that the human being who was the first son of the first human being was able to establish a city since people then lived such long lives. By city, I refer, of course, to the earthly city, not to the one named the City of God, of which it was my purpose to write when I undertook the task of composing this vast work.

XV

Whether we can believe that men of the primitive era abstained from sexual intercourse till the age when they are reported to have engendered children.

SOMEONE then will say: "Are we therefore to believe that a person who intended to produce children and was not purposely continent abstained from sexual activity for a hundred and more years, or, according to the Hebrew version, for a period not much less, that is, for eighty, seventy or sixty years, or if he did not abstain, was unable to produce any offspring?" This problem admits of two solutions: either sexual maturity came proportionally later as the years of an entire life-span were more numerous, or, more plausibly in my opinion, it is not the first-born children that were mentioned in this

memorati sunt, sed quos successionis ordo poscebat ut perveniretur ad Noe, a quo rursus ad Abraham videmus esse perventum ac deinde usque ad certum articulum temporis, quantum oportebat signari etiam generationibus commemoratis cursum gloriosissimae civitatis in hoc mundo peregrinantis et supernam patriam requirentis.

Quod enim negari non potest, prior omnibus Cain ex coniunctione maris et feminae natus est. Neque enim illo nato dixisset Adam quod dixisse legitur: *Adquisivi hominem per Deum*, nisi illis duobus ipse fuisset homo nascendo additus primus. Hunc secutus Abel, quem maior frater occidit, praefigurationem quandam [1] peregrinantis civitatis Dei, quod [2] ab impiis et quodam modo terrigenis, id est terrenam originem diligentibus et terrenae civitatis terrena felicitate gaudentibus, persecutiones iniquas passura fuerat,[3] primus ostendit. Sed quot annorum erat Adam cum eos genuit non apparet.

Exinde digeruntur generationes aliae de Cain, aliae de illo quem genuit Adam in eius successionem [4] quem frater occidit; et appellavit nomen illius Seth dicens, ut scriptum est: *Suscitavit enim mihi Deus semen aliud pro Abel, quem occidit Cain*. Cum itaque istae duae series generationum, una de Seth, altera de Cain, has duas, de quibus agimus, distinctis

---

[1] praefiguratione quadam *a few MSS.*
[2] quod esset *some MSS.*
[3] fuerat *omitted in two MSS.*
[4] successione *some MSS.*

---

[1] Genesis 4.1.
[2] Genesis 4.25, where, according to the Septuagint and the

connexion, but those that were required for the line of succession to arrive at Noah. As we can see, the line extended from Noah, in turn, to Abraham and from the latter to a certain point of time, up to which it was essential to mention the successive generations in order to indicate the course of that most glorious city that sojourns in this world and seeks its homeland above.

Undeniably, Cain was born before all others from the union of man and woman. For if he had not been the first person to be added by birth to that original couple, Adam would not have said at his birth what we read that he did say: " I have gotten a man with God's help." [1]   Abel, who came next and was slain by his older brother, was the first to fore-shadow in a way the City of God during its sojourn on earth—that it was destined to suffer unjust perse-cutions from wicked and, as it were, earth-born men, that is, from those who are enamoured of their earthly origin and delight in the earthly happiness of the earthly city. But it is not revealed how old Adam was when he had those sons.

The generations that follow divide into two branches, the one descending from Cain, the other from him whom Adam engendered to replace the son slain by his brother; he called this son Seth, say-ing, according to Scripture: " For God has raised me up another seed for Abel, whom Cain slew." [2] Thus there are these two lineages, one descending from Seth, the other from Cain, and they suggest by

Hebrew text, it was Eve who bestowed on him the name of Seth. Augustine's version, like the Vulgate, must have been somewhat ambiguous here.

ordinibus insinuent civitates, unam caelestem in terris peregrinantem, alteram terrenam terrenis, tamquam sola sint, gaudiis inhiantem vel inhaerentem, nullus de progenie Cain, cum dinumerata sit, connumerato Adam, usque ad octavam generationem, quot annorum fuisset expressus est quando genuit eum qui commemoratur post eum. Noluit enim spiritus Dei in terrenae civitatis generationibus tempora notare ante diluvium sed in caelestis maluit tamquam essent memoria digniores.

Porro autem Seth quando natus est, non quidem taciti sunt anni patris eius, sed iam genuerat alios, et utrum solos Cain et Abel adfirmare quis audeat? Non enim quia soli nominati sunt propter ordines generationum quas commemorare oportebat, ideo consequens videri debet solos fuisse tunc generatos ex Adam. Cum enim, silentio coopertis omnium nominibus ceterorum, legatur eum genuisse filios et filias, quota fuerit ista proles eius quis praesumat adserere si culpam temeritatis evitat?

Potuit quippe Adam divinitus admonitus dicere, postea quam Seth natus est: *Suscitavit enim mihi Deus semen aliud pro Abel,* quoniam talis erat futurus qui impleret illius sanctitatem, non quod ipse prior post eum temporis ordine nasceretur. Deinde quod scriptum est: *Vixit autem Seth quinque et ducentos annos* (vel, secundum Hebraeos, *quinque et centum*

---

[1] Cf. Genesis 5.3, where Adam's age is given as 130 years in the Vulgate, but as 230 years in the Septuagint.

their separate genealogies these two cities which we are discussing, one the heavenly city sojourning on earth, the other the earthly city craving for or clinging to earthly joys as though they were the only ones. Yet in the case of Cain's progeny, though it is enumerated from Adam down to the eighth generation, there is no statement of the age that anyone had attained when he became father of the one who is mentioned after him. For the spirit of God chose not to express the chronology down to the flood in terms of the lineage of the earthly city but preferred to use the line of the heavenly city, implying that it was more worthy of being so recorded.

Moreover, when Seth was born, his father's age was not indeed left unmentioned,[1] but Adam had already had other children, and who would venture to say for certain whether Cain and Abel were the only ones? For it should not be inferred that they were the only children of Adam at that time just because they alone were named to provide for the lines of descent that it was essential to mention. Though the names of all the others are shrouded in silence, we read that he became father of sons and daughters. Would anyone then who tries not to be guilty of temerity presume to state where Seth stood numerically in this group of Adam's progeny?

Adam may have said under divine inspiration after Seth was born: " For God has raised me up another seed for Abel," because Seth was destined to be the one to carry on his brother's holiness, not because he was the first to be born after Abel in point of time. Further, when it is written: " Seth lived two hundred and five years (or, according to the Hebrew

annos), *et genuit Enos*, quis possit nisi inconsideratus adseverare hunc eius primogenitum fuisse, ut admirantes merito requiramus quo modo per tot annos inmunis fuerit a conubio sine ullo proposito continentiae vel non genuerit coniugatus, quando quidem etiam de ipso legitur: *Et genuit filios et filias, et fuerunt omnes dies Seth duodecim et nongenti anni, et mortuus est?*

Atque ita deinceps quorum anni commemorantur, nec filios filiasque genuisse reticentur. Ac per hoc non apparet omnino utrum qui nominatur genitus ipse fuerit primogenitus. Immo vero, quoniam credibile non est patres illos aetate tam longa aut inpuberes fuisse aut coniugibus caruisse vel fetibus, nec illos eorum filios primos eis natos fuisse credibile est. Sed cum sacrae scriptor historiae ad ortum vitamque Noe, cuius tempore diluvium factum est, per successiones generationum notatis temporibus intenderet pervenire, eas utique commemoravit, non quae primae suis parentibus fuerint, sed quae in propagationis ordinem venerint.

Exempli gratia, quo id fiat apertius, aliquid interponam unde nullus ambigat fieri potuisse quod dico. Evangelista Matthaeus generationem dominicae carnis per seriem parentum volens commendare memoriae, ordiens a patre Abraham atque ad David primitus ut perveniret intendens: *Abraham*, inquit,

---

¹ Genesis 5.6.   ² Genesis 5.7–8.

texts, a hundred and five years) and became the father of Enos,"[1] could anyone but a thoughtless person maintain that the latter was his first-born? Thus in our wonderment we justly ask why for so many years he abstained from sexual union without any deliberate intention to remain continent, or, if he did engage in intercourse, why he did not have children, for we read also concerning him: "And he had sons and daughters, and all the days of Seth were nine hundred and twelve years, and he died."[2]

And so it is with all the others whose ages are mentioned, nor is the fact that they had sons and daughters omitted. Hence it is by no means indicated whether the person born whose name is given was actually the first-born. No, the contrary rather is the case, for since it is impossible to believe that those fathers either were sexually immature or lacked wives or offspring for so long a time, it is equally impossible to believe that those sons were their first-born. But since it was the purpose of the writer of the sacred history to trace chronologically the succession of generations down to the birth and life of Noah, in whose time the flood occurred, the offspring that he mentioned were assuredly not the first children born to their parents but those that belonged to the line of descent.

To make my argument clearer, I shall introduce at this point an illustration which will serve to dispel all doubt that what I am saying might have happened. When the evangelist Matthew wished to record the descent of the Lord's flesh through a line of ancestors, he began with father Abraham and, aiming to come down first to David, said: "Abraham was the father

genuit Isaac. Cur non dixit Ismael, quem primitus genuit? *Isaac autem,* inquit, *genuit Iacob.* Cur non dixit Esau, qui eius primogenitus fuit? Quia scilicet per illos ad David pervenire non posset. Deinde sequitur: *Iacob autem genuit Iudam et fratres eius.* Numquid Iudas primogenitus fuit? *Iudas,* inquit, *genuit Phares et Zarat.* Nec istorum geminorum aliquis fuit primogenitus Iudae, sed ante illos iam tres genuerat. Eos itaque tenuit in ordine generationum per quos ad David atque inde quo intenderat perveniret. Ex quo intellegi potest veteres quoque homines ante diluvium non primogenitos, sed eos fuisse commemoratos per quos ordo succedentium generationum ad Noe patriarcham duceretur, ne serae pubertatis illorum obscura et non necessaria quaestio nos fatiget.

XVI

De iure coniugiorum, quod dissimile a subsequentibus matrimoniis habuerint prima conubia.

CUM igitur genus humanum post primam copulam viri facti ex pulvere et coniugis eius ex viri latere marium feminarumque coniunctione opus haberet ut gignendo multiplicaretur, nec essent ulli homines nisi qui ex illis duobus nati fuissent, viri sorores suas coniuges acceperunt. Quod profecto quanto est

---

[1] Matthew 1.2.   [2] Matthew 1.3.

of Isaac." [1] Why did he not say Ishmael, who was his first son? "And Isaac," he continued, " was the father of Jacob." Why did he not say Esau, who was Isaac's first-born? The reason, plainly, is that he could not come down to David through these other sons. Next we read: "And Jacob was the father of Judah and his brothers." Was Judah then actually his first-born? " Judah," he continues, " was the father of Phares and Zara." [2] And neither of these twins was Judah's first-born, for he had already had three children before them. Thus the evangelist included in the genealogy only those who enabled him to arrive at David and then at the final goal that he had set. From this we can deduce that the early men too who were mentioned before the flood were not the first-born but those through whom the line of successive generations could be brought down to the patriarch Noah. Thus we need not weary ourselves with the obscure and needless problem of their delayed sexual maturity.

XVI

On the law of matrimony, which was not the same in the first unions as in later marriages.

Now, after the first union between a man, created from dust, and his spouse, fashioned from the man's side, the human race required the mating of males and females to reproduce and multiply, and the only other human beings who then existed had been born from those first two parents. Since this was the case, men took their sisters as wives. This

antiquius conpellente necessitate, tanto postea factum est damnabilius religione prohibente. Habita est enim ratio rectissima caritatis ut homines, quibus esset utilis atque honesta concordia, diversarum necessitudinum vinculis necterentur, nec unus in uno multas haberet sed singulae spargerentur in singulos ac sic ad socialem vitam diligentius conligandam plurimae plurimos obtinerent. Pater quippe et socer duarum sunt necessitudinum nomina. Ut ergo alium quisque habeat patrem, alium socerum, numerosius se caritas porrigit. Utrumque autem unus Adam esse cogebatur et filiis et filiabus suis quando fratres sororesque conubio iungebantur. Sic et Eva uxor eius utrique sexui filiorum fuit et socrus et mater. Quae si duae feminae fuissent, mater altera et socrus altera, copiosius se socialis dilectio conligaret. Ipsa denique iam soror, quod etiam uxor fiebat, duas tenebat una necessitudines, quibus per singulas distributis ut altera esset soror, altera uxor, hominum numero socialis propinquitas augeretur.

Sed hoc unde fieret tunc non erat quando nisi fratres et sorores ex illis duobus primis nulli homines erant. Fieri ergo debuit quando potuit, ut, exi-

practice, of course, respectable as it may have been
when it was dictated by necessity, later became no
less reprehensible when it was forbidden by religion.
For love was accorded its due importance so that
men, for whom harmony was useful and honourable,
might be bound by ties of various relationships.
The underlying purpose was that one man should not
comprise many relationships in his one self but that
these connexions should be severally distributed
among individuals and in this way serve to weld
social life more securely by covering in their multiplicity a multiplicity of people. For father and
father-in-law are terms describing two relationships.
Thus, when each individual has one person for a
father and another for a father-in-law, love extends
over a greater number of people. The one Adam
was compelled to be both to his own sons and daughters since brothers and sisters were joined in wedlock.
Similarly, his wife Eve too was both mother-in-law
and mother to her children of either sex. But if
these relationships had involved two women, one as
mother and another as mother-in-law, the bond of
social affection would have embraced a wider circle.
Finally, even a sister, in virtue of becoming also a
wife, comprised in her one person two relationships.
But if these roles had been bestowed each on a
different woman, that is, if one had been a sister and
another a wife, the number of people united by close
ties would have been increased.

There was, however, no possibility of this happen-
ing at a time when there were no human beings
except the brothers and sisters sprung from the
first couple. Accordingly, the change took place

stente copia, inde ducerentur uxores quae non erant
iam sorores, et non solum illud ut fieret nulla necessitas esset verum etiam si fieret nefas esset. Nam si
et nepotes primorum hominum, qui iam consobrinas
poterant accipere coniuges, sororibus matrimonio
iungerentur, non iam duae sed tres in homine uno
necessitudines fierent, quae propter caritatem nume-
rosiore propinquitate nectendam disseminari per
singulos singulae debuerunt. Esset enim unus homo
filiis suis, fratri scilicet sororique coniugibus, et pater
et socer et avunculus; ita et uxor eius eisdem
communibus filiis et mater et amita et socrus;
idemque inter se filii eorum non solum essent fratres
atque coniuges verum etiam consobrini quia et
fratrum filii.

Omnes autem istae necessitudines, quae uni
homini tres homines conectebant, novem conecterent
si essent in singulis singulae, ut unus homo haberet
alteram sororem, alteram uxorem, alteram conso-
brinam, alterum patrem, alterum avunculum, alterum
socerum, alteram matrem, alteram amitam, alteram
socrum. Atque ita se non in paucitate coartatum,
sed latius atque numerosius propinquitatibus crebris
vinculum sociale diffunderet.

Quod, humano genere crescente et multiplicato,

when the possibility arose; for, as soon as there was the requisite population, men became obliged to choose from it wives who were not already their sisters; and not only was there no necessity for brothers to marry their sisters, but if they did, it was an abomination. For if even the grandchildren of the first human beings were joined in marriage with their sisters, though they could already receive cousins as wives, one person would embody not just two but three relationships, which should have been severally distributed among different individuals to unite in love a more numerous kinship. One man would be both father and father-in-law and uncle to his own children, that is, to the brother and sister who were wedded. Similarly, his wife would be at once mother and aunt and mother-in-law to their common children; and these very same children of theirs would be to each other not only brother or sister and husband or wife but also cousins because they would be the children of brothers and sisters as well.

All these relationships, however, which combined three persons in one, would have united nine if they were each limited to one person. For then a single man would have one person as a sister, another as a wife, another as a cousin, another as a father, another as an uncle, another as a father-in-law, another as a mother, another as an aunt and another as a mother-in-law. And thus the social bond would not be restricted to a small circle, but would extend more widely to embrace a greater number of people through the abundant ties of kinship.

With the growth and increase of the human race,

SAINT AUGUSTINE

etiam inter impios deorum multorum falsorumque
cultores sic observari cernimus ut, etiamsi perversis
legibus permittantur fraterna coniugia, melior tamen
consuetudo ipsam malit exhorrere licentiam, et cum
sorores accipere in matrimonium primis humani
generis temporibus omnino licuerit, sic aversetur
quasi numquam licere potuerit. Ad humanum enim
sensum vel adliciendum vel offendendum mos valet
plurimum. Qui cum in hac causa inmoderationem
concupiscentiae coherceat, eum dissignari atque cor-
rumpi merito esse nefarium iudicatur. Si enim est
iniquum aviditate possidendi transgredi limitem
agrorum, quanto est iniquius libidine concumbendi
subvertere limitem morum! Experti autem sumus
in conubiis consobrinarum etiam nostris temporibus
propter gradum propinquitatis fraterno gradui proximum quam raro per mores fiebat quod fieri per leges
licebat quia id nec divina prohibuit et nondum
prohibuerat lex humana. Verum tamen factum
etiam licitum propter vicinitatem horrebatur inliciti,
et quod fiebat cum consobrina paene cum sorore
fieri videbatur quia et ipsi inter se propter tam pro-
pinquam consanguinitatem fratres vocantur et paene
germani sunt.

Fuit autem antiquis patribus religiosae curae, ne
ipsa propinquitas se paulatim propaginum ordinibus

---

¹ According to pseudo-Aurelius Victor, *Epitome de Caesari-
bus* 48.10, and Ambrose, *Epistulae* 60.8 (*ad Paternum*), such
marriages were forbidden by Theodosius.

this principle, as we observe, is respected even among
the impious worshippers of many false gods. For
though their perverse laws may allow marriages
between brother and sister, nevertheless they tend
in their superior practice to be repelled by this
licence; and, though it was entirely permissible to
marry a sister when the human race was in its infancy,
such unions are now so completely abhorred that it
seems as if they could never have been allowed.
Custom is a very powerful force in attracting or
revolting human feeling. And since in this case
custom serves to restrain immoderate lust, we are
right in considering it abominable to annul or infringe
it. For if it is wrong to cross the boundary of a field
motivated by greed of gain, how much worse it is
to subvert a moral boundary motivated by lust for
sexual indulgence! Moreover, we have also learned
from experience that even in our own times marriages
between cousins were rare because of the degree of
kinship only once removed from that of brother and
sister, and they were rare by moral sanction though
not illicit by law, for such marriages were not forbidden by divine law and had not yet been forbidden
by human law.[1] Nevertheless, there was a revulsion
from doing something which, lawful though it was,
bordered close on something unlawful, and to have
to do with a cousin did not seem very different from
having to do with a sister, for even among themselves, because of their close relationship, cousins
are called brothers and sisters and are in fact almost
that by blood.

The ancient fathers, however, feared that kinship
itself, gradually loosening its ties as generations

dirimens longius abiret et propinquitas esse de-
sisteret, eam nondum longe positam rursus matri-
monii vinculo conligare et quodam modo revocare
fugientem. Unde, iam pleno hominibus orbe terrarum, non quidem sorores ex patre vel matre vel ex
ambobus suis parentibus natas, sed tamen amabant
de suo genere ducere uxores. Verum quis dubitet
honestius hoc tempore etiam consobrinorum prohibita esse coniugia, non solum secundum ea quae
disputavimus, propter multiplicandas adfinitates ne
habeat duas necessitudines una persona cum duae
possint eas habere et numerus propinquitatis augeri,
sed etiam quia nescio quo modo inest humanae
verecundiae quiddam naturale atque laudabile, ut,
cui debet causa propinquitatis reverendum honorem
ab ea contineat, quamvis generatricem, tamen libidinem, de qua erubescere videmus et ipsam pudici-
tiam coniugalem.

Copulatio igitur maris et feminae, quantum adtinet
ad genus mortalium, quoddam seminarium est civitatis. Sed terrena civitas generatione tantummodo,
caelestis autem etiam regeneratione opus habet ut
noxam generationis evadat. Utrum autem aliquod
fuerit, vel si fuit, quale fuerit corporale atque visibile
regenerationis signum ante diluvium, sicut Abrahae
circumcisio postea est imperata, sacra historia tacet.
Sacrificasse tamen Deo etiam illos antiquissimos
homines non tacet, quod et in duobus primis fratri-

---

[1] Cf. Genesis 17.10–14.   [2] Cf. Genesis 4.3–4.

succeeded one another, might increasingly grow apart and cease even to exist. To forestall this, they religiously arranged to weld it again with the bond of marriage while it was not yet far distant and in a sense to recall it as it sped away. Hence, when the world was already full of people, though they did not marry sisters by one parent or both parents in common, they nevertheless preferred to take wives from their own clan. Yet no one surely doubts the greater propriety of the present-day ban on marriage even between cousins. For, as I have already argued, it multiplies ties of kinship and prevents one individual from occupying two relationships since two persons can hold them and thus increase the number of kindred. But there is a further reason: human nature is somehow commendably endowed with a certain sense of shame, so that if kinship entitles a woman to honour and respect, it keeps from her that passion which, though it results in offspring, is still carnal lust and, as we see, causes a blush even in chaste wedlock.

Accordingly, so far as the race of mortals is concerned, the intercourse of male and female represents, as it were, the seedbed of a city. But whereas the earthly city needs only generation, the heavenly city needs regeneration as well to escape the corruption of generation. The sacred history, however, does not tell us whether there was some bodily and manifest sign of regeneration before the flood, as circumcision was later enjoined upon Abraham,[1] or if there was, what form it took. Yet we are told that even those earliest human beings sacrificed to God, as was seen in the case of the first two brothers;[2]

509

SAINT AUGUSTINE

bus claruit; et Noe post diluvium, cum de arca fuisset egressus, hostias Deo legitur immolasse. De qua re in praecedentibus libris iam diximus non ob aliud daemones arrogantes sibi divinitatem deosque se credi cupientes sibi expetere saqrificium et gaudere huius modi honoribus nisi quia verum sacrificium vero Deo deberi sciunt.

XVII

De duobus ex uno genitore procreatis patribus atque principibus.

Cum ergo esset Adam utriusque generis pater, id est et cuius series ad terrenam et cuius series ad caelestem pertinet civitatem, occiso Abel atque in eius interfectione commendato mirabili sacramento, facti sunt duo patres singulorum generum, Cain et Seth, in quorum filiis, quos commemorari oportebat, duarum istarum civitatum in genere mortalium evidentius indicia clarere coeperunt.

Cain quippe genuit Enoch, in cuius nomine condidit civitatem, terrenam scilicet, non peregrinantem in hoc mundo sed in eius temporali pace ac felicitate quiescentem. Cain autem interpretatur possessio, unde dictum est quando natus est sive a patre sive a matre eius: *Adquisivi hominem per Deum.* Enoch vero dedicatio; hic enim dedicatur terrena civitas ubi conditur, quoniam hic habet eum quem intendit et

---

[1] Cf. Genesis 8.20.
[2] Cf. above, 10.4–6 and 26.
[3] Genesis 4.1.

510

and we read that after the flood, when Noah had
come forth from the ark, he offered victims to God.[1]
We have already discussed this subject in preceding
books, where the point is made that the demons,
who arrogate divinity to themselves and wish to be
considered gods, demand sacrifices and rejoice in such
tribute only because they know that true sacrifice is
due to the true God.[2]

XVII

On the two fathers and leaders sprung from one parent.

ADAM, then, was the father of both branches, that
is, of the branch whose line belongs to the earthly
city and of the branch whose line belongs to the
heavenly city. But after Abel was murdered and
a wonderful mystery was conveyed in his slaying,
there was a father for each of the two lines, Cain and
Seth, and through their sons, whose names were to
be mentioned, signs of these two cities, as they exist
among mankind, began to appear more conspicuously.

For Cain became the father of Enoch and in his
name founded a city. This was the earthly city,
which does not sojourn merely as an alien in this
world but is at ease amid its temporal peace and
happiness. Cain means acquisition, in reference to
which either his father or mother said at his birth:
" I have gotten a man by God's help." [3] Enoch, on
the other hand, means dedication, for the earthly
city is dedicated here where it is built, since it has
here the end at which it aims and to which it aspires.

appetit finem. Porro ille Seth interpretatur resurrectio et Enos filius eius interpretatur homo, non sicut Adam. Et ipsum enim nomen homo interpretatur, sed commune perhibetur esse in illa lingua, id est Hebraea, masculo et feminae. Nam sic de illo scriptum est: *Masculum et feminam fecit illos et benedixit illos et cognominavit nomen eorum Adam.* Unde non ambigitur sic appellatam fuisse feminam Evam proprio nomine ut tamen Adam, quod interpretatur homo, nomen esset amborum. Enos autem sic interpretatur homo ut hoc non posse feminam nuncupari periti linguae illius adseverent, tamquam filius resurrectionis, ubi *non nubent neque uxores ducent.* Non enim erit ibi generatio, cum illuc perduxerit regeneratio.

Quare et hoc non[1] incassum notandum arbitror, quod in eis generationibus quae propagantur ex illo qui est appellatus Seth, cum genuisse filios filiasque dicantur, nulla ibi genita nominatim femina expressa est. In his autem quae propagantur ex Cain, in ipso fine quo usque pertendunt,[2] novissima femina genita nominatur. Sic enim legitur: *Mathusael genuit Lamech. Et sumpsit sibi Lamech duas uxores; nomen uni Ada et nomen secundae Sella. Et peperit Ada Iobel; hic erat pater habitantium in tabernaculis pecuariorum. Et nomen fratris eius Iobal; hic fuit qui ostendit psalterium et citharam. Sella autem peperit et*

---

[1] non ut puto *some MSS.*
[2] pertenduntur *some MSS.*

Further, Seth means resurrection and the name of his son Enos means man, but not in the same sense as Adam. For though Adam's name too means man, yet it is said to apply to male and female alike in Hebrew. Thus in Scripture we read concerning it as follows: " Male and female he created them, and he blessed them and named them Adam." [1] Hence there is no doubt that, though the woman received the name Eve as her own, Adam, which means man, was the name of both. Enos, on the other hand, means man in a sense which, according to scholars of the Hebrew language, does not allow it to be applied to a woman; it stands for son of resurrection, where people " will neither be given in marriage nor marry." [2] For there will be no generation at the resurrection, when they have arrived there through regeneration.

It is therefore worthwhile, I think, to observe that among the offspring deriving from the man called Seth, though they are said to have had sons and daughters, no woman born in that line is expressly mentioned by name. Among those, however, that sprang from Cain, at the very end reached by their line, the last woman to be born is named. For we read as follows: " Methusael was the father of Lamech. And Lamech took two wives; the name of the one was Adah, and the name of the other Zillah. Adah bore Jabal; he was the father of those who dwell in tents and have cattle. And his brother's name was Jubal; it was he who introduced the harp and the lyre. Zillah too bore Tubal; and he was a

---

[1] Genesis 5.2.
[2] Luke 20.35.

ipsa Tobel; et erat malleator et aerarius [1] *aeramenti et ferri. Soror autem Tobel Noemma.*

Hoc [2] usque porrectae sunt generationes ex Cain, quae sunt omnes ab Adam octo adnumerato ipso Adam, septem scilicet usque ad Lamech, qui duarum maritus uxorum fuit, et octava est generatio in filiis eius, in quibus commemoratur et femina. Ubi eleganter significatum est terrenam civitatem usque in sui finem carnales habituram generationes, quae marium feminarumque coniunctione proveniunt. Unde et ipsae, quod praeter Evam nusquam reperitur ante diluvium nominibus propriis exprimuntur uxores illius hominis qui nominatur hic novissimus pater. Sicut autem Cain, quod interpretatur possessio, terrenae conditor civitatis, et filius eius, in cuius nomine condita est, Enoch, quod interpretatur dedicatio, indicat istam civitatem et initium et finem habere terrenum, ubi nihil speratur amplius quam in hoc saeculo cerni potest, ita Seth, quod interpretatur resurrectio, cum sit generationum seorsus commemoratarum pater, quid de filio eius sacra haec historia dicat intuendum est.

[1] malleator et aerarius *most MSS.* (*cf. Vulg.:* malleator et faber): malleator aerarius *two MSS.* (*cf. Septuagint:* σφυροκόπος χαλκεύς).
[2] huc *many MSS.*

smith who worked in bronze and iron. The sister of Tubal was Naamah." [1]

This is the point reached by the generations deriving from Cain. Starting from and including Adam, they add up to eight in all; that is, there are seven down to Lamech, who was the husband of two wives, and the eighth generation is represented by his children, among whom a woman is also mentioned. Thus it is neatly intimated that the earthly city will to its very end have carnal generations brought forth by the union of men and women. Hence even the wives too of this man who is the last father [2] to be named in the above passage are presented under their own names, and, except for Eve, this is not found elsewhere before the flood. Cain, then, whose name means possession, is the founder of the earthly city, and Enoch, whose name means dedication, is the son in whose name it was founded. Through them it is shown that this city has both its beginning and its end on earth with no hope of anything beyond what can be seen in this world. But Seth, whose name means resurrection, is the father of generations that are separately recorded, and so we must now examine what this sacred history says about his son.

---

[1] Genesis 4.18–22.
[2] That is, Lamech.

SAINT AUGUSTINE

XVIII

Quid significatum sit in Abel et Seth et Enos quod appareat ad Christum et corpus eius, id est ecclesiam, pertinere.

Et Seth, inquit, *natus est filius, et nominavit nomen eius Enos; hic speravit invocare nomen Domini Dei.* Nempe clamat adtestatio veritatis. In spe igitur vivit homo filius resurrectionis; in spe vivit, quamdiu peregrinatur hic, civitas Dei, quae gignitur ex fide resurrectionis Christi. Ex duobus namque illis hominibus, Abel, quod interpretatur luctus, et eius fratre Seth, quod interpretatur resurrectio, mors Christi et vita eius ex mortuis figuratur. Ex qua fide gignitur hic civitas Dei, id est homo qui speravit invocare nomen Domini Dei.

Spe enim salvi facti sumus, ait apostolus. *Spes autem quae videtur non est spes. Quod enim videt quis, quid sperat?*[1] *Si autem quod non videmus speramus, per patientiam expectamus.* Nam quis vacare hoc existimet ab altitudine sacramenti? Numquid enim Abel non speravit invocare nomen Domini Dei, cuius sacrificium scriptura tam acceptum Deo fuisse commemorat? Numquid ipse Seth non speravit invocare

[1] quid sperat *V and many other MSS., Vulg.:* quid et sperat *a few MSS. (cf. the Greek:* τί καὶ ἐλπίζει).

XVIII

On the symbolism found in Abel, Seth and Enos and the relevance that it clearly has to Christ and his body, that is, the Church.

SCRIPTURE says: " To Seth also a son was born, and he called his name Enos; this son hoped to call upon the name of the Lord God."[1] Here indeed is testimony crying out the truth. It is in hope then that man, son of resurrection, lives, in hope that the City of God, which springs from a belief in the resurrection of Christ, lives so long as it sojourns on earth. For since Abel's name means mourning and his brother Seth's means resurrection, the death of Christ and his coming to life from among the dead are foreshadowed in these two men. And belief in this gives rise here on earth to the City of God, that is, to a man who " hoped to call upon the name of the Lord God."

" For in hope," as the Apostle says, " we were saved. Now hope that is seen is not hope. For why does a man hope for what he sees? But if we hope for what we do not see, we wait for it with patience."[2] No one could fail to realize that a profound mystery is implied in these words. For did not Abel hope to call upon the name of the Lord God, to whom his sacrifice, according to Scripture, was so pleasing? Did not Seth himself hope to call

[1] Genesis 4.26. Augustine's discussion here of the virtue of hope is based upon a mistranslation of the Hebrew, which means ' began to call,' as indicated by the Vulgate.

[2] Romans 8.24–25.

nomen Domini Dei, de quo dictum est: *Suscitavit enim mihi Deus semen aliud pro Abel?*

Cur ergo huic proprie tribuitur quod piorum omnium intellegitur esse commune, nisi quia oportebat in eo qui de patre generationum in meliorem partem, hoc est supernae civitatis, separatarum primus commemoratur exortus praefigurari hominem, id est hominum societatem quae non secundum hominem in re felicitatis terrenae, sed secundum Deum vivit in spe felicitatis aeternae? Nec dictum est: "Hic speravit in Dominum Deum," aut: "Hic invocavit nomen Domini Dei," sed: *Speravit,* inquit, *invocare nomen Domini Dei.* Quid sibi hoc vult *Speravit invocare* nisi quia prophetia est exorturum populum qui secundum electionem gratiae invocaret nomen Domini Dei?

Hoc est quod per alium prophetam dictum apostolus de hoc populo intellegit ad Dei gratiam pertinente: *Et erit, omnis qui invocaverit nomen Domini salvus erit.* Hoc ipsum enim quod dicitur: *Et nominavit nomen eius Enos, quod interpretatur homo,* ac deinde additur: *Hic speravit invocare nomen Domini Dei,* satis ostenditur quod non in se ipso spem ponere debeat homo. *Maledictus* enim *omnis* (sicut alibi legitur) *qui spem suam ponit in homine,*[1] ac per hoc nec in se ut sit civis alterius civitatis, quae non secundum filium Cain

---

[1] in homine *V and most other MSS., Vulg.:* in hominem *a few MSS. (cf. Septuagint:* ἐπ᾽ ἄνθρωπον).

---

[1] Genesis 4.25.	[2] Genesis 4.26.
[3] Cf. Romans 11.5.	[4] Joel 2.32.
[5] Cf. Romans 10.13.	[6] Jeremiah 17.5.

upon the name of the Lord God? In reference to Seth Scripture says: " God has raised me up another seed in place of Abel." [1]

Why, therefore, should that be said of Enos in particular which is known to be true of all godly men equally? The reason is this: he is mentioned as the first offspring of the father of the generations that have been reserved for a better portion, that is, are to participate in the city above; and it is therefore fitting that we should have foreshadowed in him the man, that is, the society of men, that lives not according to man in the actuality of earthly happiness, but according to God in the hope of eternal happiness. Now it was not said: " He hoped in the Lord God," or: " He called upon the name of the Lord God." Rather Scripture states: " He hoped to call upon the name of the Lord God." [2] The words " he hoped to call " can only mean, prophetically, that a people would arise which, chosen by grace,[3] would call upon the name of the Lord God.

Another prophet has said: "And it shall come to pass that all who call upon the name of the Lord shall be delivered." [4] This passage is taken by the Apostle to refer to this people who belong to the grace of God.[5] For the words: "And he called his name Enos," which means man, and those that follow: " He hoped to call upon the name of the Lord God," make it sufficiently plain that man should not place his hope in himself. As we read elsewhere, " Cursed is everyone who places his hope in man "; [6] and thus no one should place his hope in himself either if he is to be a citizen of that other city, which is not dedicated, after the manner of Cain's son, in

dedicatur hoc tempore, id est mortalis huius saeculi labente transcursu, sed in illa inmortalitate beatitudinis sempiternae.

XIX

De significatione, quae in Enoch translatione monstratur.

NAM et ista propago cuius est pater Seth in ea generatione habet dedicationis nomen quae septima est ex Adam, adnumerato Adam. Septimus enim ab illo natus est Enoch, quod interpretatur dedicatio. Sed ipse est ille translatus quoniam placuit Deo, et insigni numero in ordine generationum quo sabbatum consecratum est, septimo scilicet ab Adam. Ab ipso autem patre istarum generationum quae discernuntur a progenie Cain, id est a Seth, sextus est; quoto die factus est homo et consummavit Deus omnia opera sua. Sed huius Enoch translatio nostrae dedicationis est praefigurata dilatio.

Quae quidem iam facta est in Christo, capite nostro, qui sic resurrexit ut non moriatur ulterius, sed etiam ipse translatus est. Restat autem altera dedicatio universae domus cuius ipse Christus est fundamentum, quae differtur in finem, quando erit omnium resurrectio non moriturorum amplius. Sive autem domus Dei dicatur sive templum Dei sive

---

[1] Cf. Genesis 5.24; Hebrews 11.5–6. See above, 15.10 (p. 463, note 1).

[2] Cf. Ephesians 2.20.

this present time, that is, in the transience of this mortal age, but in the immortality of everlasting bliss.

XIX

On the symbolic meaning manifested in Enoch's translation.

FOR the name that means dedication also occurs in the line of descent through Seth. We find it in the seventh generation from Adam, if we include him in our count. For Enoch, whose name means dedication, was born seventh in the line beginning with Adam. But he is the very one who was translated because he found favour with God;[1] and his number in the line of descent, namely, seventh from Adam, is the same notable number as that by which the Sabbath was consecrated. On the other hand, he is sixth from Seth, the father of the line that is distinguished from the offspring of Cain; and it was on the sixth day that man was created and God completed all his works. But the translation of this Enoch is a foreshadowing of the postponement of our own dedication.

This dedication has already been realized in Christ, our head, who rose again never to die any more, but he too was translated. There remains another dedication, that of the entire house of which Christ himself is the foundation.[2] This dedication is postponed till the end of time, when there will be a resurrection of all those who are to die no more. But whether we call it the ‘ House of God ’ or the

civitas Dei, id ipsum est nec abhorret a Latini eloquii consuetudine. Nam et Vergilius imperiosissimam civitatem domum appellat Assaraci, Romanos volens intellegi, qui de Assaraco per Troianos originem ducunt, et domum Aeneae eosdem ipsos quia, eo duce Troiani cum Italiam venissent, ab eis condita est Roma. Imitatus namque est poeta ille litteras sacras, in quibus dicitur domus Iacob iam ingens populus Hebraeorum.

XX

De eo quod Cain successio in octo ab Adam generationes clauditur et in posteris ab eodem patre Adam Noe decimus invenitur.

DICET aliquis: "Si hoc intendebat scriptor huius historiae in commemorandis generationibus ex Adam per filium eius Seth, ut per illas perveniret ad Noe, sub quo factum est diluvium, a quo rursus contexeretur ordo nascentium quo perveniret ad Abraham, a quo Matthaeus evangelista incipit generationes quibus ad Christum pervenit, aeternum regem civitatis Dei, quid intendebat in generationibus ex Cain et quo eas perducere volebat?" Respondetur: Usque ad diluvium, quo totum illud genus terrenae civitatis absumptum est; sed reparatum est ex

---

[1] Cf. Virgil, *Aeneid* 1.284.
[2] Cf. Virgil, *Aeneid* 3.97.

' Temple of God ' or the ' City of God,' it is all the same and not at variance with idiomatic Latin usage. For Virgil too refers to the supreme imperial city as the ' house of Assaracus,' [1] by which he means the Romans, who derive their origin from Assaracus through the Trojans. And he refers to these same Romans as the ' house of Aeneas ' [2] because Rome was founded by the Trojans after they had come to Italy under the leadership of Aeneas. In so doing, that celebrated poet followed the practice of holy Scripture, where the Hebrew people is called the ' house of Jacob ' even after it has grown enormous.

XX

Why Cain's line of succession terminates in the eighth generation from Adam while Noah is found to belong to the tenth generation of descendants from the same father Adam.

Now someone may say: " Let us grant that the purpose of the writer of this history in recording the generations from Adam through his son Seth was to come through them down to Noah, in whose day the flood occurred, and then to trace the succeeding line of offspring from Noah down to Abraham, with whom the evangelist Matthew begins his account of the generations leading to Christ, the eternal king of the City of God. But what then was his purpose in recording the generations from Cain and to what point was it his intention to trace them? " The answer is: Down to the time of the flood, when the entire race of the earthly city was wiped out; but it

filiis Noe. Neque enim deesse poterit haec terrena
civitas societasque hominum secundum hominem
viventium usque ad huius saeculi finem, de quo
Dominus ait: *Filii saeculi huius generant et generantur.*
Civitatem vero Dei peregrinantem in hoc saeculo
regeneratio perducit ad alterum saeculum cuius filii
nec generant nec generantur.

Hic ergo generari et generare civitati utrique commune est, quamvis Dei civitas habeat etiam hic
multa civium milia quae ab opere generandi se
abstineant. Sed habet etiam illa ex imitatione
quadam, licet errantium. Ad eam namque pertinent etiam qui deviantes ab huius fide diversas
haereses condiderunt; secundum hominem quippe
vivunt, non secundum Deum. Et Indorum gymnosophistae, qui nudi perhibentur philosophari in
solitudinibus Indiae, cives eius sunt et a generando se
cohibent. Non est enim hoc bonum nisi cum fit
secundum fidem summi boni, qui Deus est. Hoc
tamen nemo fecisse ante diluvium reperitur, quando
quidem etiam ipse Enoch septimus ab Adam, qui
translatus refertur esse, non mortuus, genuit filios et
filias antequam transferretur, in quibus fuit Mathusalam, per quem generationum memorandarum ordo
transcurrit.

Cur ergo tanta paucitas successionum commemoratur in generationibus ex Cain si eas usque ad diluvium
perduci oportebat nec erat diuturna aetas prae-

---

[1] Cf. Luke 20.34, which Augustine freely paraphrases here.
[2] See above, 14.17 (p. 361).

was later reconstituted from the offspring of Noah. In fact, this earthly city and society of men living according to man cannot possibly disappear until the end of this world, concerning which the Lord says: " The children of this world engender and are engendered." [1] On the other hand, the City of God, which sojourns as an alien in this world, is brought by regeneration to another world whose children neither engender nor are engendered.

In this world, accordingly, the citizens of both cities alike are engendered and engender, although even here the City of God has many thousands of citizens who abstain from the act of procreation. The other city too has citizens who imitate them in a way, but these are in error. For this earthly city also includes people who have strayed from the faith of the heavenly city and established various sects; they live of course according to man and not according to God. The Indian gymnosophists too, who are said to live as naked philosophers in the jungles of India,[2] are citizens of the earthly city, and yet they refrain from procreation. For such continence is good only when it is practised by faith in the highest good, which is God. Yet we find no one who lived so before the flood. Indeed, even Enoch himself, who was seventh in line from Adam and was, we are told, translated without dying, became the father of sons and daughters prior to his translation. And among Enoch's children was Methuselah, who belonged to the line that was to be recorded.

Why then do we find so few generations mentioned in the line of descent from Cain if they were to be traced down to the time of the flood and their sexual

veniens pubertatem quae centum vel amplius annos
vacaret a fetibus? Nam si non intendebat auctor
libri huius aliquem ad quem necessario perduceret
seriem generationum, sicut in illis quae veniunt de
semine Seth intendebat pervenire ad Noe, a quo
rursus ordo necessarius sequeretur, quid opus erat
praetermittere primogenitos filios ut perveniretur ad
Lamech, in cuius filiis finitur illa contextio, octava
generatione scilicet ex Adam, septima ex Cain,
quasi esset inde aliquid deinceps conectendum unde
perveniretur vel ad Israeliticum populum, in quo
caelesti civitati etiam terrena Hierusalem figuram
propheticam praebuit, vel ad Christum *secundum carnem, qui est super omnia Deus benedictus in saecula*,
supernae Hierusalem fabricator atque regnator, cum
tota progenies Cain diluvio sit deleta?

Unde videri potest in eodem ordine generationum
primogenitos fuisse commemoratos. Cur ergo tam
pauci sunt? Non enim usque ad diluvium tot esse
potuerunt, non vacantibus usque ad centenariam
pubertatem patribus ab officio generandi si non erat
tunc proportione longaevitatis illius etiam sera
pubertas. Ut enim peraeque triginta annorum
fuerint cum filios generare coeperunt, octiens triceni

---

[1] Cf. above, 15.2 (p. 419).
[2] Romans 9.5.

maturity was not delayed by so long a period that
they could not have children for a hundred years or
more? Now in the case of the generations descending from the seed of Seth the author of this book had in
mind to come down to Noah and, resuming with him,
to continue in due sequence. But if in the case of
Cain's progeny the writer did not have in mind someone to whom he was obliged to trace the line, what
need was there to pass over first-born sons in order to
arrive at Lamech, with whose children (that is, in the
eighth generation from Adam or the seventh from
Cain) the end of that series is reached? He must
have expected to add a link to bring the line down
either to the people of Israel, among whom the
earthly Jerusalem also prophetically prefigured the
heavenly city,[1] or to Christ " according to the flesh,
who is God supreme over all things and blessed forever," [2] the artificer and ruler of the Jerusalem
above. But how could he have done so, inasmuch
as the entire posterity of Cain was destroyed in the
flood?

Hence it looks as if first-born sons were recorded
in the genealogy under discussion. Why then are
there so few? Indeed, there could not have been
only that small number down to the time of the
flood; for the fathers did not have to wait till they
reached the age of a hundred before they were
mature enough to undertake the duty of procreation
if the age of puberty was not also delayed to correspond proportionally with the longer life-span of that
time. Let us assume that they were uniformly
thirty years old when they began to produce children;
multiplying thirty by eight (since there were eight

(quoniam octo sunt generationes cum Adam et cum eis quos genuit Lamech) ducenti et quadraginta sunt anni, num itaque toto deinde tempore usque ad diluvium non generaverunt?

Qua tandem causa qui haec scripsit generationes commemorare noluit quae sequuntur? Nam ex Adam usque ad diluvium conputantur anni secundum codices nostros duo milia ducenti sexaginta duo, secundum Hebraeos autem mille sescenti quinquaginta sex. Ut ergo istum numerum minorem credamus esse veriorem, de mille sescentis quinquaginta sex annis ducenti quadraginta detrahantur. Numquid credibile est per mille quadringentos et quod excurrit annos qui restant usque[1] diluvium progeniem Cain a generationibus vacare potuisse?

Sed qui ex hoc movetur meminerit, cum quaererem quo modo credendum sit antiquos illos homines per tam multos annos a gignendis filiis cessare potuisse, duobus modis istam solutam esse quaestionem: aut de sera pubertate, proportione tam longae vitae, aut de filiis qui commemorantur in generationibus, quod non fuerint primogeniti, sed hi per quos ad eum quem intendebat auctor libri poterat perveniri,[2] sicut ad Noe in generationibus Seth. Proinde in generationibus Cain, si non occurrit qui deberet intendi ad quem, praetermissis primogenitis, per eos qui commemorati sunt perveniri oportebat, sera

---

[1] usque *V and two other MSS.*: usque ad *most MSS.*
[2] pervenire *some MSS.*

generations if we count Adam and the children of
Lamech), we get two hundred and forty years.
Surely this cannot mean that they had no children
throughout the entire following period down to the
time of the flood.

What reason then did the writer of these accounts
have for not wanting to record the subsequent
generations? For the lapse of time from Adam to
the flood comes to two thousand two hundred and
sixty-two years according to our text, but only to one
thousand six hundred and fifty-six years according
to the Hebrew tradition. Now assuming that this
lesser number is the more correct, let us subtract
two hundred and forty from one thousand six hundred
and fifty-six years. Is it at all possible to believe
that for the one thousand and four hundred odd years
remaining till the time of the flood Cain's offspring
could have had no children?

Well, if anyone is troubled by this problem, let
him recall that when I discussed how it was possible
to believe that those men of old could have abstained
for so many years from producing children, we
arrived at a twofold solution to this question: either
their puberty was delayed to correspond proportionally with their longevity, or the sons who are recorded
in the genealogy were not the first-born, but those
through whom it was possible to arrive at the one
whom the author of the book had in mind, as, for
example, Noah in the line of descent from Seth.
Accordingly, if we do not find in Cain's line anyone
whom the writer must have had in mind as the
person necessary to reach through those who were
recorded, while he passed over the first-born, we have

pubertas intellegenda restabit, ut aliquanto post
centum annos puberes habilesque ad gignendum
facti fuerint ut ordo generationum per primogenitos
curreret et usque [1] diluvium ad numerum annorum
tantae quantitatis occurreret.

Quamvis fieri possit ut propter aliquam secretiorem
causam quae me latet usque ad Lamech et eius
filios generationum perveniente contextu commendaretur haec civitas, quam dicimus esse terrenam, ac
deinde cessaret scriptor libri commemorare ceteras
quae usque ad diluvium esse potuerunt. Potest et
illa esse causa cur non ordo generationum per primogenitos duceretur, ut necesse non sit in illis hominibus tam seram credere pubertatem, quod scilicet
eadem civitas, quam Cain in nomine Enoch filii sui
condidit, longe lateque regnare potuerit et reges
habere non simul plures, sed suis aetatibus singulos,
quos genuissent sibi successuros quicumque regnas-
sent. Horum regum primus esse potuit ipse Cain;
secundus filius eius Enoch, in cuius nomine ubi reg-
naretur condita est civitas; tertius Gaidad, quem
genuit Enoch; quartus Mevia, quem genuit Gaidad;
quintus Mathusael, quem genuit Mevia; sextus
Lamech, quem genuit Mathusael, qui est septimus
ab Adam per Cain. Non autem erat consequens ut
primogeniti regum regnantibus succederent patribus,
sed quos regnandi meritum propter virtutem terrenae utilem civitati vel sors aliqua reperiret, vel ille

---

[1] usque *V and two other MSS.*: usque ad *most MSS.*

no alternative but to assume later puberty. This would mean that they did not attain puberty and the ability to procreate until some time after the age of a hundred if the line of descent was to run through the first-born and encompass so large a number of years by the time of the flood.

And yet it is possible that for some less obvious reason that escapes me this city, which I call earthly, was represented until the succession of generations reached Lamech and his children and that the author of the book then ceased to record any others that may have existed down to the time of the flood. But it is possible to imagine still another reason why the line of descent was not traced through the first-born, and this would eliminate the necessity of believing that puberty came so late in those men. What I mean is that the city founded by Cain in the name of his son Enoch perhaps extended its dominion far and wide, yet was ruled not by several kings simultaneously but by only one at any given period, the successor in each case being a son of the reigning king. The first of these kings may have been Cain himself; the second, his son Enoch, in whose name was founded the city that would be the centre of the monarchy; the third, Gaidad, son of Enoch; the fourth, Mevia, son of Gaidad; the fifth, Mathusael, son of Mevia; the sixth, Lamech, son of Mathusael and seventh in the line from Adam through Cain. Reigning fathers, however, were not necessarily succeeded on the throne by their first-born sons, but by those who gained the kingship because of some special virtue of service to the earthly city or by those who were selected by some kind of lot; or else the father

potissimum succederet patri hereditario quodam iure regnandi quem prae ceteris filiis dilexisset.

Potuit autem, vivente adhuc Lamech atque regnante, fieri diluvium ut ipsum cum aliis omnibus hominibus, exceptis qui in arca fuerunt, quem perderet inveniret. Neque enim mirandum est si, varia quantitate numerositatis annorum interposita per tam longam aetatem ab Adam usque [1] diluvium, non aequalis numeri generationes habuit utraque progenies, sed per Cain septem, per Seth autem decem—septimus est enim, ut iam dixi, ab Adam Lamech, decimus Noe. Et ideo non unus filius Lamech, sicut in ceteris superius, sed plures commemorati sunt, quia incertum erat quis ei fuisset mortuo successurus si regnandi tempus inter ipsum et diluvium remansisset.

Sed quoquo modo se habeat sive per primogenitos sive per reges ex Cain generationum ordo decurrens, illud mihi nullo pacto praetereundum silentio videtur, quod, cum Lamech septimus ab Adam fuisset inventus, tot eius adnumerati sunt filii donec undenarius numerus impleretur, quo significatur peccatum. Adduntur enim tres filii et una filia. Uxores autem aliud possunt significare, non hoc quod nunc commendandum videtur. Nunc enim de generationibus loquimur; illae vero unde sint genitae tacitum est.

Quoniam ergo lex denario numero praedicatur,

---

[1] usque *V and one other MS.:* usque ad *most MSS.*

was succeeded on the throne through a sort of hereditary right by that particular son whom he had loved more than the rest.

The flood may have taken place during the lifetime and reign of Lamech, coming upon and destroying him along with all other people, except for those who were in the ark. And if we consider the variations in age during the long period from Adam to the time of the flood, it is no wonder that both lines of descent did not have an equal number of generations, for the line through Cain had seven and that through Seth had ten—Lamech, as I stated previously, belonging to the seventh generation, and Noah to the tenth from Adam. Moreover, Lamech, unlike the others before him, has more than one son recorded [1] because it was uncertain who would have succeeded him on his death if there had remained time for another to reign between him and the flood.

But, however this may be, whether the line of descent from Cain is traced through the first-born or through kings, I do not think it right to pass over in silence the fact that when Lamech was reached in the seventh generation from Adam, enough of his children were recorded to bring the count up to eleven, a number signifying sin. For we find three sons and one daughter added. The wives, however, may have some other special meaning but not the one that I think now calls for presentation. For we are now speaking of lines of descent, and no information is given about the origin of those wives.

Accordingly, since the law is symbolized by the

---

[1] Cf. Genesis 4.19–22; 5.28–30.

unde est memorabilis ille decalogus, profecto numerus undenarius, quoniam transgreditur denarium, transgressionem legis ac per hoc peccatum significat. Hinc est quod in tabernaculo testimonii, quod erat in itinere populi Dei velut templum ambulatorium, undecim vela cilicina fieri praecepta sunt. In cilicio quippe recordatio est peccatorum propter haedos ad sinistram futuros; quod confitentes in cilicio prosternimur tamquam dicentes quod in psalmo scriptum est: *Et peccatum meum ante me est semper.*

Progenies ergo ex Adam per Cain sceleratum undenario numero finitur, quo peccatum significatur; et ipse numerus femina clauditur, a quo sexu initium factum est peccati per quod omnes morimur. Commissum est autem ut et voluptas carnis, quae spiritui resisteret, sequeretur. Nam et ipsa filia Lamech Noemma voluptas interpretatur. Per Seth autem ab Adam usque ad Noe denarius insinuatur legitimus numerus. Cui Noe tres adiciuntur filii, unde, uno lapso, duo benedicuntur a patre, ut, remoto reprobo et probatis filiis ad numerum additis, etiam duodenarius numerus intimetur, qui et in patriarcharum et in apostolorum numero insignis est propter septenarii partes alteram per alteram multiplicatas. Nam ter quaterni vel quater terni ipsum faciunt. His ita se habentibus, video considerandum et

---

[1] Cf. Exodus 26.7.
[2] Cf. Acts 7.44.
[3] Augustine has in mind here the Last Judgement; cf. Matthew 25.33.
[4] Psalms 51.3.
[5] Cf. Genesis 9.22–27.

number ten (and hence the designation of the famous decalogue), surely then the number eleven, passing ten as it does, stands for trespassing against the law and consequently for sin. This is why eleven curtains of goats' hair were ordered to be prepared for the tabernacle of the testimony,[1] which served the people of God as a mobile temple on their wandering.[2] For the goats' hair brings sins to mind because the goats are to stand on the left;[3] and when we confess a sin, we prostrate ourselves on goats' hair as if to say in the words of the psalmist: "And my sin is ever before me."[4]

Thus the line of descendants from Adam through Cain the felon ends with number eleven, which symbolizes sin; and this number itself concludes with a woman, whose sex was responsible for initiating the sin through which we all undergo death. Moreover, a further consequence of this sin was the advent of carnal pleasure to oppose the spirit. In fact, the name of Lamech's own daughter Naamah means pleasure. On the other hand, in the line extending from Adam through Seth down to Noah we find the number ten, which is the number of law. To this the three children of Noah are added, but one of them fell into sin while the other two received their father's blessing.[5] Thus, if we subtract the one rejected and add to the number ten only the sons who were approved, we also arrive at the number twelve. This number is notable as that of the patriarchs and of the apostles because it is the product of two components of seven multiplied by one another. For three times four or four times three make twelve. Recognizing all this, I see that

commemorandum, ista utraque progenies, quae
distinctis generationibus duas insinuat civitates,
unam terrigenarum, alteram regeneratorum, quo
modo postea sic commixta fuerit atque confusa ut
universum genus humanum, exceptis octo hominibus, diluvio perire mereretur.[1]

XXI

*Qua ratione commemorato Enoch, qui fuit filius
Cain, totius generationis eius usque ad diluvium
sit continuata narratio, commemorato
autem Enos, qui fuit filius Seth, ad
conditionis humanae principium
sit reditum.*

PRIMO autem intuendum est quem ad modum,
cum ex Cain generationes enumerarentur, commemorato ante ceteros posteros eius illo in cuius
nomine condita est civitas, id est Enoch, contexti
sunt ceteri usque ad illum finem de quo locutus sum,
donec illud genus atque universa propago diluvio
deleretur. Cum vero filius Seth unus commemoratus
fuisset, Enos, nondum usque ad diluvium additis
ceteris, articulus quidam interponitur et dicitur:
*Hic liber nativitatis hominum. Qua die fecit Deus
Adam, ad imaginem Dei fecit illum. Masculum et feminam fecit illos, et benedixit illos et cognominavit nomen
eorum Adam qua die fecit illos.*

[1] perire mereretur *some MSS.:* perimeretur *other MSS.*

I should next examine and relate how these two progenies, which by their separate lines suggest two cities, one the city of the earth-born and the other the city of the reborn, later became so mixed and mingled that the entire human race, with the exception of eight people, deserved to perish in the flood.

XXI

Why it is that after the mention of Enoch, son of Cain, the account of his entire line is continued down to the flood, but after the mention of Enos, son of Seth, there is a return to the origin of man's creation.

Now we must first consider why the genealogical accounts proceed differently in the case of Cain and Seth. For in the enumeration of the generations deriving from Cain, the man in whose name the city was founded, that is, Enoch, was mentioned before the rest of the descendants, and then they were listed as far as the end of which I have spoken, that is, down to the time when that line with its entire offspring was destroyed in the flood. In the case of Seth, however, after the mention of one son, namely, Enos,[1] the other descendants were not directly added down to the time of the flood, but a short passage is interjected as follows: " This is the book of the birth of men. When God made Adam, he made him in the likeness of God. Male and female he made them, and he blessed them and named them Adam on the day when he made them." [2]

[1] Cf. Genesis 4.26.
[2] Genesis 5.1–2.

SAINT AUGUSTINE

Quod mihi videtur ad hoc interpositum, ut hinc rursus inciperet ab ipso Adam dinumeratio temporum, quam noluit facere qui haec scripsit in civitate terrena, tamquam eam Deus sic commemoraret ut non conputaret. Sed quare hinc reditur ad istam recapitulationem postea quam commemoratus est filius Seth, homo qui speravit invocare nomen Domini Dei, nisi quia sic oportebat istas duas proponere civitates, unam per homicidam usque ad homicidam (nam et Lamech duabus uxoribus suis se perpetrasse homicidium confitetur), alteram per eum qui speravit invocare nomen Domini Dei? Hoc est quippe in hoc mundo peregrinantis civitatis Dei totum atque summum in hac mortalitate negotium, quod per unum hominem quem sane occisi resurrectio genuit commendandum fuit. Homo quippe ille unus totius supernae civitatis est unitas, nondum quidem conpleta, sed praemissa ista prophetica praefiguratione conplenda.

Filius ergo Cain, hoc est filius possessionis, (cuius nisi terrenae?) habeat nomen in civitate terrena quia in eius nomine condita est. De his est enim de quibus cantatur in psalmo: *Invocabunt nomina eorum in terris ipsorum;* propter quod sequitur eos quod in alio psalmo scriptum est: *Domine, in civitate tua imaginem eorum* [1] *ad nihilum rediges.* Filius autem Seth, hoc est filius resurrectionis, speret invocare

[1] ipsorum *some MSS., Vulg.*

[1] Cf. Genesis 4.26. [2] Cf. Genesis 4.23.
[3] Psalms 49.11. [4] Psalms 73.20.

The purpose of the insertion of this passage was, I think, to begin the chronological reckoning afresh at this point from Adam himself. The writer of these words chose not to do the same in the case of the earthly city, making it appear as if God gave an account of it without including it in the count. But why, we may ask, does he go back at this point to make the recapitulation after the mention of Seth's son, a man who hoped to call upon the name of the Lord God? [1] It must be that this was the right way to present the two cities, the one by citing a slayer at its beginning and end (for Lamech too confesses to his two wives that he had committed a murder),[2] the other by citing the man who hoped to call upon the name of the Lord God. For while the City of God sojourns as an alien in the present world, this calling upon the Lord is its whole and supreme occupation in this mortal life of ours, and it was to be represented in the person of one man who was son certainly of a resurrection of a man who was slain. This one person exemplifies the unity of the entire heavenly city, which, though not yet fulfilled, is destined to be fulfilled, according to that prophetic foreshadowing which preceded it.

Let then the son of Cain, that is, the son of possession (and here, of course, earthly possession is meant) have a name in the earthly city since it was established in his name. For it is of such people that the psalmist sings: " They will call upon their names in their own lands "; [3] and hence they meet with the fate described in another psalm: " Lord, in thy city thou shalt bring their image to naught." [4] On the other hand, let the son of Seth, that is, the son of

nomen Domini Dei; eam quippe societatem hominum praefigurat quae dicit: *Ego autem sicut oliva
fructifera in domo Dei speravi in misericordia Dei.*
Vanas autem glorias famosi in terra nominis non
requirat; *beatus* est enim *vir cuius est nomen Domini
spes eius, et non respexit in vanitates et insanias mendaces.*

Propositis itaque duabus civitatibus, una in re
huius saeculi, altera in spe Dei, tamquam ex communi quae aperta est in Adam ianua mortalitatis
egressis ut procurrant et excurrant ad discretos
proprios ac debitos fines, incipit dinumeratio temporum; in qua et aliae generationes adiciuntur,
facta recapitulatione ex Adam, ex cuius origine
damnata, veluti massa una meritae damnationi
tradita, facit[1] Deus alia in contumeliam vasa irae,
alia in honorem vasa misericordiae, illis reddens quod
debetur in poena, istis donans quod non debetur in
gratia, ut ex ipsa etiam conparatione vasorum irae
superna civitas discat, quae peregrinatur in terris,
non fidere libertate arbitrii sui sed speret invocare
nomen Domini Dei. Quoniam voluntas in natura,
quae facta est bona a Deo bono sed mutabilis ab
inmutabili quia ex nihilo, et a bono potest declinare

[1] fecit *some MSS.*

---

[1] Psalms 52.8.

resurrection, hope to call upon the name of the Lord
God, for he foreshadows the society of men that says:
" Like a fruitful olive tree in the house of God, I have
put my hope in the mercy of God." [1] Let him not,
however, seek the hollow renown of a celebrated
name on earth, for " blessed is the man whose hope
is in the name of the Lord, and who has no regard
for vanities and lying follies." [2]

Thus we have the two cities set before us, one
existing in the actuality of this world and the other
in hope placed in God. They came forth by a common door, as it were, of mortality that was opened
in Adam in order to continue and complete their
respective courses to their own distinct and destined
goals. The chronological reckoning now commences;
and in this reckoning, after a recapitulation from
Adam, other generations are added. Out of Adam's
condemned beginning, as if out of a single lump
consigned to deserved condemnation, God makes,
on the one hand, vessels of wrath for dishonour and,
on the other, vessels of mercy for honour; [3] to the
former he makes a due award of punishment and to
the latter he grants a free gift of grace. His purpose
in so doing is to instruct the celestial city, which
sojourns as an alien on earth, through this comparison
made with the vessels of wrath, that it must not trust
its own freedom of will but must hope to call upon
the name of the Lord God. For while man's nature
was created good by God, who is good, yet it was
made changeable by him who is unchangeable since
it was fashioned out of nothing. Hence the will in

[2] Psalms 40.4.
[3] Romans 9.22–23.

ut faciat malum, quod fit libero arbitrio, et a malo ut
faciat bonum, quod non fit sine divino adiutorio.

XXII

De lapsu filiorum Dei alienigenarum mulierum amore
captorum, unde et omnes, exceptis octo hominibus,
diluvio perire meruerunt.

Hoc itaque libero voluntatis arbitrio, genere humano progrediente atque crescente, facta est per-
mixtio et, iniquitate participata, quaedam utriusque
confusio civitatis. Quod malum a sexu femineo
causam rursus invenit, non quidem illo modo quo ab
initio (non enim cuiusquam etiam tunc fallacia
seductae illae feminae persuaserunt peccatum viris).
Sed ab initio quae pravis moribus fuerant in terrena
civitate, id est in terrigenarum societate, amatae
sunt a filiis Dei, civibus scilicet peregrinantis in hoc
saeculo alterius civitatis, propter pulchritudinem
corporis. Quod bonum Dei quidem donum [1] est,
sed propterea id largitur etiam malis, ne magnum
bonum videatur bonis.

Deserto itaque bono magno et bonorum proprio,
lapsus est factus ad bonum minimum, non bonis
proprium, sed bonis malisque commune. Ac sic

[1] bonum *V and one other MS.*

---

[1] Cf. Genesis 6.2.

his being may fall away from good to do evil, which happens by its own free choice, and from evil to do good, which does not happen except by divine assistance.

XXII

On the fall of the sons of God who were captivated by love for alien women, in consequence of which all, except eight persons, deservedly perished in the flood.

THUS, as the human race advanced and grew, this freedom of the will in its decisions effected a blend of the two cities and caused them, as a result of their partnership in unrighteousness, to be confounded, so to speak, with each other. Though this evil too derived its origin from the female sex, yet the manner in which it came about was different from that at the beginning, for these women were not led astray as before by someone's guile so as to persuade their husbands to sin. Rather, the women who had been morally depraved from the beginning in the earthly city, that is, in the society of the earth-born, were loved for the beauty of their bodies by the sons of God,[1] those citizens of the other city sojourning in this world. This beauty is indeed a good given by God, but he bestows it also on the wicked lest the good should regard it as a great good.

Consequently, the abandonment of a major good peculiar to the good entailed a decline to a very minor good that is not peculiar to the good but common to good and bad alike. So it was that the sons of God

filii Dei filiarum hominum amore sunt capti, atque ut eis coniugibus fruerentur, in mores societatis terrigenae defluxerunt, deserta pietate quam in sancta societate servabant. Sic enim corporis pulchritudo, a Deo quidem factum, sed temporale carnale infimum bonum, male amatur, postposito Deo, aeterno interno sempiterno bono, quem ad modum, iustitia deserta, et aurum amatur ab avaris, nullo peccato auri sed hominis. Ita se habet omnis creatura. Cum enim bona sit, et bene amari potest et male, bene scilicet ordine custodito, male ordine perturbato. Quod in laude quadam cerei breviter versibus dixi:

> Haec tua sunt, bona sunt, quia tu bonus ista
> creasti.
> Nil nostrum est in eis nisi quod peccamus
> amantes,
> Ordine neglecto, pro te quod conditur abs te.

Creator autem si veraciter ametur, hoc est si ipse, non aliud pro illo quod non est ipse, ametur, male amari non potest. Nam et amor ipse ordinate amandus est quo bene amatur quod amandum est, ut sit in nobis virtus qua vivitur bene. Unde mihi videtur quod definitio brevis et vera virtutis ordo est amoris; propter quod in sancto cantico canti-

---

[1] These three verses, with some slight verbal changes in the first, constitute the introduction of a poem entitled *De Anima* and attributed to Augustine; see *Anthologia Latina*, pars prior, fasc. II (1906), ed. A. Riese, 43, no. 489.

were taken captive by love of the daughters of men, and in order to enjoy them as wives, they abandoned the godliness that they had observed in their holy society and sank into the lower morality of the earth-born society. For when physical beauty, which, though created by God, is a temporary and carnal good of the lowest sort, is loved in preference to God himself, who is an eternal, internal and sempiternal good, such love is as bad as when justice is abandoned and gold is loved by the avaricious, through no fault of the gold but of the man. So it is with every created thing. For though it is good, it can be loved both in a good way and in a bad way —in a good way, when due order is preserved, in a bad way when due order is disturbed. I expressed this thought briefly in a poem celebrating the paschal candle:

> These things are thine and are good, for thou
>   who art good didst create them.
> Nothing of ours is in them save our sin in
>   neglecting due order,
> When in thy stead we have love for that which
>   by thee is created.[1]

If, however, the Creator should be truly loved, that is, if he himself should be loved and not something else in his stead which is not he, he cannot be loved in a bad way. For we must observe due order in loving even the love itself with which we love in a good way what is worthy of love, if there is to be in us the virtue that enables us to live a good life. Hence, in my opinion, a short and true definition of virtue is ' a due ordering of love '; and this is why

545

corum cantat sponsa Christi, civitas Dei: *Ordinate
in me caritatem.* Huius igitur caritatis, hoc est
dilectionis et amoris, ordine perturbato, Deum filii
Dei neglexerunt et filias hominum dilexerunt.

Quibus duobus nominibus satis civitas utraque
discernitur. Neque enim et illi non erant filii
hominum per naturam, sed aliud nomen coeperant
habere per gratiam. Nam in eadem scriptura, ubi
dicti sunt dilexisse filias hominum filii Dei, idem dicti
sunt etiam angeli Dei. Unde illos multi putant non
homines fuisse sed angelos.

XXIII

*An credendum sit angelos substantiae spiritalis amore
speciosarum mulierum captos earundem inisse coniugia, ex quibus gigantes sint creati.*

QUAM quaestionem nos transeunter commemora-
tam in tertio huius operis libro reliquimus insolutam,
utrum possint angeli, cum spiritus sint, corporaliter
coire cum feminis. Scriptum est enim: *Qui facit*

---

[1] Song of Songs 2.4. Augustine's text seemingly follows the
Septuagint, which reads here: τάξατε ἐπ' ἐμὲ ἀγάπην. But
the latter version apparently means: "Set in order (*or* array)
your love toward me." In his interpretation of the quotation
Augustine attempts to make it conform to the important
concept of *ordinata dilectio* discussed in his *De Doctrina
Christiana* 1.27.28. He may have been influenced to adopt
this explanation of the passage by Origen's comment on the
verse in his *Homiliae in Canticum Canticorum* (translated by
Jerome into Latin) 2.8, edited by W. A. Baehrens in *Origenes
Werke* (1925), vol. 8, pp. 52–53, and, more fully, in the third
book of his *Commentarium in Canticum Canticorum* (translated

in the holy *Song of Songs* Christ's bride, the City of God, sings: " Set affection in due order within me." [1] Thus the sons of God disturbed the due ordering of this affection, that is, of attachment and love, when they became detached from God and attached to the daughters of men.

These two epithets are enough to mark the contrast between the two cities. For the sons of God too were sons of men by nature, but they began to have another name by grace. In the same passage of Scripture, where the sons of God are said to have loved the daughters of men, they are also called angels of God.[2] Hence many think that they were not men but angels.

XXIII

Whether we should believe that angels, who are of spiritual substance, were so captivated by love for beautiful women that they united with them in marriage, which led to the birth of the giants.

IN the third book of the present work we touched in passing on this question whether angels, being spirits, could have bodily intercourse with women, but we left the matter there unresolved.[3] According to Scripture, " He makes spirits his angels," [4] that

by Rufinus into Latin), edited by W. A. Baehrens, *ibid.*, pp. 186–191.

[2] Cf. Genesis 6.2, where the corrector of the codex Alexandrinus of the Septuagint has written ἄγγελοι instead of υἱοί found in other manuscripts.

[3] See above, 3.5 (vol. 1, 279).

[4] Psalms 104.4.

angelos suos spiritus, id est eos qui natura spiritus
sunt facit esse angelos suos, iniungendo eis officium
nuntiandi. Qui enim Graece dicitur ἄγγελος, quod
nomen Latina declinatione angelus perhibetur,
Latina lingua nuntius interpretatur. Sed utrum
eorum corpora consequenter adiunxerit dicendo: *Et
ministros suos ignem ardentem*, an quod caritate tamquam igne spiritali fervere debeant ministri eius
ambiguum est.

Apparuisse tamen hominibus angelos in talibus
corporibus ut non solum videri verum etiam tangi
possent eadem veracissima[1] scriptura testatur. Et
quoniam creberrima fama est, multique se expertos
vel ab eis qui experti essent, de quorum fide dubitandum non esset,[2] audisse confirmant, Silvanos et
Panes,[3] quos vulgo incubos vocant, inprobos saepe
extitisse mulieribus et earum appetisse ac peregisse
concubitum, et quosdam daemones, quos Dusios
Galli nuncupant, adsidue hanc inmunditiam et
temptare et efficere plures talesque adseverant ut
hoc negare inpudentiae videatur, non hinc aliquid
audeo definire, utrum aliqui spiritus elemento aerio
corporati (nam hoc elementum, etiam cum agitatur
flabello, sensu corporis tactuque sentitur) possint

---

[1] veracissima *V*: verissima *most MSS.*
[2] est *a few MSS.*
[3] faunos (ph-) *some MSS.*

---

[1] Cf., *e.g.*, Genesis 19.1–22; Numbers 22.23–35; Judges
6.12–22; 13.3–20.
[2] On Silvanus see above, 6.9 (vol. 2, 341–343). Pan, an
Arcadian pastoral god, was early identified with the Italian

is, he makes those who are spirits by nature his angels by laying upon them the duty of bearing messages. For the Greek term *angelos,* which appears in Latin inflexion as *angelus,* means *nuntius* in Latin, that is, ' messenger.' But it is uncertain whether the psalmist was then referring to their bodies when he went on to say: "And his ministers a flaming fire," or whether he meant that God's ministers should burn with love as with a spiritual fire.

Still, according to the entirely reliable testimony of Scripture, angels appeared to men in such bodies that they could be not only seen but also handled.[1] Moreover, there is a very widespread report, corroborated by many people either through their own experience or through accounts of others of indubitably good faith who have had the experience, that Silvans and Pans,[2] who are commonly called *incubi,* often misbehaved towards women and succeeded in accomplishing their lustful desire to have intercourse with them. And the tradition that certain demons, termed Dusii by the Gauls,[3] constantly attempt and perpetrate this foulness is so widely and so well attested that it would seem impudent to deny it. Hence I dare not make any definite statement on the question whether some spirits endowed with bodies consisting of the element air—an element that, even when merely stirred by a fan, is felt by the body with its sense of touch—are also able to

Faunus, the plural of which appears here in some manuscripts for Panes.

[3] On these Celtic demons see Ihm in Pauly-Wissowa's *Real-Encyclopädie* 5.1867–1868, *s.v.* " Dusii."

hanc etiam pati libidinem ut, quo modo possunt,
sentientibus feminis misceantur.

Dei tamen angelos sanctos nullo modo illo tempore
sic labi potuisse crediderim, nec de his dixisse
apostolum Petrum: *Si enim Deus angelis peccantibus
non pepercit, sed carceribus caliginis inferi retrudens
tradidit in iudicio puniendos reservari*, sed potius de illis
qui primum apostatantes a Deo cum zabulo [1] suo
principe ceciderunt, qui primum hominem per invidiam serpentina fraude deiecit. Angelos autem
fuisse etiam Dei homines nuncupatos eadem scriptura
sancta locupletissima testis est. Nam et de Iohanne
scriptum est: *Ecce mitto angelum meum ante faciem
tuam, qui praeparabit viam tuam;* et Malachiel propheta propria quadam, id est proprie sibi inpertita,
gratia dictus est angelus.

Verum hoc movet quosdam, quod ex illis qui dicti
sunt angeli Dei et ex mulieribus quas amaverunt non
quasi homines generis nostri sed gigantes legimus
esse natos, quasi vero corpora hominum modum
nostrum longe excedentia, quod etiam supra commemoravi, non etiam nostris temporibus nata sunt.[2]
Nonne ante paucos annos, cum Romanae urbis quod
a Gothis factum est adpropinquaret excidium,
Romae fuit femina cum suo patre et sua matre quae
corpore quodam modo giganteo longe ceteris prae-
mineret? Ad quam visendam mirabilis fiebat usque-

---

[1] zabulo *one MS.*: diabolo *most MSS.*
[2] sint *some MSS.*

---

[1] 2 Peter 2.4. [2] Mark 1.2.
[3] Cf. Malachi 2.7. [4] Cf. above, 15.9 (pp. 457–459).
[5] Rome was sacked by the Goths in A.D. 410.

experience such lust and so have intercourse in such
a way as they can with women who feel the sensation
of it.

Nevertheless, I simply cannot bring myself to
believe that the holy angels of God could thus have
fallen at that time or that it was about them that the
apostle Peter said: " For if God did not spare the
angels when they sinned, but thrust them into
dungeons of nether gloom and committed them
there to be held for punishment at the time of judgement." [1] Rather he was speaking, I think, of those
who first broke away from God and fell with their
leader, the devil, who, moved by envy, brought the
first man down through trickery in the guise of a
serpent. Our holy Scripture offers abundant testimony that men of God were also termed angels.
For example, it says of John: " Behold, I send my
angel before thy face, who shall prepare thy way "; [2]
and the prophet Malachi was called an angel because
of a certain special grace, that is, a grace that was
specially bestowed upon him. [3]

Some people, however, are disturbed by the statement that offspring from the union of the so-called
angels of God and the women whom they loved were
not like our own human kind but giants, as though
even in our own times human beings had not in
fact been born with bodies far exceeding our own
proportions, as I have also mentioned above. [4] Was
there not in Rome a few years ago, when the destruction of the city by the Goths was drawing near, [5] a
woman living with her father and mother who
towered far above the others by her almost gigantic
stature? Wherever she was, an amazing throng

quaque concursus. Et hoc erat maxime admirationi, quod ambo parentes eius nec saltem tam longi homines erant quam longissimos videre consuevimus.

Potuerunt igitur gigantes nasci et prius quam filii Dei, qui et angeli Dei dicti sunt, filiabus hominum, hoc est secundum hominem viventium, miscerentur, filii scilicet Seth filiis [1] Cain. Nam et canonica scriptura sic loquitur in quo libro haec legimus, cuius verba ista sunt: *Et factum est postquam coeperunt homines multi fieri super terram, et filiae natae sunt illis; videntes autem angeli Dei filias hominum quia bonae sunt, sumpserunt sibi uxores ex omnibus quas elegerunt.[2] Et dixit Dominus Deus: Non permanebit spiritus meus in hominibus his in aeternum propter quod caro sunt; erunt autem dies eorum centum viginti anni. Gigantes autem erant super terram in diebus illis et post illud, cum intrarent filii Dei ad filias hominum, et generabant sibi; illi erant gigantes a saeculo, homines nominati.*

Haec libri verba divini satis indicant iam illis diebus fuisse gigantes super terram quando filii Dei acceperunt uxores filias hominum cum eas amarent bonas, id est pulchras. Consuetudo quippe scripturae huius est etiam speciosos corpore bonos vocare. Sed et postquam hoc factum est, nati sunt gigantes. Sic enim ait: *Gigantes autem erant super terram in diebus illis et post illud, cum intrarent filii Dei ad filias hominum.* Ergo et ante in illis diebus et post illud.

---

[1] filiabus *a few MSS.*
[2] elegerant *some MSS., Vulg.*

---

[1] Genesis 6.1–4.

would flock to see her. And especially remarkable was the fact that both her parents were not even as tall as the tallest that we are accustomed to see.

It is possible therefore that giants were born even before the sons of God, who were also called the angels of God, united with the daughters of men, that is, of those who lived according to man, or, in other words, before the sons of Seth united with the daughters of Cain. For, in fact, our canonical Scripture says so in the book where we read this. Here are its words: "And it came to pass after men began to multiply on the face of the ground, and daughters were born to them, that angels of God saw that the daughters of men were good; and they took to wife such of them as they chose. Then the Lord God said: 'My spirit shall not abide in these men for ever, for they are flesh; but their days shall be a hundred and twenty years.' The giants were on the earth in those days and also afterwards, when the sons of God came in to the daughters of men and engendered children for themselves. These were the giants that were of old, the men of renown." [1]

These words of the divine book show plainly enough that there were already giants on earth in those days when the sons of God took as wives the daughters of men, whom they loved since they were good, that is, beautiful; for it is the custom of this Scripture to call good those too who are physically attractive. But giants were born even afterwards, for, as Scripture says, " The giants were on the earth in those days and also afterwards, when the sons of God came in to the daughters of men." Thus there were giants in those days both before and after that event.

553

Quod autem ait: *Et generabant sibi*, satis ostendit quod prius, antequam sic caderent filii Dei, Deo generabant, non sibi, id est non dominante libidine coeundi, sed serviente officio propagandi, non familiam fastus sui, sed cives civitatis Dei, quibus adnuntiarent tamquam angeli Dei ut ponerent in Deo spem suam, similes illius qui natus est de Seth, filius resurrectionis, et speravit invocare nomen Domini Dei; in qua spe essent cum suis posteris coheredes aeternorum bonorum et sub Deo patre fratres filiorum.

Non autem illos ita fuisse angelos Dei ut homines non essent, sicut quidam putant, sed homines procul dubio fuisse scriptura ipsa sine ulla ambiguitate declarat. Cum enim praemissum esset quod *videntes angeli Dei filias hominum quia bonae sunt, sumpserunt sibi uxores ex omnibus quas elegerunt*,[1] mox adiunctum est: *Et dixit Dominus Deus: Non permanebit spiritus meus in hominibus his in aeternum propter quod caro sunt.* Spiritu Dei quippe fuerant facti angeli Dei et filii Dei, sed declinando ad inferiora dicuntur homines nomine naturae, non gratiae. Dicuntur et caro desertores spiritus et deserendo deserti.

Et septuaginta quidem interpretes et angelos Dei dixerunt istos et filios Dei. Quod quidem non

---

[1] elegerant *a few MSS., Vulg.*

---

[1] Cf. Psalms 78.7.

When Scripture says: "And they engendered children for themselves," it shows plainly enough that earlier, before the sons of God fell as they did, they engendered children for God, not for themselves, that is, that sexual lust was not their master but the servant of their reproductive function, and that they did not engender a family for their own pride but citizens for the City of God, to whom they, as angels of God, would deliver a message, urging them to place their hope in God,[1] as did the son of Seth, that is, the son of resurrection, who hoped to call on the name of the Lord God. Having this hope, they would share with their offspring in an inheritance of eternal blessings and would be brothers of their own children under God the father.

These sons of God, however, were not angels of God in the sense that they were not also human beings, as some people think, but they were assuredly human beings. On this point the testimony of Scripture is unequivocal. For after the words " the angels of God saw that the daughters of men were good, and they took to wife such of them as they chose," it at once adds; " Then the Lord God said: ' My spirit shall not abide in these men for ever, for they are flesh.' " They owed their creation as angels of God and sons of God to the spirit of God, but because they sank to a lower level, they are called human beings, a name that they had by nature, not by grace. They are also called flesh since they deserted the spirit, and in deserting, they were deserted by it.

In the Septuagint too they are called both angels of God and sons of God. This reading, to be sure,

omnes codices habent, nam quidam nisi filios Dei
non habent. Aquila autem, quem interpretem
Iudaei ceteris anteponunt, non angelos Dei nec
filios Dei sed filios deorum interpretatus est. Utrumque autem verum est. Nam et filii Dei erant,
sub quo patre suorum patrum etiam fratres erant, et
filii deorum quoniam diis geniti erant, cum quibus et
ipsi dii erant iuxta illud psalmi: *Ego dixi: Dii estis
et filii Excelsi omnes.* Merito enim creduntur septuaginta interpretes accepisse propheticum spiritum, ut,
si quid eius auctoritate mutarent atque aliter quam
erat quod interpretabantur dicerent, neque hoc
divinitus dictum esse dubitaretur, quamvis hoc in
Hebraeo esse perhibeatur ambiguum, ut et filii Dei
et filii deorum posset interpretari.

Omittamus igitur earum scripturarum fabulas quae
apocryphae nuncupantur eo quod earum occulta
origo non claruit patribus, a quibus usque ad nos
auctoritas veracium scripturarum certissima et notissima successione pervenit. In his autem apocryphis
etsi invenitur aliqua veritas, tamen propter multa
falsa nulla est canonica auctoritas. Scripsisse quidem nonnulla divine [1] illum Enoch, septimum ab

---

[1] divin(a)e *some MSS.:* divina *other MSS.*

---

[1] Aquila, a contemporary of Emperor Hadrian, had translated the Old Testament into Greek. His version was regarded as accurate and faithful to the original, but he was
accused of distorting those passages which Christians interpreted as prophetically indicating the advent of Christ.

[2] Psalms 82.6.

[3] For Augustine's view of the divine inspiration of the
Septuagint see below, 18.43 (vol. 6, 29–35); cf. also his *De
Doctrina Christiana* 2.15.22.

is not attested in all the manuscripts, for some have only " sons of God." Aquila,[1] on the other hand, whom the Jews prefer to the other translators, says in his version neither angels of God nor sons of God but sons of gods. But either expression is right. For they were sons of God, under whom as father they were also brothers of their own fathers; and at the same time they were sons of gods since they were the offspring of gods, along with whom they themselves too were gods according to the words of the psalmist: " I have said, ' You are gods, sons of the Most High, all of you.' "[2] We may well believe that the seventy translators received the spirit of prophecy, and thus if they changed anything under its authority and expressed what they were trans- lating differently from the original, there can be no doubt that their words too came from God.[3] In any case, this expression, we are told, is ambiguous in the Hebrew and translatable either as sons of God or as sons of gods.[4]

Let us then pass over the tales of those writings which are called apocrypha because their origin was hidden and uncertain to the fathers, from whom the authority of the true Scriptures has come down to us by a very sure and well-known line of transmission. Although some truth is found in these apocrypha, yet they contain much that is false and for that reason have no canonical authority. Now we cannot deny that some things were written under divine inspiration by Enoch, who belonged to the seventh

---

[4] On the ambiguity of the Hebrew word *Eloim* cf. Jerome's comment on Genesis 6.2 in *Liber Quaestionum Hebraicarum in Genesim*, in *Corpus Christianorum* vol. 72, 9.

Adam, negare non possumus cum hoc in epistula canonica Iudas apostolus dicat. Sed non frustra non sunt in eo canone scripturarum qui servabatur in templo Hebraei populi succedentium diligentia sacerdotum, nisi quia ob antiquitatem suspectae fidei iudicata sunt, nec utrum haec essent quae ille scripsisset poterat inveniri, non talibus proferentibus qui ea per seriem successionis reperirentur rite servasse. Unde illa quae sub eius nomine proferuntur et continent istas de gigantibus fabulas quod non habuerint homines patres recte a prudentibus iudicantur non ipsius esse credenda, sicut multa sub nominibus et aliorum prophetarum et recentiora sub nominibus apostolorum ab haereticis proferuntur, quae omnia nomine apocryphorum ab auctoritate canonica diligenti examinatione remota sunt.

Igitur secundum scripturas canonicas Hebraeas atque Christianas multos gigantes ante diluvium fuisse non dubium est et hos fuisse cives terrigenae societatis hominum, Dei autem filios, qui secundum carnem de Seth propagati sunt, in hanc societatem, deserta iustitia, declinasse. Nec mirandum est quod etiam de ipsis gigantes nasci potuerunt—neque enim omnes gigantes, sed magis multi utique tunc fuerunt quam post diluvium temporibus ceteris. Quos propterea creare placuit Creatori, ut etiam hinc ostenderetur non solum pulchritudines verum etiam magnitudines et fortitudines corporum non magni

---

[1] Cf. Jude 14.

generation from Adam, since the apostle Jude says this in a canonical letter.[1] But these writings are with good reason not included in the canon of Scripture which was carefully kept in the temple of the Hebrew people by a succession of priests. For they were judged of dubious authenticity because of their age. It was also impossible to ascertain whether they were what Enoch had written since they were not presented by men who were found to have kept them with proper ceremony through successive generations. Hence discerning authorities are right in their judgement that the writings presented under Enoch's name with those tales about giants not having human fathers should not be attributed to him. In like manner, many writings are presented by heretics under the names of other prophets or, if they are later, under the names of the apostles, but all these too have been excluded after careful examination from canonical authority and go under the name of apocrypha.

Therefore, according to the Hebrew and Christian canonical writings, there is no doubt that there were many giants before the flood and that these were citizens of the earth-born society of men; there is also no doubt that the sons of God, who descended from Seth according to the flesh, sank to the level of this society after forsaking righteousness. And it is not surprising that their offspring could be giants —not all of them in fact, but there were more giants then than in succeeding eras since the deluge. The Creator saw fit to create them in order to make it known in this way too that the wise man should attach little importance not only to physical beauty

pendendas esse sapienti, qui spiritalibus atque inmortalibus longe melioribus atque firmioribus et
bonorum propriis, non bonorum malorumque communibus, beatificatur bonis. Quam rem alius propheta commendans ait: *Ibi fuerunt gigantes illi
nominati, qui ab initio fuerunt staturosi, scientes proelium.
Non hos elegit Dominus, nec viam scientiae dedit illis;
sed interierunt quia non habuerunt sapientiam, perierunt
propter inconsiderantiam.*

XXIV

*Quo modo intellegendum sit quod de eis qui diluvio
perdendi erant Dominus dixerit: Erunt dies
eorum centum viginti anni.*

QUOD autem dixit Deus: *Erunt dies eorum centum
viginti anni,* non sic accipiendum est quasi praenuntia-
tum sit post haec homines centum viginti annos vivendo non transgredi, cum et post diluvium etiam
quingentos excessisse inveniamus. Sed intellegendum est hoc Deum dixisse cum circa finem quin-
gentorum annorum esset Noe, id est quadringentos
octoginta vitae annos ageret, quos more suo scriptura
quingentos vocat, nomine totius maximam partem
plerumque significans. Sescentensimo quippe anno
vitae Noe, secundo mense, factum est diluvium, ac
sic centum viginti anni praedicti sunt futuri vitae

---

[1] Baruch 3.26–28.   [2] Genesis 6.3.
[3] Cf. Genesis 7.11.

but to physical size and strength as well, for the spiritual and immortal goods with which he is blest are far better and more enduring, and such as belong to the good alone and are not common to the good and wicked alike. This is the point that another prophet makes when he says: " Those giants of renown were there, who from the beginning were of great stature, expert in war. These the Lord did not choose, nor did he give them the way of knowledge; but they were destroyed because they had no wisdom, they perished through their lack of judgement." [1]

XXIV

What the Lord meant when he said concerning those
who were to be destroyed in the flood: " Their
days shall be a hundred and twenty years."

As for God's words " Their days shall be a hundred and twenty years," [2] they cannot be taken as foretelling that thereafter men would not live beyond a hundred and twenty years, since we find that after the flood, as before, men lived even beyond five hundred years. We must understand that God spoke these words when Noah was nearing the age of five hundred years, that is, was in his four hundred and eightieth year, called characteristically the five-hundredth year in Scripture, where the largest part of anything is often denoted by the name of the whole. Now the flood occurred in the second month of the six-hundredth year of Noah's life,[3] and thus what was foretold is that men who were doomed to perish would live one hundred and twenty years

561

hominum periturorum, quibus transactis diluvio delerentur.

Nec frustra creditur sic factum esse diluvium, iam non inventis in terra qui non erant digni tali morte defungi qua in impios vindicatum est—non quo quicquam bonis quandoque morituris tale genus mortis faciat aliquid quod eis possit obesse post mortem, verum tamen nullus eorum diluvio mortuus est quos de semine Seth propagatos sancta scriptura commemorat. Sic autem divinitus diluvii causa narratur: *Videns*, inquit, *Dominus Deus quia multiplicatae sunt malitiae hominum super terram et omnis quisque cogitat in corde suo diligenter super maligna omnes dies, et cogitavit Deus quia fecit hominem super terram, et recogitavit et dixit Deus: Deleam hominem, quem feci, a facie terrae, ab homine usque ad pecus et a repentibus* [1] *usque ad volatilia caeli, quia iratus sum quoniam feci eos.*

XXV

De ira Dei, quae incommutabilem tranquillitatem nulla inflammatione perturbat.

Ira Dei non perturbatio animi eius est sed iudicium quo inrogatur poena peccato. Cogitatio vero eius et recogitatio mutandarum rerum est inmutabilis ratio. Neque enim sicut hominem, ita Deum cuiusquam

[1] reptilibus *some MSS. (cf. Vulg.:* reptili).

---

[1] Genesis 6.5–7.　　[2] Cf. Numbers 23.19.

more, after which they were to be destroyed in the flood.

We have good reason for believing that the flood took place in a situation where there were no longer to be found on earth any who were not worthy of such a death as was meted out in punishment of the wicked—not that good men, who will of course die some time, can be affected by this kind of death in any way that may harm them after death, but nevertheless none of those who, according to holy Scripture, were descended from the seed of Seth did die in the flood. Here is the divinely inspired account of the reason for the flood: " The Lord God saw that the wickedness of men had multiplied on the earth and that everyone was eagerly imagining evil in his heart all his days, and God considered that he had made man on the earth, and he reconsidered and said: ' I will blot out man, whom I have created, from the face of the ground, man and beast and creeping things and birds of the air, for I am angry that I have made them.' " [1]

XXV

On the anger of God, which does not disturb his unchangeable serenity by any flaming eruption.

THE anger of God is not an agitation of his mind but a judgement imposing punishment upon sin. Moreover, his consideration and reconsideration of any matter are merely his unchangeable design for things that are subject to change. For unlike man, God does not repent anything that he has done,[2] and

facti sui paenitet, cuius est de omnibus omnino rebus tam fixa sententia quam certa praescientia. Sed si non utatur scriptura talibus verbis, non se quodam modo familiarius insinuabit omni generi hominum, quibus vult esse consultum, ut et perterreat[1] superbientes et excitet neglegentes, et exerceat quaerentes et alat intellegentes; quod non faceret si non se prius inclinaret et quodam modo descenderet ad iacentes. Quod autem etiam interitum omnium animalium terrenorum volatiliumque denuntiat, magnitudinem futurae cladis effatur, non animantibus rationis expertibus, tamquam et ipsa peccaverint, minatur exitium.

XXVI

Quod arca quam Noe iussus est facere in omnibus
Christum ecclesiamque significet.

Iam vero quod Noe, homini iusto et, sicut de illo scriptura veridica loquitur, in sua generatione perfecto (non utique sicut perficiendi sunt cives civitatis Dei in illa inmortalitate qua aequabuntur angelis Dei, sed sicut esse possunt in hac peregrinatione perfecti), imperat Deus ut arcam faciat in qua cum suis, id est uxore, filiis et nuribus, et cum animalibus quae ad illum ex Dei praecepto in arcam ingressa sunt liberaretur a diluvii vastitate, procul dubio figura est peregrinantis in hoc saeculo civitatis Dei,

---

[1] praetereat *V and several other MSS.*

---

[1] Cf. Genesis 6.9.

concerning each and every thing his decision is as
unwavering as his prescience is unerring. But if
Scripture were not to use such expressions, it would
not come home so intimately, as it were, to all mankind, for whom it chooses to take thought. For only
in this way can it frighten the proud, arouse the
remiss, keep the curious occupied and provide
nourishment for the wise; nor would it succeed in
doing this if it did not first incline and come down, as
it were, to the lowly. When it further announces
the annihilation of all animals on earth and in the
air, it is emphasizing the magnitude of the coming
disaster, not threatening the destruction of irrational
creatures as if they too had sinned.

XXVI

*That the ark which Noah was ordered to make sym-
bolizes Christ and the church in every detail.*

Now God, as we know, enjoined the building of an
ark upon Noah, a man who was righteous and, according to the true testimony of Scripture, perfect in
his generation,[1] that is, perfect, not as the citizens
of the City of God are to become in that immortal
state where they will be made equal with the angels
of God, but as they can be during their sojourn here
on earth. In this ark he was to be rescued from the
devastation of the flood with his family, that is, his
wife, sons and daughters-in-law, as well as with the
animals that came to him in the ark at God's direction. We doubtless have here a symbolic representation of the City of God sojourning as an alien in this

hoc est ecclesiae quae fit salva per lignum in quo pependit mediator Dei et hominum, homo Christus Iesus.

Nam et mensurae ipsae longitudinis et altitudinis et latitudinis eius significant corpus humanum, in cuius veritate ad homines praenuntiatus est venturus et venit. Humani quippe corporis longitudo a vertice usque ad vestigia sexiens tantum habet quam latitudo, quae est ab uno latere ad alterum latus, et deciens tantum quam altitudo, cuius altitudinis mensura est in latere a dorso ad ventrem, velut, si iacentem hominem metiaris supinum seu pronum, sexiens tantum longus est a capite ad pedes quam latus a dextra in sinistram vel a sinistra in dextram et deciens quam altus a terra. Unde facta est arca trecentorum in longitudine cubitorum et quinquaginta in latitudine et triginta in altitudine. Et quod ostium in latere accepit, profecto illud est vulnus quando latus crucifixi lancea perforatum est. Hac quippe ad illum venientes ingrediuntur, quia inde sacramenta manarunt quibus credentes initiantur. Et quod de lignis quadratis fieri iubetur, undique stabilem vitam sanctorum significat; quacumque enim verteris quadratum, stabit. Et cetera quae in eiusdem arcae constructione dicuntur ecclesiasticarum signa sunt rerum.

Sed ea nunc persequi longum est; et hoc iam fecimus in opere quod adversus Faustum Manichaeum

---

[1] 1 Timothy 2.5.   [2] Cf. John 19.34.

world, that is, of the church which wins salvation by
virtue of the wood on which the mediator between
God and men, the man Christ Jesus,[1] was suspended.

The very measurements of the ark's length, height
and breadth symbolize the human body, in the reality
of which it was prophesied that Christ would come to
mankind, as, in fact, he did come. For the length
of the human body from top to toe is six times its
breadth from one side to the other and ten times its
thickness measured on a side from back to belly.
Thus, if you measure a man lying on his back or face
down, his length from head to foot is six times his
breadth from right to left or from left to right and
ten times his elevation from the ground. This is
why the ark was made three hundred cubits in length,
fifty in breadth and thirty in height. And as for the
door that it received on its side, that surely is the
wound that was made when the side of the crucified
one was pierced by the spear.[2] This is the way by
which those who come to him enter, because from
this opening flowed the sacraments with which be-
lievers are initiated. Moreover, the order that it
should be made of squared beams contains an allusion
to the foursquare stability of saints' lives, for in
whatever direction you turn a squared object, it will
stand firm. In similar fashion, everything else mentioned in the construction of this ark symbolizes some
aspect of the church.

It would, however, be tedious to spell all this out
in detail now; besides, I have already done so in
my work *Against Faustus the Manichaean*,[3] who denied

[3] Cf. *Contra Faustum Manichaeum* 12.14; see also Philo,
Quaestiones in Genesin 2.2.

scripsimus, negantem in Hebraeorum libris aliquid
de Christo esse prophetatum.   Et fieri quidem potest
ut et nobis quispiam et alius alio exponat haec
aptius, dum tamen ea quae dicuntur ad hanc de qua
loquimur Dei civitatem in hoc saeculo maligno tamquam in diluvio peregrinantem omnia referantur, si
ab eius sensu qui ista conscripsit non vult longe aber-
rare qui exponit.

Exempli gratia, velut si quispiam quod hic scriptum est: *Inferiora bicamerata et tricamerata facies eam*,
non quod ego in illo opere dixi velit intellegi, quia
ex omnibus gentibus ecclesia congregatur, bicamera-
tam dictam propter duo genera hominum, circum-
cisionem scilicet et praeputium, quos apostolus et
alio modo dicit Iudaeos et Graecos, tricameratam
vero eo quod omnes gentes de tribus filiis Noe post
diluvium reparatae sunt.   Sed aliud dicat aliquid
quod a fidei regula non sit alienum.   Nam quoniam
non solas in inferioribus mansiones habere arcam
voluit verum etiam in superioribus (et haec dixit
bicamerata) et in superioribus superiorum (et haec
appellavit tricamerata), ut ab imo sursum versus
tertia consurgeret habitatio, possunt hic intellegi et
tria illa quae commendat apostolus, fides, spes,
caritas.   Possunt etiam multo convenientius tres
illae ubertates evangelicae, tricena, sexagena, cen-

---

[1] Genesis 6.16.
[2] *Contra Faustum Manichaeum* 12.16.
[3] Cf. Romans 1.16; 3.9; Galatians 3.28.
[4] 1 Corinthians 13.13.

that there was any prophecy concerning Christ in the
books of the Hebrews. And there is always the
possibility that someone else may be able to explain
these matters more satisfactorily than I or one man
than another. I would only stipulate that everything that is said must bear on our present subject,
the City of God, which sojourns as an alien in this
wicked world as though in a flood, if the interpreter
does not wish to stray far from the sense intended by
the author of this account.

A person, for example, may reject the interpretation that I have given in my work against Faustus of
this scriptural passage: " Make it with lower, second,
and third storeys." [1] There [2] I explained that because the church is assembled from all nations, it is
called two-storeyed for the two categories of men,
that is, the circumcised and the uncircumcised, or,
as the Apostle puts it in another way, the Jews and
the Greeks; [3] and I explain that it is called three-
storeyed because all nations were restored after the
flood from the three sons of Noah. But let this person
offer some other explanation not incompatible with
the rule of faith. For, as we know, God wanted the
ark to have quarters not only on the lower level but
also on the upper level, which was called the second
storey, and on the still higher level, which was called
the third storey, so that a third place to live in might
rise upward from the bottom. It is possible to interpret this as an allusion to those three virtues praised by
the Apostle, namely, faith, hope and charity. [4] Or
again, even much more suitably, it is possible to
interpret it as a reference to those three rich harvests
mentioned in the gospel, with a thirtyfold, sixtyfold

tena, ut in infimo habitet pudicitia coniugalis, supra
vidualis atque hac superior virginalis, et si quid
melius [1] secundum fidem civitatis huius intellegi et
dici potest. Hoc etiam de ceteris quae hic ex-
ponenda sunt dixerim, quia, etsi non uno disseruntur
modo, ad unam tamen catholicae fidei concordiam
revocanda sunt.

XXVII

De arca atque diluvio nec illis esse consentiendum qui
solam historiam recipiunt sine allegorica signi-
ficatione nec illis qui solas figuras defendunt,
repudiata historica veritate.

NON tamen quisquam putare debet aut frustra
haec esse conscripta aut tantummodo rerum gestarum veritatem sine ullis allegoricis significationibus
hic esse quaerendam aut, e contrario, haec omnino
gesta non esse sed solas esse verborum figuras aut,
quidquid illud est, nequaquam ad prophetiam ecclesiae pertinere. Quis enim nisi mente perversus
inaniter scriptos esse contendat libros per annorum
milia tanta religione et tam ordinatae successionis
observantia custoditos aut solas res gestas illic
intuendas ubi certe, ut alia omittam, si numerositas

----

[1] aliud *some MSS.*

----

[1] Cf. Matthew 13.8.

and hundredfold return;[1] according to this interpretation, the chastity of wedlock would occupy the
lowest level, that of widowhood the second and that
of virginity the highest. And perhaps it is possible
to arrive at and offer even better interpretations that
accord with the faith of this city of ours. The same
would apply also to the rest of the presentation
that is to follow here: more than one explanation
may be possible, but they must all square with the
harmonious unity of the catholic faith.

XXVII

That we should agree neither with those who accept
only the historical account of the ark and the flood
without any allegorical connotations nor with
those who reject their historical reality and
defend their symbolic significance alone.

No one should suppose, however, that this account
of the flood was written to no purpose, or that we are
to look here only for the historical reality of events
without any allegorical connotations, or, conversely,
that these events did not take place at all but represent only symbolic discourse, or that, whatever it is, it
has absolutely nothing to do with prophecy about the
church. Who but a demented person would argue
that books which have been guarded for thousands
of years so reverently and with such regard for so
orderly a transmission were written pointlessly, or
that we should see in them an account of historical
events only? For, to omit other considerations, if
it was the large number of animals that necessitated

571

animalium cogebat arcae tantam fieri magnitudinem, inmunda bina et munda septena intromitti
animalia quid cogebat cum aequalis numeri possent
utraque servari? Aut vero Deus, qui propter genus
reparandum servanda praecepit, eo modo illa quo
instituerat restituere non valebat?

Qui vero non esse gesta sed solas rerum significan-
darum figuras esse contendunt primum opinantur
tam magnum fieri non potuisse diluvium ut altissi-
mos montes quindecim cubitis aqua crescendo
transcenderet propter Olympi verticem montis,
supra quem perhibent [1] nubes non posse concrescere
quod tam sublime iam [2] caelum sit ut non ibi sit aer
iste crassior ubi venti nebulae imbresque gignuntur.
Nec adtendunt omnium elementorum crassissimam
terram ibi esse potuisse. An forte negant esse
terram verticem montis? Cur igitur usque ad illa
caeli spatia terris exaltari licuisse et aquis exaltari
non licuisse contendunt, cum isti mensores et pen-
sores elementorum aquas terris perhibeant superiores
atque leviores? Quid itaque rationis adferunt
quare terra gravior et inferior locum caeli tran-
quillioris invaserit per volumina tot annorum et
aqua levior ac superior permissa non sit hoc facere
saltem ad tempus exiguum?

Dicunt etiam non potuisse capere arcae illius
quantitatem animalium genera tam multa in utroque

[1] perhibent *adopted by Dombart from one MS.:* perhibentur
most MSS.
[2] quam *some MSS.*

---

[1] Cf. Genesis 7.2.

the construction of so huge an ark, what was the
need of including two unclean and seven clean animals of each species [1] when both kinds might have
been preserved by the same number? Can it be
that God, who ordered them to be preserved so as
to restore their species, was unable to create them
anew as he had created them before?

Others argue that we have here not an account of
actual happenings but only symbolic language to
convey hidden meanings. Their view is, first, that
it is impossible for so vast a flood to have occurred
that water rose fifteen cubits above the highest
mountains. According to them, clouds cannot form
above the summit of Mount Olympus because the atmosphere there is so high that the denser air in which
winds, clouds and rains originate is lacking. They
fail to observe that earth, the densest of all the elements, could be found there. Can they possibly
deny that the summit of the mountain is made of
earth? But if they admit that the earth could rise
to those heights in the atmosphere, why then do they
maintain that the waters could not? After all, those
scientists who measure and weigh the elements do
state that water rises higher and is lighter than earth.
What reason therefore do they adduce to explain
why earth, a heavier and lower element, could penetrate the region of the calmer atmosphere during the
course of so many years, if water, which is lighter
and rises higher, has not been allowed to do so even
for a short time?

Moreover, people say that an ark of those dimensions cannot have contained so many species of animals of both sexes, two of each kind from the unclean

573

sexu, bina de inmundis, septena de mundis. Qui
mihi videntur non conputare nisi trecenta cubita
longitudinis et latitudinis quinquaginta nec cogitare
aliud tantum esse in superioribus itemque aliud
tantum in superioribus superiorum, ac per hoc ter
ducta illa cubita fieri nongenta per centum quinquaginta. Si autem cogitemus quod Origenes non
ineleganter astruxit, Moysen scilicet, hominem Dei
eruditum, sicut scriptum est, *omni sapientia Aegyptiorum*, qui geometricam dilexerunt, geometrica
cubita significare potuisse, ubi unum quantum sex
nostra valere adseverant, quis non videat quantum
rerum capere illa potuit magnitudo?

Nam illud quod disputant tantae magnitudinis
arcam non potuisse conpingi, ineptissime calumni-
antur cum sciant inmensas urbes fuisse constructas;
nec adtendunt centum annos quibus arca illa est
fabricata—nisi forte lapis lapidi adhaerere potest
sola calce coniunctus ut murus per tot milia circum-
agatur, et lignum ligno per suscudines, epiros, clavos,
gluten bituminis non potest adhaerere ut fabricetur
arca non curvis sed rectis lineis longe lateque por-
recta, quam nullus in mare mittat conatus hominum
sed levet unda, cum venerit, naturali ordine pon-
derum, magisque divina providentia quam humana
prudentia natantem gubernet ne incurrat ubicumque
naufragium.

Quod autem scrupulosissime quaeri solet de minu-

---

[1] Cf. Origen, *In Genesim Homiliae* 2.2. [2] Acts 7.22.

and seven of each kind from the clean. But they calculate, it seems, only three hundred cubits in length and fifty in width, without considering that there is just as much space on the upper level and as much also on the still higher level, so that those dimensions in cubits are multiplied by three and thus come to nine hundred by one hundred and fifty. Further, it is possible, as Origen brilliantly suggested,[1] that Moses, a man of God " instructed," according to Scripture, " in all the wisdom of the Egyptians " [2]—and they were devoted to geometry, meant geometric cubits, of which one is said to equal six of ours. If we should follow such a line of thinking, the enormous capacity of an ark of that size would be plain to all.

When they argue that an ark of such vast dimensions could not be framed, their disparaging remarks are quite foolish since they know that enormous cities have been constructed; and, besides, they overlook the hundred years that it took to build that ark. Or if stones can be cemented together by lime alone to form a circular wall many miles long, is it possible that wood cannot be joined by tenons, pegs, nails and pitch-glue to build an ark which would extend not in curving but in straight lines throughout its length and breadth? Such an ark would not be launched into the sea by human effort but would be raised, thanks to the natural difference in specific gravity, by the flood water when it arrived; and the ark would be piloted when afloat by divine providence rather than by human prudence so as to avoid shipwreck anywhere.

Further, a question is often raised by extremely

tissimis bestiolis, non solum quales sunt mures et
stelliones verum etiam quales lucustae, scarabei,
muscae denique et pulices, utrum non amplioris
numeri in arca illa fuerint quam qui est definitus
cum hoc imperaret Deus, prius admonendi sunt quos
haec movent sic accipiendum esse quod dictum est:
Quae repunt super terram, ut necesse non fuerit con-
servari in arca quae possunt in aquis vivere, non
solum mersa, sicut pisces, verum etiam supernatantia,
sicut multae alites. Deinde cum dicitur: *Masculus
et femina erunt*, profecto intellegitur ad reparandum
genus dici, ac per hoc nec illa necesse fuerat ibi esse
quae possunt sine concubitu de quibusque rebus vel
rerum corruptionibus nasci, vel si fuerunt, sicut in
domibus esse consuerunt, sine ullo numero definito
esse potuisse. Aut si mysterium sacratissimum
quod agebatur et tantae rei figura etiam veritate
facti aliter non posset impleri nisi ut omnia ibi certo
illo numero essent quae vivere in aquis, natura
prohibente, non possent, non fuit ista cura illius
hominis vel illorum hominum sed divina. Non enim
ea Noe capta intromittebat, sed venientia et in-
trantia permittebat. Ad hoc enim valet quod dictum
est: *Intrabunt ad te,* non scilicet hominis actu sed Dei
nutu, ita sane ut non illic fuisse credenda sint quae

---

[1] Genesis 6.20.
[2] Genesis 6.19; cf. also Genesis 7.2, 3, 9, 16.
[3] Genesis 6.20.

meticulous critics about the very tiny creatures, not
only such as mice and lizards but also such as locusts,
beetles and even flies and fleas. They ask whether
the number of these creatures in that ark was not
larger than the limit set when God gave the order.
In this connexion, we must first advise those who are
perplexed by the matter that the words " That crawl
upon the earth " [1] are to be understood as implying
that it was not necessary to preserve in the ark
creatures that can live in the waters; and this would
include not only those submerged, such as fish, but
also those that swim on the surface, such as many
species of birds. Moreover, since the words " They
will be male and female " [2] must surely be taken as
referring to the renewal of the species, it was likewise unnecessary for such creatures to be at hand as
can be generated asexually from various substances
or from the putrefaction of them. Or if they were
there, just as they usually are in houses, there need
not have been any fixed number of them. On the
other hand, it may not otherwise have been possible for the very holy mystery that was being
enacted, the symbolic representation of so great an
event, to be perfectly reflected in actual history as
well unless all the creatures that were prevented by
nature from living in the waters were present there
in that specified number. But in that case this was
not a concern of one man or of many men but of God.
For Noah did not capture the creatures and put them
in; he merely let them in as they came and sought
to enter. Such is the import of the words " They
will come in to you " [3]—not, of course, through man's
doing but through God's bidding. Yet we should

SAINT AUGUSTINE

sexu carent. Praescriptum enim atque definitum est: *Masculus et femina erunt.*

Alia sunt quippe quae de quibusque rebus sine concubitu ita nascuntur ut postea concumbant et generent, sicut muscae; alia vero in quibus nihil sit maris et feminae, sicut apes. Ea porro quae sic habent sexum ut non habeant fetum, sicut muli et mulae, mirum si fuerunt ibi, ac non potius parentes eorum ibi fuisse suffecerit,[1] equinum videlicet atque asininum genus; et si qua alia sunt quae commixtione diversi generis genus aliquod gignunt. Sed si et hoc ad mysterium pertinebat, ibi erant; habet enim et hoc genus masculum et feminam.

Solet etiam movere nonnullos, genera escarum quae illic habere poterant animalia quae non nisi carne vesci putantur, utrum praeter numerum ibi fuerint sine transgressione mandati quae aliorum alendorum necessitas illic coegisset includi, an vero, quod potius est credendum, praeter carnes aliqua alimenta esse potuerunt quae omnibus convenirent. Novimus enim quam multa animalia quibus caro cibus est frugibus pomisque vescantur et maxime fico atque castaneis. Quid ergo mirum si vir ille sapiens et iustus, etiam divinitus admonitus quid cuique congrueret, sine carnibus aptam cuique generi alimoniam praeparavit et condidit?

[1] sufficerit *or* sufficeret *some MSS.*

578

not suppose that animals without sex were included
there, for it was precisely specified: " They will be
male and female."

There are, in fact, some animals that come into
being asexually from diverse kinds of matter but
later copulate to reproduce, such as flies. There are
others, like bees, that have no distinguishing sexual
characteristics. As for those animals that are sexually differentiated but without the capacity to have
offspring, like male and female mules, it would be
surprising if they were present in the ark and not
rather their parents, namely, the horse and the
ass, who would have sufficed to be there. The same
would apply in the case of any other animals that
produce some kind of creature by cross-breeding.
But if the presence of these hybrids also was essential
to the mystery, they were included; for such a
species too has male and female.

A question also arises concerning the kinds of food
that could have been available in the ark to animals
who are thought to eat only meat. For some people
often wonder whether there were on board, without
any violation of God's order, extra animals that must
have been included beyond the number prescribed
because of the need to feed the others, or whether,
as is more credible, there may have been some pro-
visions, other than meat, that were suitable for all.
We know, in fact, how many carnivorous animals
feed on vegetables and fruit, especially figs and chest-
nuts. What wonder then if that wise and righteous
man, who was also advised by God of what was appropriate for each one, prepared and stored food, apart
from meat, that was suitable for each species?

Quid est autem quo [1] vesci non cogeret fames?
Aut quid non suave ac salubre facere posset Deus,
qui etiam ut sine cibo viverent divina facilitate
donaret, nisi ut pascerentur etiam hoc inplendae
figurae tanti mysterii conveniret? Non autem ad
praefigurandam ecclesiam pertinere tam multiplicia
rerum signa gestarum, nisi fuerit contentiosus,
nemo permittitur opinari. Iam enim gentes ita
ecclesiam repleverunt, mundique et inmundi, donec
certum veniatur ad finem, ita eius unitatis quadam
compagine continentur ut ex hoc uno manifestissimo
etiam de ceteris, quae obscurius aliquanto dicta sunt
et difficilius agnosci queunt, dubitare fas non sit.

Quae cum ita sint, [si] [2] nec inaniter ista esse
conscripta putare quisquam vel durus audebit, nec
nihil significare cum gesta sint, nec sola dicta esse
significativa non facta, nec aliena esse ab ecclesia
significanda probabiliter dici potest. Sed magis
credendum est et sapienter esse memoriae litterisque
mandata et gesta esse et significare aliquid et ipsum
aliquid ad praefigurandam ecclesiam pertinere.

Iam usque ad hunc articulum perductus liber iste
claudendus est ut ambarum civitatum cursus, terrenae scilicet secundum hominem viventis et caelestis
secundum Deum, post diluvium et deinceps in rebus
consequentibus requiratur.

---

[1] quo *V and two other MSS.:* quod *most MSS.*
[2] si *bracketed by Dombart, following Duebner.*

Is there anything that hunger would not compel us to eat? Is there anything that God could not make palatable and wholesome? Indeed, he could even have enabled those creatures by his divine power to live without food if their eating were not essential to complete the symbolic representation of so great a mystery. Now no one, except a captious critic, can suppose that such manifold details of actual events do not serve to foreshadow the church symbolically. For nations have already filled the church, and people, clean and unclean, are held together, and will be until the predetermined end is reached, in the frame, as it were, of its unity. Since the prophecy is so perfectly manifest in this case, it is abominable to be doubtful about its other implications, which are put somewhat less clearly and are more difficult to detect.

No person therefore, however stubborn, will venture to suppose that this account was written to no purpose; nor can it be reasonably said that though the events happened, they do not have a symbolic significance, or that we have only symbolic words here without any basis in fact, or that it is not the church to which the symbolism refers. Rather we must believe that the transmission of this account in a written history was a wise action, that the events did take place, that they do have a symbolic significance and that this significance points figuratively to the church.

Now that the present book has reached this juncture, I must bring it to a close in order to investigate next the careers of both cities, that is, of the earthly city that lives according to man and of the heavenly city that lives according to God, during the period after the flood and from that time on in subsequent history.

Printed in Great Britain by
Richard Clay (The Chaucer Press), Ltd.,
Bungay, Suffolk

THE LOEB CLASSICAL LIBRARY

VOLUMES ALREADY PUBLISHED

Latin Authors

AMMIANUS MARECLLINUS. Translated by J. C. Rolfe. 3 Vols.

APULEIUS: THE GOLDEN ASS (METAMORPHOSES). W. Adlington (1566). Revised by S. Gaselee.

ST. AUGUSTINE: CITY OF GOD. 7 Vols. Vol. I. G. E. McCracken. Vol. II. W. M. Green. Vol. IV. P. Levine. Vol. V. E. M. Sanford and W. M. Green. Vol. VI. W. C. Greene.

ST. AUGUSTINE, CONFESSIONS OF. W. Watts (1631). 2 Vols.

ST. AUGUSTINE, SELECT LETTERS. J. H. Baxter.

AUSONIUS. H. G. Evelyn White. 2 Vols.

BEDE. J. E. King. 2 Vols.

BOETHIUS: TRACTS and DE CONSOLATIONE PHILOSOPHIAE. Rev. H. F. Stewart and E. K. Rand.

CAESAR: ALEXANDRIAN, AFRICAN and SPANISH WARS. A. G. Way.

CAESAR: CIVIL WARS. A. G. Peskett.

CAESAR: GALLIC WAR. H. J. Edwards.

CATO: DE RE RUSTICA; VARRO: DE RE RUSTICA. H. B. Ash and W. D. Hooper.

CATULLUS. F. W. Cornish; TIBULLUS. J. B. Postgate; PERVIGILIUM VENERIS. J. W. Mackail.

CELSUS: DE MEDICINA. W. G. Spencer. 3 Vols.

CICERO: BRUTUS, and ORATOR. G. L. Hendrickson and H. M. Hubbell.

[CICERO]: AD HERENNIUM. H. Caplan.

CICERO: DE ORATORE, etc. 2 Vols. Vol. I. DE ORATORE, Books I. and II. E. W. Sutton and H. Rackham. Vol. II. DE ORATORE, Book III. De Fato; Paradoxa Stoicorum; De Partitione Oratoria. H. Rackham.

CICERO: DE FINIBUS. H. Rackham.

CICERO: DE INVENTIONE, etc. H. M. Hubbell.

CICERO: DE NATURA DEORUM and ACADEMICA. H. Rackham.

CICERO: DE OFFICIIS. Walter Miller.

CICERO: DE REPUBLICA and DE LEGIBUS; SOMNIUM SCIPIONIS. Clinton W. Keyes.

CICERO: DE SENECTUTE, DE AMICITIA, DE DIVINATIONE. W. A. Falconer.

CICERO: IN CATILINAM, PRO FLACCO, PRO MURENA, PRO SULLA. Louis E. Lord.

CICERO: LETTERS to ATTICUS. E. O. Winstedt. 3 Vols.

CICERO: LETTERS TO HIS FRIENDS. W. Glynn Williams. 3 Vols.

CICERO: PHILIPPICS. W. C. A. Ker.

CICERO: PRO ARCHIA POST REDITUM, DE DOMO, DE HARUSPICUM RESPONSIS, PRO PLANCIO. N. H. Watts.

CICERO: PRO CAECINA, PRO LEGE MANILIA, PRO CLUENTIO, PRO RABIRIO. H. Grose Hodge.

CICERO: PRO CAELIO, DE PROVINCIIS CONSULARIBUS, PRO BALBO. R. Gardner.

CICERO: PRO MILONE, IN PISONEM, PRO SCAURO, PRO FONTEIO, PRO RABIRIO POSTUMO, PRO MARCELLO, PRO LIGARIO, PRO REGE DEIOTARO. N. H. Watts.

CICERO: PRO QUINCTIO, PRO ROSCIO AMERINO, PRO ROSCIO COMOEDO, CONTRA RULLUM. J. H. Freese.

CICERO: PRO SESTIO, IN VATINIUM. R. Gardner.

CICERO: TUSCULAN DISPUTATIONS. J. E. King.

CICERO: VERRINE ORATIONS. L. H. G. Greenwood. 2 Vols.

CLAUDIAN. M. Platnauer. 2 Vols.

COLUMELLA: DE RE RUSTICA. DE ARBORIBUS. H. B. Ash, E. S. Forster and E. Heffner. 3 Vols.

CURTIUS, Q.: HISTORY OF ALEXANDER. J. C. Rolfe. 2 Vols.

FLORUS. E. S. Forster; and CORNELIUS NEPOS. J. C. Rolfe.

FRONTINUS: STRATAGEMS and AQUEDUCTS. C. E. Bennett and M. B. McElwain.

FRONTO: CORRESPONDENCE. C. R. Haines. 2 Vols.

GELLIUS, J. C. Rolfe. 3 Vols.

HORACE: ODES AND EPODES. C. E. Bennett.

HORACE: SATIRES, EPISTLES, ARS POETICA. H. R. Fairclough.

JEROME: SELECTED LETTERS. F. A. Wright.

JUVENAL and PERSIUS. G. G. Ramsay.

LIVY. B. O. Foster, F. G. Moore, Evan T. Sage, and A. C. Schlesinger and R. M. Geer (General Index). 14 Vols.

LUCAN. J. D. Duff.

LUCRETIUS. W. H. D. Rouse.

MARTIAL. W. C. A. Ker. 2 Vols.

MINOR LATIN POETS: from PUBLILIUS SYRUS TO RUTILIUS NAMATIANUS, including GRATTIUS, CALPURNIUS SICULUS, NEMESIANUS, AVIANUS, and others with "Aetna" and the "Phoenix." J. Wight Duff and Arnold M. Duff.

OVID: THE ART OF LOVE and OTHER POEMS. J. H. Mozley.

2

OVID: FASTI. Sir James G. Frazer.

OVID: HEROIDES and AMORES. Grant Showerman.

OVID: METAMORPHOSES. F. J. Miller. 2 Vols.

OVID: TRISTIA and EX PONTO. A. L. Wheeler.

PERSIUS. Cf. JUVENAL.

PETRONIUS. M. Heseltine; SENECA; APOCOLOCYNTOSIS. W. H. D. Rouse.

PHAEDRUS AND BABRIUS (Greek). B. E. Perry.

PLAUTUS. Paul Nixon. 5 Vols.

PLINY: LETTERS. Melmoth's Translation revised by W. M. L. Hutchinson. 2 Vols.

PLINY: NATURAL HISTORY. 10 Vols. Vols. I.–V. and IX. H. Rackham. Vols. VI.–VIII. W. H. S. Jones. Vol. X. D. E. Eichholz.

PROPERTIUS. H. E. Butler.

PRUDENTIUS. H. J. Thomson. 2 Vols.

QUINTILIAN. H. E. Butler. 4 Vols.

REMAINS OF OLD LATIN. E. H. Warmington. 4 Vols. Vol. I. (ENNIUS AND CAECILIUS.) Vol. II. (LIVIUS, NAEVIUS, PACUVIUS, ACCIUS.) Vol. III. (LUCILIUS and LAWS OF XII TABLES.) Vol. IV. (ARCHAIC INSCRIPTIONS.)

SALLUST. J. C. Rolfe.

SCRIPTORES HISTORIAE AUGUSTAE. D. Magie. 3 Vols.

SENECA: APOCOLOCYNTOSIS. Cf. PETRONIUS.

SENECA: EPISTULAE MORALES. R. M. Gummere. 3 Vols.

SENECA: MORAL ESSAYS. J. W. Basore. 3 Vols.

SENECA: TRAGEDIES. F. J. Miller. 2 Vols.

SIDONIUS: POEMS and LETTERS. W. B. ANDERSON. 2 Vols.

SILIUS ITALICUS. J. D. Duff. 2 Vols.

STATIUS. J. H. Mozley. 2 Vols.

SUETONIUS. J. C. Rolfe. 2 Vols.

TACITUS: DIALOGUES. Sir Wm. Peterson. AGRICOLA and GERMANIA. Maurice Hutton.

TACITUS: HISTORIES AND ANNALS. C. H. Moore and J. Jackson. 4 Vols.

TERENCE. John Sargeaunt. 2 Vols.

TERTULLIAN: APOLOGIA and DE SPECTACULIS. T. R. Glover. MINUCIUS FELIX. G. H. Rendall.

VALERIUS FLACCUS. J. H. Mozley.

VARRO: DE LINGUA LATINA. R. G. Kent. 2 Vols.

VELLEIUS PATERCULUS and RES GESTAE DIVI AUGUSTI. F. W. Shipley.

VIRGIL. H. R. Fairclough. 2 Vols.

VITRUVIUS: DE ARCHITECTURA. F. Granger. 2 Vols.

3

Greek Authors

ACHILLES TATIUS. S. Gaselee.

AELIAN: ON THE NATURE OF ANIMALS. A. F. Scholfield. 3 Vols.

AENEAS TACTICUS, ASCLEPIODOTUS and ONASANDER. The Illinois Greek Club.

AESCHINES. C. D. Adams.

AESCHYLUS. H. Weir Smyth. 2 Vols.

ALCIPHRON, AELIAN, PHILOSTRATUS: LETTERS. A. R. Benner and F. H. Fobes.

ANDOCIDES, ANTIPHON, Cf. MINOR ATTIC ORATORS.

APOLLODORUS. Sir James G. Frazer. 2 Vols.

APOLLONIUS RHODIUS. R. C. Seaton.

THE APOSTOLIC FATHERS. Kirsopp Lake. 2 Vols.

APPIAN: ROMAN HISTORY. Horace White. 4 Vols.

ARATUS. Cf. CALLIMACHUS.

ARISTOPHANES. Benjamin Bickley Rogers. 3 Vols. Verse trans.

ARISTOTLE: ART OF RHETORIC. J. H. Freese.

ARISTOTLE: ATHENIAN CONSTITUTION, EUDEMIAN ETHICS, VICES AND VIRTUES. H. Rackham.

ARISTOTLE: GENERATION OF ANIMALS. A. L. Peck.

ARISTOTLE: HISTORIA ANIMALIUM. A. L. Peck. Vol. I.

ARISTOTLE: METAPHYSICS. H. Tredennick. 2 Vols.

ARISTOTLE: METEOROLOGICA. H. D. P. Lee.

ARISTOTLE: MINOR WORKS. W. S. Hett. On Colours, On Things Heard, On Physiognomies, On Plants, On Marvellous Things Heard, Mechanical Problems, On Indivisible Lines, On Situations and Names of Winds, On Melissus, Xenophanes, and Gorgias.

ARISTOTLE: NICOMACHEAN ETHICS. H. Rackham.

ARISTOTLE: OECONOMICA and MAGNA MORALIA. G. C. Armstrong; (with Metaphysics, Vol. II.).

ARISTOTLE: ON THE HEAVENS. W. K. C. Guthrie.

ARISTOTLE: ON THE SOUL. PARVA NATURALIA. ON BREATH. W. S. Hett.

ARISTOTLE: CATEGORIES, ON INTERPRETATION, PRIOR ANALYTICS. H. P. Cooke and H. Tredennick.

ARISTOTLE: POSTERIOR ANALYTICS, TOPICS. H. Tredennick and E. S. Forster.

ARISTOTLE: ON SOPHISTICAL REFUTATIONS.
On Coming to be and Passing Away, On the Cosmos. E. S. Forster and D. J. Furley.

ARISTOTLE: PARTS OF ANIMALS. A. L. Peck; MOTION AND PROGRESSION OF ANIMALS. E. S. Forster.

4